Finding a Woman's Place

Princeton Theological Monograph Series

K. C. Hanson, Charles M. Collier, D. Christopher Spinks,
and Robin Parry, Series Editors

Recent volumes in the series:

Richard Valantasis et al. editors
*The Subjective Eye: Essays in Culture, Religion,
and Gender in Honor of Margaret R. Miles*

Donald E. Gowan
The Bible on Forgiveness

J. Harold Ellens and John T. Greene, editors
Probing the Frontiers of Biblical Studies

Randall W. Reed
*A Clash of Ideologies: Marxism, Liberation Theology,
and Apocalypticism in New Testament Studies*

Lowell K. Handy, editor
Psalm 29 through Time and Tradition

Thomas J. King
*The Realignment of the Priestly Literature: The Priestly Narrative in
Genesis and Its Relation to Priestly Legislation and the Holiness School*

Hemchand Gossai
Power and Marginality in the Abraham Narrative

Finding a Woman's Place
Essays in Honor of Carolyn Osiek, R.S.C.J.

Edited by
DAVID L. BALCH
and
JASON T. LAMOREAUX

☙PICKWICK *Publications* · Eugene, Oregon

FINDING A WOMAN'S PLACE
Essays in Honor of Carolyn Osiek, R.S.C.J.

Princeton Theological Monograph Series 150

Copyright © 2011 Wipf and Stock Publishers. All rights reserved. Except for brief quotations in critical publications or reviews, no part of this book may be reproduced in any manner without prior written permission from the publisher. Write: Permissions, Wipf and Stock Publishers, 199 W. 8th Ave., Suite 3, Eugene, OR 97401.

Pickwick Publications
An Imprint of Wipf and Stock Publishers
199 W. 8th Ave., Suite 3
Eugene, OR 97401

www.wipfandstock.com

ISBN 13: 978-1-60608-989-7

Cataloging-in-Publication data:

Finding a woman's place : essays in honor of Carolyn Osiek, R.S.C.J. / edited by David L. Balch and Jason T. Lamoreux.

Princeton Theological Monograph Series 150

xl + 366 p.; 23 cm. Includes bibliographical references and indexes.

ISBN 13: 978-1-60608-989-7

1. Bible. N.T.—Criticism, interpretation, etc. 2. Bible. N.T.—Social scientific criticism. 3. Sex roles—religious aspects—Christianity. 4. Women in Christianity. 5. Church history—Primitive and early church, ca. 30–600. I. Osiek, Carolyn. II. Balch, David L. III. Lamoreaux, Jason T. IV. Title. V. Series.

BS2545 .S55 F35 2011

Manufactured in the U.S.A.

Dr. Carolyn Osiek, R.S.C.J

Contents

A Remembrance / ix

List of Contributors / xi

Carolyn Osiek, R.S.C.J.: A Bibliography / xiii

Abbreviations / xxx

Introduction—David Balch and Jason T. Lamoreaux / xxxii

The River of Life—Sharon Karam, R.S.C.J. / xl

PART ONE: Visual and Oral Documents

1. Values of Roman Women Including Priests Visually Represented in Pompeii and Herculaneum
   —*David Balch / 3*

2. The Art of Translating for Oral Performance
   —*David Rhoads / 50*

PART TWO: Synoptic Documents and Acts

3. God as "Father" in Matthew: Imperial Intersections
   —*Warren Carter / 81*

4. A Man's Place in Matthew 19:3–15: Creation and Kingdom as Transformative Space of Identity
   —*Halvor Moxnes / 103*

5. "This Widow Keeps Bothering Me" (Luke 18:5)
   —*Amy-Jill Levine / 124*

6. Symposiac Humor in Luke 14:1–24
   —*Terri Bednarz, R.S.M. / 151*

7. The Women Householders of Acts in Light of Recent Research on Families—*Margaret Y. MacDonald / 171*

PART THREE: Johannine Documents

8 Birthed from the Side of Jesus (John 19:34)
   —*Barbara Reid, O.P.* / 191

9 History and Theology in the Johannine Presentation of the Causes for the Death of Jesus: John 11:45–53 as Convergence Point—*Donald Senior* / 215

10 Til Death Do Us Part: Uniting Social-Scientific and Narrative Criticism in Johannine Exegesis
   —*Jason L. Merritt* / 233

PART FOUR: Pauline Documents

11 Seen but Not Heard: Women Prophets in Caesarea
   —*Laurie Brink, O.P.* / 253

12 Two Visions of the Lord: A Comparison of Paul's Revelation to his Opponents' Revelation in 2 Corinthians 12:1–10—*Jeremy W. Barrier* / 272

PART FIVE: Early Church Documents

13 Tertullian's Reception of Paul's Instructions about Women—*Adela Yarbro Collins* / 293

14 Women's Ordination in Hippolytus' Commentary *On the Song of Songs* and the Question of Provenance
   —*Yancy W. Smith* / 311

Index of Ancient Sources / 339

Index of Modern Authors / 359

A Remembrance

IN HONORING CAROLYN OSIEK, WE WISH TO EXTEND OUR GRATITUDE to her religious community, the *Religious of the Sacred Heart*, and, in particular, we offer a gracious remembrance of her dear friend and colleague, Sister Barbara Bowe, R.S.C.J., who passed away on March 14, 2010. Sisters Carolyn and Barbara ministered together at *Catholic Theological Union* in Chicago for some 20 years. They supported each other in their scholarly endeavors. Both were graduates of Harvard's Divinity School where Lyn focused on the New Testament and Early Christian Origins, and Barbara centered her studies on the Gospel of John. Sisters Carolyn and Barbara shared a love of biblical texts and the biblical world, they shared faith and community life along with their sisters and the CTU community, and they shared their love of the Holy Land with countless students over the years.

Many of us know personally the loss of wonderful scholars, whose life here ends earlier than we had hoped. We feel the loss even more, when such scholars are among our dearest friends. Barbara's smile and laughter, her persistent and ever present support to many of us as our professor, friend and colleague will be missed. Barbara has profoundly shaped our world through her spiritual and scholarly endeavors. We wish to honor the memory of Barbara with this well-deserved posthumous acknowledgment. Barbara's life achievements, her friendship, and sisterhood have, no doubt, shaped our own dear colleague, friend, and mentor, Carolyn Osiek.

Terri Bednardz, R.S.M.

Contributors

DAVID BALCH is Professor of New Testament at Pacific Lutheran Theological Seminary, Berkeley, California.

JEREMY W. BARRIER is Assistant Professor of Biblical Literature and Director of the Graduate Program at Heritage Christian University, Florence, Alabama.

TERRI BEDNARZ, R.S.M., is Assistant Professor of New Testament Studies at Loyola University, New Orleans, Louisiana.

LAURIE BRINK, O.P., is Assistant Professor of New Testament at Catholic Theological Union, Chicago, Illinois.

WARREN CARTER is Professor of New Testament at Brite Divinity School, Fort Worth, Texas.

ADELA YARBRO COLLINS is Buckingham Professor of New Testament Criticism and Interpretation at Yale University, New Haven, Connecticut.

JASON T. LAMOREAUX is a PhD candidate at Texas Christian University, Fort Worth, Texas.

AMY-JILL LEVINE is E. Rhodes and Leona B. Carpenter Professor of New Testament Studies at Vanderbilt University Divinity School, Nashville, Tennessee.

MARGARET Y. MACDONALD is Professor of Religious Studies at St. Francis Xavier University, Antigonish, Nova Scotia, Canada.

Jason L. Merritt recently completed his Ph.D. in New Testament at Brite Divinity School and is instructor in classical Greek at St. Peter's Classical School in Fort Worth, Texas.

Halvor Moxnes is Professor of New Testament at the University of Oslo, Norway.

Barbara Reid, O.P., is Vice President, Academic Dean, and Professor of New Testament Studies at Catholic Theological Union, Chicago, Illinois.

David Rhoads is Professor of New Testament emeritus at Lutheran School of Theology at Chicago, Illinois.

Donald Senior, is President and Professor of New Testament Studies at Catholic Theological Union, Chicago, Illinois.

Yancy W. Smith is a Bible translation consultant for World Bible Translation Center, Fort Worth, Texas.

Carolyn Osiek, R.S.C.J.
A Bibliography

1976

"Reflections on an American Spirituality." *Spiritual Life* 22.4 (1976) 230–40.

1977

Review of *Sémitismes et latinismes dans le Pasteur d'Hermas* by A. Hilhorst. *CBQ* 39.4 (1977) 592–93.

"The Church Fathers and the Ministry of Women." In *Women Priests: A Catholic Commentary on the Vatican Declaration*, edited by Leonard Swidler and Arlene Swidler, 75–80. New York: Paulist, 1977.

"The First Week of the *Spiritual Exercises* and the Conversion of Saint Paul." *Review for Religious* 36.5 (1977) 657–65.

"Journeying to the Interior." Review *of The Way of the River* by E. Ferlita; *Life to the Full* by J. Heagle; *The Bible Makes Sense* by W. Brueggemann. *National Catholic Reporter* 13.45 (1977) 10.

"Reflections on an American Spirituality." *Catholic Mind* 75 (1977) 24, 33.

1978

"The Ministry of Ordination of Women according to the Early Church Fathers." In *Women and Priesthood: Future Directions*, edited by Carroll Stuhlmueller, 59–68. Collegeville, MN: Liturgical, 1978.

"Rich and Poor in the Shepherd of Hermas." *Harvard Theological Review* 71–72 (1978–1979) 322–23.

1979

Review of *The Method and Message of Jesus' Teachings* by R. H. Stein. *Spirituality Today* 31.3 (1979) 592–93.

"Biblical Themes." In *Good News Bible, Catholic Study Edition*, li–lxi. New York: Sadlier, 1979.

The Letter of Paul to the Philippians. NCR Cassettes, 1979.

"Liturgical Presidency in the New Testament." *Emmanuel* 85.4 (1979) 204–9.

"Women in the World of Jesus." *CBQ* 41.4 (1979) 664–65.

1980

Review of *God's People in Christ: New Testament Perspectives on the Church and Judaism* by Daniel Harrington. *Theology Today* 37.3 (1980) 369–70.
Review of *Jews and Christians in Antioch in the First Four Centuries of the Common Era* by Wayne Meeks and Robert Wilken. *Journal of Ecumenical Studies* 17.4 (1980) 690–91.
Review of *Jews and Christians in Dialogue: New Testament Foundations* by John Koenig. *Theology Today* 37.3 (1980) 369–70.
Review of *Paul: Crisis in Galatia—A Study in Early Christian Theology* by George Howard. *CBQ* 42.4 (1980) 570–72.
Review of *Women and Ministry in the New Testament* by Elisabeth Tetlow. *New Catholic World* Sept/Oct (1980) 232–33.
Review of *How to Read and Pray St. Paul* by Marilyn Norquist. *Modern Liturgy* 7.8 (1980) 27–28.
Review of *Kirche und Mission im Epheserbrief (Stuttgarter Bibelstudien 86)* by Regina Pacis Meyer. *CBQ* 42.3 (1980) 414–15.
1 Corinthians: Franciscan Herald, 1980.
"Biblical Models for Ministry." *Ministries* 1.7 (1980) 10–12, 27–28.
Galatians. NT Message Series. Wilmington, DE: Glazier, 1980.
"Galatians: Paul's Gospel of Freedom." *TBT* 18.2 (1980) 82–88.
"Inspired Texts: The Dilemma of the Feminist Believer." *Spirituality Today* 32.2 (1980) 138–47.
"Jacob's Well." *TBT* 18.3 (1980) 187–89.
"Living in Faith." *RSCJ: A Journal of Reflection* 2.1 (1980) 37–47.
Poverty. NCR Cassettes, 1980.
"Scripture for Today." *National Catholic Reporter* 16 (1980) 12.
"Women in the NT Church." *Ministries* 1.4 (1980) 18–20.

1981

Review of *The Social Context of Paul's Ministry: Tentmaking and Apostleship* by Ronald F. Hock. *CBQ* 43.2 (1981) 296–97.
"Celebrant's Guide, Commentary, and Homiletic Notes for Sundays and Feast Days of Advent." *Scripture in Church* 44 (1981) 404–13, 40–52.
"Haggadah." *TBT* 19.6 (1981) 358–60.
Jesus and the Kingdom. Atlanta: Episcopal Radio-TV Foundation, 1981.
"The Jewish-Christian Community at Capharnaum." *TBT* 19.1 (1981) 36–38.
"The Ransom of Captives: Evolution of a Tradition." *Harvard Theological Review* 74.4 (1981) 365–86.
"The Relationship of Charisms to Rights and Duties in the New Testament Church." *The Jurist* 19.1 (1981) 295–313.
"The Relationship of Charisms to Rights and Duties in the New Testament Church." In *Official Ministry in a New Age*, edited by James H. Provost, 41–59. Washington, DC: CLSA/Catholic University of America, 1981.
Response To "Augustine and Prayer" By G. Jerome Knies, O.S.A. In *Proceedings of the First Institute on the Augustinian Spiritual Tradition*, 86–89. Olympia Fields, IL: Institute on the Augustinian Spiritual Tradition, 1981.

1982

Review of *Il "Mysterion" paolino: Traiettoria e costituzione* by Romano Penna. *CBQ* 44.3 (1982) 521-22.
Review of *The Revolt of the Widows: The Social World of the Apocryphal Acts* by Stevan L. Davies. *CBQ* 44.2 (1982) 318-19.
"Ancient Burials." *TBT* 20.6 (1982) 358-61.
"Critics' Choice." *Commonweal* 109.4 (1982) 118.
"Jacob's Well—Does the Bible Condemn Wealth?" *TBT* 20.1 (1982) 28-29.
"Seers' Corner: Corinth." *TBT* 20.5 (1982) 282-83.
"Wealth and Poverty in the *Shepherd of Hermas.*" *Studia Patristica* 18 (1982) 725-30.

1983

Review of *Das Visionenbuch des Hermas als Apokaylpse*, vol. 1 by David Hellholm. *CBQ* 45.3 (1983) 488-89.
Review of *The Rich Christian in the Church of the Early Empire: Contradictions and Accommodations* by L. William Countryman. *Second Century: A Journal of Early Christian Studies* 3.2 (1983) 107-9.
"Bible Terms Today: Eirene—Peace." *TBT* 21.3 (1983) 203.
"Celebrant's Guide, Commentary, and Homiletic Notes for Thirtieth and Thirty-First Sundays of the Year." *Scripture in Church* 52 (Oct-Dec 1983) 392-95, 422-26.
"Haggadah." *TBT* 21.1 (1983) 2-4.
"Reflections on Weekday Readings." *Scripture in Church* (1983) 330-34.
Rich and Poor in the Shepherd of Hermas: An Exegetical-Social Investigation. CBQMS 15. Washington DC: Catholic Biblical Association, 1983.
"The Widow as Altar: The Rise and Fall of a Symbol." *Second Century* 3.3 (1983) 159-69.
With Donald Senior. "How and Why Catholic and Protestant Bibles Differ." In *Liturgical Press*, 1983.

1984

Review of *In Memory of Her: A Feminist Theological Reconstruction of Christian Origins* by Elisabeth Schüssler Fiorenza. *Biblical Theology Bulletin* 14.4 (1984) 166-67.
Review of *Let Wives Be Submissive: The Domestic Code in 1 Peter* by David Balch. *CBQ* 46.1 (1984) 138-40.
Review of *St Paul's Corinth: Texts and Archaeology* by Jerome Murphy-O'Conner. *Biblical Theology Bulletin* 14.4 (1984) 162.
Review of *The First Urban Christians: The Social World of the Apostle Paul* by Wayne A. Meeks. *Biblical Theology Bulletin* 14.4 (1984) 165-66.
The Bible and Christian Life. Argus Videotape (with D. Bergant, D. Senior, and C. Stuhlmueller), 1984.
"Chicago Theologians on BEM, Response to WCC's *Baptism, Eucharist, Ministry*, Ed. Robert W. Bertram." *Journal of Ecumenical Studies* 21.1 (1984) 64-70.
"Commentary and Homiletic Notes for the Thirtieth Sunday of the Year." *Scripture in Church* 56 (1984) 388-400.

"How to Get Sold on the World's Best-Seller." *U.S. Catholic* 49.10 (1984) 25–31.

"Jacob's Well." *TBT* 22.3 (1984) 158–59.

"Slavery in the New Testament." *TBT* 22.3 (1984) 151–55.

"Weekday Homily Helps." 1984.

"What Social Sciences Can Do to Scripture." *National Catholic Reporter* 20.45 (1984) 9, 16.

"Working Paper on Adaptation and Renewal of Religious Life since Vatican II." *Daybreak* April (1984) 13–16.

1985

Review of *Paul, the Law and the Jewish People* by E. P. Sanders. *CBQ* 47.2 (1985) 365–66.

Review of *The Epistle to the Galatians: A Commentary on the Greek Text* by F. F. Bruce. *Journal of Biblical Literature* 104.2 (1985) 352–54.

"The Feminist and the Bible: Hermeneutical Alternatives." In *Feminist Perspectives on Biblical Scholarship*, edited by Adela Y. Collins, 93–105. Biblical Scholarship in North America 10. Chico, CA: Scholars, 1985.

"Inspired Texts: The Dilemma of the Feminist Believer." In *A Companion to the Bible*, edited by Miriam Ward. New York: Alba House, 1985.

"Jacob's Well." *TBT* 23.4 (1985) 246–47.

"The Spiritual Direction of Thinking Types." *Review for Religious* 44 (1985) 209–19.

"Twentieth and Twenty-First Weeks of the Year." *Scripture in Church* 59 (July–Sept 1985) 318–25.

1986

Review of *Christian Biblical Ethics, from Biblical Revelation to Contemporary Praxis: Method and Content* by Robert J. Daly et. al. *Biblical Theology Bulletin* 16.1 (1986) 30–31.

Review of *Feminist Interpretation of the Bible* by Letty M. Russell. *CBQ* 48.3 (1986) 584–85.

Review of *The Churches the Apostles Left Behind* by Raymond E. Brown. *Journal of Biblical Literature* 105.4 (1986) 732–34.

Review of *The Churches the Apostles Left Behind* by Raymond E. Brown. *Biblical Theology Bulletin* 16.1 (1986) 30–31.

Beyond Anger: On Being a Feminist in the Church. New York: Paulist, 1986.

"Bible Terms Today." *TBT* 24 (1986) 85–86.

But Jesus Said: New Testament Moral Concerns. Credence Cassettes, 1986.

"Decree on the Up-to-Date Renewal of Religious Life, *Perfectae Caritatis*." In *Vatican II and Its Documents: An American Reappraisal*, edited by Timothy E. O'Connell, 79–90. Wilmington, DE: Glazier, 1986.

"The Genre and Function of the *Shepherd of Hermas*." In *Semeia 36: Early Christian Apocalypticism: Genre and Social Setting*, edited by Adela Y. Collins, 113–21. Decatur, GA: Scholars, 1986.

"How to Prevent Bible Baffle." *U.S. Catholic* 51 (1986) 33–38.

"Jacob's Well: Feminist Hermeneutics." *TBT* 24.1 (1986) 18–19.

"Twenty-Ninth and Thirtieth Weeks of the Year." *Scripture in Church* 16.64 (1986) 432–36.

With Kathleen Hughes. "Constitutional Hermeneutics: On the Interpretation of Constitutions." *Review for Religious* 45 (1986) 57–68.

1987

Review of *Chiesa e Tribolazione: Il tema della thlipsis nelle Lettere di S Paolo* by Paolo Iovino. *CBQ* 49.2 (1987) 341–42.

Review of *Ignatius of Antioch: A Commentary on the Letters of Ignatius of Antioch* by William R. Schoedel. *Journal of Biblical Literature* 106.4 (1987) 734–36.

Review of *Rediscovering Paul: Philemon and the Sociology of Paul's Narrative World* by Norman R. Peterson. *Biblical Theology Bulletin* 17.1 (1987) 39.

Review of *The New Testament in Its Social Environment* by John E. Strambaugh and David L. Balch. *Bible Review* 3.1 (1987) 11–12.

Review of *Women and the Word: The Gender of God in the New Testament and the Spirituality of Women* by Sandra M. Schneiders. *Horizons* 14.1 (1987) 171–72.

Review of *Prayer and Temperament: Different Prayer Forms for Different Personality Types* by Chester P. Michael and Marie C. Norrisey. *RSCJ: A Journal of Reflection* 8.1 (1987) 157–59.

Review of *The Triumph of the Meek: Why Early Christianity Succeeded* by Michael Walsh. *New Catholic World* 232 (1987) 276.

Education as Liberation according to John. Time Consultants and Alba House, 1987.

"Jacob's Well: Johannine School." *TBT* 25.1 (1987) 19–20.

Lesser Festivals 4: Saints' Days and Special Occasions. Proclamation 3. Minneapolis: Fortress, 1987.

"Ten New Testament Truths to Live By." *Praying* 17.March-April (1987) 14–19.

1988

Review of *Early Jewish and Christian Exegesis: Response to the World and Self-Understanding according to 1 Corinthians* by Craig A. Evans and William F. Stinespring. *CBQ* 50.2 (1988) 344–45.

Review of *Hellenica et Judaica: Hommage á Valentin Nikiprowetzky* by A. Caquot et. al. *CBQ* 50.3 (1988) 551–52.

Review of *Paul the Worldly Ascetic* by Vincent L. Wimbush. *CBQ* 50.3 (1988) 549–50.

Review of *Suffering and the Spirit: An Exegetical Study of II Cor. 2:14—3:3 within the Context of the Corinthian Correspondence* by Scott Hafemann. *CBQ* 50.1 (1988) 137–38.

Review of *The Illegitimacy of Jesus: A Feminist Theological Interpretation of the Infancy Narratives* by Jane Schaberg. *CrossCurrents* 38.3 (1988) 360–61.

Review of *The New Eve in Christ: The Use of the Bible in the Debate about Women in the Church* by Mary E. Hayter. *Critical Review of Books in Religion* 1 (1988) 128–30.

Review of *Studies in the New Testament and Gnosticism* by George E. MacRae, S.J. *New Theology Review* 1.3 (1988) 97–98.

"Giving Sisters' Retreats, Or: Damned If You Do and Damned If You Don't." *The Passionist* 18 (1988) 11–20.
"The Gospel of John and the Spirituality of the Society." *RSCJ: A Journal of Reflection* 9.1 (1988) 132–39.
"Images of God: Breaking Boundaries." *Spirituality Today* 40 (1988) 333–44.
"Jacob's Well." *TBT* 26.1 (1988) 39–40.
"New New Testament." Review of new NAB. *Praying* 23 (1988) 28–29.
"Patterns of Ministry in the New Testament." In *Ministry: An Ecumenical Challenge*, edited by Wm. Powell Tuck, 10–21. Lexington: Kentucky Council of Churches, 1988.
"Paul's Prayer." In *Scripture and Prayer: A Celebration for Carroll Stuhlmueller*, edited by Carolyn Osiek, RSCJ and Donald Senior, 145–57. Wilmington, DE: Glazier, 1988.
"The Religious as Contemplative: Being Prophetic and Priestly." *Review for Religious* 47.5 (1988) 691–700.
"Rights, Responsibilities, and Homosexuality." In *The Vatican and Homosexuality: reactions to the "Letter to the bishops of the Catholic Church on the pastoral care of homosexual persons,"* edited by Jeannine Gramick and Pat Furey, 126–32. New York: Crossroads, 1988.
"Translations of Epiphanius, *Panarion* 49, 78.23, 79." In *Maenads, Martyrs, Matrons, Monastics*, edited by Ross Shepard Kraemer, 50–58, 226–27. Philadelphia: Fortress, 1988.
With Donald Senior, editors. *Scripture and Prayer: A Celebration for Carroll Stuhlmueller.* Wilmington, DE: Glazier, 1988.

1989

Review of *New Testament Tensions and the Contemporary Church* by Carl S. Dudley and Earle Hilgert. *CBQ* 51.1 (1989) 150–51.
Review of *The Eucharist in the New Testament* by Jerome Kodell. *Worship* 63.4 (1989) 383–84.
Review of *The World that Shaped the New Testament* by Calvin J. Roetzel. *Biblical Theology Bulletin* 19.1 (1989) 40.
Review of *Transforming Grace: Christian Tradition and Women's Experience* by Anne Carr. *Biblical Theology Bulletin* 19.2 (1989) 70–71.
Review of *The Beginnings of the Church* by Frederick J. Cwiekowski. *New Theology Review* 2.2 (1989) 96.
Review of *Reading Corinthians: A Literary and Theological Commentary* by Charles H. Talbert. *The Catholic World* (Nov–Dec 1989) 276–77.
Review of *Quest for Sanctity: Seven Passages to Growth in Faith* by Gerald R. Grosh. *Review of Religious* 48 (1989) 946–47.
Review of *Dirt, Greed and Sex: Sexual Ethics in the New Testament and Their Implications for Today* by L. William Countryman. *New Theology Review* 2.4 (1989) 98–99.
Review of *Galilee, Jesus and the Gospels: Literary Approaches and Historical Investigations* by Sean Freyne. *New Theology Review* 2.4 (1989) 97–98.
"Control, Surrender, and Type." In *Teach Us to Pray*, edited by Ackerman. Minneapolis: Westminster Presbyterian Church, 1989.

"Critics' Choice." *Commonweal* 116.5 (1989) 156–57.
"The Feminist and the Bible: Hermeneutical Alternatives." *Religion and Intellectual Life* 6.3–4 (1989) 96–109.
"Jacob's Well: Resurrection and Immortality." *TBT* 27.3 (1989) 166–67.
"The Jesus of John's Gospel, a Breed Apart." *Church* 5 (1989) 24–27.
"The Liberation Theology of the Gospel of John." *TBT* 27 (1989) 210–18.
"The New Handmaid: The Bible and the Social Sciences." *Theological Studies* 50.2 (1989) 260–78.
"The Resurrection: Prism of New Testament Faith." *TBT* 27 (1989) 133–39.
"Second-Century Church Writers." In *New Jerome Biblical Commentary*, 1346–50. Englewood Cliffs: Prentice Hall, 1989.
"Seers' Corner: Palestinian Rock Tombs." *TBT* 27.3 (1989) 168–70.

1990

Review of *A Church in Crisis: Ecclesiology and Paraenesis in Clement of Rome* by Barbara E. Bowe. *Theological Studies* 51.1 (1990) 175–318.
Review of *Sisters Rejoice: Paul's Letter to the Philippians and Luke-Acts as Received by First-Century Women* by Lillian Portefaix. *CBQ* 52.2 (1990) 359–60.
Review of *Women in the Earliest Churches* by Ben Witherington III. *Journal of Biblical Literature* 109.2 (1990) 359–60.
Review of *Early Christianity as a Social Movement* (Toronto Studies in Religion 5) by Anthony J. Blasi. *Patristics* 19.1 (1990) 4–5.
"Biblical Images of Feminine: Some Alternatives." *TBT* 28.6 (1990) 342–46.
"Christian Prophecy: Once Upon a Time?" *Currents in Theology and Mission* 17.4 (1990) 291–97.
"Early Christian Theology of Martyrdom." *TBT* 28 (1990) 153–57.
Every Catholic's Guide to the Sacred Scriptures. Nashville: Nelson, 1990.
"Jacob's Well: God's Will and Ours." *TBT* 28.4 (1990) 242–43.
"The Second Century through the Eyes of Hermas: Continuity and Change." *Biblical Theology Bulletin* 20.3 (1990) 116–22.
Women, Jesus, and Paul. Alba House Cassettes, 1990.

1991

Review of *Knowing the Truth: A Sociological Approach to New Testament Interpretation* by Howard Clark Kee. *CBQ* 53.1 (1991) 140–41.
Review of *Sociology in the Jesus Movement* by Richard A. Horsley. *CBQ* 53.2 (1991) 329–31.
Review of *The Male Woman: A Feminine Ideal in the Early Church* by Kerstin Aspegren. *Theological Studies* 52.4 (1991) 778.
Review of *Faith and Wealth: A History of Early Christian Ideas on the Origin, Significance, and Use of Money* by Justo L. Gonzalez. *New Theology Review* 4.2 (1991) 112–13.
Review of *Responses to 101 Questions on the Bible* by Raymond R. Brown. *Theology Today* 48.2 (1991) 261.
Review of *Slavery as Salvation: The Metaphor of Slavery in Pauline Christianity* by Dale B. Martin. *Thought* 66.263 (1991) 413.

"Avila." *The Critic* 46.2 (1991) 70–79.
"Jesus and Money, or—Did Jesus Live in a Capitalist Society?" *Chicago Studies* 30 (1991) 17–28.
Jesus; the Prophets; Male and Female Imagery. Alba House Cassettes, 1991.
"Literal Meaning and Allegory." *TBT* 29 (1991) 261–66.
"The Middle East in Biblical Perspective." *Critic* 45 (1991) 24–32.
"Evidence for the Ordination of Women to the Priesthood in the Early Church." *New Women, New Church* 14:4–6/15.1 (1991–1992) 1, 17.

1992

Review of *Sociology and the New Testament: An Appraisal* by Bengt Holmberg. *CBQ* 54.2 (1992) 353–54.
Review of *The Corinthian Women Prophets: A Reconstruction through Paul's Rhetoric* by Antoinette Clark Wire. *Biblical Theology Bulletin* 22.1 (1992) 44.
Review of *Conflict at Rome: Social Order and Hierarchy in Early Christianity* by James S. Jeffers. *Journal of Biblical Literature* 111.4 (1992) 731–33.
Review of *Die Wahrnehmung sozialer Wirklichkeit im Hirten des Hermas* by Martin Leutzsch. *CBQ* 54.3 (1992) 575–77.
Review of *Farewell Addresses in the New Testament* by William S. Kurz. *New Theology Review* 5 (1992) 96–97.
Review of *Women in the New Testament: A Select Bibliography* by Inger Marie Lindboe. *CBQ* 54 (1992) 577–77.
"BTB Reader's Guide: Slavery in the Second Testament World." *Biblical Theology Bulletin* 22.4 (1992) 174–79.
"Fullness of Life." *TBT* 30 (1992) 133–37.
"Galatians." In *The Women's Bible Commentary*, edited by Carol A. Newsom and Sharon H. Ringe, 333–37. Louisville: Westminster/ John Knox, 1992.
"Jacob's Well: The Words of Life." *TBT* 30.3 (1992) 158–59.
"The Social Function of Female Imagery in Second Century Prophecy." *Vetera Christianorum* 29.1 (1992) 55–74.
"The Social Sciences and the Second Testament: Problems and Challenges." *Biblical Theology Bulletin* 22.2 (1992) 88–95.
What Are They Saying about the Social Setting of the New Testament? Rev. and exp. ed. New York: Paulist, 1992.
"With John for the Long Haul." *New Theology Review* 5.1 (1992) 76–80.
With Barbara Ellen Bowe, Kathleen Hughes, and Sharon Karam, editors. *Silent Voices, Sacred Lives: Women's Readings for the Liturgical Year*. New York: Paulist, 1992.

1993

Review of *Der Hirt des Hermas* by Norbert Brox. *CBQ* 55.4 (1993) 799–800.
Review of *Social History of the Matthean Community: Cross-Disciplinary Approaches* edited by David Balch. *CBQ* 55.4 (1993) 833–35.
Review of *The Social Setting of the Ministry as Reflected in the Writings of Hermas, Clement and Ignatius* by Harry O. Maier. *CBQ* 55.1 (1993) 171–73.
Review of *The Future of Early Christianity: Essays in Honor of Helmut Koester* edited by Birger A. Pearson. *CBQ* 55.1 (1993) 199–201.

Review of *The Voice of the Turtledove: New Catholic Women in Europe* edited by Anne Brotherton. *Catholic World* 236.1414 (1993) 185.
Review of *Sacred Violence: Paul's Hermeneutic of the Cross* by Robert G. Hamerton-Kelly. *New Theology Review* 6.3 (1993) 88–90.
"Captivity and Slavery: Early Christian Experience." *TBT* 31 (1993) 348–52.
"The City: Center of Early Christian Life." *TBT* 31 (1993) 17–21.
"The Cultural Context of the United States of America." *Connections: Toward a Global Consciousness (RSCJ Publication)* 3.1 (1993) 146–48.
Interpreting the Apocalypse for Today. Convention Seminar Cassettes, 1993.
"Ordering, Relatedness, Self-Sacrifice." In *Biblical Social Values and Their Meaning*, edited by John J. Pilch and Bruce J. Malina, 126–28, 55–60. Peabody, MA: Hendrickson, 1993.
"The Women at the Tomb: What Are They Doing There?" *Ex Auditu* 9 (1993) 97–107.
Women, Image of Christ, Christ, Image of Woman. Convention Seminar Cassettes, 1993.

1994

Review of *But She Said: Feminist Practices of Biblical Interpretation* by Elisabeth Schüssler Fiorenza. *Journal of Religion* 74.1 (1994) 92–93.
Review of *Death and Desire: The Rhetoric of Gender in the Apocalypse of John* by Tina Pippin. *CBQ* 56.2 (1994) 382–83.
Review of *La christologie chez Clément de Rome et dans le Pasteur d'Hermas* by Phillipe Henne. *CBQ* 56.4 (1994) 796–98.
Review of *The Four Gospels*, 3rd ed., by L. Thomas Hold. *CBQ* 56.1 (1994) 186–90.
Review of *Death and Desire* by Tina Pippin. *CBQ* 56 (1994) 382–83.
Review of *The Lost Gospel: The Book of Q and Christian Origins* by Burton L. Mack. *New Theology Review* 7 (1994) 104–5.
Review of *What Is Social Science Criticism?* by John H. Elliott. *New Theology Review* 8.4 (1994) 110–11.
"Getting to Know the Women in the Bible." *U.S. Catholic* 59.6 (1994) 13–14.
"Philippians." In *Searching the Scriptures: A Feminist Commentary*, edited by Elisabeth Schüssler Fiorenza, 237–49. New York: Crossroad, 1994.
"The Prayer of the Departing Jesus." *TBT* 32 (1994) 151–55.
"Reading the Bible as Women." In *New Interpreter's Bible*, 181–87. Nashville: Abingdon, 1994.
"The Shepherd of Hermas: An Early Tale That Almost Made It into the New Testament." *Biblical Research (Washington, D.C.)* 10.5 (1994) 48–54.
"Women in the Ancient Mediterranean World: State of the Question—New Testament." *Biblical Research* 39 (1994) 57–61.
"Women in the Church: Where Do We Go from Here?" *TBT* 32 (1994) 228–33.

1995

Review of *Origins and Method: Towards a New Understanding of Judaism and Christianity: Essays in Honor of John C Hurd* edited by B. H. McLean. *CBQ* 57.3 (1995) 629–30.

Review of *Philologia Sacra: Biblische und patristische Studien für Herman J Frede und Walter Thiele zu ihrem siebzigsten Geburtstag*, Bd 1: Altes und Neues Testament; Bd 2: *Apokryphen, Kirchenväter, Verschiedenes* edited by Roger Gryson. *CBQ* 57.1 (1995) 208–10.
Review of *The Biblical Commission's Document, The Interpretation of the Bible in the Church: Text and Commentary* by Joseph A. Fitzmyer. *CBQ* 57.3 (1995) 590.
Review of *The Jewish Family in Antiquity* by Shaye Cohen. *CBQ* 57.4 (1995) 836–37.
Review of *When Women were Priests: Women's Leadership in the Early Church and the Scandal of their Subordination in the Rise of Christianity* by Karen J. Torjesen. *Biblical Research (Washington, D.C.)* 11.4 (1995) 14–15.
Review of *The New Testament World: Insights from Cultural Anthropology* rev. ed. by Bruce J. Malina. *New Theology Review* 8.3 (1995) 93–94.
"Church in the Round." *Catholic World* 238 (1995) 89–89.
"Discipleship of Equals." *New Theology Review* 8 (1995) 113–15.
"The New Testament and the Family." *Concilium* 4 (1995) 1–9.
"Putting Away Childish Things." *National Catholic Reporter* 31 (1995) 31.
With Harry J. Leon. *The Jews of Ancient Rome*. Updated ed. Peabody, MA: Hendrickson, 1995.

1996

Review of *Lydia's Impatient Sisters: A Feminist Social History of Early Christianity* by Luise Schottroff. *Theological Studies* 57.3 (1996) 525–26.
Review of *Religious Propaganda and Missionary Competition in the New Testament World: Essays Honoring Dieter Georgi* edited by Lukas Borman et al. *CBQ* 58.2 (1996) 372–74.
Review of *The Synagogues and Churches of Ancient Palestine* by L. Hoppe. *CBQ* 58.1 (1996) 155–318.
Review of *Sociology of the Jesus Movement* by Richard A. Horsley. *New Theology Review* 9.2 (1996) 91–92.
"Apocalyptic Eschatology." *TBT* 34 (1996) 341–45.
"Evolving Leadership Roles in the Early Church." *TBT* 34 (1996) 72–76.
"The Family in Early Christianity: 'Family Values' Revisited." *CBQ* 58.1 (1996) 1–25.
"Jesus and Galilee." *TBT* 34.3 (1996) 153–59.
"Women in Early Christianity: Contradictions and Challenges." *RSCJ Occasional Papers* (Spring 1996) 3–14.

1997

Review of *The Christian Inscription at Pompeii* by Paul Berry. *CBQ* 59.3 (1997) 570–71.
Review of *The Ladies and the Cities: Transformation and Apocalyptic Identity in Joseph and Aseneth, 4 Ezra, the Apocalypse and the Shepherd of Hermas* by Edith McEwan Humphrey. *CBQ* 59.1 (1997) 158–59.
Review of *The Social World of the First Christians: Essays in Honor of Wayne A Meeks* edited by L. Michael White and O. Larry Yarbrough. *CBQ* 59.1 (1997) 200–202.
Review of *Woman at the Altar: The Ordination of Women in the Roman Catholic Church* by Lavinia Byrne. *New Theology Review* 10.4 (1997) 111.

Review of *The Archaeology of Early Christianity: A History*, by William H. C. Frend. *Biblical Theology Bulletin* 27.3 (1997) 117–18.
"Building Bridge of Hope: Education for Relationship." *RSCJ Occasional Papers* Winter (1997) 10–20.
"Changing Images of God and Christ." *Journal of Constructive Theology* 3.2 (1997) 3–12.
"The Feminist and the Bible: Hermeneutical Alternatives." *Hervormde teologiese studies* 53 (1997) 956–68.
"First Corinthians Seven and Family Questions." *TBT* 35 (1997) 275–79.
"Homily for Silver Jubilee." *RSCJ Occasional Papers* Fall (1997) 12–13.
"Jesus and Cultural Values: Family Life as an Example." *Hervormde teologiese studies* 53 (1997) 800–14.
"The Shepherd of Hermas in Context." *Acta patristica et byzantina* 8 (1997) 115–34.
"The Women at the Tomb: What Are They Doing There?" *Hervormde teologiese studies* 53 (1997) 103–18.
With David L. Balch. *Families in the New Testament World: Households and House Churches*. The Family, Religion, and Culture. Louisville: Westminster John Knox, 1997.

1998

Review of *Early Christian Women and Pagan Opinion: The Power of the Hysterical Woman* by Margaret Y. MacDonald. *CBQ* 60.3 (1998) 579–80.
Review of *Voluntary Associations in the Greco-Roman World* edited by John S. Kloppenborg and Stephen G. Wilson. *CBQ* 60.4 (1998) 797–99.
Review of *The Birth of Christianity* by John Dominic Crossan. *America* 179.15 (1998) 23–24.
"Discipleship, Equality and the Bible." In *The Changing Face of the Church*, edited by Timothy Fitzgerald and Martin F. Connell, 95–113. Chicago: LTP, 1998.
"The Ephesian Household Code." *TBT* 36.6 (1998) 360–64.
"Families in Early Christianity." In *The Family Handbook*, edited by Herbert Anderson et al., 287–90. Louisville: Westminster John Knox, 1998.
"John, a Gospel for Our Time." *TBT* 36 (1998) 72–78.
"Marriage and Family Life in the Bible." *Scripture from Scratch* 998 (Sept 1998).
"The Oral World of Early Christianity in Rome: The Case of Hermas." In *Judaism and Christianity in First-Century Rome*, edited by Karl P. Donfried and Peter Richardson, 151–72. Grand Rapids: Eerdmans, 1998.
"Women in House Churches." In *Common Life in the Early Church: Essays Honoring Graydon F. Snyder*, edited by Julian V. Hills et al., 300–15. Harrisburg, PA: Trinity, 1998.

1999

Review of *Friendship, Flattery, and Frankness of Speech: Studies on Friendship in the New Testament* by John T. Fitzgerald. *CBQ* 61.1 (1999) 191–93.
Review of *Paul and Empire: Religion and Power in Roman Imperial Society* edited by Richard Horsley. *Currents in Theology and Mission* 26.1 (1999) 63.

Review of *Constructing Early Christian Families: Family as Social Reality and Metaphor* edited by Halvor Moxnes. *CBQ* 61.2 (1999) 405–07.
Review of *Feminist Interpretation: The Bible in Women's Perspective* by Luise Schottroff, Silvia Schroer, and Marie-Theres Wacher. *Theological Studies* 60.2 (1999) 353–55.
Review of *Religious Experience in Earliest Christianity: A Missing Dimension in New Testament Studies* by Luke T. Johnson. *Christian Spirituality Bulletin* 7.2 (1999) 29–30.
"Call to Sanctification." *National Catholic Reporter* 35 (1999) 41.
"Challenges and Features of the Millennium Church." *Beyond Frontiers* (1999) 8–9.
"Characters: The Spice of the Story." *TBT* 37 (1999) 276–80.
"Gospel and Enculturation: The Long Road." *Religion and Theology* 6.1 (1999) 83–92.
Shepherd of Hermas: A Commentary. Hermeneia. Minneapolis: Fortress, 1999.

2000

Review of *Ancient and Modern Perspectives on the Bible and Culture: Essays in Honor of Hans Dieter Betz* edited by Adela Yarbro Collins. *CBQ* 62.2 (2000) 386–88.
Review of *Fidelidades en Conflicto: La Ruptura con la Familia por Causa del Discipulado y de la Misión en la Tradición Synóptica* by Santiago Guijarro Oporto. *Biblical Theology Bulletin* 30.1 (2000) 38–39.
Review of *Inculturation of the Jesus Tradition: The Impact of Jesus on Jewish and Roman Cultures* by Graydon Snyder. *CBQ* 62.4 (2000) 763–65.
Review of *Rhetoric and Ethic: The Politics of Biblical Studies* by Elisabeth Schüssler Fiorenza. *Theological Studies* 61.3 (2000) 553–55.
Review of *The Choice between Two Cities: Whore, Bride, and Empire in the Apocalypse* by Barbara R. Rossing. *CBQ* 62.3 (2000) 567–69.
Review of *Following Christ: Models of Discipleship in the New Testament* by Andrew Ryder. *New Theology Review* 13 (2000) 83–84.
Matthew's Gospel: Embracing Our Jewish Roots. St. Anthony Messenger Press Tapes, 2000.
Philippians, Philemon. Abingdon New Testament Commentaries. Nashville: Abingdon, 2000.
Visions of the End and New Beginnings: Apocalypse as Text of Hope. Convention Seminar Cassettes, 2000.
Woman and Apocalyptic Literature: The Outside View. Convention Seminar Cassettes, 2000.
"Women and Ministry in the Early Church." *RSCJ Occasional Papers* (Fall 2000) 3–9.
With Laurie Brink. "Two Women, a Generation Apart, View Religious Life." *National Catholic Reporter* 36 (2000) 22–23.

2001

Review of *The Jesus Movement: A Social History of Its First Century* by Ekkehard W. Stegemann and Wolfgang Stegemann. *CBQ* 63.3 (2001) 561–63.

Review of *Building God's House* by L. Michael White. *Religious Studies Review* 27.3 (2001) 228–31.
Review of *The Social Origins of Christian Architecture. 4, House Churches and the Demographics of Diversity* by L. Michael White. *Religious Studies Review* 27.3 (2001) 228–31.
Review of *Families and Family Relations as Represented in Early Judaisms and Early Christianities: Texts and Fictions* edited by Jan Willem Van Henten and Athalya Brenner. *CBQ* 63.2 (2001) 382–84.
Review of *Knowing Her Place: Gender and the Gospels* by Anne Thurston. *New Theology Review* 14.1 (2001) 88–89.
Review of *Women and Christian Origins* edited by Ross Shepard Kraemer and Mary Rose D'Angelo. *CBQ* 63.4 (2001) 788–89.
Review of *The World according to Eve: Women and the Bible in Ancient Times* by Cullen Murphy. *Shofar* 19.2 (2001) 142–43.
"Called to Give Witness." In *Bicentennial Homily, Holy Family Church, Nov. 18, 2000*, 107–11. Society of the Sacred Heart, 2001.
"Philippians." In *New Oxford Annotated Bible*, edited by Bruce M. Metzger et al., 328–33. Oxford: Oxford University Press, 2001.
"Transculturality and Cultural Specificity in Religious Life." *RSCJ Occasional Papers* (Fall 2001) 22–30.

2002

Review of *Honor, Patronage, Kinship and Purity: Unlocking New Testament Culture* by David deSilva. *CBQ* 64.1 (2002) 156–57.
Review of *Roman Women* by Augusto Fraschetti. *Journal of Religion* 82.3 (2002) 449–50.
Review of *The Ancient Church as Family* by Joseph Hellerman. *Journal of Religion* 82.4 (2002) 625–26.
Review of *The Letter to Philemon* by Markus Barth and Helmut Blanke. *Biblica* 83.2 (2002) 293–96.
Review of *The Quest for Home: The Household in Mark's Community* by Michael F. Trainor. *CBQ* 64.4 (2002) 780–81.
Review of *"A Hard Saying": The Gospel and Culture* by Francis J. Moloney. *New Theology Review* 15.4 (2002) 89–90.
Review of *Women Officeholders in Early Christianity: Epigraphical and Literary Studies* by Ute E. Eisen. *CBQ* 64.3 (2002) 571–72.
"Archaeological and Architectural Issues and the Question of Demographic and Urban Forms." In *Handbook of Early Christianity: Social Science Approaches*, edited by Anthony J. Blasi et al., 83–103. Walnut Creek, CA: AltaMira, 2002.
"The Bride of Christ (Ephesians 5:22–33) A Problematic Wedding." *Biblical Theology Bulletin* 32.1 (2002) 29–39.
"Perpetua's Husband." *Journal of Early Christian Studies* 10.2 (2002) 287–90.

2003

Review of *Biblical Religion and Family Values: A Problem in the Philosophy of Culture* by Jan Newman. *Interpretation* 57.1 (2003) 100.

Review of *Philippians: From People to Letter* by Peter Oakes. *CBQ* 65.2 (2003) 297–98.
Review of *The Churches and Catacombs of Early Christian Rome: A Comprehensive Guide* by Matilda Webb. *Journal of Early Christian Studies* 11.1 (2003) 123–24.
Review of *The Cult of Saint Thecla: A Tradition of Women's Piety in Late Antiquity* by Stephen J. Davis. *Journal of Early Christian Studies* 11.3 (2003) 422–24.
"Pietas in and out of the Frying Pan." *Biblical Interpretation* 11.2 (2003) 166–72.
"Second Corinthians." In *The Interpreter's Study Bible*, 2061–77. Peabody, MA: Abingdon, 2003.
With David L. Balch, editors. *Early Christian Families in Context: An Interdisciplinary Dialogue*. Religion, Marriage and Family. Grand Rapids: Eerdmans, 2003.

2004

Review of *La Domus Tardoantica: Forme e rappresentazioni dello spazio domestico nelle città del Mediterraneo* by Isabella Baldini Lippolis. *Journal of Early Christian Studies* 12.1 (2004) 137–38.
Review of *Mary Magdalene, The First Apostle: The Struggle for Authority* by Ann Graham Brock. *Journal of Religion* 84.1 (2004) 100–101.
Review of *The Resurrection of Mary Magdalene: Legends, Apocrypha, and the Christian Testament* by Jane Schaberg. *Biblical Theology Bulletin* 34.2 (2004) 379.
"Did Early Christians Teach, or Merely Assume, Male Headship?" In *Does Christianity Teach Male Headship?* edited by David Blankenhorn, Don Browning and Mary Stewart Van Leeuwen, 23–27. Grand Rapids: Eerdmans, 2004.
"The New Testament Letter as Mass Communication." *TBT* 42.1 (2004) 5–11.
"Romans 'Down the Pike': Glimpses from Later Years." In *Celebrating Romans: Template for Pauline Theology: Essays in Honor of Robert Jewett*, edited by Sheila E. McGinn, 149–61. Grand Rapids: Eerdmans, 2004.
"Who Did What in the Church of the New Testament." In *Lay Ministry in the Catholic Church, Conference on the Catholic Church in the Twenty-First Century*, edited by Richard W. Miller II, 1–12. Kansas City: Liguori, 2004.
"Who Submits to Whom? Submission and Mutuality in the Family." In *Mutuality Matters: Family, Faith, Just Love*, edited by Herbert Anderson et. al., 57–64. Lanham, MD: Rowman & Littlefield, 2004.

2005

Review of *Divorce and Remarriage in the Bible: The Social and Literary Context* by David Instone-Brewer. *Journal of Semitic Studies* 50.2 (2005) 379–81.
Review of *Marriage and Family in the Biblical World* edited by Ken M. Campbell. *CBQ* 67.2 (2005) 378–79.
Review of *Putting Jesus in His Place: A Radical Vision of Household and Kingdom* by Halvor Moxnes. *Journal of Religion* 85.2 (2005) 302–03.
Review of *Reading Women's Stories: Female Characters in the Hebrew Bible* by John Peterson. *Theological Studies* 66.4 (2005) 930.
Review of *L'achat et la vente des esclaves dans l'Egpte romaine: Contribution papyrologique à l'étude de l'esclavage dans une province orientale de l'empire*

romain (Archiv für Papyrusforschung und verwandte Gebiete, Beiheft 14) by Jean A. Straus. *Bryn Mawr Classical Review* (2005).

Review of *When Children Became People: The Birth of Childhood in Early Christianity* by O. M. Bakke. *RBL* Online (2005).

"Catholic or catholic? Biblical Scholarship at the Service of the Church." *Heart* 3.1 (2005) 19–22.

"DaVinci Code Remedy." *Vital Theology* 1.17 (2005) 4.

"*Diakonos* and *Prostatis*: Women's Patronage in Early Christianity." *Hervormde teologiese studies* 61.1–2 (2005) 347–70.

"Family Matters." In *Christian Origins*, edited by Richard A. Horsley, 201–20. A People's History of Christianity 1. Minneapolis: Fortress, 2005.

"Introduction of David L. Petersen." *Journal of Biblical Literature* 124.1 (2005) 4–5.

"The Study of Women in the Early Church." *TBT* 43.5 (2005) 277–82.

With Kevin Madigan. *Ordained Women in the Early Church: A Documentary History*. Baltimore: Johns Hopkins University Press, 2005.

2006

Review of *Reconceptualising Conversion: Patronage, Loyalty, and Conversion in Religions of the Ancient Mediterranean* by Zeba A. Crook. *BMCR* Online (2006).

"Catholic or catholic? Biblical Scholarship at the Center [Presidential Address]." *Journal of Biblical Literature* 125.1 (2006) 5–22.

"The New Testament Teaching on Family Matters." *Hervormde teologiese studies* 62.3 (2006) 819–43.

"Paul and His Writings: Reading Guides to Romans, 1–2 Corinthians, Galatians, Ephesians, Philippians, Colossians, 1–2 Thessalonians, 1–2 Timothy, Titus, Philemon." In *The Catholic Study Bible*, edited by Donald Senior and John J. Collins, 439–95. 2nd ed. Oxford: Oxford University Press, 2006.

"The Self-Defining Praxis of the Developing Ecclesia." In *Origins to Constantine*, edited by Margaret M. Michell and Frances M. Young, 274–92. Cambridge History of Christianity 1. Cambridge: Cambridge University Press, 2006.

With Margaret Y. Macdonald and Janet H. Tulloch. *A Woman's Place: House Churches in Earliest Christianity*. Minneapolis: Fortress, 2006.

2007

Review of *The Lost Apostle* by Rena Pederson. *U S. Catholic* 72.1 (2007) 45.

Review of *Mulier Potens: Realtà femminile nel mondo antico* by Nicoletta Francesca Berrino. *BMCR* online (2007).

Review of *Women's Letters from Ancient Egypt, 300 BC—AD 800* edited by Roger Bagnall and Rafaela Cribiore. *RBL* online (2007).

Review of *Poverty in the Roman World* by Margaret Atkins and Robin Osbourne. *Journal of Economic History* 67.4 (2007) 1065–66.

"The Fourth Commandment: A Call to Fidelity." *TBT* 45.2 (2007) 105–10.

"In Memorium: Sullivan, Kathryn Lois, 1905–2006." *CBQ* 69.1 (2007) 104–5.

"Interview: Grave Mistake?" *TCU Magazine* (2007) 20.

"Kathryn Sullivan, RSCJ (1905–2006) Woman of the Word." *TBT* 45.1 (2007) 5–10.

"Marcela, Paula, Melania La Anciana Y Melania La Joven." In *Mujeres con Autoridad en El Cristianismo Antiguo*, edited by Carmen Bernabé Ubieta, 183–208. Navarra: Verbo Divino, 2007.

"Motivation for Conversion of Women in Early Christianity: The Case of Pentecostalism." In *In Other Words: Essays on Social-Science Method and the New Testament in Honor of Jerome H. Neyrey*, edited by Anselm C. Hagdorn, Zeba A. Crook, and Eric Stewart, 186–201. Sheffield: Phoenix, 2007.

"Why Do We Have Four Gospels?" *TBT* 45.3 (2007) 155–59.

With Margaret Y. Macdonald and Janet H. Tulloch. *El Lugar de la Mujer en la Iglesia Primitiva*. Salamanca: Sígueme, 2007.

2008

Review of *From Clement to Origen: The Social and Historical Context of the Church Fathers* by David Rankin. *Journal of Early Christian Studies* 16.1 (2008) 106–07.

Review of *Lo, I Tell You a Mystery: Cross, Resurrection, and Paranesis in the Rhetoric of 1 Corinthians* by David A. Ackerman. *Biblical Theology Bulletin* 38.4 (2008) 191–92.

Review of *Roman Women* by Eve D'Ambra. *Biblical Theology Bulletin* 38.3 (2008) 144–44.

Review of *Origine delle catacomb Romane. Atti della giornata tematica dei Seminari de Archeologia Cristiana* by Vicenzo Fiocchi-Nicolai. *BMCR* online (2008).

"The Bride of Christ (Ephesians 5:22–33): A Problematic Wedding." In *Sacred Marriages: The Divine-Human Sexual Metaphor from Sumer to Early Christianity*, edited by Martti Nissinen and Risto Uro, 371–92. Eisenbrauns, 2008.

"Mujeres, Honor Y Contexto En La Antiguedad Mediterranea." In *Reimaginando los Origenes del Cristianismo: Relevancia Social y Ecclesial de los Estudios Sobre Origenes del Cristianismo: Libro Homenaje a Rafael Aquirre en Su 65 Cumpleanos*, edited by Carmen Bernabé and Carolos Gil, 353–71. Navarra: Verbo Divino, 2008.

"The Patronage of Women in Early Christianity." In *Feminist Companion to Patristic Literature*, edited by Amy-Jill Levine and Maria Mayo Robbins, 173–92. London: T. & T. Clark, 2008.

"Roman and Christian Burial Practices and the Patronage of Women." In *Commemorating the Dead: Texts and Artifacts in Context—Studies of Roman, Jewish, and Christian Burials*, edited by Laurie Brink and Deborah Green, 243–70. New York: de Gruyter, 2008.

"Women, Honor, and Context in Mediterranean Antiquity." *Harvard Theological Review* 64.1 (2008) 323–37.

2009

"Early Christian Family." In *Proceedings of the American Benedictine Academy Conventions, August 10–13, 2006*, edited by Renée Branigan, 1–12. 2009.

"The Politics of Patronage and the Politics of Kinship: The Meeting of the Ways." *Biblical Theology Bulletin* 39.3 (2009) 143–52.

""When You Pray, Go into Your *Tameion*" (Matthew 6:6) But Why?" *CBQ* 71.4 (2009) 723–40.

"Women Leaders of Households in Early Christianity." *Emmanuel* 115.2 (2009) 141–43, 146–52.

2010
"Accusers, Mourners, Disciples: Women in Luke's Passion Narrative." *TBT* 48.2 (2010) 75–59.
"Constructions of Gender in the Roman Imperial World." In *Understanding the Social World of the New Testament*, edited by Dietmar Neufeld and Richard E. Demaris, 44–56. Oxford: Routledge, 2010.

Abbreviations

AB	Anchor Bible
ABRL	Anchor Bible Reference Library
ANRW	*Aufstieg und Niedergang der römischen Welt*
BDAG	Walter Bauer, Frederick W. Danker, William F. Arndt, and F. Wilbur Gingrich, *A Greek-English Dictionary of the New Testament and Other Early Christian Literature*, 3rd ed. Chicago: University of Chicago Press, 2000
BETL	Bibliotheca ephemeridum theologicarum lovaniensium
BibInt	*Biblical Interpretation*
BibIntSer	Biblical Interpretation Series
BibSem	Biblical Seminar
BJS	Brown Judaic Studies
BR	*Biblical Research*
CBQ	*Catholic Biblical Quarterly*
CDiosc	Casa dei Dioscuri (VI 9,6.7) in Pompeii
CIL	*Corpus Inscriptionum latinarum*
CR:BS	*Currents in Research: Biblical Studies*
FCNT	Feminist Companion to the New Testament and Early Christian Writings
HTR	*Harvard Theological Review*
ICC	International Critical Commentaries
Int	*Interpretation*
Inv.	Inventory number
JBL	*Journal of Biblical Literature*
JFSR	*Journal of Feminist Studies in Religion*
JRS	*Journal of Roman Studies*
JSNT	*Journal for the Study of the New Testament*
JSNTSup	Journal for the Study of the New Testament Supplements
JTS	*Journal of Theological Studies*
KJV	King James Version of the Bible

LCL	Loeb Classical Library
LNTS	Library of New Testament Studies
MANN	Museo Archeologico Nazionale di Napoli
NAB	New American Bible
NICNT	New International Commentary on the New Testament
NJB	New Jerusalem Bible
NovTSup	Novum Testamentum Supplements
NRSV	New Revised Standard Version of the Bible
NTS	*New Testament Studies*
NTTS	New Testament Tools and Studies
OCD	*Oxford Classical Dictionary*, 3rd ed. (2003)
PP	La pitture pompeiana, eds. Irene Bragantini and Valeria Sampaolo (2009)
PPM	Ida Baldassare, ed., *Pompei: pitture e mosaici* (1990–2003; supplement 1995)
RM	*Mitteilungen des deutschen archaeologischen Instituts, Römischen Abteilungen = Römischen Mitteilungen*
RSV	Revised Standard Version of the Bible
SacPag	Sacra Pagina
SBL	Society of Biblical Literature
SBLMS	Society of Biblical Literature Monograph Series
SBT	Studies in Biblical Theology
SecCent	*Second Century*
SNTSMS	Society for New Testament Studies Monograph Series
SSAP	Studi della soprintenza archeologica di Pompei
TBT	*The Bible Translator*
TDNT	*Theological Dictionary of the New Testament*. Edited by Gerhard Kittel and Gerhard Friedrich. Translated by Geoffrey W. Bromiley. Grand Rapids: Eerdmans, 1964–76
WBC	Word Biblical Commentary
WUNT	Wissenschaftliche Untersuchungen zum Neuen Testament

Introduction

David Balch *and* Jason T. Lamoreaux

PROFESSOR CAROLYN OSIEK'S BIBLIOGRAPHY REVEALS THAT SHE HAS either written or reviewed some of the most provocative books published during her professional career. I will introduce this volume honoring her contributions by a highly selective focusing on a recurrent theme announced in the subtitle of her recent book with Margaret MacDonald, "house churches," that is, the lives, and worship of patrons, women, slaves, and children in domestic spaces, including their meals together and the architecture of those spaces. Second, I will briefly illustrate that Prof. Osiek's publishing has been both academic and pastoral, that is, also concerned for the church and her contemporaries' struggle with how to live faithful lives. The co-editor, Jason T. Lamoreaux, who originally suggested this Festschrift and who has done the lion's share of editing, will comment on Prof. Osiek from a doctoral student's perspective.

Professor Osiek published her dissertation,[1] written at Harvard with the guidance of Helmut Koester, which already reveals her interest in social history: chapter 6 concerns "Rich and Poor in Second Century Rome." The next year she published an overview, asking *What Are They Saying about the Social Setting of the New Testament?*[2] This booklet dealt with questions of ethnicity (Part I: Jew and Greek), status (Part II: Slave and Free), and gender (Part III: Male and Female), the latter already addressing the household code and its implications.

---

1. Osiek, *Rich and Poor in the Shepherd of Hermas*, 1983. Having spent years writing the dissertation, a decade and a half after having published it, she authored *Shepherd of Hermas: A Commentary*, 1999, commenting, e.g., on "The Woman Church, the principal revealer in the *Visions* ... This female guide has no true precedent in Western literature" (16).

2. Osiek, *What Are They Saying about the Social Setting of the New Testament?* 1984.

Early too Prof. Osiek wrote a commentary on Galatians,³ later on Philippians.⁴ The few pages allowed in *The Women's Bible Commentary* on "Galatians" drew her remarks on "no male and female (3:28)," "God as 'Father' (4:4–7)," "Paul as Mother to the Galatian Christians (4:21–31)," the "Allegory of Sarah and Hagar (4:21–31)," as well as on "Freedom in Christ (5:1, 13)." In chapter 5 Osiek wrote, "Paul may be doing something quite radical: He is holding up traditionally feminine values as ideals for everyone, male and female . . . Bearing the cross in freedom does not mean enduring abuse and victimhood, but living genuinely for others out of one's own inner freedom" (337).

After the turn of the millennium, Prof. Osiek published an amazing series of extraordinarily insightful articles and books. Her article on "Archaeological and Architectural Issues and the Question of Demographic and Urban Forms"⁵ is simply the best available on the subject. She surveys housing forms in early Palestine, later Roman Jerusalem, the Greek peristyle house and terrace houses of Roman Ephesus, as well as the *domus* and *insula* of Pompeii, Herculaneum, and Ostia. She collects four texts that distinguish how women function in Greek houses from their roles in Roman houses (89, 93). Then she turns to imagining how Christian groups would have related when worshipping. One of the most significant contributions during these years is her discussion of patronage,⁶ including women who were leaders of house churches, noting the Roman example of Quadratilla (Pliny the Younger, *Ep.* 7.24), who planned her own dinner entertainment; she must have presided at table, something that would have been thought quite un-

---

3. Osiek, *Galatians* (1980). Compare her later "Galatians," in *The Women's Bible Commentary* (1992), 333–37. On Romans, compare Osiek, "Romans 'Down the Pike': Glimpses from Later Years" (2004), 149–61, commenting on 1) the considerable cultural and theological diversity in the Roman church, 2) the strong Jewish component, 3) the tendency to choose moderate rather than extreme positions, and 4) the early lack of a centralized organization.

4. Osiek, *Philippians Philemon*, Abingdon New Testament Commentaries (Nashville: Abingdon, 2000).

5. Osiek, "Archaeological and Architectural Issues and the Question of Demographic and Urban Forms," in *Handbook of Early Christianity: Social Science Approaches*, ed. Anthony J. Blasi, Jean Duhaime, and Paul-André Turcotte (Walnut Creek, CA: Altamira, 2002) 83–103.

6. Compare her later summary, Osiek, "The Patronage of Women in Early Christianity," (2008) 173–92.

usual, but which also presented possibilities for Christian women.[7] Strikingly, she notes[8] that 1 Cor 14:30 implies that most in attendance are sitting rather than reclining, which possibly means that some reclined in a triclinum, while most others sat outside in the peristyle.

A symposium[9] provided her an opportunity to summarize the results of her research. The Service of Word and the Service of Altar were the reverse of our contemporary practice, that is, first believers ate and then the symposium followed, that is, the wine and entertainment, including the philosophical discussion.[10] She points out that patronage meant that the powerful protected and nourished others under their care, which involved mutuality, but not equality. She posits an architectural change about 140–150 CE, when Christians moved out of the dining room into the hall. Buildings may have looked like private houses but were remodeled on the inside. So the groups no longer reclined or sat at a meal but stood or sat on the floor. Both the *Didaskalia* and Justin Martyr assume such arrangements, along with the Christian house discovered at Dura Europus.[11] Pastoral care was no longer in the hands of private patrons. She summarizes in three points: 1) there have always been designated leaders, but the forms of leadership have evolved flexibly. In the first and early second centuries, no clear understanding of clergy or ordination had developed. 2) Society was hierarchical. 3) She asks, can we, should we, try to go back to any of these forms? Her response and assertion is, probably we cannot go back, but we certainly can go forward. Based on the knowledge of what has been, a freedom is given to us to evolve new forms, new understandings, new interpretations, and new ways of meeting real needs. So knowledge of history is enlightening—to know what has been helps us imagine what will be. But it will never be exactly the same; it will be different.

With Kevin Madigan she then published *Ordained Women in the Early Church*.[12] To note a couple of points: the preponderance of evi-

---

7. Osiek, "Archaeological and Architectural Issues" 98.

8. Ibid., 99.

9. Osiek, "Who Did What in the Church in the New Testament?" (2004) 1–12.

10. Ibid., 3.

11. Ibid., 7.

12. Madigan and Osiek, *Ordained Women in the Early Church* (2005). I will not select comments from *A Woman's Place: House Churches in Earliest Christianity*; it is, and for some time will surely remain, the standard in the field.

dence for female deacons is clearly in the East, but the West is not without its references, often conciliar prohibitions.[13] It is a false assumption that all women officeholders were celibate, either virgin or widowed. Finally, a quote: "Except in monastic traditions, those in today's liturgically impoverished West, with its fixation on sacrament and preaching, can too easily forget that recitation of the Divine Office is an essential component of the liturgy. There is ample evidence that female deacons exercised leadership in this role. Then there are the intriguing pieces of evidence of female presbyters who do indeed seem to have exercised a ministry at the altar, even in the West."[14]

Second, as indicated, I will briefly illustrate that Prof. Osiek's publishing has not only been academic, but also pastoral. An article that illustrates both concerns provides a transition: "Who Submits to Whom?"[15] The question concerns the interaction of revelation and culture. To what extent do faithful and observant believers accommodate to cultural norms and are fully citizens of their world, and to what extent must they say "no" to some cultural norms or practices in order to affirm their identity as believers?[16] The author of Revelation (2.14, 20) refused to compromise the Jewish ritual prohibition against eating meat, a contrast with Paul's playing rather loose with his advice to Corinth (1 Cor 8.1–13; 10.27–33). Prof. Osiek's extensive travels around the world are reflected in her observation of another contrast, one between contemporary Asian and African cultures and the West. Age remains a determining factor in the former; but deference to elders often favors males over females. In the New Testament, the problem is illustrated by the household codes, eliciting her comment: the tendency of elite males to make of themselves the center of the universe is very ancient. The idea of social equality could be entertained among this elite group without extending it to all men.[17] Prof. Osiek's evaluation is informed

13. Ibid., 3.

14. Ibid., 5. The authors cite Mary Ann Rossi, "Priesthood, Precedent, and Prejudice: On Recovering the Women Priests of Early Christianity," *Journal of Feminist Studies in Religion* 7/1 (1991), 73–94. Translation with introduction of Georgio Otranto, "Note sul sacerdozio femminile nell'antichità in margine a una testimonianza di Gelasio I," *Vetera Christianorum* 19 (1982), 341–60.

15. Osiek, "Who Submits to Whom? Submission and Mutuality in the Family," (2004) 57–64. Compare her recent "Family Matters," (2005) 201–20.

16. Osiek, "Who Submits to Whom?" 57.

17. Ibid., 59.

by the following insight: It follows from Aristotle that the concept of the person in these ancient societies was very different from what it is today in Western society. The effects of the Enlightenment, the democratic experiments of modern countries, and the psychological and technological revolutions have completely changed our ideas of what it is to be a person in community, from subordinate or ruling member of society, depending on one's birth, to free and autonomous individual with inalienable rights.[18] Her subsequent discussion is a pastoral interpretation of Gal 3.28 in relation to diverse, contemporary interpretations of the New Testament household codes, concluding as follows: "here is a message perhaps more timely than all the discussion of submission, pro and con. Can we learn to relate to each other, not hierarchically, not anti-hierarchically, but with the give and take that characterizes mature relationships in which persons are secure enough to establish a rhythm of taking and receiving, of ceding and affirming"?[19]

Very early Prof. Osiek published her pastoral *Beyond Anger*.[20] Our author encourages embracing the cross, not as passive victims, but as free agents capable of sustaining the liberating and redemptive suffering that is necessary in order that women's continuing presence in the church can effect needed changes according to the pattern of the gospel.

Among the many, I choose to mention two more pastoral contributions, including an article for which Prof. Osiek has received as many requests as any other: "The Spiritual Direction of Thinking Types."[21] Most literature in the field is written by "feelers" for "feelers, and members of most religious communities, post Vatican II, are feelers." Prof. Osiek, therefore, writes on "how to survive in religious life as a personality type minority." Spiritual directors should NOT advise a thinker in her prayer to "get out of your head into your heart! This also affects one's image of God; Jesus as strong, just, and reliable relate especially to the thinking function."[22] But reason does not govern the dark night, loss of control, powerlessness, the chaos of life. A sense of being abandoned by God may bring a new integration, the discovery of dimensions of life

---

18. Ibid., 61.
19. Ibid., 64.
20. Osiek, *Beyond Anger* (1986).
21. Osiek, "The Spiritual Direction of Thinking Types" (1985), 209–19.
22. Ibid., 213.

beyond previously accepted limits. One more insight: while feelers find it more difficult to forgive, thinkers find it more difficult to admit that they are wrong and ask forgiveness.

Finally, with three of her R.S.C.J. sisters, Prof. Osiek researched and published *Women's Readings for the Liturgical Year*,[23] now regrettably out of print. Women ask: Where are our voices? Where are our memories? Where are our hopes? Why are prominent women from the Hebrew and Christian scriptures missing from the lectionary or included in such an abbreviated fashion? The sisters do not call this an alternative lectionary, but one that "enriches our liturgical year." Enriching readings for the first week of advent, for example, are: First Sunday of Advent: Rev 12.1–6; Monday: 1 Enoch 42.1–3; Tuesday: Sirach 1.1–10; Wednesday: Sirach 4.11–18; Thursday: Sirach 6.18–31; Friday: Sirach 24.1–12; Saturday: Sir 24.13–14, 19–21.

This selection of articles and books is obviously not extensive, but meant to be suggestive of the many listed in the bibliography. I had the pleasure and intellectual excitement first of being Prof. Osiek's co-author and later her colleague teaching at Brite Divinity School. Lyn, may your generativity continue to bless others in your retirement!

While David had the honor of working with Dr. Osiek for many years, I, Jason T. Lamoreaux, have been her graduate student. In this introduction, I will briefly comment on the student articles submitted in Dr. Osiek's honor with a view toward illuminating some of the characteristics Dr. Osiek has as a teacher and mentor. Her patience, professionalism, and guidance are central to why students have come to study under her tutelage, but once a student has had Dr. Osiek for a class, it becomes clear that her humor, spirituality, and ease with others also contributes to the praise she receives from her pupils.

In this collection honoring Dr. Osiek, four of her graduate students have submitted essays. The essays are pieces of dissertation topics or papers written under the guidance of Dr. Osiek. A testament to Dr. Osiek's breadth of knowledge, the essays delve into issues concerning the opponents to Paul in 2 Corinthians (Barrier), humor in the Gospel of Luke (Bednarz), women's ordination in the Georgian text of Hippolytus' commentary on Song of Songs (Smith), and literary and social-science

---

23. Barbara Bowe, Kathleen Hughes, Sharon Karam, and Carolyn Osiek, R.S.C.J. *Silent Voices, Sacred Lives: Women's Readings for the Liturgical Year* (New York: Paulist, 1992).

criticism in the Johannine tradition (Merritt). Furthermore, these essays reflect Dr. Osiek's own concerns about women in the early church and their roles within leadership. While this is the case, Dr. Osiek always encouraged her students to find their own voices and pursue their own interests.

Barrier sums up Dr. Osiek's care for her students in his first footnote: "The motivation for revising this article in a Festschrift for Carolyn Osiek is due to the fact that she approached me immediately after attending my lecture in Irving, Texas, and encouraged me to continue to develop this essay for publication." Dr. Osiek often encouraged her students' work and pushed them to excel in publications, teaching, learning, and oral presentations at conferences. But this shows the serious side of a far more down to earth personality. Dr. Osiek not only endears herself to her students through her breadth of knowledge and encouragement but also through her sharp wit and sense of humor. In this regard, Bednarz' article is an apt tribute, not only to the academic life of Dr. Osiek, but also to her personality. Bednarz gives a glimpse into Dr. Osiek's interactions with students when she states, "I cannot recall ever attending a feast with Lyn that she did not engage in some serious discussion of the biblical world in one moment and enjoy amusing anecdotes and teasing in next moment." Many of her students can attest to this very experience.

Personally, I arrived at Brite Divinity School in the fall of 2005. While I was meeting the faculty at Brite, some for the first time, one faculty member commented, "Lyn walks on water." The comment was neither snide nor sarcastic but said in admiration. Some years later, I had asked for a recommendation letter. In granting my request, Dr. Osiek noted that her influence might not give me an advantage for this particular job. Needless to say, I was taken aback and replied that she was mistaken. I mention this anecdote in order to contrast it with the aforementioned faculty comment. While many speak highly of her, Dr. Osiek remains humble and demonstrates a rarely found harmony in her life. As her bibliography reflects, Dr. Osiek is not only concerned with matters of scholarship but also of spiritual wellbeing.

As the articles in this volume indicate, Dr. Osiek's scholarship has touched many in the guild, far more than we could have included. While discussing the contents of the volume, David Balch, Barbara Bowe, and I decided it was prudent to narrow the topics within which to find contributors. We decided to stay within the topics represented by the majority of Dr. Osiek's publications: Women, the Second Testament, and the Early Church. Regrettably, this excluded Intertestamental and First Testament colleagues. If all who admired Dr. Osiek could have contributed, we could have collected enough essays for a multi-volume work.

Lastly, we, the editors, think it is important not only to honor Dr. Osiek with this volume, but also to show gratitude in memory of Dr. Osiek's good friend and fellow sister in her order, Dr. Barbara Bowe. Barbara Bowe was originally a co-editor on this volume and was extremely excited to present it to Carolyn, her longtime colleague and good friend. During the planning process for this volume, Barbara Bowe discovered she had brain cancer. The cancer rapidly took over and Barbara passed on March 14, 2010.

> The challenge of faith begins—for every person—with the invitation to know the mysterious deity we call "God." But soon we learn that no name, no affirmation about God, no set of descriptors or dogmatic formulas can fully capture the One who is Holy Mystery and so we begin, as Moses did, in every God encounter by taking our sandals off in recognition that we are on holy ground."—Barbara Bowe, R.S.C.J.

The River of Life

Contemplative at heart
globetrotter with such ease
complex in thinking
yet delighted by nature's simplest offering,
your library is far-flung now
among colleagues and former students.
Your lecture notes now enhance
the courses of your newly-minted scholars,
and the seeds you have planted of the Word
you have learned and loved bears fruit
in who knows how many lands and languages?
      And your work is done.
Not quite!
      The work of your life was never wholly
      behind the podium or in academia
      but in reports from your contemplation,
      as you drew *water joyfully from the springs of salvation*.
And the pilgrims you have taken to River Jordan and beyond
And the students you have taken to the Heart of Life
And the organizations you have led with grace and clarity
And the collaborative work on books which expand our vision
And the tenacity with which you push to the truth,
all the while taking joy in a garden,
testify to your living legacy.
The river of your life now brings you back to what you love—
Research, translation, and searching out the stories of pioneer women,
Lives not fully celebrated until your words flesh them out.
Delight then, dear master teacher, in this new chapter of life,
but know that we do not believe your tours are done,
or the last lecture given.
Enjoy the time to relish what your life is most intensely about,
a time of *drawing water joyfully from the springs of salvation,*
this time not far from the mighty Mississippi,
which brought the undaunted Philippine Duchesne almost 200 years ago.
Your grateful students do the same from your words and example.
                              Sharon Karam rscj

PART ONE

Visual and Oral Documents

1

Values of Roman Women Including Priests
Visually Represented in Pompeii and Herculaneum

David Balch

Introduction: Professor Carolyn Osiek, RSCJ

I WRITE TO EXPRESS ADMIRATION OF AND GRATITUDE TO CAROLYN Osiek, a former colleague. Professor Osiek and I co-authored a book, responding to an invitation from Prof. Don Browning, and then, utilizing funds granted a second time by Prof. Browning through the Lily Endowment, we invited the outstanding authors whom we had discovered and cited in our footnotes to an interdisciplinary conference to dialogue face to face. Later still, we became colleagues at Brite Divinity School, and, then on the same faculty, enjoyed teaching gifted MDiv and PhD students. I like to think that Lyn moved south solely because of the quality of our faculty, staff, and students, but occasionally admit that Chicago's frigid winters might also have motivated her. She was a continual blessing to us all.

In the book we co-authored, her paragraphs on "women teachers of women"[1] are especially innovative. In her conference paper, Prof. Osiek again typically made new observations, this time in reference

---

1. Osiek and Balch, *Families in the New Testament World*, 167–73: "Despite all the recent interest in women's history, one aspect of women's lives that is not frequently spoken of is the intergenerational family activity whereby women in traditional societies convey wisdom and practical knowledge from mother to daughter and surrogate mother to surrogate daughter." Compare Setälä and Savunen, *Female Networks and the Public Sphere in Roman Society*.

to women slaves.² In concert with Margaret Y. MacDonald and Janet H. Tulloch, she developed these and other insights and descriptions of early Christian women.³ Further, with Kevin Madigan, Prof. Osiek collected all the evidence for ordained women, deacons and presbyters in the early church, just a historical study, she claimed—with a gleam in her eye.⁴ Already by the time of the conference that we co-sponsored, my interests had shifted toward visual representations in the Greco-Roman world. Therefore, I offer Prof. Osiek this study of Roman visual representations of some feminine values, including the visualization of women priests.

Commenting on Paul's address in Philippians 1:1–2, Osiek writes:

> . . . the Roman genius for order and organization has expressed itself earlier in the Roman colony of Philippi than elsewhere. It is likely that the *episkopoi* are a council formed of the natural leaders of the house-churches in the city. We know that women who were heads of households were also leaders of house churches from the beginning (Acts 12.12; 16.15, 40; Col 4.15). We also know that there were women *diakonoi*, notably Phoebe of Cenchrae (Rom 16.1; probably also 1 Tim 3.11). Because of the corroborating evidence, it is simple bias to assume that the *episkopoi* and *diakonoi* of Phil 1.1 must be exclusively male. Indeed, Euodia and Syntyche [Phil 4.2] may be among either group.⁵
>
> What best fits is that Euodia and Syntyche, important enough to be called "coworkers" by Paul, were in fact *episkopoi*, that is, heads of local house churches and thus strategic members of the church.⁶

---

2. Osiek, "Female Slaves, *Porneia*, and the Limits of Obedience," in Balch and Osiek, eds., *Early Christian Families* (2003), 255–56: "It has become customary and helpful to distinguish between sex and gender . . . In most slave systems, while slaves undeniably have a sex, they do not have gender. Thus a male slave is not a man . . . Consequently a female slave is not a woman (*gune, mulier*), and thus cannot have feminine traits ascribed to her nor the social expectations of a woman in her culture placed on her, nor can she claim any status privileges inherent in the cultural construct of womanhood. Therefore the safeguards built into the culture to protect women are not to be applied to female slaves, which is an added degree of alienation."

3. Osiek and MacDonald, *A Woman's Place*.

4. Madigan and Osiek, *Ordained Women in the Early Church*.

5. Osiek, *Philippians*, 35.

6. Ibid., 111–12.

Osiek and MacDonald, *A Woman's Place*, chapter 7, also concerns "Women Leaders of Households and Christian Assemblies," and chaps. 8–10 concern other aspects of women's leadership and agency among early Christians in the Roman world. The two authors begin their

> study of the lives of wives with an ironic scene, a gathering in the house of Nympha, where the hierarchical household code is being proclaimed (Col. 3:18—4:1). The irony lies in the fact that Nympha is clearly a woman leader of a house church, yet the epistle that is being read in her house recommends the subjugation of wife to husband in a manner that makes the endorsement of Nympha's role in Col. 4:15–16 surprising. The apparent contradiction has frequently been dismissed ... [But] it is surprising to find the explicit reference to her leadership of a house church in a document that marks the beginning of a trend in early church literature of the latter half of the first century CE: the tendency to instruct subordinate members of the household to be subject to the *paterfamilias* (the husband, father, and master of slaves) ...[7]

Casa dei Dioscuri (VI 9,6.7; plate 1) in Pompeii: Heroic Masculine and "Universal" Feminine Paradigms

Lucia Romizzi has argued that the differentiation between the male patriarchal world and the world of women is visually represented in the Casa dei Dioscuri = CDiosc (VI 9,6.7) in Pompeii, a grand complex (1520 square meters) restructured in the Neronian/Flavian eras with two atria and two peristyles.[8] I briefly summarize Romizzi's suggestions about the decorative scheme in this house as an example of distinctions within the domus noticed by Osiek and MacDonald. Three other authors study the visual representations in this Pompeian domus, including L. Richardson, Jr.[9] and Irene Bragantini.[10] An important fourth

---

7. Osiek and MacDonald, *A Woman's Place*, 18.

8. Romizzi, "La Casa dei Dioscuri," which I cite. Compare her *Programmi decorative*, 382–86, on this house.

9. Richardson, *Pompeii*.

10. Bragantini, "Casa dei Dioscuri." Note: Richardson employs an older system of numbering the rooms of the house, Bragantini a more recent system; I follow Bragantini. For Richardson the vestibule is #3, for Bragantini #33. For Richardson the Corinthian atrium is #7, for Bragantini #37. For Richardson the tablinum is #26, for Bragantini

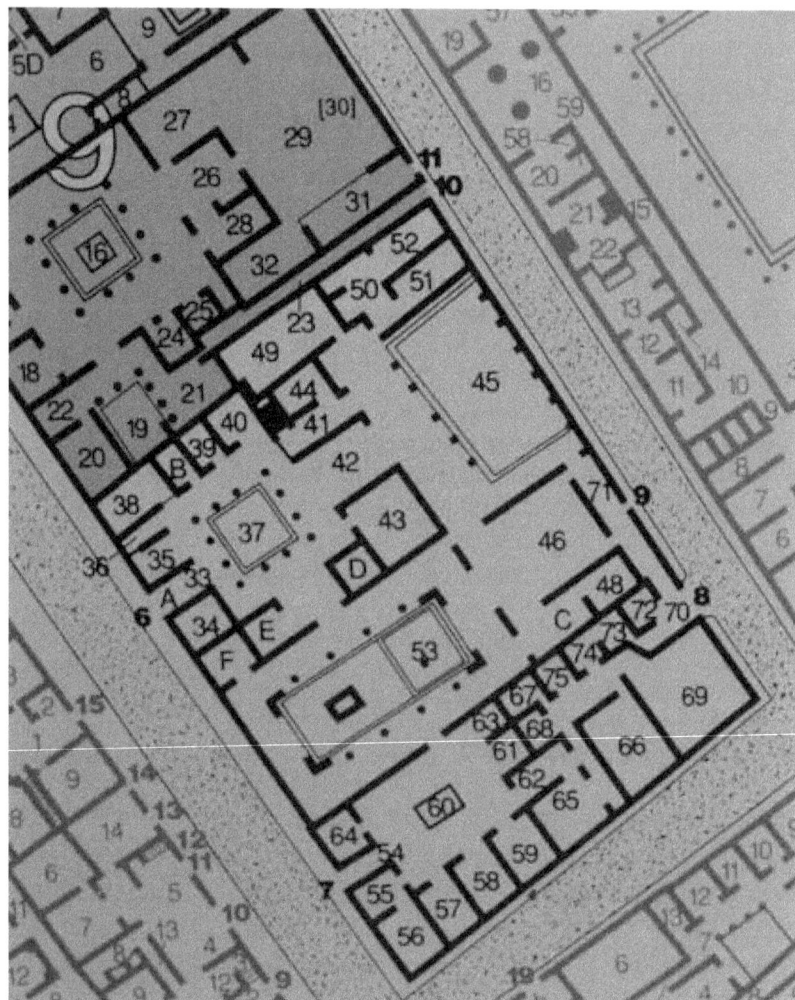

PLATE 1: Casa dei Dioscuri (VI 9,6.7), plan, from PPM IV (1993) 860

source is the new catalogue of the permanent exhibit at the National Archaeological Museum in Naples,[11] color plates 129–145, which reproduce frescoes from the CDiosc; captions for these plates were written by Fiorenza Grasso. But this article is most indebted to the formulations of

---

#42. For Richardson the pseudo-peristyle is #33, for Bragantini #45. For Richardson the great, south peristyle is #45, for Bragantini #53.

11. Bragantini and Sampaolo, eds., *La pittura pompeiana*

Romizzi,[12] who adds[13] that the *tabulae pictae* in the CDiosc is similar to the scheme of visual representations in the Pompeian macellum (VII 9,7),[14] a rare public edifice in the ancient world where the cycle of images is preserved. In a careful study Richardson[15] concludes, "the seven painters of the CDiosc cannot be regarded as a fair cross section of the Fourth Style painters of Pompeii, for the house was so splendid that only superior artists were chosen to decorate it."[16] Romizzi[17] argues that the decorative program of the CDiosc can be schematized as follows:

A. Atrium area
    1. vestibule (33)   status: *ordo equestris* (Dioscuri)
    2. Corinthian atrium (37) world of gods/goddesses
    3. tablinum (42)   heroic masculine paradigm (virtue of Achilles)
B. Eastern peristyle area (45) world of Dionysus: the sacred, nature, theater
C. South peristyle area (53)   models of comportment for the "universal" feminine: wife and mother (mythic heroines)

The vestibule (33) and tablinum (42) visually celebrate social status, that is, the equestrian order, those males for whom the Dioscuri are protectors and Achilles the noble ideal, while the grand fourth style frescoes of

---

12. I have not been able to utilize Esposito, "La 'Bottega dei Vettii.'"

13. Romizzi, "La Casa dei Dioscuri," 82.

14. Romizzi was anticipated by Bragantini's note at 972, #219. See Sampaolo, "Macellum."

15. Richardson, *Pompeii*, 159.

16. Ibid., 115–60, discusses the seven painters of the CDiosc in detail, comparing the frescoes in this house with those elsewhere in Pompeii and Herculaneum, e.g. the "Dioscuri painter" worked also in the Casa dei Vettii (pp. 121–22), the "Io painter" in the Macellum and in the Tempio d'Iside (pp. 124, 131, 134) as well as in the Casa dei Vettii (pp. 129, 131), and the "Perseus painter," who was responsible for the great peristyle (Bragantini, "Casa dei Dioscuri," #53) of the CDiosc, worked also in the Casa dei Vettii (pp. 156, 159). The concluding quotation above is from Richardson, *Pompeii*, 159.

17. Romizzi, "La Casa dei Dioscuri," 139. I have placed quotation marks around Romizzi's adjective "universal," because it does not fit early Jewish and Christian evidence, e.g., Philo, *Contemplative Life*, 18–19, 83, 88; 1 Cor 7:10–11, 25–27; Luke 18:28–30; Acts 21:8–9.

the south peristyle (53) visually represent examples of mythic heroines. This collection of women incarnates virtues of the family: the young wife (Andromeda) and the faithful wife (Penelope), as well as counter examples, a murderous mother (Medea) and an impious mother (Niobe).[18] The feminine *exempla* are presented in three diverse areas of the south peristyle: 1) two frescoes on the north and south walls of the great peristyle (53: Penelope, a priestess), 2) two now faded frescoes on the pilastri closest to oecus (46: Andromeda, Medea), and 3) the killing of the sons and daughters of Niobi on the eastern surface of the western pilastri, facing but on the end of the garden most distant from oecus (46).[19] In relation to these images of women, Romizzi quotes Ovid: "But whatever is said to men, deem also said to you, ye women: we give arms to the opposing sides, and if aught thereof concerns not your needs, yet by example it can teach much" (*Remedies of Love* 53–54, trans. Mozley in LCL). In more detail,[20] the CDiosc has two axes, the first major axis from the entrance vestibule (33), through the Corinthian atrium (37)[21]

---

18. For domestic frescoes that function as ethical counterpoints, see Balch, *Roman Domestic Art*, 210–11. For moral contrasts in the textual world, see Malherbe, "Hellenistic Moralists" 284–85, 297–98, quoting, e.g., Seneca *ep.* 6.5–6; 52.8; also *Paul and the Popular Philosophers* 39–48. Pliny *Nat. Hist.* 35.40.147–48 catalogues "women artists," which means that they might have been among the crafts persons who painted these frescoes. Pliny remembers that "when Marcus Varro [116–27 BCE] was a young man, Iaia of Cyzicus . . . painted pictures with the brush at Rome, . . . chiefly portraits of women, as well as a large picture on wood of an Old Woman at Naples, and also a portrait of herself . . . No one else had a quicker hand in painting, while her artistic skill was such that in the prices she obtained she far outdid the most celebrated portrait painters of the same period . . . , whose pictures fill the galleries." (trans. Rackham in LCL) See Roux and Barré, *Herculaneum und Pompeji*, vol. 1, Tafeln 1–2, 13–14, 58; vol. 2, Tafel 11–13, 48. Two visual representations of women artists painting occur in Pompeii: Casa dei Chiurgo (VI 1,10; inventory 9018 MANN; *PPM* IV 75; see plate 2) and perhaps Casa dell'Imperatrice di Russia (VI 14,42; inventory 9017 MANN; see plate 3). Pliny reports that Iaia painted "chiefly portraits of women," which fits both Romizzi's description of the Casa dei Dioscuri, south peristyle ("La Casa dei Dioscuri," 53) and Barringer's description of the Pompeian macellum (see below).

19. See Romizzi, "La Casa dei Dioscuri," 139–40.

20. Here I follow Richardson closely, but employ Bragantini's room numbers. I am re-presenting Romizzi's thesis and describe only some of the visual representations, giving little architectural detail, enough of the latter to indicate the visual representations' location.

21. Richardson (*Pompeii*, 8) observes that there are only four Pompeian atria that are truly Corinthian, defined by more than four columns supporting the compluvium; this one has twelve columns.

PLATE 2: Woman artist painting (Casa dei Chiurgo [VI 1, 10; PPM IV 75; PP 102; and Bergmann 157–59])

and its impluvium, then through the tablinum (42) into the porticoed pseudo-peristyle/garden (45), a major axis running from (south)west to (north)east, which concludes in a lararium standing against the east wall.[22] A second minor axis lies at ninety degrees to the major one, beginning at the north(west) rim of the impluvium in the Corinthian atrium (37), and running south(east) through the impluvium and then through a wide, decorated door (2.32 m. wide x 2.27 m. high[23]) into the great south peristyle (53).[24]

22. Ibid., 45.
23. Ibid., 51.
24. Ibid., 8.

PLATE 3: Woman artist painting (perhaps Casa dell'Imperatrice di Russia [VI 14,42; 14, 42; see PP 102])

The façade of the house was decorated with images of Hermes/Mercury, god of business, and Fortuna holding a horn of plenty.[25] The entrance (door #6) vestibule (33) is decorated with two monumental vignettes of the Dioscuri, divine twins, Castor and Pollux (each 63 cm; plate 4).[26] Mythological images in vestibules are rare in Pompeii. These divine twins are protectors of equestrians, suggesting an owner who belongs to that order.[27]

25. Bragantini, "Casa dei Dioscuri," #9; Romizzi, "La Casa dei Dioscuri," fig. 4.

26. Romizzi, "La Casa dei Dioscuri," 87, plate 2 gives measurements. Richardson, *Pompeii*, plates XV.1–2; Bragantini, "Casa dei Dioscuri," #14–15 (color); Romizzi, "La Casa dei Dioscuri," Figs. 5a-5a (color); Grasso, plates 129–130 (color).

27. Romizzi, "La Casa dei Dioscuri," 138. Romizzi (88–89) points out connections to other equestrian spaces and images in Pompeii: Fig. 6, Terme del Sarno, atrium (b; see

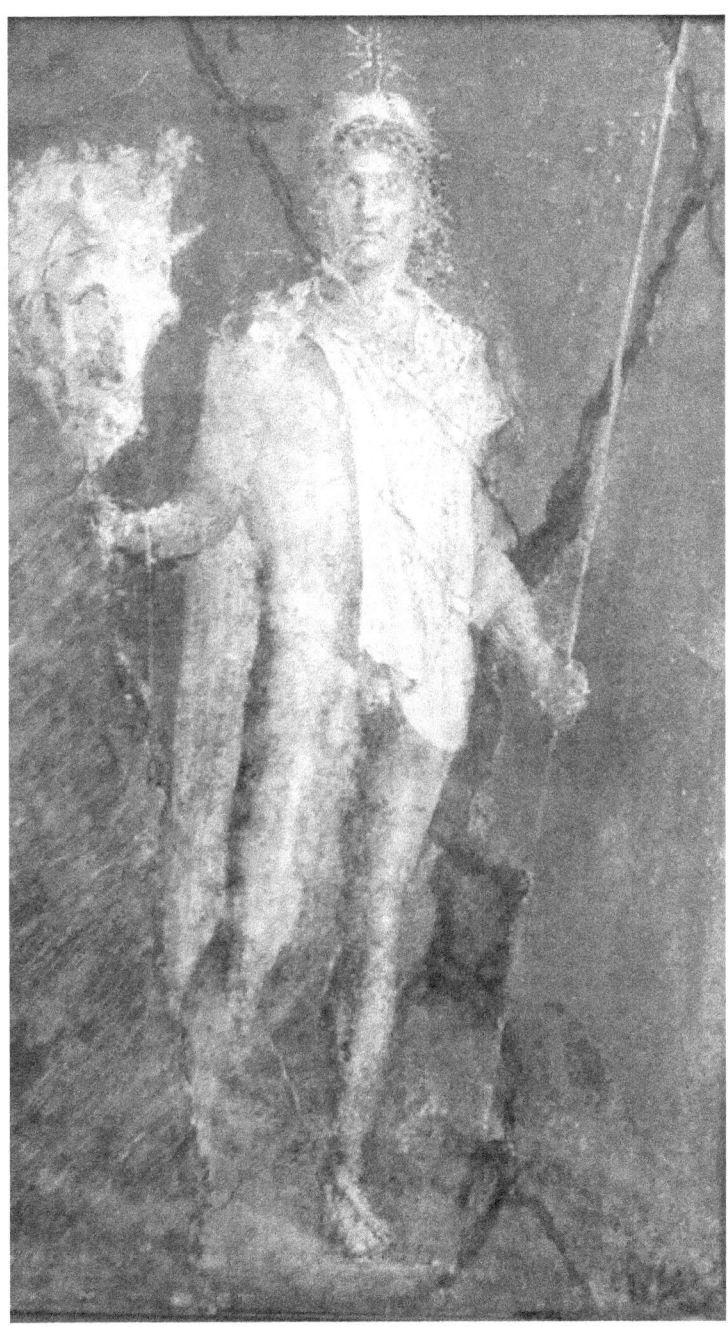

PLATE 4A: Dioscuri, Castor and Pollux, divine twins, protectors of equestrians. At entrance door (#6), Casa dei Dioscuri. Inventory 9453 and 9455 MANN.

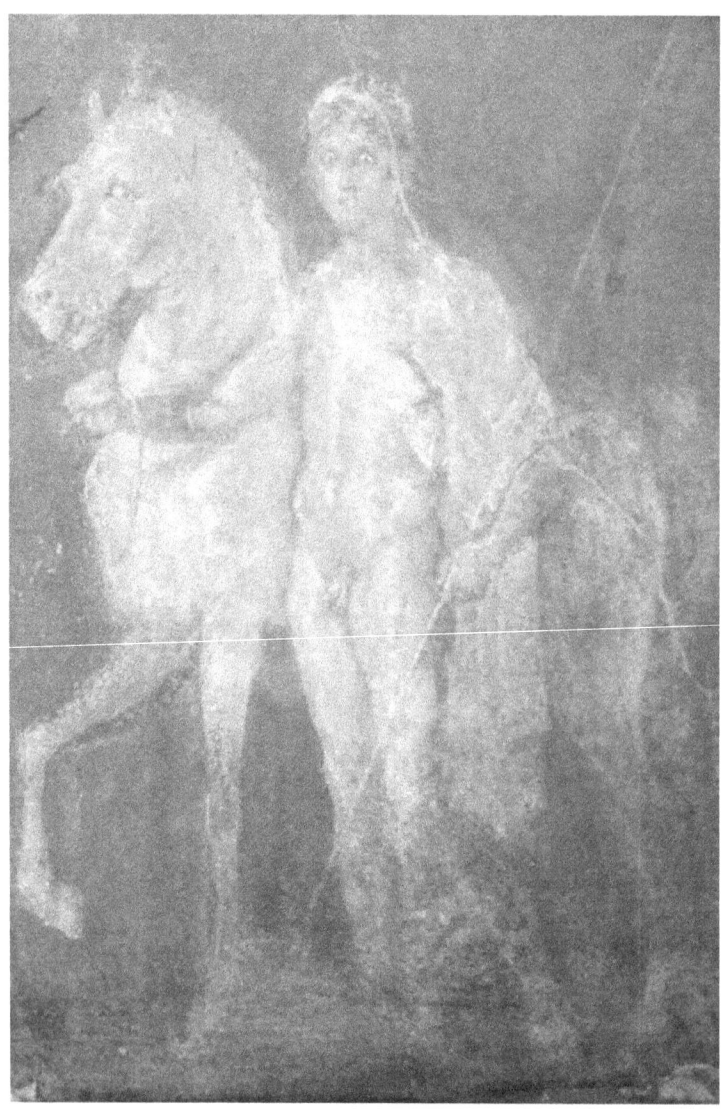

PLATE 4B: Dioscuri, Castor and Pollux, divine twins, protectors of equestrians. At entrance door (#6), Casa dei Dioscuri. Inventory 9453 and 9455 MANN.

A visitor, passing through the vestibule, would then enter the Corinthian atrium (37) with its crowd of monumental divine images in the fourth style. Jupiter enthroned, crowned by victory (plate 5) appears on the west, entrance wall.[28] The same west wall, south of the entrance, has another figure of Fortuna. The south wall, on either side of a bay opening into peristyle (53), has a Bacchus (plate 6) and a Victory in flight. In that bay on the west side of the door was a figure of Demeter/Ceres (plate 7),[29] a maternal, benevolent goddess who liberates from fear of death, and on the east side, of Apollo. On the east wall, opposite the entrance door, was a Saturn (plate 8), and perhaps also Mercury and a woman. The north wall has space for four figures, but we know only of a Mars,[30] a group of divine figures all painted on red grounds that confer *majestas* on the space.[31]

Continuing along the major axis into the tablinum (42), one again sees fourth style representations, on the south wall the discovery of Achilles on Scyros (plate 9), and on the north wall the quarrel between Achilles and Agamemnon (plate 10),[32] both celebrating military virtues and referring to Greek paideia.[33]

In oecus (43), a room adjacent to and south of the tablinum but with a door opening only onto the atrium in the atrium's southeast cor-

---

also *PPM* VIII 117 and Romizzi, Figs. 7ab). Also in Moregine, edificio dei Triclini, vano (B), Dioscuro. For the images of the Dioscuri in Moregine, triclinio (B), see Guzzo, *Tales from an Eruption*, 174–75; Mastroroberto, "Una visita di Nerone a Pompei," 500–501; and Mastroroberto, "L'*aurea aetas* neroniana," 62, 64–65, all in color.

28. Richardson, *Pompeii*, 12.

29. Kozakiewicz, "Appendix," 141, notices that the visual representation of Demeter/Ceres holding a long torch twined with a beaded fillet is similar to the fillet represented on the head of the statue of a priestess in the Macellum (see below).

30. Richardson, *Pompeii*, 14.

31. Ibid., plates XVI.1–2; XVII.1–2; Bragantini, "Casa dei Dioscuri," #53–54, 56, 60, 62 (all color); Romizzi, "La Casa dei Dioscuri," Figs. 10abcde (color); Grasso, plates 131–34 (color).

32. Richardson, *Pompeii*, plates XXXII–XXXIII, XXXVIII.1; Bragantini, "Casa dei Dioscuri," #82, 84, 88 (color); Romizzi, "La Casa dei Dioscuri," Figs. 23 (color), 24; Grasso, plates 136, 139 (color).

33. Richardson, *Pompeii*, 34.

PLATE 5: Zeus/Jupiter enthroned, crowned by victory. Corinthian atrium (37), western wall. Inv. 9551 MANN.

Plate 6: Dionysus/Bacchus and satyr. Corinthian atrium (37), western wall. Inv. 9268 MANN.

PLATE 7: Demeter/Ceres. Corinthian atrium (37), south wall. Inv. 9454 MANN.

PLATE 8: Saturn. Corinthian atrium (37), east wall opposite the entrance. Inv. 8837 MANN.

PLATE 9: Achilles on Scyros. Tablinum (42), south wall. Inv. 9104 MANN.

PLATE 10: Achilles confronting Agamemnon. Tablinum (42), north wall. Inv. 9110 MANN.

ner, two rare mythological subjects appear, on the north wall the Birth of Adonis[34] and on the west wall Minos and Scylla.[35]

Walking through the tablinum into the porticoed pseudo-peristyle (45), a center of family life,[36] one enters a refined residential area with oeci and triclinia, including a wide portico (4.7 m) whose length runs north/south between the atrium and the peristyle, sheltering some rooms (41–44) from the sun as well as having its own shade all day.[37] Between portico and garden there are five Doric columns, and others continue around the north and east walls, but not along the south wall. On the east wall, on either side of the opening to the tablinum, there were two theatrical frescoes, one of tragedy the other of comedy.[38] At the west end of the north wall was an image of Io and Argos (plate 11).[39] In the middle of the south wall a complicated building of two stories with open porches was visually represented:

> Before it stands a woman in priestly dress carrying a flaming torch in her right hand and a patera in her left. In the foreground is a low cylindrical altar, its top covered with offerings, beside which stands a dog. At the right, on one of the porches of the building, sits a fisherman wearing a *causia* [Macedonian hat] and holding a rod from which he unhooks a fish he has just caught. On a little pedestal at the left side of the building is a Priapic herm. The background is filled with trees and mountains (plate 12).[40]

34. Ibid., plate XXV; Bragantini, "Casa dei Dioscuri," #107; Romizzi, "La Casa dei Dioscuri," Fig. 30ab. An Easterner, whose name varies, is one of those who aroused the love of Aphrodite, who bore Adonis.

35. Richardson, *Pompeii*, 29 and plate XXV; Bragantini, "Casa dei Dioscuri," #107, 130; Romizzi, "La Casa dei Dioscuri," 125 and Figs. 30ab, 31. Scylla, daughter of the king of Megara, Nisus, betrayed the city to a besieging general, Minos, either for a bribe (Aeschylus *Choephori* 612–22) or for love (Ovid *Met.* 8.1–151), so this is yet another family story that is visually represented.

36. Richardson, *Pompeii*, 40.

37. Ibid., 41.

38. Ibid., 43 and plates LI.1–2; Bragantini, "Casa dei Dioscuri," #166–67; Romizzi, "La Casa dei Dioscuri," Figs. 27–28 ; Grasso, plate 135.

39. Bragantini, "Casa dei Dioscuri," #169 (color); Romizzi, "La Casa dei Dioscuri," Fig. 26 (color).

40. Richardson, *Pompeii*, 44. Gell (engravings by Gandy), online: http://www.mediterranees.net/voyageurs/gell/Chapter_13.html, immediately after describing the Phaedra and Hipplytus fresco, writes as follows: "In the same part of the portico, or *xystus*, at no. 30, is a singular picture. A priestess, with a torch in one hand and a dish of fruits in the other, is seen placed before a temple, or habitation, decorated with festoons

PLATE 11: Io and Argos. Porticoed pseudo-peristyle (45), west end of north wall. Inv. 8998 MANN.

Richardson admits that interpretation of the scene is difficult, but observes that similar paintings, perhaps by the same artist, recur repeatedly in Pompeii.[41] On the same south wall, east of the doorway from the

of verdure and torches. In front of her is an altar, the offerings upon which are pomegranates. Behind the dwelling is a man, in a peaked hat, fishing."

41. Richardson, *Pompeii*, 44 n. 253 cites the source of the image: Zahn 3, plate 48, and notes that Rostowzew, 96, n.1, interpreted the painting as a rite of the dead, so that the building shown was a tomb, an opinion Richardson finds attractive. Rostowzew (see his Tafel XI.1) draws a parallel to two fourth-style landscapes in the Casa della fontana piccola (VI 8,23.24; *PPM* IV 621–59, peristilo [10], #40–41), both landscapes with two-story buildings, a person fishing, and a priestess in a long robe. Both landscapes are also discussed by Frölich, who has the clearest figures (#5–6). This image from the Casa dei Dioscuri is not reproduced by Richardson, Bragantini, Romizzi, or Grasso.

PLATE 12: Priest carrying flaming torch in her right hand, patera in her left, with low cylindrical altar in foreground, top covered with offerings, building with porches in background, from porch of which a fisherman unhooks a fish from a rod. Priapic herm is to viewer's left; background is filled with trees and mountains. Porticoed pseudo-peristyle (45), middle of south wall. Source: W. Zahn, *Die schönsten Ornamente und merkwürdigsten Gemälde aus Pompeji* 3 (1859), plate 48.

pseudo-peristyle (45) to the great oecus (46), was a fresco of Phaedra,[42] daughter of Minos, in love with her son, Hippolytus,[43] which seems to have a proleptic function, preparing for the south peristyle (53), where the orientation is feminine.[44]

The enormous Rhodian peristyle (53) to the south is among the rare *oeci cyziceni* (see Vetruvius 6.3.10) with a floor of *opus sectile*, sheets of precious marble, the only one discovered in Pompeii, large enough for two triclinia to be arranged in the middle of the room.[45] Along the minor axis of the domus, one walks from the Corinthian atrium (37) through an opening framed by three landscape frescoes, whose subjects anticipate mythical themes of the peristyle itself. Above the doorway Pan and a hermaphrodite[46] suggest Dinonysiac leisure (*otium*). Landscapes to the right and left celebrate heroines: Europa and the bull, and Perseus' fight with the suitors of Andromeda, of which no drawings or photos remain.[47]

Richardson[48] affirms that the decoration of the peristyle was carried out in a single scheme in the north, south, and west porticoes, and in a richer but related and harmonious scheme in the Rhodian portico on the east; that is, there was a planned vista from the *oecus cyzicenus* (46), where entertainers would perform for diners.[49] The east portico had two magnificent visual representations on the east faces of the L-shaped piers at the corners of the garden near the great oecus (46). Medea meditating the murder of her children (plate 13) is represented on the east face of the north pier,[50] Perseus liberating Andromeda (plate 14) on the south pier.[51] On the north face of the Medea-pier, there was

42. Bragantini, "Casa dei Dioscuri," #163 ; Romizzi, "La Casa dei Dioscuri," Fig. 29.

43. Richardson, *Pompeii*, 43.

44. Romizzi, "La Casa dei Dioscuri," 138.

45. Richardson, *Pompeii*, 65, n. 371.

46. Ibid., plate XXIII.1; Bragantini, "Casa dei Dioscuri," #57; Romizzi, "La Casa dei Dioscuri," Fig. 22 (color).

47. Richardson, *Pompeii*, 15.

48. Ibid., 55.

49. Ibid., 63, 65.

50. Richardson, *Pompeii*, plate LIV; Bragantini, "Casa dei Dioscuri," #163, 221, 223; Romizzi, "La Casa dei Dioscuri," Fig. 39 (color); Grasso, plate 142 (color).

51. Richardson, *Pompeii*, plate LIII; Bragantini, "Casa dei Dioscuri," #222, 224; Romizzi, "La Casa dei Dioscuri," Fig. 38 (color); Grasso, plate 143 (color). Berg, "Wearing Wealth," Fig.11 is of Andromeda fettered to a rock in House I 7,7 in Pompeii; Fig. 2 is of Achilles among women at Skyros, a fresco in the House of M. Lucretius Fronto (V 4a).

PLATE 13: Medea meditating the murder of her children. South peristyle (53), east face the north pier, at east end of the garden near the great oecus (46). Inv. 8977 MANN.

Plate 14: Perseus, holding head of Medusa, liberating Andromeda, with sea moster below. South peristyle (53), east face of south pier, at east end of the garden near the great oecus (46). Inv. 8998 MANN.

26   PART ONE: VISUAL AND ORAL DOCUMENTS

a visual representation of "a priestess with a sacred serpent, sometimes identified as Hygeia, . . . a girl in a green chiton with a white mantle and white shoes. In her right hand she held a silver tray on which were a pine cone, figs, and eggs. A crested and bearded serpent wound about her body and descended over her shoulders to feed from the tray."[52] The vista down the garden was further enriched by two large panels on the east faces of the piers at the west end of the garden, most distant from but still facing the great oecus (46), on the south pier the sons of Niobe as they fall wounded (plate 15), on the north pier, the daughters of Niobe (plate 16), both frescoes dominated by an enormous Delphic tripod.[53] On the north wall there was a visual representation of Odysseus/Ulysses and Penelope, an almost identical copy of which was painted in the Pompeian macellum (VII 9,7; PPM VII 336–39[54]). "On the south wall was a painting of uncertain subject; in most accounts it is described as Achilles arming himself, but the discovery of a second copy of the same subject in the Casa di Spurio Messori that supplies most of the missing parts of the composition makes it clear that it is a religious scene, probably a rite of expiation."[55] To summarize, Romizzi observes that the vestibule (33) and the tablinum (42) of the Casa dei Dioscuri visually present a male patriarchal world of aristocratic social status (the Dioscuri) and military values (Achilles), while the magnificent south peristyle (53) visually presents models that Romans considered good (Andromeda, Penelope) and evil (Medea, Niobe) wives and mothers.

---

52. Richardson, *Pompeii*, 61. Gell (http://www.mediterranees.net/voyageurs/gell/Chapter_html), plate 68 is of this priestess (cited by Bernstein 535, n. 33). Gell identifies her as Hygeia, but Richardson and Bernstein as a priestess.

53. Bragantini, "Casa dei Dioscuri," #220, 226–27; Romizzi, "La Casa dei Dioscuri," Fig. 40; Grasso, plates 144–45 (color).

54. Richardson, *Pompeii*, plates XXVI, XXX.3, who also (55, n. 320) gives other examples of the same subject; Bragantini, "Casa dei Dioscuri," #216–19; Romizzi, "La Casa dei Dioscuri," Fig. 36.

55. Richardson, *Pompeii*, 56 n. 321 observes that there is no published photograph or drawing of this painting. Bragantini, "Casa dei Dioscuri," #231 gives a picture of the deteriorated wall, with little left of the fresco; Romizzi, "La Casa dei Dioscuri," Fig. 37, offers the image from the Casa di Spurio Messori [VII 3,29, triclinio (l); *PPM* VI 921 (color)], in which a priestess pours purifying water over the head of a hero (Achilles, Hercules, or Orestes). Compare Balch, *Roman Domestic Art*, 219–20 for discussion of a similar visual representation of the expiation of a hero by a priestess in the Casa del Centenario (IX 8,3.7; *PPM* IX 1027).

PLATE 15: Son of Niobe, falling wounded, killed by Apollo, enormous Delphic tripod in center. South peristyle (53), east faces of south and north piers, at west end of the garden, distant from the great oecus (46). Inv. 9302 MANN.

PLATE 16: Daughter of Niobe, falling wounded, killed by Artemis, enormous Delphic Tripod in center. South peristyle (53). Inv. 9304 MANN.

Strikingly, just before a person leaves the pseudo-peristyle (45), on the left one would see "woman in priestly dress carrying a flaming torch in her right hand and a patera in her left. In the foreground is a low cylindrical altar, its top covered with offerings." Walking a step or two further, just as a person entered the south peristyle (53) and faced the L-shaped pier at that northwestern corner of the garden, one would see "a priestess with a sacred serpent . . . wound about her body and descended over her shoulders." Looking then to the right, to the far south wall of the peristyle garden, a planned view from the great oecus (46) on the left, one would see a third priestess pouring purifying water over a hero (Achilles, Hercules, or Orestes).

"The Mythological Paintings in the Macellum at Pompeii"[56]

Romizzi[57] argues that the exceptional corpus of fourth style mythological frescoes in the Casa dei Discouri is similar to the decorative program in the Pompeian Macellum, a rare public edifice in the ancient world that conserves a cycle of *tabulae pictae*, and that both are related to decorative schemes in the Casa dei Vettii (VI 15,1), the Casa del Citarista (I 4,5.25), the Temple of Isis (VIII 7,28), the dining complex at Moregine,[58] and the Basilica at Herculaneum.[59] She argues that this selection of myths was not casual, but symbolic, agreeing with Karl Schefold that certain social groups adopt a particular iconography, a conclusion also adopted by Paul Zanker. Judith Barringer agrees: "myths are not simply used as wall decoration in domestic contexts, but are sometimes combined in ingenious and sophisticated narrative programs designed to educate as well as to entertain the viewer."[60] Barringer further argues that the wall paintings in the Pompeian Macellum, while utilizing Greek motifs, are "infused with peculiarly Roman features . . . to forge moralizing *exampla* expressive of Roman values."

Here I focus on comparing the scheme in the Casa dei Discouri with the story lines in the Pompeian Macellum, relying on and sum-

---

56. The title of an article by Barringer, which I summarize below.
57. Romizzi, "La Casa dei Dioscuri," 82, 140, 147.
58. See Guzzo, *Tales from an Eruption*; also Mastroroberto.
59. See Najbjerg.
60. Barringer, "The Mythological Paintings," 149.

marizing the intriguing article by Barringer. Two mythological paintings of about 65 CE still grace the interior north and west walls of the Macellum (VII 9,4–12), Io and Argos on the west wall,[61] Odysseus and Penelope on the north.[62] Aeschylus wrote a now lost *Penelope*, expressing a somber, melancholy mood, which characterizes her in the Macellum visual representation, which originated then in the theater.[63] "Penelope is especially noteworthy for her elegant profile and right arm, and for her voluminous drapery . . . She is the picture of nobility with her meticulously detailed spindle, distaff, and bracelets," symbols of her domestic skill, cunning, and virtue.[64] Barringer denies that such characterizing of Penelope can be shown to draw directly on Greek prototypes, and points rather to Roman interest in moments of quiet tension just before action, sexual or violent. Unlike all earlier depictions, Penelope here meets the gaze of Odysseus, rather than averting her eyes, perhaps indicating sexual longing, the union of an aristocratic lady with a beggar, who happily turns out to be her husband.[65]

Barringer writes that "these two myths do not appear together elsewhere."[66] In the Casa dei Discouri the Io and the Penelope frescoes do not appear in the same room, but indeed in the same domus, the former on the north wall of the pseudo-peristyle (45), the latter on the north wall of the great peristyle (53). As we have seen, Romizzi analyzes the decorative scheme of the whole house, that is, the comparison and contrast between visual representations even though they occur in different domestic areas.[67] The Io and Penelope frescoes were created as a pair and juxtaposed in the Macellum,[68] and the same two visual representations were also, I would argue, part of one synchronic decorative scheme in the Casa dei Dioscuri.

    61. Ibid., plate 1.
    62. Ibid., plate 2.
    63. Ibid.,153–54.
    64. Ibid., 155, 157.
    65. Ibid., 156.
    66. Ibid., 158, n. 46, lists other visual representations of Io in Pompeii, including the Casa dei Dioscuri.
    67. Compare the argument for analyzing an entire domus in Balch, *Roman Domestic Art*, 178; 183, n. 48.
    68. Barringer, "The Mythological Paintings," 158.

Other mythological visual representations do not survive in the Macellum, but we have nineteenth century descriptions of them, of Medea contemplating murdering her children, of Thetis delivering weapons to Achilles, and of Phrixos riding on the golden ram,[69] all three on the north wall with the Penelope panel, all of which visually represent a pregnant moment.[70] Achilles receives arms from his mother, Thetis, just before entering battle. Medea contemplates, just before the murder of her children. Phrixos is seated on the golden ram, whose hooves are just touching ground, perhaps just before the ram is sacrificed. Barringer[71] sees "several images of calm moments just before sex (Penelope) or violence (Io, Medea, Achilles, perhaps Phrixos)."

Further, there is a "clear thematic program designed to instruct, as well as to entertain the viewer."[72] There are two categories of myth, two frescoes related to the Trojan War, the other two to events surrounding Jason on Colchis (see n. 69).

> One painting is of Penelope, the ideal wife who waits faithfully for her husband for twenty years... She is also offered as a singular example of loyalty, patience, and virtue by various Greek and Roman authors... In another painting, we see Thetis, a dedicated mother, providing weapons to her son, who will shortly take vengeance on Patroclus' killer. The two paintings, then, can be said to represent the definition of a good woman: a good wife and a good mother.
>
> The other two paintings on this wall, which refer to the adventures of Jason, are also complements of each other. In one, the mother Medea, contemplates the murder of his children; in the other, Phrixos, a stepchild, escapes from his murderous stepmother, Ino, with the help of his own loving mother, Nephele ... In both paintings we see references to the actions of a bad mother (or stepmother).

69. Barringer (ibid., plate 4), who also (159) explains that Phrixos and his sister Helle were threatened by their stepmother Ino; their biological mother, Nephele, arranged their escape through the air on a golden ram. While crossing water below, Helle fell in, and the sea was then named the Hellespont. Phrixos landed safely in Colchis (east Georgia, the eastern coast of the Black Sea). The ram was offered to Zeus, and its famous golden fleece hung in a tree, which Jason later seeks, aided by the Colchian princess Medea, who had fallen in love with him, whose children she bears and then murders.

70. Ibid., 158–59.

71. Ibid., 160

72. Ibid., 161.

32 PART ONE: VISUAL AND ORAL DOCUMENTS

> Taken as a whole, then, the four panels illustrate the concept of a good woman/bad woman as moralizing exempla, designed to instruct the viewer as to the virtues of being a good mother and wife, and the honor that this brings on a woman ...[73]

I have summarized Barringer's art historical analysis, which she develops in further fascinating artistic and moral detail, with many references to contemporary Greek and Latin literature, e.g. noting Brilliant's argument[74] that such visual programs correspond to rhetorical controversies enunciated in the work of the Elder Seneca and to ethical views in the plays of the Younger Seneca, e.g., his *Medea*.

For whom were these entertaining and moral visual representations intended?

> The least likely person to do the marketing was a free-born aristocratic male ... The clientele was probably comprised of male and female slaves, and freed or free-born men and women without servants ... But [since there were shrines in the Macellum,] perhaps free-born aristocratic inhabitants came to the Macellum for reasons other than marketing.[75]

Romizzi's and Barringer's artistic analyses demonstrate intriguing correspondences between the decoration on the walls and piers of the south peristyle (53) in the Casa dei Discouri and visual representations on the walls of the Macellum, in the former, women whom Romans considered good (Andromeda, Penelope) and evil (Medea, Niobe) wives and mothers, and in the latter also, a good wife (Penelope) and good mothers (Thetis, Nephele) contrasted with a murderous mother and stepmother (Medea, Ino). In the Roman patriarchal world, some patrons have chosen visually to represent feminine virtues and vices, additionally in the Casa dei Discouri in contrast with male values, that is, Achilles, whose mother is also visually represented in the Macellum. In both spaces, domestic and commercial, Penelope and Medea are moral counterpoints, juxtaposed somehow to Io.

---

73. Barringer, "The Mythological Paintings," 162–63. Alternatively, Schefold (*Pompejanische Malerei*, 100) argues that the misfortunes of Io are compared with those of Penelope and Medea, and that Medea and Penelope are positive and negative examples of love.

74. Brilliant, *Visual Narratives*, 69–71.

75. Barringer, "The Mythological Paintings," 165.

Plate 17: Marble statue of priest wearing dress of Roman matron, holding libation dish in her right hand, and box of incense in the left, with fillet of twisted wool on her head, as well as garland of myrtle, so a priestess of Venus. The only restoration is of the right arm, from the elbow through the patera. Macellum (VII 9,7), Pompeii. Inv. 6041 MANN. I thank Dr. Marinella Lista, Dr. Rosaria Ciardello and Ivan Varrialle for arranging and allowing me to take these photos (July 2010).

34   PART ONE: VISUAL AND ORAL DOCUMENTS

PLATE 18

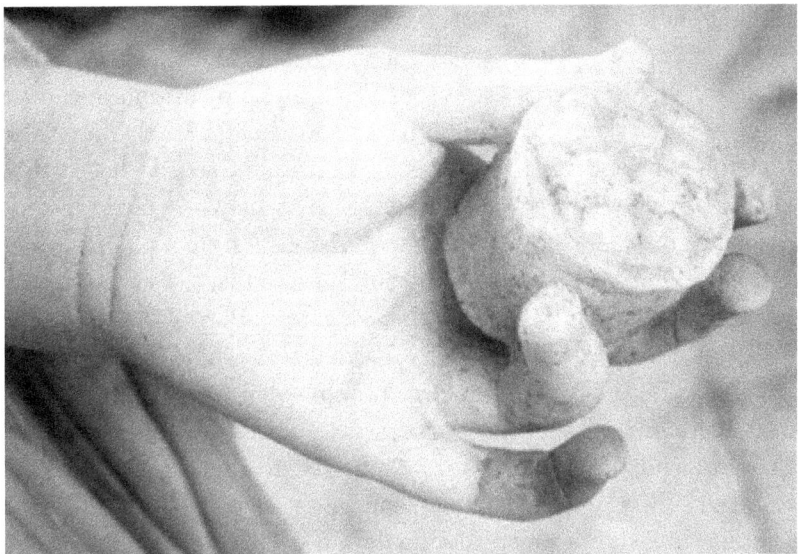

PLATE 19

There is another crucial correspondence between these two spaces: two marble statues are prominently displayed in the Macellum, one of a woman priest (plates 17–19).[76] She wears the characteristic three-layered dress of a Roman matron, a long, wide outermost garment (*palla*) with which she veils the back of her head, and below this a sleeveless *stola*, which identifies a married woman, held by straps over the shoulders, and which falls with soft folds across the breasts. Under these a sleeved tunic, which has buttons from her shoulders down her arms. The *palla* is gathered and falls over her left arm, and her right leg is bent. Her hands reach forward, the right hand holding a libation dish (*patera*), the left a box with grains of incense. She is dressed for cultic activity, which clarifies the ornamentation on her head, a fillet, a heavy band of twisted wool worn by priests (*infula tortilis*; see n. 29), and also a garland of berries and flowers, myrtle, the garland worn over continuous rows of her curls. Myrtle was a plant sacred to Venus, often represented in Pompeii in relation to *Venere Pompeiana*, which means

---

76. See Adamo Muscettola, "I Nigidi Mai di Pompei," Figs. 2–5; Small, "Shrine of the Imperial Family," Figs. 7–8; Cooley and Cooley, 102, Plate 5.5; Torelli, Tavole 93.1; Romizzi, "La Casa dei Dioscuri," Figs. 47, 50; Barnabei, "I Culti di Pompei," Fig. 41; Small, "Religion in the Roman Period," 206 n. 104; Welch, "portrait sculpture" 560–64.

that the statue visually represents a priestess of Venus.[77] Citing similar statue types, Adamo Muscettola[78] concludes that the Pompeian example is Neronian.[79] Several priestesses of Venus are known from the era of Augustus and Tiberius, but only one is known epigraphically from later times, Alleia Nigidia Maia, priestess of Venus and Ceres,[80] whose father, Cn. Alleius Nigidius Maius, was equestrian and may have reconstructed the macellum.[81] Small[82] identifies her rather as Agrippina II, mother of Nero.[83] Torelli,[84] followed by Barnabei,[85] argues that the statue visually represents Holconia, public priestess, daughter perhaps of M. Holconius Celer, married perhaps to Spurius Turranius Proculus Gellianus. In a later article Small[86] notes the three proposals for her identity and admits, "certainty is impossible." In any case, whether both the Casa dei Dioscuri and the macellum are connected to the Nigidii family, as Romizzi argues, or not, both the domestic peristyle (53) of the Casa dei Dioscuri and the commercial macellum just off the forum emphasize the function of (a) priestess(es), just as frescoes in both spaces visually represent feminine *exempla*, good and evil Roman wives and mothers.

The Nigidii family and the Casa dei Dioscuri

Romizzi[87] draws attention to a graffito drawn on the façade of the CDiosc (CIL IV 1293), which seems to celebrate the slaughter of the Nucerians

---

77. This description is based on Adamo Muscettola, "I Nigidi Mai di Pompei," 199; and Small, "Shrine," 120.
78. Adamo Muscettola, "I Nigidi Mai di Pompei," 205–6.
79. Small, "Shrine," 120, agrees with the Neronian date.
80. See Castrén, 73, n. 3. The inscription honoring her is translated by Cooley and Cooley, 102; see 96.
81. Adamo Muscettola, "I Nigidi Mai di Pompei," 206.
82. Small, "Shrine," 126–30.
83. Small (ibid., 121, n. 30) says there is no explicit evidence for a connection between the statue and the rebuilding of the macellum. Small continues (132) arguing that the altar in the Macellum was dedicated to Emperor Claudius by Cn. Alleius Nigidius Maius, and that the area was not actually a macellum, but a public triclinium for feasts of the emperor cult.
84. Torelli, "culto imperiale" 264–65.
85. Barnabei, "I Culti di Pompei," 79.
86. Small, "Religion," 206, n. 104.
87. Romizzi, "La Casa dei Dioscuri," 141.

in the riot of 59 CE.[88] There are two figures, one wearing legionary armor and standing on a platform probably representing the amphitheater, the other standing on a stair and carrying a shield (*scutum*). The man standing at the top of the amphitheater seems to attack the other with a lance. Richardson[89] translates the accompanying epigram: "Campani, in victory you perished together with the Nucerians." Richardson refers this to the involvement of a Pompeian *collegium iuuenum* in the riot, a *collegium* in which the Nigidii as Samnite aristocracy were members, which was then dissolved by the Roman senate (Tacitus *Ann.* 14.17). Romizzi[90] connects this graffito with several inscriptions celebrating Cn. Alleius Nigidius Maius as a giver of games and concludes that he was himself the owner of the Casa dei Dioscuri, and that his daughter, Alleia Maia, *sacerdos Veneris et Cereris*, had an important influence in this powerful family. An inscription celebrating her was found broken into four fragments in the Sarno Bath complex[91]: "Alleia, daughter of Maius, priestess of Venus and Ceres, to herself, in accordance with a decree of the town counselors, with [public] money" (*Ephemeris Epigraphica* VIII 855).[92] Further, as noted above, Romizzi[93] connects the decorative scheme in the Casa dei Dioscuri with those in the Terme del Sarno, the dining complex in Moregine, and the Macellum,[94] the first three of these related to equestrians, and all four related to the imperial cult. Especially the CDiosc and the Macellum share specific aesthetic subjects (Io and Argos, Medea, Penelope and Odysseus/Ulysses, and *xenia*), a theme (the familial world of women), and further, employment of the same workshop that painted both the domestic and the commercial spaces. The priestess, then, visually represented in marble in the Macellum is Alleia Maia, which corresponds with three striking visual representations of priestesses in the domestic peristyle (53).[95] One can almost imagine Alleia Maia herself planning the decorative scheme in

88. A graffito reproduced by Cooley and Cooley 63, Figure 4.6.
89. Richardson, *Pompeii*, 89.
90. Romizzi, "La Casa dei Dioscuri," 141–42.
91. Franklin, "Cn. Alleius Nigidius Maius," 436 n. 15.
92. Trans. Cooley and Cooley, 102, E49.
93. Romizzi, "La Casa dei Dioscuri," 144–47
94. See the first paragraph above under the subheading "The Mythological Paintings in the Macellum at Pompeii."
95. Romizzi, "La Casa dei Dioscuri," 148, 151.

the peristyle (53) of the CDiosc, differentiating herself and her values from the male scheme in the vestibule and tablinum.

Unfortunately for this attractive hypothesis, Franklin[96] disputes the interpretation: Tacitus (*Ann.* 14.17) reports explicitly not only that illegal associations were dissolved, but that the leaders of the riot of 59 CE were exiled, and our Cn. Alleius Nigidius Maius was not; on the contrary, he flourished twenty more years in Pompeii. Some of the Nigidii family lived in the Casa dei Dioscuri, but probably not Maius and Alleia.

Other aspects of Richardson's discussion[97] of the "family of the Casa dei Dioscuri" are convincing. Many names of inhabitants of Pompeii are known from bronze seals found in the houses and from inscriptions painted on their exterior walls. Such a seal—for stamping bread sent to the public ovens—was found in the CDiosc, as were inscriptions. The latter name three persons, including a Fuscus and a Vaccula, who belonged to the rich and powerful Nigidii family.[98] M. Nigidius Vaccula, gave several pieces of bronze furniture to the public baths of Pompeii; in the apodyterium of the Forum Baths, archaeologists found three elegant bronze benches supported on legs shaped like calves' legs inscribed M.NIGIDIVS.VACCVLA.P.S (CIL X 818), and also a large bronze brazier supported on legs shaped like sphinxes, with a plaque on one side showing a heifer, a play on the name Vaccula. A similar brazier was found in the Stabian baths, on the side of which was a plaque of a heifer and the inscription M.NIGIDIVS P.S (CIL X 8071.48). Richardson[99] concludes that M. Nigidius Vaccula was probably an occupant of the CDiosc, as was N. Nigidius Fuscus, related as father (Fuscus) and son (Vaccula). The father was candidate for the quinquennial duumvirate, many years before Pompeii was destroyed; the son made the gifts to the baths. "Yet the relations of these Nigidii to Alleius Nigidius Maius are uncertain."[100]

Gentilitial names ending in –*idius* are Oscan, so native to Campania and common in Pompeii. The most outstanding member of the family, Cn. Alleius Nigidius Maius, was *duumuir quinquennalis* in 55–56, priest

---

96. Franklin, "Cn. Alleius Nigidius Maius," 439–40.
97. Richardson, *Pompeii*, chap. II.
98. Ibid., 82, 85.
99. Richardson, *Pompeii*, 83, 85.
100. Franklin, "Cn. Alleius Nigidius Maius," 435.

of Caesar Augustus (*flamen Caesaris Augusti*, in the reign of Claudius, Nero, or Vespasian), leader of the colony (*princeps coloniae*), owner of a troupe of gladiators, and a leading games-giver,[101] e.g., CIL IV 7991[102], in black and red: "20 pairs of gladiators of Gnaeus Alleius Nigidius Maius, quinquennial, and their substitutes will fight without any public expense at Pompeii." The "substitutes" are gladiators who take the place of defeated fighters in subsequent bouts. Also CIL IV 1180[103], in red, outside the main entrance of the Gladiatorial Barracks, on the external wall of the Large Theater, 70–79 CE: "For the well-being of the [emperor Vespasian] Caesar Augustus and of his children, [and on account of the] dedication of the altar, [the gladiatorial troupe] of Gnaeus [All]eius Nigidius Maius, priest of Caesar Augustus, will fight at Pompeii, without delay, on the 4 July. There will be a hunt and awnings." The altar mentioned has been identified by some with the finely carved altar in the so-called "Temple of Vespasian" in the forum. Cooley and Cooley prefer a date to Vespasian's reign, as their bracketed insertion above demonstrates, but Dobbins[104] dates it with the altar originally to the Augustan period, renaming it "The Sanctuary of the Genius of Augustus."[105] The "awnings" mentioned would shield spectators from the sun, as seen in the fresco visually representing the riot painted in House of Actius Anicetus (I 3,23; PPM I 80).[106]

Another advertisement (CIL IV 7993, in red and black, House of Trebius Valens (III 2,1) reads: "At the dedication Ocella of the *opus tabularum* of Gnaeus Alleius Nigidius Maius, at Pompeii on the 13 June, there will be a procession, hunt, athletics, and awnings. Greetings to Nigra [picture of a head]."[107] Scholars dispute the identity of the *opus*

---

101. Richardson, *Pompeii*, 83 n. 25 cites van Buren; the latest, best article is by Franklin. Compare Sabbatini Tumolesi 32–44 for the inscriptions, Latin and Italian, and also Cooley and Cooley, 52–54 for English translations, "games presented by Gnaeus Alleius Nigidius Maius, leading games-giver."

102. Trans. Cooley and Cooley D20.

103. Ibid., D23.

104. Dobbins, "Sanctuary of the Genius of Augustus."

105. Franklin, "Cn. Alleius Nigidius Maius," 445 accepts Dobbins's date for the original Augustan temple, but thinks that the altar may have been rededicated by Maius to Vespasian.

106. See Balch, *Roman Domestic Art*, CD 122.

107. Trans. Cooley and Cooley, 54, D21.

tabularum. Franklin[108] identifies it with "a series of panels depicting varieties of gladiators and wild animal scenes belonging to the Fourth Pompeian style installed surrounding the amphitheater arena."[109]

A rental notice advertising urban property gives an idea of his sources of income: "To let from the 1st July next in the *Insula Arriana Polliana*, now owned by Gnaeus Alleius Nigidius Maius: shops with upper rooms, quality apartments and houses. Lessees contact Primus, slave of Gnaeus Alleius Nigidius Maius" (CIL IV 138).[110] Another source of his wealth may have been the public priestess Eumachia, since members of his family were buried in her tomb, which implies that the branch of the Alleii, into which Nigidius Maius was adopted,[111] were beneficiaries of the Eumachii. His wife, Alleia Decimilla, was a *sacerdos publica Cereris*, and as noted above, his daughter, Alleia, was *sacerdos Veneris et Cereris*.[112]

Franklin[113] concludes that Cn. Alleius Nidigius Maius played a major role in Pompeii for four decades, having begun his career c. CE 25; he was an active sixty-five when Vesuvius brought his career to an end. He rose to office in Claudian days, withdrew in the Neronian years, but then identified himself with Vespasian's interests in the amphitheater. We do not know the exact family relationship between Maius and the other members of the Nigidii family who lived in the CDiosc. We also do not know whether Maius' daughter, Allia, is the priestess visually represented by a marble statue in the Macellum, nor her relationship, if any, to the CDiosc peristyle (53) focused on feminine themes. Nevertheless, we can observe the striking similarities in the iconographical programs in the south peristyle (53) of the CDiosc and in the Macellum, both focused on feminine themes that include priestesses, the former juxtaposed with the male world visualized in other areas of the house.

---

108. Franklin, "Cn. Alleius Nigidius Maius," 442–44.

109. See *PPM*, supplemental volume, *La documentazione nell'opera di disegnatori e pittori dei secoli XVII e XIX* (1995) 105–11 for these images in color.

110. Trans. Cooley and Cooley, 172–73 [H50]; see Franklin, "Cn. Alleius Nigidius Maius," 441–42; De Albentiis; Sampaolo, "Casa di Pansa"; Pirson, "Rental accommodation."

111. Richardson, *Pompeii*, 83, with n. 27.

112. Franklin, "Cn. Alleius Nigidius Maius," 436.

113. Ibid., 446.

The Vesting of a Priestess in Herculaneum

The walls, floors, and rooms of Campania exhibit many professional women. Since New Testament scholars have been so absorbed with texts, we have rarely seen these women, whom their contemporaries visually represented two millennia ago. Because one particular fresco is directly related to the subject of this paper, to Osiek's commentary on Philippians, to Osiek and MacDonald's discussions of women's leadership, and to Madigan and Osiek's book on *Ordained Women*, I add a description of the "vesting of a priestess" in Herculaneum, hoping to entice scholars to further research.

On February 21, 1761, excavators discovered four small frescoes,[114] each c. 44 x 44 cm, which had all already been detached from the Palaestra walls and placed on the ground, perhaps awaiting a restoration, paintings dating c. 30–40 CE. I describe one of the four, the "vesting of a priestess" (inventory 9022).

The fresco (plate 20)[115] visually represents two older and two younger women, each dressed differently. To the viewer's left, an older woman is seated on a high chair that has gold veneer but no backrest. She wears a very fine transparent tunic that delicately reveals her breasts. With her left hand she pulls aside a white cloak with a blue border, a narrow piece of which she uses to veil her head. The elaborate hairstyle is held by a gold diadem, complemented by a pair of earrings and a necklace set with precious stone(s). The older woman has placed her right arm around a young woman standing to her right, who with her right elbow leans on an arm of the older woman's chair, the pose of the muse Polimnia. The younger woman wears a sumptuous golden gown and also has an elegant hairstyle. Her back extends outside the frame of the visual representation into the space of viewers. She gazes at a young woman to the viewers' right, who is also standing and who gazes directly out at viewers. An older, taller slave woman, a status indicated by her white cap and a darker, simpler robe, is arranging her hair. The

---

114. The four are #45 ("vesting of a priestess"), #46 ("concert"), #47 ("actor dressed as a king"), and #48 ("two heroes"), pp. 162–65, in the catalogue *La pitture pompeiana*, eds. Bragantini and Sampaolo (2009). The concert (#46) is directed by a woman, and the actor (#47) gazes at a young woman, who kneels before a marble stele to write a dedication, perhaps to record a victory at a theatrical contest. See Ragghianti, *Pittori di Pompei*, Tavole 22, also 7, 54.

115. Sources for this description are Kraiker, "Stuckgemälde"; Sirano; and Grasso.

PLATE 20: "Vesting of a priestess." Palaestra (II 4,19), Herculaneum. Inv. 9022 MANN.

young priestess wears a long violet tunic hemmed with a darker fringe enriched with gold, a bright upper vest, with a cape thrown over her left shoulder and hanging down alongside her left arm. Her long hair may be seen from the nape of her neck lying along her right shoulder. Two diadems wrap around her hair; she wears pearl earrings, a necklace with a central precious stone, and two armbands. The room is a *gynaikonitis*, shown by the presence of a small wooden table with lion feet, on which one sees a box and a violet band, and on which green plants grow. A glass pitcher rests on the floor under the table.

Earlier scholars were dazzled by the quality of these four frescoes and suggested a classical Greek origin for them all.[116] However, aspects

---

116. Kraiker, "Stuckgemälde," 133–35.

of the painting technique belong to a Roman workshop.[117] Both the long-necked glass pitcher under the table and the round wooden table itself with lion paw feet are typically Pompeian, a type of table often used in a cult; earlier such Greek tables typically had deer legs.[118] Laurel (bay) branches are seen on top of the table, as is a small box with ivory inlay. Still, the four feminine figures are not *in* the image; they *are* the image, which is classically Greek[119]. The young priestess gazing directly at the viewer, Kraiker suggests,[120] is found on Attic grave monuments from c. 320 BCE. The young woman leaning on the older woman's chair is a late addition to the classical type, which focused on three figures.[121] Kraiker concludes[122] that the young priestess herself is not only present but is represented as "consciously present."

A Caution

Gerd Theissen[123] argues, "primitive Christian ethics often consists of making the values and norms of the upper class accessible to all. One could speak of a 'democratization' of an ancient aristocratic ethic . . ." This brings the "radicalization of demands . . . when ordinary people . . . take over not only the substance of norms but also the aristocratic self-confidence which is associated with them: the claim to do things better than others."[124] Barringer has shown that artists visualized aristocratic ethics, so that to some extent, the themes of moralists who wrote and those who painted corresponded. If she is correct about those who viewed the Macellum visual representations, "male and female slaves, and freed or free-born men and women without servants",[125] the frescoes were powerful exponents of this Greco-Roman aristocratic ethic also for the lower classes, both on the forum and in domestic spaces.

Roman houses and certainly markets were open, so that Jews and Christians would have been among the viewers of such frescoes in

---

117. Ibid., 141.
118. Ibid., 139, 144–45 with n. 48.
119. Ibid., 143.
120. Ibid., 146.
121. Ibid., 147–48.
122. Ibid., 149.
123. Theissen, *Religion*, 82.
124. Ibid., 116.
125. Barringer, "The Mythological Paintings," 165.

Rome and also in the Roman colonies such as Corinth and Philippi.[126] To pose the problem by stating questions, would Christians also have internalized Thetis as a "good" mother? Would Christians have related to the slave woman "vesting the priestess" as a person with an identity (see n. 2 above[127])? Did Christians, whether female or male, who became deacons and presbyters in early house churches (see n. 4 above), celebrate the same aristocratic values visualized both in the CDiosc and the Pompeian Macellum? Would they have supported the amphitheater games of the priestess Alleia Maia's father, as she most probably did? Deutero-Pauline Christians, who lived and worshipped in Roman houses, did indeed adopt the aristocratic, patriarchal, male Aristotelian household code (Col 3.18–4.1[128]).

An Imaginative Conclusion

We have no evidence of Christians in Pompeii or Herculaneum.[129] However, many of the artistic themes discussed above did not originate in Campania and would appear, adapted by local artists, in other Roman cultural settings, for example, in Rome and the Roman colonies Corinth and Philippi. Even though the artist who painted the "vesting of a priestess" in Herculaneum did not know Christians, might we not imagine the older seated woman as Nympha (Col 4.15) or Grapte (Hermas *Vis.* 2.4.3[130]), leaders in Roman households who taught women? Do we not see the older woman instructing the younger women of her household, as Osiek suggests (see n. 1 above)? Might we not imagine the priestess as one of those young women who so disturbed deutero-Pauline authors (1 Tim 4:11–15)?

We might also imagine her as Euodia, *episcopos*, head of a household and house church in Philippi (1:1; 4:2). We do not know what generated tensions between the two leaders, Euodia and Syntyche; in

---

126. Balch, *Roman Domestic Art*, 34–38; also Balch, "Pompeii and Corinth."

127. Osiek and MacDonald, chap. 5: "Female Slaves: Twice Vulnerable," in *A Woman's Place* give dismally realistic answers to this question.

128. See Balch, *Domestic Code.*

129. See Lampe, *From Paul to Valentinus*, 7 n. 3. For the presence of Jews in these cities see Giordano and Kahn, also Varone, as well as Cooley and Cooley, 76, 84, 109–10.

130. See Osiek and MacDonald, *A Woman's Place*, 12–13, 42, 75–76, 92, 158, 162, 214, 236.

the Roman world it is easy to imagine that "the nub of the problem was status . . . they seek their own interests"[131] (see Phil 2:3–4). Possible specific issues might have been doctrinal, or attitudes toward Judaism, Roman authorities, or toward Paul.[132] I suggest that we do know Euodia's attitude toward Paul. A few verses after referring to tensions between these two leaders, Paul recalls "the early days of the gospel," their having "shared with me in the matter of giving and receiving" (4:15). Fast-forwarding to the present, "I have received from Epaphroditus the gifts you sent, a fragrant offering (*osmen euodias*) . . ." (4:18 [NRSV]). Should we not translate that last phrase "a Euodian fragrance/offering"? Osiek[133] suggests the possibility of a pun, the kind of play that Paul makes on the name of the slave Onesimus (Phlm 20).[134] In this Roman colony we see one of the earliest patrons/leaders of a Christian community who utilized her influence for the *ekklesia* and her resources for Paul.

In both the visual and the textual worlds, we see and hear symbols of the leadership of women priests and presbyters. The marble statue of a priestess in the Macellum in Pompeii, three frescoes of women priests related to the south peristyle (53) in the Casa dei Dioscuri, and the extraordinary fresco of the "Vesting of a Priestess" found in the Palaestra in Herculaneum, all exhibit women priests, which may expand our imaginations concerning actual possibilities for early Christian women.

---

131. Reumann, *Philippians*, 633.
132. Ibid., 628–29.
133. Osiek, *Philippians* 123.
134. Ibid., 141.

Bibliography

Adamo Muscettola, Stefania. "I Nigidi Mai di Pompei: far politica tra l'età neronia e l'età flavia." *Rivista dell'istituto nazionale d'archeologia e storia dell'arte* 3/14–15 (Rome, 1991–1992) 193–218 with 17 figures.

Balch, David L. *Let Wives be Submissive: The Domestic Code in 1 Peter*. SBLMS 26. Chico: Scholars, 1981.

———. *Roman Domestic Art and Early House Churches*. WUNT 228. Tübingen: Mohr/Siebeck, 2008.

———. "Women Prophets/Maenads Visually Represented in Two Roman Colonies: Pompeii and Corinth." In *The Interface of Orality and Writing: Seeing, Speaking, Writing in the Shaping of New Genres*, edited by Annette Weissenrieder and Robert B. Coote, 236–59, with 12 plates. WUNT 1/260. Tübingen: Mohr/Siebeck, 2010.

Balch, David L., and Carolyn Osiek, editors. *Early Christian Families in Context: An Interdisciplinary Dialogue*. Religion, Marriage, and Family. Grad Rapids: Eerdmans, 2003.

Baldassarre, Ida. *Pompei: pitture e mosaici*. 10 vols., with a supplement, *La documentazione nell'opera di disegnatori e pittori dei secoli XVIII e XIX* (1995). Rome: Istituto della Enciclopedia Italiana, 1990–2003.

———. *La documentazione nell'opera di disegnatori e pittori dei secoli XVIII e XIX*. Rome: Istituto della Enciclopedia Italiana, 1995.

Barnabei, Lorenza. "I Culti di Pompei: Raccolta Critica della Documentazione." *Contributi di archeologia vesuviana III: I culti di Pompei*. SSAP 21. Rome: "L'Erma" di Bretschneider, 2007, pp. 76–81: "Culto imperiale: il sacello nel macellum."

Barringer, Judith M. "The Mythological Paintings in the Macellum at Pompeii." *Classical Antiquity* 13 (1994) 149–66 with 5 figures.

Berg, Ria. "Wearing Wealth. *Mundus Muliebris* and *Ornatus* as Status Markers for Women in Imperial Rome." In *Women, Wealth and Power in the Roman Empire*, edited by Päivi Setälä, 15–75 with 17 figures. Acta Instituti Romani Finlandiae 25. Rome: Institutum Romanum Finlandiae, 2002.

Bergmann, Bettina. "Staging the Supernatural: Interior Gardens of Pompeian Houses," 53-69, with Catalogue plates, pp. 110–68. Pompeii and the Roman Villa: Art and Culture Around the Bay of Naples, ed. Carol C. Mattusch. Washington, DC: National Gallery of Art, 2008.

Bernstein, Frances. "Pompeian Women." In *The World of Pompeii*, edited by John J. Dobbins and Pedar W. Foss, 526–37 with 3 figures. New York: Routledge, 2007.

Bragantini, Irene. "Casa dei Dioscuri (VI 9,6–7)." In *PPM* (1993) IV 860–1004 with 286 plates.

Brilliant, Richard. *Visual Narratives: Storytelling in Etruscan and Roman Art*, 65–83. Ithaca: Cornell University Press, 1984.

Castrén, Paavo. *Ordo Populusque Pompeianus: Polity and Society in Roman Pompeii*. Acta Instituti Romani Finlandiae 8. Rome: Bardi, 1975.

Cooley, Alison E., and M. G. L. Cooley. *Pompeii: A Sourcebook*. New York: Routledge, 2004.

De Albentiis, Emidio. "Indagini sull'*Insula Arriana Polliana* di Pompei." *Dialoghi di archeologia* 3.7 (1989) 43–84.

Dobbins, John J. "The Altar in the Sanctuary of the Genius of Augustus in the Forum at Pompeii." *RM* 99 (1992) 251–61 with Tafeln 72–74.

———. "Problems of Chronology, Decoration, and Urban Design in the Forum at Pompeii." *American Journal of Archaeology* 98 (1994) 629–94 with 61 figures.

———. "The Pompeii Forum Project 1994–95." In *Sequence and Space in Pompeii*, edited by Sara E. Bon and Rick Jones, 73–87. Oxbow Monograph 77. Oxford: Oxbow, 1997.

———. "The Forum and Its Dependencies." In *The World of Pompeii*, edited by John J. Dobbins and Pedar W. Foss, 150–83. New York: Routledge, 2007.

Duncan-Jones, R. P. Review of Castrén, *Ordo Populusque Pompeianus* (1975) in *JRS* 67 (1977) 195–98.

Esposito, D. "La 'Bottega dei Vettii': vecchi date e nuove acquisizioni." *Rivisti di Studi Pompeiani* 10 (1999) 23–61.

Franklin, James L. Jr. "Cn. Alleius Nigidius Maius and the Amphitheatre: Munera and a Distinguished Career at Ancient Pompeii." *Historia: Zeitschrift für alte Geschichte* 46 (1997) 434–47.

Frölich, Thomas. "Die Wanddekorationen des Peristyle der Casa della Fontana Piccola in Pompeji." In *Functional and Spatial Analysis of Wall Painting*, edited by Eric M. Moormann, 72–81 with 11 figures. Proceedings of the Fifth International Congress on Ancient Wall Painting, Amsterdam, 8–12 September, 1992. BABESCH Supplement 3. Leiden: BABESCH, 1993.

Gell, William, with engravings by J. P. Gandy. *Pompeiana: The Topography, Edifices, and Ornaments of Pompeii*. London, 1832. Online: http://www.mediterranees.net/voyageurs/gell/Chapter_13.html.Adamo.

Giordano, Carlo, and Isidoro Kahn. *The Jews in Pompeii, Herculaneum, Stabiae and in the Cities of Campania Felix*. Translated by Wilhelmina F. Jashemski. Rome: Bardi, 2001.

Grasso, Fiorenza. Captions to color plates 45 and 129–45, frescoes from the Insula Orientalis (II 4,19), Ercolano, and from the Casa dei Dioscuri (VI 9,6.7), Pompei, pp. 162 and 302–21 in Irene Bragantini and Valeria Sampaolo, eds., *La pittura pompeiana*. Naples: Electa, 2009.

Guzzo, Pier Giovanni, editor. *Tales from an Eruption: Pompeii Herculaneum Oplontis*. Rome: Electa, 2003, pp. 166–79 with 10 plates: "Moregine, The Valiante Estate; the Suburb on the River; the Building of the Triclinia."

Kaufmann-Heinimann, Annemarie. "Religion in the House." In *A Companion to Roman Religion*, edited by Jörg Rüpke, 188–201. Oxford: Blackwell, 2007.

Kozakiewicz, Maria. "Appendix [to Small, "The Shrine of the imperial family in the Macellum at Pompeii"]: The headgear of the female statue," pp. 137–41.

Kraiker, Wilhelm, "Das Stuckgemälde aus Herculaneum: 'Schmückung einer Priesterin.'" *RM* 60–61 (1953–1954) 133–49 with Tafeln 56–58.

Lampe, Peter. *From Paul to Valentinus: Christians at Rome in the First Two Centuries*. Translated by Michael Steinhauser. Edited by Marshall Johnson. Minneapolis: Fortress, 2003.

Madigan, Kevin, and Carolyn Osiek. *Ordained Women in the Early Church: A Documentary History Edited and Translated*. Baltimore: Johns Hopkins University Press, 2005.

Malherbe, Abraham J. "Hellenistic Moralists and the New Testament." In *Aufstieg und Niedergang der römischen Welt* II.26.1 (1992) 267–333.

———. *Paul and the Popular Philosophers*. Minneapolis: Fortress, 1989.

Mastroroberto, Marsia. "Una visita di Nerone a Pompei: le deversoriae tabernae di Moregine." In *Storie da un'eruzione. Pompei Ercolano Oplontis; Napoli, Museo*

Archeologico Nazionale, 20 marzo-31 agosto 2003, edited by Antonio d'Ambrosio, Pier Giovanni Guzzo, and Marisa Mastroroberto, 479–523 with color plates. Milan: Electa, 2003.

———. "L'*aurea aetas* neroniana sulle pareti dipinte di Moregine a Pompei." In *Rosso Pompeiano. La decorazione pittorica nelle collezioni del Museo di Napoli e a Pompei. Rome, Museo Nazionale Romano Palazzo Massimo alle Terme, 20 dicembre 2007—31 marzo 2008*, edited by Maria Luisa Nava, Rita Paris, and Rosanna Friggeri, 60–73. Milan: Electa, 2007.

Moeller, Walter O. "Gnaeus Alleius Nigidius Maius, Princeps Coloniae." *Latomus* 32 (1973) 515–20.

Mouritsen, Henrik and Ittai Gradel. "Nero in Pompeian Politics: *Edicta Munerum* and Imperial Flaminates in Late Pompeii." *Zeitschrift für Papyrologie und Epigraphik* 87 (1991) 145–56.

Najbjerg, Tina. "A Reconstruction and Reconsideration of the So-Called Basilica in Herculaneum." *Journal of Roman Archaeology*, supplement 47 (2002) 122–65.

———. "From Art to Archaeology: Recontextualizing the Images from the Porticus of Herculaneum." In *Antiquity Recovered: The Legacy of Pompeii and Herculaneum*, edited by Victoria C. Gardner Coates and Jon L. Seydl, 59–72 with 5 figures. Los Angeles: J. Paul Getty Museum, 2007.

Osiek, Carolyn. *Philippians. Philemon*. Abingdon New Testament Commentaries. Nashville: Abingdon, 2000.

———. "Female Slaves, *Porneia*, and the Limits of Obedience." In *Early Christian Families in Context: An Interdisciplinary Dialogue*, edited by David L. Balch and Carolyn Osiek, 255–74. Grand Rapids: Eerdmans, 2003.

Osiek, Carolyn, and David L. Balch. *Families in the New Testament World: Households and House Churches*. The Family, Religion and Culture. Louisville: Westminster John Knox, 1997.

Osiek, Carolyn, and Margaret Y. MacDonald, with Janet H. Tulloch. *A Woman's Place: House Churches in Earliest Christianity*. Minneapolis: Fortress, 2006.

Pirson, Felix. "Rented Accommodation at Pompeii: The Evidence of the Insula Arriana Polliana VI.6," 165–82. *Journal of Roman Archaelolgy*, Supplementary Series 22: *Domestic Space in the Roman World: Pompeii and Beyond*, edited by R. Laurence and A. Wallace-Hadrill (1997).

Ragghianti, Carlo Ludovico. *Pittori di Pompei*. Monumenti d'arte italiana 4. Milan: Milione, 1963.

Reumann, John. *Philippians: A New Translation with Introduction and Commentary*. AB 33B. New Haven: Yale University Press, 2008.

Richardson, L., Jr. *Pompeii: The Casa dei Dioscuri and Its Painters*. With 58 plates. Memoirs of the American Academy in Rome 23. Rome: American Academy in Rome, 1955.

Romizzi, Lucia, "La Casa dei Dioscuri di Pompei (VI 9,6.7): una nuova lettura." In *Contributi di archeologia Vesuviana II*, 80–160 with 26 plates. SSAP 18. Rome: Electa, 2006.

———. *Programmi decorative di III e IV stile a Pompei. Un'analisi sociologica ed iconological*. Quaderni di Ostraka 11. Naples: Loffredo, 2006.

Rostowzew, M. "Die hellenistisch-römische Architektur Landschaft." *RM* 26 (1911) 1–186 with 11 Tafeln.

Roux, H., and L. Barré. *Herculaneum und Pompeji: Vollständige Sammlung der daselbst Entdeckten zum Teil noch Uneditierter Malereien, Mosaiken und Bronzen*. 6 vols. Hamburg: Meissner, 1841.

Sabbatini Tumolesi, Patrizia. *Gladiatorvm Paria: Annunci di spettacoli gladiatorii a Pompei*. Rome: Edizioni di Storia e Letteratura, 1980.

Sampaolo, Valeria. "Casa di Pansa (VI 6,1)." In PPM (1993) IV 357–61.

———. "Macellum (VII 9,7)." In *PPM* (1997) VII 328–52.

Schefold, Karl. *Pompejanische Malerei: Sinn und Ideengeschichte*. Basel: Schwabe, 1952.

———. *Die Wände Pompejis: Topographisches Verzeichnis der Bildmotive*. Berlin: de Gruyter, 1957.

Setälä, Päivi and Liisa Savunen, editors. *Female Networks and the Public Sphere in Roman Society*. Acta Instituti Romani Finlandiae 22. Rome: Solin, 1999.

Sirano, Francesco. Caption for the "Vesting of a Priestess," from the Palestra, Insula Orientalis (II 4,19), Ercolano, p. 146 in *Rosso Pompeiano. La decorazione pittorica nelle collezioni del Museo di Napoli e a Pompei. Rome, Museo Nazionale Romano Palazzo Massimo alle Terme, 20 dicembre 2007 – 31 marzo 2008*, edited by Maria Luisa Nava, Rita Paris, and Rosanna Friggeri. Milan: Electa, 2007.

Small, Alastair. "The Shrine of the Imperial Family in the Macellum at Pompeii." In *Subject and Ruler: The Cult of the Ruling Power in Classical Antiquity. Papers Presented at a Conference Held in the University of Alberta on April 13–15, 1994, to Celebrate the 65th Anniversary of Duncan Fishwick*, edited by Alastair Small, 115–36 with 12 figures. Journal of Roman Archaeology Supplementary Series 17. Ann Arbor: Journal of Roman Archaeology, 1996.

———. "Urban, Suburban and Rural Religion in the Roman Period." In *The World of Pompeii*, edited by John J. Dobbins and Pedar W. Foss, 184–211 with 5 figures. New York: Routledge, 2007.

Theissen, Gerd. *The Religion of the Earliest Churches: Creating a Symbolic World*. Translated by John Bowden. Minneapolis: Fortress, 1999.

Torelli, Mario. "Il culto imperiale a Pompei." In *I culti della campania antica: Atti del Convegno Internazionale di Studi in ricordo di Nazarena Valenza Mele, Napoli, 15–17 Maggio 1995*, 245–70 with Tavole 83–93. Rome: Bretschneider, 1998.

———. ""Conclusioni," pp. 285–90 in "Moregine: Suburbio 'portuale' di Pompei. Una giornata di studio," Ferrara, 2003. *Ostraka* 12 (2003) 239–96.

Van Andringa, William. Chapter 7: "Le *macellum* de Pompéi." In *Quotidien des Dieux et des Hommes: La Vie Religieuse dans les Cités du Vésuve à l'Époque Romaine*. Bibliothèque des Écoles Françaises d'Athènes et de Rome 337. Rome: École Française de Rome, 2009.

Van Buren, A. W. "Gnaeus Alleium Nigidius Maius of Pompeii." *American Journal of Philology* 68 (1947) 382–93.

Varone, Antonio. *Presenze giudaiche e cristiane a Pompei*. Naples: D'Auria, 1979.

Welch, Katherine E. "Pompeian Men and Women in Portrait Sculpture." In *The World of Pompeii*, edited by John J. Dobbins and Pedar W. Foss, 550–58. New York: Routledge, 2007.

Zahn, Wilhelm. *Die schönsten Ornamente und merkwürdigsten Gemälde aus Pompeji, Herculaneum und Stabiae nebst einigen Grundrissen und Ansichten nach den am Ort und Stelle gemachten Originalzeichnungen*. 3 vols. Berlin: Reimer, 1828–1859.

Zanker, Paul. "Mythenbilder im Haus." In *Proceedings of the XVth International Congress of Classical Archaeology: "Classical Archaeology towards the Third Millennium: Reflections and Perspectives,"* edited by Roald F. Docter and Eric M. Moormann, 40–48. Allard Pierson Series 12. Amsterdam: Allard Pierson Museum, 1999.

2

The Art of Translating for Oral Performance

David Rhoads

CAROLYN OSIEK HAS A RARE COMBINATION OF PERSONAL TRAITS THAT have made her a premier scholar, an outstanding teacher, a wonderful colleague, a good friend, and a fine human being. I have been privileged to know her over the course of many years, and my life is all the richer for it. One of the areas of New Testament studies that we shared was the performance of early Christian writings and the translation of them as oral literature, an interest that is reflected in her commentary on *The Shepherd of Hermas*. It is a delight to be able to present this essay in her honor.

Translation is an *art*, because the act of rendering biblical works into contemporary languages is more than a purely technical process. It is an artistic achievement. Translation involves, first, understanding the profound content, the significant artistry, and the powerful impact of the original languages of the writings in the Bible in their context. Second, translation involves finding contemporary ways to express the meanings, the power, the vibrancy, the passion, and the potential impacts of the original compositions in modern tongues. In these efforts, theorists of translation have sought to address the following functions of communication: expressive, cognitive, interpersonal, informative, imperative, performative, emotive, and aesthetic.[1] The art of translation requires that those who do translation bridge the world of biblical scholarship and the needs of the contemporary church.

Now we are entering a new development that makes translating even more challenging because it places both biblical discourse and

---

1. Listed in Noss, "A Translator's Trail," 25–31.

contemporary translation squarely in the context of the *art of oral performance*. My own limited forays into translation have been in preparation for oral performances of biblical compositions. Over the last three decades, as part of my vocation as a New Testament scholar, I have offered memorized performances of several New Testament writings in dramatic form before gathered audiences of students, church communities, and academic societies: the *Gospel of Mark*, the *Sermon on the Mount*, selections from *Luke*, scenes from *John*, *Galatians*, *Philemon*, *James*, *1 Peter*, and the *Book of Revelation*. In some of these performances, I have adapted the translations of others. In most instances, however, I have developed my own translations.

In these efforts, I have come to appreciate as a scholar the orality of the original compositions and the challenge of translating them for performance in contemporary contexts. Many New Testament scholars have begun to study various aspects of the orality of early Christianity and the oral dynamics of biblical compositions.[2] In recent years, I have sought to articulate a framework of "biblical performance criticism" for our common study of the orality of the New Testament writings.[3] Similarly, there is also now emerging a movement on the part of professional biblical translators to translate for orality. Although this movement relates to the entire Bible, my focus here is on the New Testament.

Common Approaches to Translation for Print

Most of us are aware of the common distinction between a "literal" word-for-word approach to translation and a freer "dynamic equivalence" approach that seeks to replicate/reproduce meaning more freely in ways appropriate to particular contemporary cultures of reception. We may also be aware that the most widely-used translations are prepared mainly for public reading of selected passages in the context of worship and education and/or for private devotional reading. These translations are done almost exclusively out of a print mentality—trans-

---

2. For information on current developments in this field and extensive bibliography, go to www.biblicalperformancecriticism.org. See also the volumes in the series on Biblical Performance Criticism published by Cascade Books.

3. See Rhoads, "Performance Criticism: Part I"; and "Performance Criticism: Part II."

lating from ancient written texts in order to produce printed texts in a contemporary language. Even when the translation is intended for one of the considerable number of oral cultures that remain in the world, the goal is a written text—for use not only in Bible reading but also as an opportunity to teach literacy to people who are non-literate.

With a print mentality, the focus is on a text rather than on an oral performance. As such, the emphasis falls more on a single meaning of a text than on the "meaning potential"[4] that might be brought out in different ways in performance; more on faithfulness to the original than on creativity in the oral register of the receptor language; more on the intention of the author/text than on the potential impacts upon an audience; more on the effect on an individual reader than on the collective experience of a gathered community; more on the cognitive sense made by a reader than on the emotional experience of the listeners. This model rooted in a print mentality has been critiqued in recent years by post-modernists who argue that meaning does not inhere in a text but is multivalent—negotiated and renegotiated between text, reader (audience), and context.[5] It has also been critiqued by post-colonial scholars who point to the power dynamics in the presumed assumption of the superiority of a printed text and of literacy itself over orality.[6]

There have been significant efforts in recent years to expand and reorient traditional models of translation. Advances include a move from dynamic equivalence to a more-encompassing "functional equivalence"—which goes beyond a focus on "meaning" to include significant analysis also of the "form" of the passage to be translated, such as its genre as well as its patterns of discourse, and a consequent effort to find comparable patterns of discourse in the receptor language.[7] The most significant endeavors in this regard go beyond a *communication model*, which focuses on finding the [single?] meaning/form in the lan-

---

4. See Cosgrove, *Meanings*.

5. For a review of these issues, see Rhoads, "Introduction," 4–18.

6. Discussed by Porter, "Assessing." See also, Porter's earlier essay, "Some Issues."

7. Noss, "A Translator's Trail," 353–54. On the important field of biblical discourse analysis, see Porter and Carson, *Discourse Analysis*; Reed, "Discourse Analysis"; Porter and Reed, *Discourse Analysis*; Westfall, *Discourse Analysis*, 22–87. For an excellent workbook on the smaller units of discourse analysis, see Levinsohn, *Discourse Features*. Other sources listed above seek to give detailed analyses of entire literary pieces as integrated units of discourse. The many insights from discourse analysis can be reoriented and reconceived in terms of their function as "oral arts."

guage of the originating text and then attempts to replicate that meaning/form in the receptor language. In the new efforts, the movement is toward an *engagement model*, which takes more seriously the potential *impacts* of translation on audiences. This shift of emphasis from original text to audience impact involves a somewhat freer rendering in the idiom and culture of reception so as to create a more powerful experience and a more emotional encounter with the Bible on the part of cultures of reception.[8] In addition, there is another movement urging that translations include relevant information regarding local customs and culture-specific worldviews—of ancient texts and modern contexts—so as to make the translations more understandable and relevant in the receptor language.[9] Finally there have been experiments to translate biblical texts into new media, such as video renditions of biblical stories and the format of graphic novels and comic books.

Now we are on the threshold of another new dynamic in translation theory and practice, namely, immersing the whole process in the medium of orality.[10] Because it is a change in medium and because it is relevant to the full spectrum of discourse levels and functions, orality is not "added on" as though it were just another factor to be considered. Rather, the shift from translating for print to translating for oral performance represents a fundamental paradigm shift.[11] It involves analyzing the original text as a witness to oral performances in the ancient world. And it involves several other new factors: seeing translation as an embodiment, attending to the oral arts, discerning the potential meanings

---

8. Noss, "A Translator's Trail," 354–56. A recent essay by Scott Elliott of the Nida Institute for Biblical Scholarship emphasizes open creativity in the shift to address receptor audiences. He writes: "No longer concerned primarily with equivalence or fidelity, modern Translation Studies now attends to frames of reference, ethics, ideology, identity, and so forth." S. S. Elliott, "Translation."

9. Porter, "Assessing," 138–44. For further discussion of relevance theory along with bibliography, see Maxey, "Performance Criticism." The danger of making the source language relevant in the receptor language is that we so domesticate it in the new context as to lose the cultural meaning and impact of the original. On this point, see Rohrbaugh, "Foreignizing."

10. On the issue of *media* shifts in relation to translation (including electronic media), see Boomershine, "Bible Translation"; Boomershine, "Transmediation Theory"; Loubser, "How Do You Report"; Loubser, *Oral and Manuscript Culture*.

11. On paradigm shifts, see Kuhn, *Structure*. For a very helpful brief example of the shift to orality, see Rebera, "Translating." On the paradigmatic nature of the shift in biblical studies represented by orality studies, see "Orality, Print Culture, and Biblical Interpretation," a film by Eugene Botha (www.eugenebotha.co.za).

of a composition in performance, assessing the rhetorical impacts on gathered audiences, appreciating the emotional experiences of an audience, and allowing for the possibility of spontaneous creativity between performer and audience in the course of a performance. Fresh efforts are being made by biblical scholars and translators alike to explore these dynamics of oral translation.

The oral approach to translation is driven in part as a response to the need for new approaches to translations in oral cultures or predominantly oral cultures still existing throughout the world. And it is in response to a growing interest in performing biblical texts in predominantly literate/electronic cultures.[12] However, as I have suggested, it is also driven by new developments in biblical scholarship involving both the study of the biblical world as a predominantly oral culture and the rise of biblical performance criticism. What follows is an effort to unpack some of the work emerging in biblical studies and to point to some cutting edge work in oral translation.

The New Testament as Performance Literature

Biblical performance criticism is an effort to recover the oral performative nature of biblical materials at their origins—through an understanding of the oral cultures of antiquity, the mechanics of writing, reading, and memory work, and the dynamics of performance scenarios as well as through an appreciation for the difference that performance can make in our interpretation and understanding of biblical writings.[13] The New Testament is a collection of narratives and letters that were originally composed in the genre of stories and letters (not originally composed *as* scripture) that were primarily presented and received as oral performances, each probably presented in its entirety in a performance event. I understand "performance event" as an expressive presentation of a gospel or letter or the book of *Revelation* by a storyteller

---

12. There is an extensive Network of Biblical Storytellers fostering performance in many venues (www.nbsint.org and www.gotell.org). See also the website on Biblical Performance Criticism for a variety of performers (www.biblicalperformancecriticism.org).

13. A movement to understand anew the orality of early Christianity began with the publication of Kelber, *The Oral and the Written Gospel* and the work of the SBL Seminar, "The Bible in Ancient and Modern Media" under the leadership of Thomas Boomershine.

composing/re-composing from memory in performance or by a lector performing from a scroll to a gathered audience in a particular time and place.

In the first century, virtually everyone would have experienced these compositions now in the New Testament as expressive readings or performances to gathered communities. It is considered likely that more than ninety to ninety-five percent of the people in the Mediterranean world, including Israel in Palestine, were non-literate.[14] Even the two or three percent who were fully able to write and read were also steeped in orality. Some scholars are now considering whether some of the gospel materials, particularly the *Gospel of Mark* and the re-constructed Q, may well have originally been composed mentally/orally. Compositions such as we see with the letters of Paul were composed mentally/orally and then dictated to a scribe. Many if not most performances were done without a script.[15] Virtually all reading was aloud at a public or private gathering. Everything we know about storytellers and orators in the ancient world suggests that storytelling and public reading alike would have been animated, emotional, and engaging.

The handwritten scrolls that retain "transcriptions" of these oral presentations were nothing like our printed Bibles. These handwritten scrolls with continuous script—one upper-case letter after another without spaces between words, with no sentence or paragraph markers, and having no punctuation or accents—were fundamentally a phonetic storehouse of sounds-in-syllables waiting to be put back into orality, like scores for music. It is unlikely that an 'author' would have composed in the act of scribing such a manuscript. As with musical compositions, composers of stories or speeches probably would have been composed in imagination or sounded out what they were composing—and later transcribed it. In fact, they likely visualized their whole embodied performance—gestures, movements, and facial expressions—as they composed ahead of actually performing.[16] The scrolls served mainly to assist a performer's memory and, particularly in relation to the letters,

---

14. For a summary of these assessments of literacy and their implications, with relevant bibliography, see P. J. J. Botha, "Greco-Roman Literacy."

15. The study of memory in the ancient world is as important as the analysis of orality and literacy. See Small, "*Wax Tablets.*"

16. See similar comments on a performer's visualization in Shiell, *Reading Acts*," 100.

to enable performances to be repeated on new occasions and in other locations, even though it is also likely that compositions would also have passed in memory from oral performance to oral performance without the aid of a manuscript. Obviously, we are extremely fortunate to have these writings preserved for us. They are virtually the only sources we have as witnesses to the life of Jesus and the life of the early church. Nevertheless, these scrolls originally functioned in a predominantly oral culture in ways that are unfamiliar to us today. As such, they are also virtually the only sources we have as witnesses for oral performances.

The writings preserved for us in the New Testament are like fossil remains of living oral performances.[17] Walter Ong has said that the New Testament writings contain a high degree of "residual orality"—traces of oral features of language embedded in written texts. He was referring to oral arts cultivated in oral cultures as means to communicate in memorable and persuasive ways.[18] Now that we are taking seriously the biblical world as oral culture, we are able to see the extent of the presence of oral arts in the New Testament writings. Consider, for example, the number of oral poetic features in the *Gospel of Mark* that have been identified in the work of Joanna Dewey and Whitney Shiner: interconnections, patterns of repetition, type scenes, forecasts and echoes, hook words, inclusios, intercalations, frames, parallelism, chiastic patterns, ring compositions, series of three, a paratactic style, non-linear plot developments, among others.[19] John Harvey and Casey Davis have done a similar analysis of the oral features of letters of Paul, finding formulaic language, topical introductions, quotations, antithesis, synonymy, vagueness, metaphor, compactness, wordplay, many forms of repetition, rare words chosen to have an impact, mnemonic devices, bridge words, run-on sentences, resonance, chiastic patterns, and various forms of

---

17. I attribute this insightful analogy to Dennis Dewey.

18. Ong, *Orality*, 30–77. One of the challenges of performance criticism is to distinguish oral arts from literary arts, if such a distinction can be made. Since we know that the early Christian writings were indeed performed orally by memory or by reading, we can assume that the structural features and sounds of the text did indeed function as oral art, whatever their origin. So we need to ask how indeed they worked as oral art.

19. Dewey, "Mark as Oral Narrative"; Dewey, "The Gospel of Mark"; Dewey, "Oral Methods"; Dewey, "Mark as Interwoven Tapestry"; and Shiner, *Proclaiming*.

parallelism.[20] Learning to listen to the Greek will assist us in appreciating these oral arts and in being able to discern them in sound.[21]

Translations for performance will differ in many ways from translations for reading. For example, a translation for performance can include the use of the "historical present." One can shift back and forth with facility from past to present tense in oral performance in a way that seems very awkward in writing. Furthermore, one can preserve word order in oral narration that does not make sense or is misleading in a text for reading. Such word order in the translation can bring out the suspense and the emphases of the original. Seeking to replicate onomatopoetic words and the sounds of the Greek sentences as they relate to the content being presented are helpful in translations for performance. The lengths of sentences, clues to punctuation, places for pauses and stops, along with contractions and elision are features that are crucial for performance. In the translation of a given text, the choice to use the same word or cognate in the receptor language as means to translate repeated occurrences of the same Greek word (even when they have somewhat different nuances of meaning) becomes important for performance. Such verbal repetitions serve to "forecast" and to "echo" events and motifs. Parallelism and chiastic patterns become significant dimensions of translation, because they contribute to rhythm and pace.

In addition, however, the writings contain not only residual traces of oral arts of sound, they also contain residual traces of the *arts of performance*. The text is a record of a performance which, by its very nature, could also serve as a "script" for subsequent performances. As such, the writings contain "stage directions" for voice inflection, volume, gestures, movement, body language, and emotions. As the story is told, directions for performing the story are also suggested. These "suggestions" occur in virtually every episode of the gospel stories and are present throughout the letters and the *Book of Revelation*: "He cried in a loud cry . . ." (voice volume of what follows); "They were astonished . . ." (tone, facial expression); "He sighed deeply in his spirit . . ." (sound, body posture); "He stretched out his hand and touched him . . ." (gesture, pace); "He looked up to heaven . . ." (head gesture, facial expression); " . . . gave to

---

20. Davis, *Oral Biblical Criticism* and Harvey, *Listening*.

21. See (or hear!) Simon, *Greek-Latin New Testament*; and Phemister. *Audio Greek New Testament*.

me and to Barnabas the right hand of partnership." (hand gesture); "The sixth angel poured his bowl over . . ." (gesture, tone of suspense); ". . . and in his mouth it tasted bitter" (facial expression). And the composition implies other performance features by virtue of grammar, syntax, word order, position of subordinate clauses, various forms of parallelism, length of sentences, choice of words, and devices of discourse, such as irony and innuendo, questions, depictions of characters by word and action, descriptions of movement, and so on.

Note that inflection, gestures, non-verbal sounds, and facial expressions are not just illustrative of meaning. They do not simply accompany words. Rather, they are features that can also *determine* meaning. In an oral performance, the meaning of a line is conveyed not only by *what* one says but also by *how* one says it. In performance studies, the implicit message on how a line is delivered is called the "subtext." In performance, all lines have a subtext as well as a text. Most lines can be inflected with different subtexts, which reflect different meanings and connotations and which generate different impacts. Of course, in performance, *how* a line is delivered includes the expression of the whole person. Facial expressions and gestures are not add-ons; they are part of one integrated act of delivery. Facial expressions of a smile or a frown or a grimace or a raised eyebrow can bring out different meanings of a line or intensify its emotional effects. A gesture alone can "be worth a thousand words." Recent studies show that gestures were very important to the ancients in communication. Attention to these features in the New Testament writings reveals hundreds of gestures depicted or implied for performance.[22]

Furthermore, a study of the writings as witnesses to oral performance leads to reflection on the whole performance event as integral to the determination of meaning and impact: the physical location, the cultural context, the situation of the audience, the social location of the audience, the possible impact of the performance upon the audience, the reaction of the audience, and the part that an audience takes in shaping the performance-in-progress.[23] When we think of orality, we are dealing with a performer who is composing and re-composing in

---

22. See Shiner, *Proclaiming*, 127–42; and J. Elliott, "A Dog." Both of these resources have extensive bibliography.

23. For examples of the dramatic ways that audiences shape, indeed may take over, performances in oral cultures, see Tymoczka, "Translation."

the act of performance in light of the circumstances and in interaction with the audience. The "embodied composition" is not fixed. Rather, to a greater or lesser degree, it is fluid. Also, we cannot ignore the fact that a performance was meant to transform an audience, to generate action and commitment, to create a certain kind of community of the audience. From what we know of ancient audiences, they were very involved, responding verbally and emotionally throughout a performance. How can we as biblical scholars faithfully imagine how a performance may have affected its ancient audiences?

Moving Toward Oral Translation

All of this analysis suggests that the writings now in the New Testament are the "written remains" of what were originally oral compositions in performance to gathered communities. Regarding translation, some of the questions we may be led to ask are: When we translate, do we take seriously the fact that the writings reflect features of the sounds and actions of performance? Are we translating the written text taking into account all the oral arts and performative dynamics to which the written text gives witness? And what are we translating? Are we translating the text alone? Could we go even further and consider the possibility of translating an imagined oral performance upon which the written text was originally based? And could we orient the translation to the implied rhetorical impact such a performance may have had upon an ancient audience? Then these questions arise: How could we think about translating something that was once oral into a contemporary culture of reception? How would it "transfer"? What would such a translation be like? What process of translation might take place to keep it within the parameters of orality?

In two interesting articles on ideophones, Philip Noss points us in some intriguing directions.[24] An ideophone is a word that "expresses what is perceived by the five senses, sound, sight, smell, taste, and feeling, both physical and emotional."[25] Such sounds punctuate the common conversation and performance dynamics of many cultures, particularly in Africa. In a Gabaya-French dictionary, almost one-fourth of the

---

24. Noss, "Translator's Trail"; and Noss, "Ideophone."
25. Noss, "Translator's Trail," 362.

words are ideophones.²⁶ Ideophones (idea+sound) encompass a range of words. Some are simple sound representations that might stand alone, such as "whoosh" or "snap." Others are onomatopoetic words used in sentences, such as "the man *ripped* his clothes" or "she *whacked* him over the head," both of which have connotations as well as denotations.

However, ideophones in African languages are more profound and complex. They convey an experience and have complex cultural associations. These are not easy to grasp. A possible example in English might be the word "sizzle," which depicts the hissing sound (and maybe the sight) of something cooking or burning up over a high heat. It can also be used metaphorically of someone "sizzling" with anger or it can refer to a hot entertainer as one who is "sizzling." Noss gives some examples in Gbaya: *hafafa* ("a swallow's flight over the surface of the water as it catches insects"); *hufuk* ("the action of tossing one's opponent to the ground in a wrestling match"); *bereng* ("reddish bright color of the evening sky"); *gete-gete* ("the action of breaking apart into small pieces"); and *lek-lek* ("the consuming action of flames as they burn and devour").²⁷ These sound-words can function as adverbs, adjectives, nouns, verbs, or stand alone; and they can be used literally and metaphorically. Again, they may comprise a large part of the vocabulary and convey whole actions as well as experiences and emotions related to sensation expressed in sound. In Noss's view, they should be used with caution and can be overdone.²⁸ Nevertheless, a performance peppered with such words can "sizzle"—stimulate the imagination, generate empathy, and provoke engagement on the part of an audience.

The question Noss raises is this: If Hebrew and Greek have only a few ideophones, what license do translators have to use them generously in a receptor language? Using the *engagement model* of translation (noted above), Noss answers that we should use them carefully but generously in the receptor language when ideographs are native to that language and because they increase the power of the biblical message and its potential impact upon the culture of reception.²⁹ The point is that translation can creatively draw upon the *oral* features of the language of reception. I believe that this step opens the door in translation to

26. Noss, "Ideophone," 423.
27. Ibid., passim.
28. Ibid., 429.
29. Noss, A Translator's Trail," 369–70.

include many aspects of orality—as well as dynamics of performance—that are distinctive to each culture of reception.

But Noss takes a second and more significant step. He suggests that transposition to a *new medium* may allow for an even greater freedom of translation in relation to ideophones. He refers, for example, to the United Bible Societies' transposition from print to video, a medium in which sounds are integral to the presentation. He also names the comic book genre and illustrated novels.[30] In these media, words like "Bonk!" and "Thunk!" are common. These are stand-alone ideophones that actually add to the text being translated and can enhance or determine meaning in that genre.

What if we extended the points Noss is making about the *sound* of ideophones to the *physicality* of performance? To start with, we would be preparing a printed translation for contemporary performances making liberal use of the oral arts of the receptor culture.[31] But what if we made use not only of the oral arts but also the performative arts? Here we could even take the bold step of going to a wholly new medium—embodiment in a performance? What if the translation was actually a live performance?[32] I do not just mean that there would be a printed translation designed *for* performances (presumably by professional or cultural storytellers), although these are desirable and significant. Nor do I mean an audio or a video rendering. Rather, I mean that live performances would *be* the translations in a new medium. Here we would be dealing not just with ideophones but also with noises, gestures, movement, facial expressions, volume and inflection, pace, and so on. Performers would work to bring to expression the explicit and implicit suggestions for performance in the original text. And we would be working with the new cultural context to explore for translation not only the oral arts but also the performance arts common to that culture as a basis for bringing out the full potential of the original—in performance.

In a sense, oral performance would not actually be a new medium, because it would correlate with the original oral performance medium of the biblical writings themselves. However, obstacles abound. For example, although we have the written text in the original language, we have quite limited ideas about the actual inflections or facial expres-

---

30. Ibid., 371–73.
31. This is the focus of the work of Ernst Wendland and the Thomases (see below).
32. This is what James Maxey is also proposing and exploring (see below).

sions or gestures from ancient performances. However, even though we cannot recover the actual performance techniques, we do have evidence that ancient performances were very expressive and emotional. Efforts are now being made by means of a study of ancient rhetorical handbooks, descriptions of performances, and artistic depictions to discern what specific ancient gestures might have accompanied and expressed such actions as a curse or a blessing or an act of mourning, and so on.[33] Although we have no way of knowing precisely what an ancient performer may have done with these stage directions, we do have good reason to think *something* is being called for on the part of the performer—a gesture, a raised voice, a bodily show of an emotion. Although we may not know precisely what physical expression we are translating, we could nevertheless be fairly confident that there was *something* there as part of an ancient performance *to be translated* into a contemporary performance.

The most appropriate approach may be to extend and extrapolate on what Noss suggests: supply culture-specific expressions of performance arts in the culture of reception, even when they are not explicit in the original. For example, an ancient storyteller may have originally performed of the *Gospel of Mark* in a popular style that today's audiences might consider to be overly dramatic and therefore somewhat distracting.

Oral Approaches to Translation

In the last decade or so, articles and books on translation have been moving in the direction of incorporating issues of orality into translation.[34] Now there are two full-length monographs that have placed

---

33. On gestures, see Shiner, *Proclaiming*, 127–42; J. Elliott, "A Dog"; E. Botha, "Pragmatic Models"; and Sheill, *Reading Acts*, 34–101. The ancient handbooks describing rhetorical gestures were written for the upper classes. However, the gestures would likely have been universally understood. What additional gestures the popular storytellers may have used are obviously difficult to recover.

34. See, for example, Bartsch, "Oral Style"; E. Botha, "Pragmatic Models"; de Vries, "Bible Translation"; Fry, "An Oral Approach"; Noss, "The Oral Story"; Noss, "The Ideophone"; van Niekerk and Pauw, "Understanding"; and Scott, "A New Voice." The first monograph devoted to the orality of a New Testament writing for translators was Thomas and Thomas, *Structure*.

translation squarely within the theory and the practice of oral performance in ancient and modern contexts.

An Oratorical-Performative Approach to Translation

The first volume is entitled *Finding and Translating the Oral-Aural Elements in Written Language: The Case of the New Testament Epistles* by Ernst Wendland. Wendland applies performance criticism to the biblical materials as a foundation for developing what he calls an *oratorical-performative* approach to translation.[35] He begins with the assumption that the original contexts for the writings now in the New Testament were oral performances. He seeks to understand these performance events and the traces of oral arts embedded in the writings. And he is eager to provide translations that facilitate oral reading/oral performance events in contemporary cultures. Therefore, he brings the dynamics of ancient oral performance into the translation *process* as well as the translation *text*.

Wendland's oratorical-performative approach addresses translation in three areas.[36] The *oral-meaning dynamic* follows the traditional semantic approach placed now in the context of orality. Taking seriously performative features of the text, Wendland considers that meaning can also include the "para-linguistic" features implied by the text (tone, pace, rhythm, inflection) as well as the "extra-linguistic" (non-verbal) features suggested by the text (gestures, posture, movement). Then there is the *oral-stylistic dynamic* that involves all of the ancient oral arts embedded in the texts—an effort to find comparable or at least compatible oral arts—in the culture for which the translation is intended. Finally, there is the *oral-impact dynamic* that seeks to discern the rhetorical effects that the oration (in part and as a whole) may have had on an ancient listening audience in an effort to replicate a similar impact upon a listening audience in a particular modern culture. Wendland focuses primarily on the oral arts of the original as a means to prepare printed translations for public oral performance in a new cultural context.

I highlight briefly four aspects of Wendland's work: oral arts, sound, memory, and context. First, Wendland pays particular attention to the oral arts, drawing upon many different ways to assess the features

---

35. Wendland, *Finding*, 275.
36. Ibid., passim.

of language in an oral culture.[37] Ken and Margaret Thomas also display these features in their analysis and translation of 1 Peter.[38] Second, he includes acoustic dynamics such as onomatopoetic words, sound repetition, wordplay, and sound structuring. Here the work of Wendland is considerably amplified by the studies of Lee and Scott[39] and Shiner,[40] who focus on the impact of the "sound" of the original language. Third, Wendland believes that features of ancient oral art that facilitated memory—mnemonic techniques—were also embedded in the biblical writings. These were designed both to assist the performer in remembering and to aid the audience in recalling.[41] For further exploration of memory arts, consult Shiner's very helpful chapter explaining ancient memory techniques.[42] Finally, in Wendland's view, a translation may need to bear some minimal situational and cultural knowledge from the contemporary context in order for an audience to understand the meaning and to experience the impact in a way faithful to the original.

Wendland offers examples of translations of selections from four New Testament letters: *James, Philemon, 1 John,* and *1 Peter*.[43] In his treatment of each letter, he provides a fairly comprehensive study of the oral arts of the Greek. He also sets out the Greek and English in schemata that feature what he sees to be their oral patterns and structures. Then he gives excerpts from a number of contemporary English translations as well as translations into Chewa, a Bantu language widely spoken in south-central Africa. And he gives "back-translations" from Chewa into English to illustrate how translation can feature oral arts from a predominantly oral culture in the contemporary world. It poses a significant challenge to biblical scholars and to translators to incorporate the plenum of oral features in the biblical writings into the translation process in another cluture.[44] To assist with this, Wendland offers a

---

37. For a comprehensive list of oral features, see ibid, 24–31. Wendland draws substantially upon the work of Walter Ong, who discusses the following traits of language in an oral culture: formulas, repetition, contrasts, traditional, experiential, colorful, hyperbolic, emotionally-charged, and acoustically-oriented, in *Orality*, 37–57.

38. Thomas and Thomas, *Structure*, passim.

39 Scott, "A New Voice." See also Lee and Scott, *Sound Mapping the New Testament*.

40. Shiner, *Proclaiming*, 162–65.

41. Wendland, *Finding*, 18–22.

42. Shiner, *Proclaiming*, 103–26. See also Kelber, "The Oral."

43. Wendland, *Finding*, chapters 2–6.

44. This is especially challenging when there is no comparable parallel in the cul-

brief step-by-step procedure to do an oral-rhetorical analysis of a biblical writing and to prepare an oratorical-performative translation.[45]

A Translation-as-Performance Approach

My second example is a volume called *From Orality to Orality: A New Paradigm for Contextual Translation of the Bible* by James Maxey. Maxey aims for "translations for performance."[46] This approach involves the radical step of making performance itself part of the translation process and the goal of the endeavor. Maxey seeks to understand and analyze the biblical materials in the imagined context of *performance events* of the early church, with a full understanding of the performative arts, the audience participation, and the rhetorical impact this might involve.[47] At the same time, he is seeking to place the translation in the context of performance events of a contemporary oral culture. He describes his experiences working with the Vuté people of Cameroon.[48] This is a predominantly oral culture that now, thanks to Maxey's earlier work with them, has attained literacy and a printed Bible translation. Recently, Maxey facilitated an opportunity for storytellers from among the Vuté people to develop translations-in-performance of five stories from the Gospel of Mark. The performers made their own translations-in-performance for the Vuté community.

In his experience of their work, Maxey learned much about performance in an oral culture. He details some of the features of their translations-in-performance: the occasional addition of information about the first century to clarify a storytelling point; selection of vocabulary that *evokes* emotion rather than just *describing* it; a preference for direct speech; a preference for short, less complex sentences with briefer clauses; the use of ideophones; the incorporation of meaning-making gestures that are culture-specific to the Vuté community; questions directed to the audience to engage them; interactions with

---

ture of reception, as, for example, there might not be with regard to genre such as an apocalypse.

45. Wendland, *Finding*, 367–82, 383–84.

46. See also Maxey, "Performance Criticism."

47. Maxey, *From Orality*, 134–38. For Maxey's reflections on his own experience of memorizing and performing Paul's *Letter to Philemon*, see ibid., 147.

48. Maxey, *From Orality*, p. 1–14, 167–92.

audience responses; interjections emphasizing local Vuté values, such as gratitude and humor; effective use of pace and silence; pointing to imagined props and characters in the story; and the use of costumes, actual props, and staging.[49] When we consider that the performance *is* the translation in voice and action, this list represents a fascinating array of oral-effective features.

In this context, translation is fluid and somewhat open-ended, probably much like the performances in the oral cultures of the early church. The end product is not necessarily a printed Bible to be reproduced and distributed, unless it is a working text or one that changes over time from performance to performance. Rather, the goal is to create fleeting, ephemeral moments of performance—events that occur and are gone. The translation happens *in* the performance, not just in preparation for it. The translation is the performance unfolding in real time. There would be as many translations as there are performances. If there is a text, it would include references to the para-linguistic and extra-linguistic aspects of the stories as they are displayed in performance (see below). Or there might be a video tape, with regard to which, Maxey laments, much is lost in comparison to a live performance event. Yet, for Maxey, the goal of the biblical story is "transformation"—such that the stories live on in the telling and retelling in homes and village events (in story and song) in the lives of those who have told and heard them. Through this process, the stories have entered their collective life and memory and now belong to the people.[50] The scriptures are embodied in the people as well as in a book. The stories have gone from the orality implied in the biblical materials to the orality of the Vuté people.

Three Key Issues

Here let me highlight three key issues that relate to this overall paradigm shift from a print orientation to orality: the desire to capture the artistry and even the beauty of the original language in translation; the innovative efforts to "format" translations for performance; and the dynamics of power in the translation process.

---

49. Ibid., 218–23.
50. Ibid., 232.

Artistry and Beauty

The ancient world valued the *artistry* of speaking, not just in terms of delivery but also in regard to all the verbal arts in a wide range of performances: epic recitation, storytelling, rhetorical speeches, orations of letters, and so on. Rhetorical handbooks and other writings touted the engaging beauty and power of the euphony, the flow, the imagery, the stories, and even the argumentation of speeches. The choice of words, the arrangement, the patterns of repetition with variation, the pleasantness of sound to the ear, the memorable nature of sayings and images, and the developing power of the persuasion—all these worked together to produce riveting experiences for ancient audiences. Outstanding orators and engaging orations were highly valued as central to public and private life both for elites and for the populace. We are fortunate to have extant in writing some of the handbooks on the art of persuasion as well as some Greco-Roman orations. These sources provide the context for our study of the oral traditions that have survived in written form in the New Testament. Although the rhetorical handbooks are products of elites, there is good reason to believe that native storytellers were quite skilled in the dynamics of telling engaging stories. Those of us who engage in translation in New Testament studies have much to learn from our colleagues in classical studies who are engaged in the translation of epic stories and rhetorical orations.[51]

Appreciation for the beauty of oral traditions is also expressed by those who explore the oral roots of the New Testament writings. Ernst Wendland wants to reproduce: "at least part of the artistic *beauty* and rhetorical *power* that are present in the original text ... the energy and vibrancy of the language as a whole, including in particular the entire *phonological* dimension of a biblical discourse in translation—the varied rhythms and euphony of speech as this is orally communicated to a *listening* audience."[52] Ken and Margaret Thomas devote a chapter to the "beauty and meaning of the language" of *I Peter*.[53] Not only do they explore the "phonological resonances"[54] or the sound repetitions. They also explore the beauty and persuasiveness of various figures of

---

51. See for example, Edwards, *Sound* and Foley, *The Singer*.
52. Wendland, *Finding*, v, 146.
53. Thomas and Thomas, *Structure*, 37–54.
54. Ibid., *Structure*, 3. This is a term they have drawn from Ernst Wendland.

speech, such as metaphors, similes, and substitution because, they argue, "Figurative speech can draw upon the hearer's imagination, excite attention, and expand meaning."[55] The goal of translation is to capture not just the signification of this imagery but also the beauty of it and its capacity to provoke vivid imaging in an audience. Just as translation committees have often included poets and prose writers on their teams, we might now also consider the inclusion of people gifted in oratory and storytelling in the work of translation, as Maxey has done, for example, with the Vuté people.[56]

Formatting

Traditional formatting—chapters, verses, brief paragraphs, headings—may not be adequate when considering translations for an oral performance or for a performative reading. Formatting itself is not neutral, and new features may need to be brought into play as means to reflect performance in print.

Folklorists have developed schemata to record an oral performance in print in such a way as to preserve some of the oral artistry involved in the performance.[57] The efforts involve notations and annotations about the use of the voice and the physical gestures and the movement of the performers. Translators are "reversing" the transcription process so that the notations may not only record a performance but they may also serve as directions for subsequent performances, much as a script for a play might function. When we imagine a script for oral performance we see also the analogy with musical scores, which include such things as notes designating various lengths, rests, signs for repetition, codas for endings, slurring, and staccato, as well as verbal directions for tempo, tone, volume, intensity, and style.[58]

In a similar way, translations that presume performance might use the following in creative ways: punctuation; spacing between words, sentences, and even letters; typing features such as bold, italics, and underlining; a choice of varying fonts—all as means to suggest pace,

---

55. Ibid., 37.

56. Maxey, *From Orality*, 167–91.

57. Hymes, *Now I Know*; Joubert, "Defining"; Fine, *The Folklore Text*; and Tedlock, *Finding*.

58. See Cosgrove, "English Bible."

volume, emphasis, intensity, and so on. Wendland identifies a number of the following "graphic" signals: "increased type size, distinctive font faces, unjustified right margins, rhythmic lineation, indentation, and judicious use of white space to visually display prominent verbal patterns."[59] Print layout, he argues, "should provide suitable clues for reading."[60] John Miles Foley uses different levels of superscript to convey inflection.[61] Maxey includes also extralinguistic features. He has developed a schema of three columns in which the translation is in the center column formatted to reflect rhythm and pace; to the left are notes on the paralinguistic features illustrating uses of the voice; and to the right are extralinguistic notes identifying gestures and other physical expressions.[62]

Furthermore, the formatting of lines could also reflect identification of utterance units (cola) that facilitate the performer with breathing and pace and that assist the audience in understanding. The format might also reflect the patterns and structures of oral arts such as parallelism, chiasms, chain formulations, link/stitch words, and various patterns of repetition in words, themes, grammar, syntax, and sound. Some of these patterns of discourse also work as features that assist memory for the performer and enhance memorability for the audience. Furthermore, the translation format might highlight formulaic sayings, proverbs, rhyme, rhythm, onomatopoetic words, ideophones, alliteration, wordplays, unusual words, and the repetition of sounds that structure discourse. Obviously, this can become quite complex, There may be a need to lay out the same passage in different formats to capture all that the translators want to feature.[63] These translation schemes do not limit a performer or a reader to one thing or another, but they do clearly place the printed text in performative space and no doubt make clear that, even with specific directions, no two performances will be the same.

As a performer of New Testament writings,[64] I am acutely aware of the limitations of these schemes and notations. I want to add de-

---

59. Wendland, *Finding*, 374; Wendland, "Duplicating."
60. Ibid., n. 373.
61. Foley, *How to Read*, 95–108.
62. See Maxey, *From Orality*, 186–88 for a schematic translation of Mark 2:1–12.
63. This is what Wendland does in his analysis of letters, *Finding, passim*.
64. See Rhoads, "Performing," 176–201.

scriptions of what I am doing in performance and note more of the oral arts at work. As aids to translation and performance, we may want to consider performance commentaries or a translation/performance notebook that expresses the multiple physical and verbal things that go into the enactment of each line of what may appear on the surface to be a simple act of storytelling or the oration of an epistle. In addition to providing a translation, a performance commentary might include notes on such matters as voice, physical expressions, movement, memory devices, impact, relevant information from the life world context, issues of power, among others. The notes could highlight *diverse* ways by which a composition may be played in performance.

Power Dynamics of Translation

The dynamics of translation are fraught with complex power issues. Usually a dominant, colonial culture is providing a translation for a suppressed culture, seeking to convert them to Christianity.[65] Recently, translators have begun to be sensitive to issues of power. For example, there are efforts to engage the local culture more fully in the translation process. Wendland, for example, wants translations to be tested and approved by the culture of reception.[66] Maxey is especially sensitive to issues of power and to his own presence and bias as a native of dominant United States culture.[67] He takes into account the power dynamics of the history of translation and seeks to counter an imperialist approach. He is aware that every translation is biased and situated. He knows the complex issues of control negotiated by translation agencies. He is aware also of the bias among translators that privileges writing over orality—how the goal of translation groups is a printed text, how the translation process often involves literacy programs, and how colonial-

---

65. On power dynamics in translation, see Bailey and Pippin, editors, *Race*; Sugirtharajah, *Postcolonial Criticism*; West, "African Biblical Hermeneutics"; Yorke, "Bible Translation"; Venuti, *The Translator's Invisibility*; and Bassnett and Trivedi, *Postcolonial Translation*.

66. Wendland, *Finding*, 374.

67. Maxey, *From Orality*, 42–48.

izing cultures use writing to dominate.⁶⁸ Maxey critiques the sometimes unilateral nature of the translation process.⁶⁹

As expressed by his subtitle, Maxey proposes a "new paradigm of contextual translation." It is based on models of "contextual theology" developed in mission studies.⁷⁰ This model seeks to respect the culture for which the translation is being made, entrusts the translation process more fully into the hands of that culture, and seeks for the relationship to be mutually informative. There are two foci to this approach. First, Maxey recognizes both the contextual nature of the biblical materials and the distinct contextual nature of contemporary culture. As such, he acknowledges and honors the power of the new culture to develop its own indigenous expressions of biblical translation. Maxey expects to learn and be transformed by his experience. Second, the model is liberationist in putting the oral translation process primarily in local hands so that the new culture can be engaged in the process of translation from the start and involved in composing their translations in and for performance.⁷¹ The key to this new model is that it takes seriously the *oral* nature of the contemporary culture. While Maxey honors and promotes the literacy of the culture, he has seen how liberating it is for a traditional oral culture to develop translations in their preferred media of performance and song.⁷²

Trajectories

I have focused on efforts by key figures to translate for oral or predominantly oral cultures. We may also want to consider what performance translations might look like in print/electronic cultures. Surely performance is one way to get the "word" off the printed page and away from an electronic text and reinvigorate it in lively, embodied inter-relationship with an audience. How can we make the oral arts of the biblical text transparent? How can we make use of techniques of oral performance of literature so as to enliven the printed translation by performances? How can we make the translation relevant in a way that will address and

68. Ibid., 91–92.
69. Ibid., 40.
70. Bevans, *Models*; Gittins, *Life*; and Schreiter, *Constructing*.
71. Maxey, *From Orality*, 51, 231–36.
72. Ibid., 228–31.

challenge audiences in their context? How can we speak and move and gesture in the ordinary language of various cultures and subcultures of society? How can we translate/ perform in such a way as to open up space for interaction with the audience? How can we generate freedom in performance to translate afresh as the performance unfolds?

Where do we go from here in the collaborative efforts of biblical scholarship and translation for orality? I would like to suggest five avenues.

1. Seek to embrace the paradigm shift to an oral medium. This is not easy, because it requires us to imagine anew the early church, reconfigure the biblical writings as oral performances, and rethink translation in terms of orality.

2. Attend carefully to the oral arts and performance arts embedded in the biblical writings. This will require us to develop new tools and learn new methods of analysis.

3. Learn how to listen—both to the Hebrew/ Greek originals and to translations. And learn how to read the biblical languages aloud with facility. Consider how translations will sound, what their emotional impact might be, how they might impel an audience to action, and what worlds they seek to create. Analyze just what it is about a biblical composition that would generate such effects.

4. Seek to imagine the performance events of the early church: performer, performance, physical location, social context, audience participation, rhetorical impact, and so on. The more concretely we can place biblical writings in performance space, the closer we will get to grasping their persuasive power.

5. Perform biblical materials yourself in translation in your native language. Absolutely, there is no better way to embrace the paradigm shift to orality than to perform a text as an act of persuasion before a live audience. Recently, New Testament scholar Margaret Lee took up the challenge to translate, memorize, and perform the *Sermon on the Mount*, which she had been studying as oral text for some time. Her comment: "I learned more about the Sermon on the Mount from my few weeks of performance preparation than I have in the entire five years since I wrote my

dissertation on that passage. The experience was an awakening for me, replete with new possibilities for my work... I anticipate rich returns on the efforts I intend to lavish in a new scholarly direction."

Conclusion

As a biblical scholar, I have consistently grown through the years in my appreciation for the task of translating. Translation is a demanding and exacting discipline, even while being significantly artful and creative. I have found that the act of translating for performance (and in performance) is one of the most helpful means to understand a biblical text. Translating for performance leads one to grasp in fresh ways the potential meanings of the original composition, the oral arts evident in the text, the significance of sound as a medium for communicating, and the experience of the rhetorical impact on an audience. I believe that translating for orality can enhance the exegetical process such that exegetes become oral translators and that translators become exegetes of the oral—and that both try their hand at performing!

Bibliography

Bailey, Randall C., and Tina Pippin, editors. *Semeia 76: Race Class, and Politics of Biblical Translation.* Atlanta: Scholars, 1996.

Bartsch, Carla. "Oral Style, Written Style, and Bible Translation." *Notes on Translation* 11 (1997) 41–48.

Bassnett, Susan, and Harish Trivedi. *Postcolonial Translation: Theory and Practice.* Translation Studies. London: Routledge, 1999.

Bevans, Stephen B. *Models of Contextual Theology.* 2nd ed. Maryknoll, NY: Orbis, 2002.

Boomershine, Thomas E. "Bible Translation and Communication Technology." *United Bible Societies Bulletin* 160/161 (1991) 14–19.

———. "A Transmediation Theory of Biblical Translation." *United Bible Societies Bulletin* 170/171 (1994) 49–57.

Botha, Pieter J. J. "Greco-Roman Literacy as Setting for New Testament Writings." *Neotestamentica* 26 (1992) 195–215.

Botha, J. Eugene. "Pragmatic Models of Text Interpretation and Bible Translation: Speech-Act Theory and Non-Verbal Communication." Paper presented at SNTS, Sibui, Romania, 2007.

Cosgrove, Charles H. *The Meanings We Choose: Hermeneutical Ethics, Indeterminacy, and the Conflict of Interpretations.* London: T. & T. Clark, 2004.

———. "English Bible Translation Postmodern Perspective: Reflections on a Critical Theory of Holistic Translation." In *The Challenge of Bible Translation: Communicating God's Word to the World*, edited by Glen Scorgie et al., 159–74. Grand Rapids: Zondervan, 2003.

Davis, Casey Wayne. *Oral Biblical Criticism: The Influence of the Principles of Orality on the Literary Structures of Paul's Epistle to the Philippians.* JSNTSup 172. Sheffield: Sheffield Academic, 1999.

Dewey, Joanna. "Mark as Oral Narrative: Structures as Clues to Understanding." *Sewanee Theological Review* 36 (1992) 45–56.

———. "The Gospel of Mark as an Oral-Aural Event: Implications for Interpretation." In *The New Literary Criticism and the New Testament*, edited by Elizabeth Struthers Malbon and Edgar McKnight, 145–61. Sheffield: Sheffield Academic, 1994.

———. "Oral Methods of Structuring Narrative in Mark." *Int* 43 (1989) 32–44.

———. "Mark as Interwoven Tapestry: Forecasts and Echoes for a Listening Audience." *CBQ* 53 (1991) 221–31.

Edwards, Mark W. *Sound, Sense, and Rhythm: Listening to Greek and Latin Poetry.* Martin Classical Lectures. Princeton: Princeton University Press, 2002.

Elliott, J. "A Dog, Shoes, and Subtabular Crumbthrowing: Gestural Communication in the Shift from Oral to Written Communication, with a Focus on the Gospel of Mark." Paper presented at a conference on "Orality and Literacy in Antiquity" in San Anselmo, CA, March 13–4, 2009.

Elliott, Scott S. "Translation and Narrative: Transfiguring Jesus." Atlanta: SBL Publications, 2009. No pages. Online: http://www.sbl-site.org/publication/article.aspx?articleId=828.

Fine, Elizabeth C. *The Folklore Text: From Performance to Print.* Bloomington: Indiana University Press, 1984.

Foley, John Miles. *How to Read an Oral Poem*. Urbana: University of Illinois Press, 2002.

———. *The Singer of Tales in Performance*. Voices in Performance and Text. Bloomington: Indiana University Press, 1995.

Fry, Euan M. "An Oral Approach to Translation." *TBT* 55 (2004) 506–10.

Gittins, Anthony. *Life and Death Matters: Doing Inculturation in Africa*. Nettetal: Steyeler, 2000.

Harvey, John D. *Listening to the Text: Oral Patterning in Paul's Letters*. Grand Rapids: Baker, 1998.

Hymes, Dell H. *Now I Know Only So Far: Essays in Ethnopoetics*. Lincoln: University of Nebraska Press, 2003.

Joubert, Annekie. "Defining and Working in an Oral Culture: Between Oral and Written Transmission—The Problems of Textualizing Performance Events." Paper presented at SNTS meeting, 2004.

Kelber, Werner H. *The Oral and the Written Gospel: The Hermeneutics of Speaking and Writing in the Synoptic Tradition, Mark, Paul, and Q*. Bloomington: Indiana University Press, 1987.

Kuhn, Thomas S. *The Structure of Scientific Revolutions*. 3rd ed. Chicago: University of Chicago Press, 1996.

Lee, Margaret Ellen, and Bernard Brandon Scott. *Sound Mapping the New Testament*. Salem, OR: Polebridge, 2009.

Levinson, Stephen H. *Discourse Features of New Testament Greek*. 2nd ed. Dallas: SIL International, 2000.

Loubser, J. A. (Bobby). "How Do You Report Something that was Said with a Smile?—Can We Overcome the Loss of Meaning When Oral-Manuscript Texts Are Represented in Modern Print Media?" *Scriptura* 87 (2004) 296–314.

———. *Oral and Manuscript Culture in the Bible: Studies in the Media Texture of the New Testament*. Stellenbosch: Sun, 2007.

Maxey, James A. "Performance Criticism and Its Implications for Bible Translation." Paper presented at the SNTS meeting, Sibiu, Romania, 2007.

———. *From Orality to Orality: A New Paradigm for Contextual Translation of the Bible*. Eugene, OR: Cascade Books, 2009.

Niekerk, A. van, and C. J. Pauw. "Understanding and/or Participation? The Goal of Making the Bible Available in Oral Context." *Scriptura* 74 (2000) 249–57.

Noss, Philip Andrew. "The Oral Story and Bible Translation." *TBT* 32 (1981) 301–18.

———. "The Ideophone in Bible Translation: Child or Stepchild." *TBT* 36 (1985) 423–30.

———. "A Translator's Trail: From Engagement to Ideophones to Engagement." In *Translating the Hebrew Bible: From the Septuagint to the Nouvelle Bible Second*, edited by Robert David and Manuel Jinbachian. Montreal: Mediaspaul, 2005.

Ong, Walter. *Orality and Literacy: The Technologizing of the Word*. London: Routledge, 1982.

Phemister, M. *Audio Greek New Testament: Westcott and Hort Greek New Testament*. Grand Rapids: Christian Classics Ethereal Library, 2003.

Porter, Stanley E. "Some Issues in Modern Translation Theory and Study of the Greek New Testament." *CR:BS* 9 (2001) 350–82.

———. "Assessing Translation Theory: Beyond Literal and Dynamic Equivalence." In *Translating the New Testament: Text, Translation, and Theology*, edited by Stanley E. Porter and Mark J. Boda, 117–45. Grand Rapids: Eerdmans, 2009.

Porter, Stanley E., and D. A. Carson. *Discourse Analysis and Other Topics in Biblical Greek*. JSNTSup 113. Sheffield: Sheffield Academic, 1995.

Porter, Stanley E., and Jeffrey T. Reed. *Discourse Analysis and the New Testament: Approaches and Results*. Sheffield: Sheffield Academic, 1999.

Rebera, Basil. "Translating a Text to Be Spoken and Heard: A Study of Ruth 1." *TBT* 43 (1992) 230–36.

Reed, Jeffrey T. "Discourse Analysis." In *Handbook to Exegesis of the New Testament*, edited by Stanley E. Porter, 189–218. NTTS 25. Leiden: Brill, 1997.

Rhoads, David, editor. *From Every People and Nation: The Book of Revelation in Intercultural Perspective*. Minneapolis: Fortress, 2005.

———. "Introduction." In *From Every People and Nation: The Book of Revelation in Intercultural Perspective*, edited by David Rhoads, 1–27. Minneapolis: Fortress, 2005.

———. "Performance Criticism: An Emerging Methodology in Second Testament Studies, Part I." *Biblical Theology Bulletin* 36 (2006) 1–16.

———. "Performance Criticism: An Emerging Methodology in Second Testament Studies, Part II." *Biblical Theology Bulletin* 36 (2006) 164–84.

———. "Performing the Gospel of Mark." In *Reading Mark, Engaging the Gospel*, 176–201. Minneapolis: Fortress, 2004.

Rohrbaugh, Richard L. "Foreignizing Translation." In *The Social Sciences and Translation* edited by Dietmar Neufeld, 11–24. SBL Symposium Series 41. Atlanta: Society of Biblical Literature, 2008.

Schreiter, Robert J. *Constructing Local Theologies*. Maryknoll: Orbis, 1985.

Scott, Bernard Brandon. "A New Voice in the Amphitheater: Full Fidelity in Translation." In *Fidelity and Translation: Communicating the Bible in the New Media*, edited by Paul Soukup and Robert Hodgson, 101–18. Franklin, WI: Sheed & Ward, 1999.

Shiell, William David. *Reading Acts: The Lector and the Early Christian Audience*. BibIntSer 70. Leiden: Brill, 2004.

Shiner, Whitney Taylor. *Proclaiming the Gospel: First Century Performance of Mark*. New York: Trinity, 2003.

Simon, John. *Greek-Latin New Testament Audio Reading Series*. Austin, TX: greek-latinaudio.com, 1999.

Small, Jocelyn Penny. *Wax Tablets of the Mind: Cognitive Studies of Memory and Literacy in Classical Antiquity*. London: Routledge, 1997.

Soukup, Paul A., and Robert Hodgson, editors. *Fidelity and Translation: Communicating the Bible in the New Media*. Franklin, WI: Sheed and Ward, 1999.

Sugirtharajah, R. S. *Postcolonial Criticism and Biblical Interpretation*. Oxford: Oxford University Press, 2002.

Sundersingh, Julian. "Toward a Media Based Translation: Communicating Biblical Scriptures to Non-Literates in Rural Tamilnadu, India." Ph.D. diss., Fuller Theological Seminary, 1999.

Tedlock, Dennis. *Finding the Center: The Art of Zuni Storytelling*. 2nd ed. Lincoln: University of Nebraska Press, 1999.

Thomas, Kenneth J., and Margaret Orr Thomas. *Structure and Orality in 1 Peter: A Guide for Translators*. United Bible Societies Monograph Series 10. New York: United Bible Societies, 2006.

Tymoczko, Maria. "Translation in Oral Tradition as a Touchstone for Translation Theory and Practice." In *Translation, History, and Culture*, edited by Susan Bassnett and André Lefevere, 46–55. London: Printer Publishers Limited, 1990.

Venuti, Lawrence. *The Translator's Invisibility: A History of Translation*. Translation Studies. London: Routledge, 1995.

de Vries, Lourens. "Bible Translation and Primary Orality." *TBT* 51 (2000) 101–14.

Waard, Jan de, and E. Nida. *From One Language to Another: Functional Equivalence in Biblical Translation*. Nashville: Nelson, 1986.

Wendland, Ernst R. "Duplicating the Dynamics of Oral Discourse in Print." *Notes on Translation* 7 (1993) 26–44.

———. *Finding and Translating the Oral-Aural Elements in Written Language: The Case of the New Testament Epistles*. Lewiston, NY: Mellen, 2008.

West, Gerald O. "African Biblical Hermeneutics and Bible Translation." In *Interacting with Scriptures in Africa*, edited by Jean-Claude Loba-Mkole, 3–29. Nairobi: Acton Publishers, 2005.

Westfall, Cynthia Long. *A Discourse Analysis of Hebrews: The Relationship between Form and Meaning*. LNTS 297. New York: T. & T. Clark, 2006.

Yorke, Gosnell. "Bible Translation in Anglophonic Africa and Her Diaspora: A Postcolonialist Agenda." *TBT* 22 (2004) 153–66.

PART TWO

Synoptic Documents and Acts

God as "Father" in Matthew
Imperial Intersections

Warren Carter

ANCIENT HOUSEHOLDS HAVE BEEN A FOCUS OF LYN OSIEK'S EXTRAORdinary scholarly work. With her feet firmly planted on (excavated) ground, she has astutely examined, for example, physical space,[1] family life,[2] roles of women,[3] slaves,[4] and house churches.[5]

Not surprisingly, household structures, roles, and relationships, so integral to human society, have not been confined to the peristyle or *insulae*. Households have, for example, been a frequent source for religious structures and language. Forty-four times, for instance, Matthew's Gospel identifies God as "Father"[6] thereby picturing God presiding over a household in which Jesus' disciples are appropriately named "children" (5:45).

The image "Father" has also been utilized for political language and structures. At least since Aristotle, patriarchal households have been identified as the basic unit of kingdoms/empires (*Pol.* 1.1.5–12; 1.5.1–7). In naming, for example, the emperor *pater patriae* (and *parens*), father of the fatherland, the Roman empire depicts itself as a patriarchal structure, a household presided over by the Father-emperor who faithfully provides for and protects his children-subjects and to

---

1. Osiek, "Archaeology," 5–35.
2. Osiek, "The Family in Early Christianity"; Osiek, "Family Matters."
3. Osiek, MacDonald, Tulloch, *A Woman's Place*.
4. Osiek, "Female Slaves, *Porneia*, and the Limits."
5. Osiek, "Women in House Churches."
6. For discussion, see Mowery, "God, Lord, and Father"; Mowery, "From Lord to Father"; Pennington, *Heaven and Earth*. I set aside references to human fathers.

whom loyalty and obedience are due.[7] Interestingly, Matthew also links God-as-Father with empire language:[8] "the righteous will shine like the sun in the empire/kingdom of their Father" (13:43); "Come, you that are blessed by my Father, inherit the empire/kingdom" (25:34), and "Our Father in Heaven ... your empire/kingdom come" (6:9–10).[9] Matthew's link constructs discipleship as participation in a cosmic household presided over by God the Father.

I want, then, to put these two conceptions—Matthew's God as Father presiding over a cosmic household, and the imperial depiction of the emperor as Father presiding over a household of some sixty million people—into conversation. What might the interface between the two gendered, patriarchal households produce? What might this interface indicate about how this early "Christian" text, the product of a group subjugated to Roman power, negotiated the Roman empire-as-household? I will argue that Matthew's presentation resembles, even participates in, imperial usage in many regards, yet several differences contest aspects of the imperial household.

To be clear, my interest lies with intertextuality and function, not source. Nor am I claiming imperial use as the only textual horizon for Matthew's use, an impossible claim given Israel's lengthy traditions involving the image,[10] the household uses noted above, or the identification of Zeus/Jupiter as Father.[11] Nor is my focus on the historical

---

7. For the standard discussion, Alföldi, *Der Vater*.

8. Matthew's term, often translated "kingdom," is basilei/a which often denotes empires; so Dan 1:20; 2:37–45; 6:4; 1 Macc 1:6, 16, 41; 8:18; 11:1; Josephus *C. Ap.* 1.150; *J.W.* 1.40; 5.409; 7.44; *Ant.* 18.120. See Carter, *Matthew and Empire*, 60–64.

9. Chilton ("God as 'Father,'" 166–67) calls Matthew's connections of "Father" with "kingdom" both "innovative" and "odd."

10. Schrenk and Quell, "πατήρ"; Pennington, *Heaven and Earth*, 217–30; Chilton ("God as 'Father,'" 166–69) argues Matthew predominantly shares the thematic concerns of the Pseudepigrapha and Targumim in seeing God as "Father" in relation to prayer, visions, power over creation, and relationship between God and elect people, concluding (169) "Matthew's Jesus does not say anything radically new about God in calling him 'father.'"

11. Horace *Odes* 1.2.2; 1.12.13–17: "the Father, who directs the destinies of men and gods, who rules the sea and lands and the sky with its shifting seasons? From whom is begotten nothing greater than himself"; Ovid *Tristia* 2.37, Jupiter is "the father (*genitor*) and ruler of the gods"; Pliny *Panegyricus* 88.8, "he is the father (*parens*) of gods and men." On Zeus' evolution from a violent tyrant to loving figure, Stevenson, "The Ideal Benefactor and the Father Analogy," esp. 432–33.

Jesus.[12] Rather, within the limits of the present format, I am exploring one interface with an eye on the larger issue of early "Christian" negotiation of imperial power.

The Emperor as Father of the Fatherland

By the late first century CE, the designation *pater patriae* was widely used, especially in elite communications, to construct an idealized relationship between ruler and ruled, expressing the duties and obligations of the benign and beneficent patron-emperor and his client-subjects, the father's children.[13] The metaphor simultaneously functioned to mask the brutalities of an unbalanced power relationship marked by tyranny, exploitation, and subjugation.

The term "father" gained prominence as a political title in the republic in the first century BCE in two interrelated contexts. First, it described Romulus as founder of Rome.[14] Second, it honored those who, like Romulus, "refounded" or saved Rome from internal and external enemies and who preserved and/or renewed its life.[15]

Significant, though, are its appearances in literary texts,[16] coins,[17] and inscriptions[18] for Julius Caesar. Weinstock argues that in addition to ascribing glory to Caesar, "father" now recognized Caesar's position

---

12. D'Angelo, "*ABBA* and 'Father.'"

13. For more elaborate discussion, Carter, *John and Empire*, 236–47, abbreviated here.

14. Weinstock, *Divus Julius*, 201. Ennius (*Ann.* 113 V) "*o pater, o genitor*," father and founder; Cicero (*Div* 1.3) "father (*parens*) of this city." Livy (1.16.3), "a god and a god's son, the king and Father (*regem parentumque*) of the Roman city."

15. Weinstock, *Divus Julius*, 175–84, 201–2. Livy (5.49.7) names Camillus (died c. 365 BCE), Cicero (*In Defense of Rabirius*, 27) and Plutarch (*Mar* 27.9) describe Gaius Marius (died 86 BCE); Plutarch identifies Cicero (Plutarch, *Cicero* 22.5; 23.6; cf Cicero, (*In Pisonem* 6; *Pro Sestio* 121).

16. Appian, *Civil Wars* 2.16.106 πατὴρ πατρίδος, *pater patridos*; 2.20.144, "the father of his country, πατέρα πατρίδος *patera patridos*, the benefactor, the peerless protector"; Suetonius, *Deified Julius*, 76.1 *patris patriae*; Dio Cassius 44.4.4, πατέρα πατρίδος *patera patridos*.

17. Weinstock, *Divus Julius*, 180–84, 200–203; coins facing 208, plate 17, 1–2, *parens patriae*.

18. Ibid., 200, a column with the inscription "Parenti patriae" (Suetonius, *Deified Julius*, 85).

as Rome's permanent leader and ruler, thereby defining the relationship between ruler and ruled. It presented his "unlimited political power" not in terms of tyranny but in terms of *patria potestas*, binding his fellow citizens to him like sons to a father in *pietas*, the loyalty or allegiance of appropriate familial duties and obligations. And in turn it defined Caesar's relationship to them as that of "the patron to his clients (rather than that of an autocrat)."[19]

Dio Cassius, several centuries later, has Caesar articulate this relationship in a speech set in 46 BCE when Caesar returns to Rome victorious. In contrast with previous conquerors, Dio has Caesar renounce the role of tyrant (43.17.2) and appeal for his children-subjects to "love each other without suspicion." He instructs them: "you will conduct yourselves toward me as toward a father (πρὸς πατέρα, *pros patera*) enjoying the forethought and solicitude which I shall give you . . . and I will take thought for you as for my children . . ." (43.17.5–6).[20] In his fatherly role, marked by love, he exhorts his children to suspend their suspicions and accept the perspective (practice the self-deception?) that their ruler has their best interests in view rather than his own. The title thus presents an idealized relationship between ruler and ruled in which the latter are to render obedience and duty, while the ruler lovingly seeks their wellbeing, rewards their efforts, punishes the non-compliant, and preserves the life of the city and its empire (43.17.6).

This sense of "father of the fatherland" defining and idealizing the relationship between ruler and ruled is secured with Augustus. In 2 BCE Augustus officially accepted the title after lengthy resistance, perhaps because, whatever his demurrals, it named too explicitly the dominating power relationship that he often sought to disguise (*Res Gestae* or *Acts of Augustus* 35). Suetonius' account (a century or so later) of Augustus' acceptance of the title emphasizes several important dimen-

---

19. Ibid., 204–17. Gradel (*Emperor Worship*, 187) claims that the decisive shift to defining a constitutional relationship of ruler and ruled does not occur until the reigns of Caligula and Claudius. Certainly the designation becomes more common through the century, but given *Res Gestae*, 35 and Suetonius' account (below), it is erroneous to claim that "the title *pater patriae* had indeed seemed to disappear with Augustus" (187).

20. Cicero contrasted "a cruel tyrant" with his own consulship as a "tender parent" (*mitissimum parentem*, *De Domo Sua* 94). A century later, Pliny contrasts the tyrant Domitian with Trajan, a "fellow-citizen not a tyrant, one who is our father not our over-lord" (*Panegyricus* 2.3).

sions (*Deified Augustus*, 58). The title is offered to Augustus three times by the "whole body of citizens with a unanimous impulse." The repeated offering secures an escalating expression of submission to and gratefulness for his rule.[21] Suetonius presents the people's consent—whatever the reality and no one polled the non-elite—as a crucial element in defining his rule not as tyranny but as paternal care. But the title not only expresses the people's submission. It also reminds Augustus to fulfill his role of ensuring the empire's security and eternity.[22] In hailing Augustus as "Father of the Fatherland," the senator Valerius Messala declares, "we feel that we are praying for lasting prosperity for our country and happiness for our city" (*felicitatem*, blessedness; Suetonius, *Deified Augustus* 58). The ruled depend on the ruler as father to preserve and prosper the life of city and empire. Duties and obligations, not tyranny and submission, shape the relationship.

This relationship of ruler and ruled is elaborated by Augustus' work, *Res Gestae*. Augustus wrote this account of his "accomplishments" in his seventy-sixth year (13 CE), a year before his death (*Res Gestae* 35). Yet he ends his account with the "senate and the equestrian order as well as the whole of the Roman people" naming him "father of the country," an event that happened in 2 BCE (*Res Gestae* 35).[23] The narrative effect of ending the work with the bestowal of this title is that the designation "father of the fatherland" functions to summarize the ruler-ruled relationship. Augustus elaborates it in terms of his accomplishments and roles as creator, benefactor, and preserver of Rome's world. These accomplishments and roles can be categorized into six overlapping areas.

Savior and Benefactor of Life

Augustus begins his first-person account by presenting himself in the *pater patriae* tradition of saving the empire from external and internal enemies. He "made the entire world subject to the power of the Roman people" and he "freed the republic oppressed by the tyranny of a faction" (*Res Gestae*, 1). "As victor [over internal and external foes], I spared all citizens who asked for forgiveness" (3). Subsequently he gave life to the freed republic through numerous benefactions: supplying grain

---

21. Ando, *Imperial Ideology*, 146–47.
22. Charlesworth, "Providentia and Aeternitas," esp. 110, 113, 122.
23. Text with notes in Eck, *Augustus*, 134–52.

by which "I liberated the whole city (Rome) from immediate fear and present danger" (5, 15, 18), making repeated financial gifts to the plebs in Rome (at least "250,000 men") and to soldiers who were colonists (15), buying land for veterans as colonists in Italy and the provinces (16), donating his money to the treasury (17), building the senate house, numerous temples, and other public works including aqueducts to ensure water supply (18–21), paying for entertainments and games including a naval battle (22–23), and restoring temples in Asia damaged by Mark Antony (24). Such actions present Augustus as the supreme father-patron or benefactor of the empire whose euergetism comprises benefactions for his children-clients.

Ruler of the World

Augustus' fatherly role ensured Rome's security and extended "the power of the Roman people" over "the entire world" (1). He did so by filling political offices at the senate's behest (1, 7), by waging battles "throughout the whole world" and extending mercy where appropriate (3), by subduing and administering Spain and Gaul (12), by "securing peace on land and on sea ... by victories throughout the whole empire of the Roman people" (13), by overcoming pirates, returning rebellious slaves to their owners, by securing with oaths of loyalty the allegiance of "all of Italy" and "the provinces of Gaul, Spain, Africa, Sicily, and Sardinia" (25), by enlarging "the territory of all provinces of the Roman people," pacifying Gaul, Spain, Germany, the Alps, and Arabia and Ethiopia where "great forces of both peoples were cut down in battle and many towns captured" (26), by adding Egypt, subduing Armenia, and recovering the provinces from the Adriatic to the east (27), by recovering military standards lost in battle in Spain, Gaul, Dalmatia, and Parthia (29), by extending the "authority of the Roman people" over Pannonia, Illyricum, and Dacia (30), and by friendships and alliances with various eastern (client) kings (31–33).[24] As ruler of the world he extended the empire "where the ocean encloses it" (26). His benefaction was peace through submission to Roman will and rule. "The doorway of (the temple of) Janus Quirinus" had been shut—to signify "peace on land and on sea"— only twice "from the time of the city's foundation until before my birth"

---

24. Bosworth ("Augustus,") sees the work emphasizing benefaction and world conquest as Augustus' "record of achievement which earned immortality" (18).

but during Augustus' time "the senate ordered it shut three times" (13). Through these acts he rules his household-empire.

Judge and Law-Giver

Augustus presents himself as committed to justice, the one who enforces order in the household-empire. He avenges the murder of his father Julius Caesar through exile, war, and "legal proceedings" (2). He accepts the task bestowed by "the senate and the Roman people" of being "the guardian of laws and morals with supreme power" (6). He passes laws to revive "many exemplary customs of our ancestors," passing on "models of conduct to be imitated" (8). He fulfills his father's will (15). Constantly he claims to attain offices and power from and for the benefit of the Roman people and at the behest of the senate in accord with "the customs of our ancestors" (e.g., 5, 6, 34). His commitment to justice is celebrated in the golden shield "given to me by the senate and the Roman people" (34).

Creator of a People, Shaper of a Community

Augustus introduces his accomplishments as being "for the republic and for the Roman people." His fatherly role means he has created a freed people who had been "oppressed by the tyranny of a faction" (1). He establishes law and order (6), increasing the number of patricians and taking a census of the people followed by a *lustrum* or purification ritual that "symbolized the newly constituted citizenry"[25] (8). He provides this people with "peace on land and on sea secured by victories" (13). His military victories and alliances forcibly expanded the empire's membership as a household subjugated to Rome (25–30). Others sought "friendship" by sending embassies (29, 31, 32). "Many other peoples . . . have experienced the trust/faithfulness of the Roman people" (32). Augustus does not use the language of love highlighted by Cicero and Dio Cassius, but his account evidences his self-understanding as a "tender father" of the Roman people.

---

25. Eck, *Augustus*, 149.

Sender of Agents

Augustus emphasizes his own role in bringing about his accomplishments, but he also acknowledges the contributions of those he as father commissions as agents of his power. Soldiers are prominent. He has "five hundred thousand soldiers ... under a military oath of allegiance." He settles "more than three hundred thousand ... in colonies," as agents of Roman control and culture throughout the empire, and he returned others to their municipalities (3, also 16). He refers to "campaigns led successfully by me or my legates under my auspices on land or on sea" (4). His sons Gaius and Lucius Caesar were designated consuls (14). "All of Italy" and "the provinces of Gaul, Spain, Africa, Sicily, and Sardinia" swore an oath of allegiance to Augustus thereby binding themselves to his purposes. More than 700 senators "served under my standards," eighty-three of whom were consuls and one hundred and seventy priests (25). He "founded colonies for soldiers ... in Africa, Sicily, Macedonia, both Spains, Achaia, Asia, Syria, Gallia Narbonensis, Pisidia. Italy also has twenty-eight colonies founded by my authority" (28).

Recipient of Honors

As head of the household, Augustus is the constant recipient of honors that expressed the expected gratitude of his children and submission of the ruled for his benefactions and accomplishments. Some honors he "humbly" declines (e.g., 4, 5). He receives ovations, triumphs and political office (4–6, 10), vows and offerings "for my health" (9), annual sacrifices (11), the dedication of an altar of Augustan Peace (12), the threefold honor of having the doorway of Janus Quirinus closed in recognition of his establishing worldwide peace (13), and honors for his two sons (14). He receives embassies and ambassadors (31–32), the name Augustus, and a golden shield celebrating his virtue, clemency, justice, and piety (34). In this idealized relationship of ruler and ruled, there is no room for protest, dissent, or ungratefulness. Augustus' crowning honor is receiving the name "father of the fatherland" (35).

Augustus' work *Res Gestae* elaborates his identity, roles, and relationship with his subjects as "father of the fatherland." The work describes and constructs the ruler-ruled relationship. He is giver of life and benefactions, ruler of the world, judge and law-giver, creator of a people, sender of agents, and recipient of honors. Others had used the title of him in similar ways, including in the provinces.[26] Inscriptions from Asia Minor around 2 BCE, for example, indicate that elite provincials make explicit their participation in his fatherly rule by adding "and of the entire human race" to the title "father of the fatherland" (πατὴρ τῆς πατρίδος καὶ τοῦ σύμπαντος τῶν ανθπώπων γένους; *pater tes patridos kai tou sumpantos ton anthropon genous*).[27]

The title "father of the fatherland" gains prominence through the century. The cluster of themes associated with it in Augustus' *Res Gestae* comes to be associated with emperors Tiberius,[28] Gaius Caligula,[29]

---

26. Sherk (*The Roman Empire*, 12–13) cites an inscription from the people of Narbonese, Gaul, detailing celebrations of the imperial cult, dedicating an altar to Augustus in 11 CE, twice identifying him as "father of his country" (lines A7 and B6), recognizing "his command over the whole world," and that he "reconciled the judgments of the people with the decurions." Ovid constructs a similar relationship of ruler and ruled for Augustus addressing him as

> Holy Father of thy Country (*sancte pater patriae*) . . . yet didst thou also receive, though late, thy title true; long time hadst thou been Father of the World (*pater orbis*). Thou bearest on earth the name which Jupiter bears in high heaven; of men (sic) thou art the father (*pater*), he of the gods . . . Caesar by his guardian care makes great thy (Romulus') city walls." (*Fasti* 2.127–134)

Ovid, though banished by Augustus, recognizes Augustus' restraint: "Do thou also, seeing thou art called ruler and father of our native land (*patriae pater*) follow the way of the god who has the same title. And that thou dost; no one has ever been able to hold the reins of power with more restraint" (*Tristia* 2.39–42). He appeals for more: "by our native land which is safe and secure under thy fatherly (*parente*) care . . . Spare me, father of our country (*pater patriae*)" (*Tristia* 2.157–58, 181).

27. Ando, *Imperial Ideology*, 403.

28. For Tiberius, Valerius Maximus, *Memorable Doings and Sayings;* Suetonius (*Tiberius* 26) says Tiberius declined "the surname of Father of his Country" (*patris patriae*).

29. For coins, Mattingly, *Coins*, vol. 1, page 150, no. 29, plate 27.24; page 150, no. 32, plate 27.26; page 152, no. 38, plate 28.5 (all with oak wreath); page 157, no. 67, cf. Plate 28.3 (with 5 soldiers bearing an aquila); page 157, no. 69, Plate 29.14 (with seated Pietas, and sacrifice in front of the temple of Divus Augustus); page 157, no. 70, Plate 30.2; page 158, no. 72, Plate 30.1 (with Vesta on throne).

Claudius,[30] Nero,[31] Vespasian and Titus,[32] Domitian,[33] and Trajan.[34] The literary expressions, coins, and inscriptions attest a consistent and pervasive cluster of motifs associated with the title that define the relationship of ruler and ruled.

From the third century, the provincial Dio Cassius sums up developments and emphases associated with "father of the fatherland."

---

30. For coins, Mattingly, *Coins*, vol. 1, page 170, no. 42, Plate 32.2 (oak wreath); page 172, no. 57, Plate 32.12 (with female figure of *Constantiae Augustae*, also nos. 58–60, 199–201); page 173, no. 61, Plate 32.17 (with female figure Nemesis, and dedicated to *Paci Augustae*, also nos. 62–66, 68–71); page 174, no. 72, Plate 32.24 (with Agrippina, also nos.73–76); page 174, no. 79, Plate 33.3 (with young Nero, also nos. 80–81); page 190, no. 185, Plate 36.1 (with oak wreath, also nos. 186); page 191, no. 188, Plate 36.2 (with triumphal arch, soldier on horseback, trophies and spear, also nos. 189–191); page 191, no. 192, Plate 36.3 (with *Spes Augusta*, also nos. 193–96); page 191, no. 197, Plate 36.4 (with Ceres and corn ears, also 198); page 192, no. 202, Plate 36.6 (with *Libertas Augusta*, also 203–205); page 192, no. 207, Plate 36.7 (with helmeted Minerva); page 192–93, nos. 208–223, Plates 36.8–9; 37.1–2, 9 (with various imperial figures). For inscriptions, Sterk, *Roman Empire*, 90–91, 94, 95, 96, 99, 100.

31. For coins, Mattingly, *Coins*, vol. 1, pages 200–284, nos. 9, 10, 12–51 (variously with Roma, Ceres, Virtus), 79–80 (with Jupiter), 113 (with Temple of Janus), 114–21 (Roma), 122–30 (with soldiers), 130–224, 234, 240, 251–60; etc. Inscriptions confirm the same identity, Sterk, *Roman Empire*, 106, 106–7, 110–12. Petronius (d. 65 CE; *Satyricon* 60) has guests at Trimalchio's dinner party rise and shout, "Good fortune to the emperor, Father of the Fatherland" (*patri patriae*). Seneca in his work addressed to Nero *On Mercy* elaborates "the duty of a father, and it is also the duty of a prince, whom not in empty flattery we have been led to call 'the Father of his Country' (*Patrem Patriae*)" (*On Mercy* 1.14.1–3).

32. For inscriptions recognizing Vespasian and Titus as "father of his country," see Sherk, *Roman Empire*, 126–30, 134–35; for coins, Mattingly, *Coins*, vol. 2, pages 95–103, nos. 451–52, 453 (with Ceres), 454 (with Concordia), 455–56, 457–58 (with Victory and dedicated to *Paci Augustae* "to Augustan peace"), 459–61 (*Paci Orbis* "for the peace of the world"). Compare Burnett et al, *Roman Provincial Coinage*, vol. 2, nos. 814–35, 850, 850A, 851–54.

33. On Statius, Newlands, *Statius' Silvae*. Martial (*Epigrams* 7.7) honors Domitian as "the world's supreme ruler and earth's parent" (*parens orbis*) and "supreme subjugator of the Rhine and father of the world" (9.5.1). For coins with *pater patriae*, Mattingly, *Coins*, vol. 2, pages 297–420, nos. 7–35, 37–50A, 70–129A, 139–140, 145–70, 176–98, 200–7, 214–226, 230–37, 248, 260–86, 323–67, 371–452, 458–80, 512–20; for inscriptions, Sherk, *Roman Empire*, 137, line 5; 145, line 13; 150, line 23 (Pergamum).

34. Pliny (*Panegyricus*) identifies Trajan as a "fellow-citizen not a tyrant, one who is our father not our over-lord" (2.3). Pliny's discussion exemplifies all six themes for Trajan as "father of the country" (*pater patriae*, 57.5), "father of us all" (*parentis publici* 67.1) who secures the eternity of the empire (67.3).

> The term "Father" perhaps gives them (emperors) a certain authority over us all—the authority which fathers once had over their children; yet it did not signify this at first but betokened honor and served as an admonition both to them, that they should love their subjects as they would their children, and to their subjects, that they should revere them as they would their fathers." (Dio 53.18.3)

Matthew: God as Father

In examining Matthew's presentation of God as Father, I employ the six categories evident in Augustus' elaboration of the title, *pater patriae* in *Res Gestae*. As will become clear, these categories are fluid in their boundaries and considerable overlap will be evident yet they encompass all of Matthew's forty-four uses.

Savior and Benefactor

For Matthew, God as father is a benefactor to all human beings. In 5:45 God acts through creation to benefit all creation, both material and human, providing sunshine for the evil and the good, and rain for the righteous and unrighteous.[35] The claim is of course rooted in the creation story of Gen 1 whereby all creation expresses God's purposes that embrace all people. In such a context Matthew asserts God's fatherly provision in the created world for all people.[36]

Other Father references express the theme. God's benefaction for the created world forms the basis for greater care for disciples. In 6:8, the Father knows what disciples need, even before they ask. In 6:26, God's fatherly care means providing food for the birds, even though "they neither sow nor reap nor gather into barns." The father's care and benefactions extend beyond the birds to disciples since the Father

---

35. Such a claim has imperial interface. Jupiter or other gods were understood to provide wind and rain to ensure the earth's fertility (Horace *Carmen saeculare*, lines 22–24, 29–32; Seneca *De Ben* 3.31.4–5; 4.26.1). The sun-god Helios, widely understood to direct the universe, appeared on Nero's coins, thereby aligning cosmic order and benefaction with imperial power. Rudolph, "Helios," 123–25.

36. This comprehensiveness somewhat modifies Foster's claim ("Why on Earth Use 'Kingdom of Heaven'?" esp. 490) that Matthew's father language reinforces an exclusive identity of disciples over against "formative Judaism."

knows they need food, drink, and clothing (6:32). In 7:11, the Father's benefactions are contrasted with, and thereby greater than, those of an evil but loving parent who, nevertheless, provides "good gifts to your children." Moving from the lesser to the greater, "how much more" does the Father provide "good things" (what is necessary?) in response to prayer (also 18:29). Another "lesser to greater" argument provides reassurance of the Father's benefaction in 10:29 where his[37] care for a sparrow underscores God's greater care for disciples (10:31). In 6:14–15, one of God's benefactions comprises forgiveness, but it requires disciples to extend forgiveness to others. Withholding forgiveness from another means the Father withholds it from disciples.

As Father, God is a benign benefactor, extending his benefactions throughout a household that comprises the world, including creation and those who do not live according to God's purposes. Disciples know God's benefactions in special ways.

Ruler of the World

A distinctive feature of Matthew's presentation of God as father is the association of the image with "heaven."[38] Twenty of the Gospel's forty-four uses of Father for God make this connection, either by the prepositional, attributive phrase ὁ πατὴρ ὁ εν [τοῖς] ουρανοῖς (13x) or the attributive adjective ὁ πατὴρ ὁ ουράνιος (7x). While some have understood the linking of Father and heaven to emphasize immanence and transcendence, I have argued elsewhere that heaven denotes the sphere or abode of God (cf.5:34).[39] Recently, Jonathan Pennington has expanded this notion to argue that Matthew's broader discourse about heaven and earth contrasts the former, as God's abode, with the latter as that of sinful humanity, a tension that will have eschatological resolution.[40] Important for our purposes here is that the constant association of God as Father with heaven establishes God's fatherhood as cosmic in scope.[41] In part, this cosmic association underscores the Father's ongoing benefaction to creation and disciples. But it also emphasizes that

---

37. I use the masculine pronoun reluctantly throughout because of the referent.
38. Mowery, "God, Lord, and Father," 27.
39. Carter, *Matthew and the Margins*, 93, 139, 155, 257.
40. Pennington, *Heaven and Earth*, 231–41.
41. Betz, *Sermon on the Mount*, 315–18.

heaven or the heavens are already under the Father's sway, as the origin of God's rule/empire being extended to earth (4:17; 6:10).

What does this rule look like? It is manifested by Jesus (4:17) to whom the Father has entrusted all things as son or agent of the Father's rule (11:27). The Lord's Prayer in 6:9–13, addressed to "our Father in Heaven," sketches some aspects.[42] It centers on honoring God's name and establishing God's kingdom or empire and will on earth as it is in heaven (6:9b-10). This rule challenges the existing order on earth that is not shaped by the Father's will and is determined apart from heaven, the Father's abode. The Father's will in heaven has ultimacy on earth and is manifested in providing bread (6:11) and in a community marked by cancelled debts (6:12). The Father's will overcomes a time of trial and the action of the evil one (6:13).

The Father's rule over the world is evident in creation: making the sun to shine and rain to fall (5:45), feeding the birds (6:26), caring for the sparrows (10:29). It is also evident in the behavior of disciples: loving enemies just as the Father does (5:44–45), forgiving others as the Father does (6:14–15; 18:35), structuring households that comprise one-flesh, husband-wife relationships, where all are children and slaves, and wealth is redistributed to the poor (chs 19–20).[43] Disciples recognize the authority or rule of only one father. No one called Father on earth has legitimate authority or rule. Instead disciples recognize only the one father in Heaven (23:9). The heavenly Father's rule will be fully established eschatologically when God's empire, which has existed from the foundation of the world, embraces those "blessed by the Father" (25:34).

Appropriately, Jesus addresses the Father as "Lord of heaven and earth" (11:25) in which "heaven and earth" designates all creation subject to God's rule (Gen 1:1). The Gospel is clear, though, that God the Father does not employ violence to establish or express this rule. The Father does not dispatch twelve legions of angels (26:53).[44]

---

42. Carter, "Recalling the Lord's Prayer"; Carter, *Matthew and the Margins,* 163–69. Foster ("Why on Earth," 492) claims that God's will is done only in the community of disciples.

43. Carter, *Households and Discipleship.*

44. These claims have imperial interface. Statius calls the emperor Domitian "Lord of the earth" (*Silv.* 3.4.20), "Great Father of the World," (4.1.17), and "ruler of the nations" (4.2.14–15). Philostratus identifies him as "master of sea and land" (*Apollonius* 7.3). Rome's reliance on its legions is well-known.

Judge and Lawgiver

Doing the will of God as Father is to be normative on earth (6:10). It is expected of disciples (12:50) just as Jesus does the Father's will (26:29, 42). This will is revealed by the Father through Jesus (11:25–27). Doing or not doing the Father's will on earth now is set in eschatological context where the Father is encountered as judge in vindication or condemnation. Those who do the will of the Father will be rewarded since he sees what they do (6:1, 4, 6, 18). Those who do not forgive do not encounter the Father's forgiveness (6:15) and will be condemned (18:35). The obedient will enter the Father's reign or empire, unlike those who address God as Lord but do not live accordingly (7:21). Those who are loyal to Jesus and live his mission without fear "acknowledge" or advocate for him before others (10:32, cf. 10:7–8, 16–31). In turn Jesus "acknowledges" or advocates for them on the day of judgment "before my Father in heaven" (10:15, 32). But those who deny Jesus are denied by him before the Father in the judgment (10:32–33). The righteous will "shine . . . in the empire of their Father" (13:43) where the Father will uproot or destroy elite societal leaders who do not enact God's vision (15:13). The Father's will is that every "little one" be vindicated (18:14). But only the Father knows who that will be (20:23), along with the hour when the Father's empire is established (24:36). Only those who have fed the hungry and thirsty, welcomed the stranger, clothed the naked, cared for the sick, and visited the imprisoned are blessed by the Father to inherit his empire (25:34).

Creator of a People/Shaper of Community

People become children in the Father's household by imitating the Father's inclusive and gracious benefactions, even to enemies and persecutors (5:45). Being perfect or whole as the Father is, knowing *and* doing the Father's will, is crucial for belonging to this household (5:48; 7:21; 12:50; 26:39, 42). Practices such as loving enemies and providing for the needy (5:44; 24:36) are central. Hence the Father reveals this will through Jesus the son not to "the wise and intelligent" (elites) but to the marginal and vulnerable (infants; 11:25–27; 16:17 Simon). The Father's commitment to and protection of these "little ones" or disciples is evident in the observation that they have angelic representatives in the Father's presence in heaven (18:10).[45] In turn, disciples offer the Father exclusive obedience and loyalty (23:9) until their vindication in the establishment of the Father's empire (26:29). In the meantime, this household marked by doing the Father's will seeks to include as many as possible in the household by going among the nations, making disciples, baptizing them in the name of the Father, Son and Holy Spirit, and teaching them to do what Jesus has revealed from the Father (28:18–20).

Sender of Agents

The Father's household or community is commissioned by the Father to be in mission to the world and to work on behalf of the Father (28:18–20). The household is the Father's agent in doing his will (7:21; 12:50). The "Spirit of the Father" will help them speak faithfully in difficult situations (10:20). This commission is revealed to the household as a result of the Father commissioning Jesus the son to be an agent and revealer of the Father's purposes (11:25–27). In so commissioning Jesus, the Father revokes or refuses to recognize the agency of some others such as the Rome-allied elite leaders who will be condemned for their social practices and structures (15:13). And Jesus refuses to imitate imperial practices of violence by calling on the Father to send twelve legions of angels (approximately 72,000 angels!) as agents to counter the crowd with swords and clubs sent to arrest him (26:53).

Recipient of Honors

Members of the household honor the Father. They acknowledge him as Lord of Heaven and earth (11:25). He is "our father," the one who defines this community (6:9) and secures its destiny (26:29). He receives its worship (5:16) and its prayers (6:6, 9; 11:25–26; 26:39, 42) that recognize His will is supreme on earth (6:10) and especially among household children (12:50).

---

45. For discussion, Davies and Allison, *Matthew*, 2:769–72.

Matthew's Household and the Emperor's Household

What happens, then, in the interface between the presentation of the emperor as the "father of the fatherland" presiding over the Roman empire as a household, and Matthew's God as "Father, Lord of Heaven and Earth" (11:25), presiding over a cosmic household?

Immediately evident from the discussion are the similarities between the two gendered presentations. The six dimensions of the title *pater patriae* that emerge in Augustus' *Res Gestae*—savior and benefactor, ruler of the world, judge and lawgiver, creator of a people/shaper of a community, sender of agents, recipient of honors—embrace the Gospel's forty-four references to God as Father. Both imperial and Gospel texts clearly employ this patriarchal and imperial model. Both Fathers preside over households in which they actively exert benefactions. Both direct the way of life of household members and hold them accountable for their living. Both create a people focused on the Fathers, thereby shaping a community. Both have agents or representatives who carry out their will and purposes. Both receive honors from their householders.

That two such similar households exist simultaneously raises the question of their interface. The fundamental similarities in the use of the image "Father" and the structures of human interaction thereby depicted suggests that the gospel is at home in, resembling, accommodated to, imitative of, inscribing imperial, patriarchal structures. The Father of Jesus is an imperial figure, paralleling the emperor as father. But what happens when the two Fathers interface? Happy coexistence seems unlikely since exclusive and excluding rule seems to be part of the father paradigm. There is one *pater patriae* whose authority, Augustus and his successors repeatedly emphasize, is to be recognized, whether voluntarily or by force. Likewise, Matthew's injunction to "call no one your father on earth, for you (children/disciples) have one Father – the one in heaven" (23:9) seems equally clear in its exclusive and excluding focus.

Does either Father exert a greater or more compelling claim? Perhaps the gospel's language of "earth" and "heaven" supplies a competitive edge, that of greater power and more extensive influence. Matthew's Father rules not only on earth but also in heaven (6:9; 11:25), a realm beyond the influence of the emperors. So 11:25 confidently asserts a totality and finality of will and rule already established in its address to God as "Father, Lord of heaven and earth." Reinforcing that sense of established fatherly ownership and care are Matthew's frequent references to the Father's active rule over and care for creation in a way that the emperor cannot replicate (5:45; 6:26). Matthew's Father appears as a benefactor of greater reach.

Yet while the emperor's rule over Rome's empire on earth is constantly celebrated (albeit as an extension of Jupiter's rule and will from heaven), Matthew's Father's rule on earth seems somewhat shaky. Children/disciples are to pray for the Father in Heaven's will to be "done on earth as it is in heaven" (6:10). The petition recognizes its establishment in the heavenly realm and suggests struggle and resistance on earth since so many do not acknowledge this Father (15:13). Such a petition certainly cannot match the confident declarations of Augustus' accomplishments in establishing worldwide rule. Matthew's recognition of the potentiality, rather than the actuality, of the Father's universal rule could be understood to counter the ideology of established imperial control and unity exuded by Augustus' *Res Gestae*.

While Matthew's spatial edge is somewhat ambiguous, the matter of temporal reach is less ambiguous. Matthew's well-known eschatological framework is evident in that the Father has an "empire/kingdom prepared for you from the foundation of the world" (25:34) for which the vindicated are destined. Matthew's Father is presented as controlling the beginning and destiny of, as well as the timetable for, the world that outlasts any emperor and empire that does not acknowledge Jesus, the Father's agent (10:32–33). Augustus is but a relative newcomer and temporary ruler. While the struggle for the Father's will to be done in the present remains, Matthew's Father seems to win the competition for greater temporal power and influence. That is to say, the empire of Matthew's Father "out-caesars" the emperor, exhibiting how deeply ingrained and inscribed the imperial patriarchal paradigm is in the gospel and its presentation of God.[46]

How do the respective households compare? Both presentations emphasize obedience to the Father's will as foundational. Both Fathers recognize threats to their households and will, though they deal with it in different ways. The prayer of Matt 6:9–13, for example, seeks to create

---

46. For critique of human patriarchy in 19:3–12, see Carter, *Households and Discipleship*, 56–89; Carter, *Matthew and the Margins*, 378–84.

an order focused on God's honor, empire, and will, against three threats; sin or more accurately debts, a time of testing, perhaps best understood as the present-time whereby children doubt the Father's presence and ability to deliver on promises to establish God's order, and the evil one or the devil whom Matthew consistently presents as opposing God's purposes.[47] These continuing threats require the intervention of "Our Father in Heaven," conceived ultimately eschatologically, to establish the Father's will. Similarly, *Res Gestae* presents Augustus the *pater patriae* as having already intervened to save the empire from threat and danger from external and internal enemies. Apparently much more successfully than Matthew's Father, Augustus establishes his will, sometimes by making treaties and friends, and sometimes by military might. Matthew's Father does not intervene forcibly or by military means, at least in the present. That option is explicitly rejected in 26:53 when Jesus does not ask his Father to send twelve legions of angels. But such renouncing of violence is temporary. In Matthew's eschatological scenes, the Father imposes his will and condemns the resistant, thereby again imitating and reinscribing imperial ways.[48]

A further aspect concerns who belongs to and is valued in the household.[49] We have noted 11:25–27 with its claims that the Father has concealed his purposes from the wise (elites) but revealed them through the Son to infants. The children-recipients are those whose lives are marked by vulnerability, powerlessness, and low status. The marginal occupy a valued place in this Father's household. Accordingly those who enter the Father's empire/kingdom are those who share their (limited) resources with the vulnerable. They have fed the hungry and thirsty, welcomed the stranger, clothed the naked, cared for the sick, and visited the imprisoned (25:34). In Matthew's Father's household, these are defining actions that do the Father's will.

The vulnerable and powerless are numerous in the household of the *pater patriae*.[50] Augustus the father-patron celebrates financial gifts

---

47. Carter, *Matthew and the Margins*, 161–70.

48. For eschatological violence, Carter, *Matthew and the Margins*, 294, 374–75; Carter, "Constructions of Violence."

49. If space permitted, a consideration of the reconfigured relationships within human households in chaps. 19–20 would be appropriate; Carter, *Households*; Carter, *Matthew and the Margins*, 376–410.

50. Whittaker, "The Poor."

to the plebs, donations of (seized) land to veterans, supplies of grain and water, and the widespread gift of peace. But Augustus does not exhort others to similar actions for the vulnerable and make such actions definitive for obedience to him or for membership in his household. Augustus' emphasis falls on military conquest and allied-subjugated peoples. And of course his purposes are paraded for, utilize, and benefit the elite.

The difference here, though, is not just one of two differently privileged groups. The two groups and practices intersect. Matthew's Father values those who are casualties of and damaged by imperial structures. As Peter Garnsey has established, "for most people [in the Roman empire] life was a perpetual struggle for survival."[51] Poor quality and quantity of food, inadequate housing, and abundant disease are the direct consequences of imperial structures and practices, notably the systematic removal of resources from non-elites in order to sustain the conspicuous consumption of the elite.[52] Matthew's Father values such people and requires practices that not only sustain them in the midst of the emperor's household but also confront, counter, and repair its damage. Augustus' benefits reinforce his hierarchical household structure.

Consistent with the renouncing of violence, valuing of the vulnerable, and repairing of imperial damage, it is not surprising that both households value different agents. Crucial for the *pater patriae*, and it is everywhere evident in *Res Gestae,* are soldiers and elite officials such as consuls and senators who maintain the status quo and its hierarchical structure. For Matthew's Father, there are three categories of quite different agents. One comprises the angelic legions restrained in the heavens. The second comprises the Son, Jesus, who dies at the hands of the empire but is raised and expected to return, revealing both the antipathy between the two Fathers and the limits of the emperor-father's power as ultimately subject to Matthew's Father. As agent of the Father's purposes, he commissions not soldiers and elite officials to a worldwide mission to secure the household, but disciples, the infants, the vulnerable and powerless. As representatives of the Father, Son, and Spirit, their mission comprises living out the words given to Jesus by the Father in actions that repair imperial damage (11:25–27; 28:18–20). But even as the Gospel distinguishes this way of life for the Father's household and

51. Garnsey, *Food and Society in Classical Antiquity,* xi.
52. Carter, "Matthew's People," esp. 156–61.

enters into contestive interaction with imperial practices, it shares the *pater patriae*'s notion of worldwide mission.

Conclusion

In setting in conversation the presentation of the emperor as the "father of the fatherland," presiding over the Roman empire as a household, and Matthew's God as "Father, Lord of Heaven and Earth" presiding over a cosmic household, it is evident how similar the two gendered, patriarchal presentations are. The Gospel participates deeply in this imperial paradigm. Some distinctions are evident, though, in the non-violent, non-military way that Matthew's Father is at work in the present (the eschatological future is another question), in some features of the lifestyle of his children (non-violent, valuing the powerless, repair of imperial damage), and in the identity and mission of his agents as the vulnerable. Even in naming these distinctives that contest aspects of the imperial household, the pervasive influence of the imperial household remains very evident. Such ambiguity of interaction is not surprising in a text that has emerged among subjugated people in an imperial context. The intersections of the two images neither exclusively alienate hearers of the Gospel from the empire, nor exclusively set them in imitative relationship. Rather they participate in the act of creating a hybrid identity that permits, employs, and restricts imperial engagement.

Bibliography

Alföldi, Andreas. *Der Vater des Vaterlandes im Römischen Denken.* Darmstadt: Wissenschaftliche Buchgesellschaft, 1971.
Ando, Clifford. *Imperial Ideology and Provincial Loyalty in the Roman Empire.* Berkeley: University of California Press, 2000.
Betz, Hans Dieter. *The Sermon on the Mount.* Hermeneia. Minneapolis: Fortress, 1995.
Bosworth, Brian. "Augustus, The *Res Gestae* and Hellenistic Theories of Apotheosis." *JRS* 89 (1999) 1–18.
Burnett, Andrew, Michel Amandry, and Ian Carradice. *Roman Provincial Coinage*, Vol. 2: *From Vespasian to Domitian (AD 69–96).* London: British Museum Press, 1999.
Carter, Warren. "Constructions of Violence and Identities in Matthew's Gospel." In *Violence in the New Testament,* edited by Shelly Matthews and Leigh Gibson, 81–108. New York: T. & T. Clark, 2005.
———. *Households and Discipleship: A Study of Matthew 19–20.* JSNTSup 103. Sheffield: Sheffield Academic, 1994.
———. *John and Empire: Initial Explorations.* New York: T. & T. Clark, 2008.
———. *Matthew and Empire: Initial Explorations.* Harrisburg, PA: Trinity, 2001.
———. *Matthew and the Margins: A Socio-Political and Religious Reading.* Maryknoll, NY: Orbis, 2000.
———. "Matthew's People," In *Christian Origins,* edited by Richard A. Horsley, 138–61. A People's History of Christianity 1. Minneapolis: Fortress, 2005.
———. "Recalling the Lord's Prayer: The Authorial Audience and Matthew's Prayer as Familiar Liturgical Experience." *CBQ* 57 (1995) 514–30.
Charlesworth, Martin. "*Providentia* and *Aeternitas*." *HTR* 29 (1936) 107–32.
Chilton, Bruce. "God as 'Father' in the Targumim, in Non-Canonical Literatures of Early Judaism and Primitive Christianity, and in Matthew." In *The Pseudepigrapha and Early Biblical Interpretation,* edited by James H. Charlesworth and Craig Evans, 151–69. Journal for the Study of the Pseudepigrapha Supplements 14. Sheffield: JSOT Press, 1993.
D'Angelo, Mary Rose. "*Abba* and "Father": Imperial Theology and the Jesus Traditions." *JBL* 111 (1992) 611–30.
Davies, W. D., and Dale Allison. *The Gospel according to Matthew.* 3 vols. ICC. Edinburgh: T. & T. Clark, 1988–97.
Eck, Werner. *The Age of Augustus.* Malden, MA: Blackwell, 2007.
Foster, Robert. "Why on Earth Use 'Kingdom of Heaven'? Matthew's Terminology Revisited." *NTS* 48 (2002) 487–99.
Garnsey, Peter. *Food and Society in Classical Antiquity.* Cambridge: Cambridge University Press, 1999.
Gradel, Ittai. *Emperor Worship and Roman Religion.* Oxford: Clarendon, 2002.
Mattingly, Harold. *Coins of the Roman Empire in the British Museum,* Vol. 1: *Augustus to Vitellius;* Vol. 2: *Vespasian to Domitian.* London: British Museum Press, 1966.
Mowery, Robert. "From Lord to Father in Matthew 1–7." *CBQ* 59 (1997) 642–56.

———. "God, Lord, and Father: The Theology of the Gospel of Matthew." *BR* 33 (1998) 24–33.

Newlands, Carole E. *Statius' Silvae and the Poetics of Empire*. Cambridge: Cambridge University Press, 2002.

Osiek, Carolyn. "Archaeology." In *Families in the New Testament World: Households and House Churches*, by Carolyn Osiek and David Balch, 5–35. Louisville: Westminster John Knox, 1997.

———. "The Family in Early Christianity: 'Family Values' Revisited." *CBQ* 58 (1996) 1–24.

———. "Family Matters." In *Christian Origins*, edited by Richard A. Horsley, 201–20. A People's History of Christianity 1. Minneapolis: Fortress, 2005.

———. "Female Slaves, *Porneia*, and the Limits of Obedience." In *Early Christian Families in Context: An Interdisciplinary Dialogue*, edited by David Balch and Carolyn Osiek, 255–74. Grand Rapids: Eerdmans, 2003.

———. "Women in House Churches." In *Common Life in the Early Church*, edited by Julian V. Hills, 300–15. Harrisburg, PA: Trinity, 1998.

Osiek, Carolyn, and David L. Balch. *Families in the New Testament World: Households and House Churches*. The Family, Religion, and Culture. Louisville: Westminster John Knox, 1997.

Osiek, Carolyn, and Margaret Y. MacDonald, with Janet H. Tulloch. *A Woman's Place: House Churches in Earliest Christianity*. Minneapolis: Fortress, 2006.

Pennington, Jonathan. *Heaven and Earth in the Gospel of Matthew*. NovTSup 126. Leiden: Brill, 2007.

Rudolph, Kurt. "Helios." In *Anchor Biblical Dictionary*, edited by David Noel Freedman, 3:123–25. New York; Doubleday, 1992.

Schrenk, Gottlob, and Gottfried Quell. 1967. "πατήρ." In *Theological Dictionary of the New Testament*, edited by Gerhard Kittel and Gerhard Friedrich, 5:945–1014. Translated by Geoffrey W. Bromiley. Grand Rapids, Eerdmans, 1967.

Sherk, Robert, editor. *The Roman Empire: Augustus to Hadrian*. Cambridge: Cambridge University Press, 1988.

Stevenson, Tom. "The Ideal Benefactor and the Father Analogy in Greek and Roman Thought." *Classical Quarterly* 42 (1992) 421–36.

Weinstock, Stefan. *Divus Julius*. Oxford: Clarendon, 1971.

Whittaker, Charles. "The Poor." In *The Romans*, edited by Andrea Giardina, 272–99. Chicago: University of Chicago Press, 1993.

A Man's Place in Matthew 19:3–15

Creation and Kingdom as Transformative Spaces of Identity

Halvor Moxnes

A Man's Place

To speak of "a man's place" points to the central role of place for the construction of gender. This is a perspective that has been often overlooked in studies of sexuality and gender both in modern societies and in New Testament studies. Over the last generation there have been many feminist studies of the New Testament and Early Christianity, many of them focusing on the role of women in the Jesus movement and early Christian groups. Their focus has primarily been on social relations and interactions, with less attention to place. But Carolyn Osiek very early saw the importance of place in terms of house and material structures for family and gender studies.[1] Significantly, her last major study in this area together with Margaret Y. MacDonald signals the importance of place in its title, *A Woman's Place*.[2] The subtitle indicates the place that is most significant in a study of women: *House Churches in Earliest Christianity*. The importance of so much of the work by Osiek lies in the way she combines these perspectives and makes the role of

---

1. Osiek and Balch, *Families;* Balch and Osiek, eds., *Context*. Shared interests in gender, family, and place studies made me especially happy to be able to establish and co-chair together with Lyn the Early Christian Families group in the SBL 2000–2003.

2. Osiek and MacDonald, *A Woman's Place*.

women, free and slaves, the main approach to studies of households and house churches.

"A man's place" in the title of this essay suggests that I will attempt a similar approach to a study of Matthew 19, by integrating the study of masculinity and that of place, i.e., household. This is an attempt at a new approach to that chapter. A couple of studies have used house and households as the main paradigm to understand the role of disciples and discipleship in Matthew,[3] and in particular in Matthew 19–20, but they did not raise the question of masculinity. This is understandable because they were written before masculinity studies in the New Testament emerged. There have been some studies of masculinity in Matthew,[4] but they have not combined gender and place. However, Anderson and Moore in their study of masculinity in Matthew and Carter in his study of household in Matthew 19–20, make observations that seem to converge. Anderson and Moore suggest that Matthew 19 presents reversals of "traditional hegemonic masculine values,"[5] and Carter suggests that chapters 19–20 represent an "inverted household code" compared to the values represented by the traditional household codes.[6]

I will follow up on these suggestions and use place theory to study how these different forms of masculinity, hegemonic and alternative, can be associated with different place locations, especially "household," creation, and "Kingdom" within Matt 19:3–15.[7]

---

3. Crosby, *House of Disciples;* Carter, *Household and Discipleship.*

4. Anderson and Moore, "Matthew and Masculinity," Neyrey, "Jesus, Gender and the Gospel of Matthew."

5. Anderson and Moore, "Matthew and Masculinity," 90. Neyrey ("Jesus, Gender and the Gospel of Matthew," 65–66) concludes that Matthew portrays Jesus in line with traditional expectations of the honorable man, where also his departures from male stereotypes are viewed as honorable in the eyes of God.

6. Carter, *Household and Discipleship,* 216.

7. Limitations of space and time makes it practically impossible to include Matt 19:16–30, a passage that shares many similarities with 19:3–15 in terms of its focus on male roles, household and renunciation, see Anderson and Moore, "Matthew and Masculinity," 90–91; and Carter, *Household and Discipleship,* 115–16. In addition, the thematic parallels between the three sections of Matt 19:3–15 and *Gos. Thom.* 22 provide justification for a separate treatment of this unit.

Place and Gender

The discourse in Matthew 19 is itself located in a male space. The issues that are brought to Jesus are specially addressed to men: the question of a husband's right to divorce his wife (19:3–9), and the question of a young, wealthy man of how to lead his life to secure eternal life (19:16–22). Other questions come from the male disciples, about marriage (19:10–12) or about their rewards for having left their households to follow Jesus (19:27). Thus, the interlocutors are all male; the issues addressed have men as their primary subjects. These discourses and narratives are primarily inter-male discussions although they may have had a broader audience including women disciples. They have the behaviour and role identities of men as their main subject. And the issues are all concerned with the role of a man as head of the household as a working, sustaining and procreating community, as husband with a dominant position over his wife and children, as protector of his wealth as a basis for his position.

These issues place the discussions in Matthew 19 as participants in the discourse of masculinity in the Greco-Roman world.[8] The passages in Matthew reflect the tensions and conflicts within the Jesus movement and early Christian groups over male roles and male identities. Within the narrative structure of Matthew 19, I suggest that the tensions become visible in the way the moral discourse of the hegemonic masculine role in the household is juxtaposed with alternative male roles in images of creation and of the Kingdom.

Masculinity as Spatial Construction

It is this interaction between discussions of a man's place in the house and household and images of social roles and relations in creation and the Kingdom that makes a spatial analysis of this text appropriate. The scholarly interest in the relations between identity and space is a result of the "spatial turn" in postmodernity. The introduction of space as an interpretative category that can be applied to many areas in humanities and social sciences was mainly due to the French philosophers Henri

---

8. In addition to Anderson and Moore, and Neyrey (see note 3), see also Conway, *Behold the Man*, 107–25.

Lefebvre and Michel Foucault.[9] Their approaches were developed theoretically and adapted within sociology, geography and architecture especially by David Harvey and Edward W. Soya.[10]

To look at male relations in space, I will use Lefebvre's model of three dimensions in the analysis of space as it has been developed by Harvey and Soya. Lefebvre speaks of these dimensions as "the experienced, the perceived, and the imagined."[11] Spatial experience is that which actually happens in space. In Matthew 19 these experiences are first of all related to household and village. It is generally recognized that in ancient Mediterranean societies the household represented the basic social unit of social and economic life. In literary texts the household is not always mentioned, since it was so obvious and taken for granted. The role of the individual cannot be understood without its place within the household. Therefore, to "leave everything," as the disciples had done, is explained in terms not only of family members, they are placed within the context of "houses" and "land" indicating the "material spatial practice" where they belonged (19:27, 29).[12]

House and household were always gendered, not necessarily in terms of physically separate areas of the house, but in social and ideological terms with regard to tasks and responsibilities, and relations.[13] The role of the husband and the husband/wife relationship were at the center of the household, with social and economic aspects interwoven (19:3–9). The children brought to Jesus were part of and belonged in a household (19:13–15).

The second dimension of an analysis of space is the ideological level where the spatial practice is discussed in light of thought processes and ideology. These discussions raise questions like: How can a spatial practice, for instance a man's right to divorce or to preserve the household property, be defended and justified, so that it will be accepted as "natural"? There is a power aspect involved in this, since this justifica-

9. Foucault, *Power/Knowledge*; Lefebvre, *The Production of Space*.

10. Harvey, *Condition of Postmodernity*; Soja, *Thirdspace*.

11. Harvey, *Condition of Postmodernity*, 219. Harvey himself speaks of "material spatial practices," "representations of space," and "spaces of representation" or "imagination." In order to distinguish this third dimension from the second I used the term "imagined places" in *Putting Jesus in His Place*, 14.

12. For the collectivistic understanding of self, see Malina, "The Mediterranean Self."

13. See the summary in Osiek and MacDonald, *A Woman's Place*, 244–50.

tion is most often provided by the elite. In the context of Matthew the Torah is often used in the argumentation, as in the reference to Moses in 19:7–8. These two forms of spaces, first and second, represent the generally accepted order in a society, so to speak, the common ground.

But there is also a third dimension that breaks with this binary system of material practice and cultural, ideological levels. Lefebvre and Harvey speak of this category as "spaces of imagination" or "lived space" with possibilities for new meanings and practices, for the utopian.[14] Soya has developed this perspective and turned it into a criticism of accepted epistemology, and a challenge to the way we as scholars construct the world. He has coined the term Thirdspace for this last form, in an attempt to break with the common categories of the two first ways to look at space.[15] That makes it difficult to give a definition of Thirdspace within our traditional categories. Soja characterises such spaces as "the terrain for the generation of 'counterspaces,' spaces of resistance to the dominant order arising precisely from their subordinate, peripheral or marginalized positioning."[16] The Thirdspace perspective undermines all claims to a settled binary relationship between "real" firstspace and "imagined" secondspace. It seeks to open up new ways of seeing space, "an –Otherness . . . a strategic and heretical space 'beyond' what is presently known and taken for granted."[17]

In the constructions of masculinities in Matthew 19, I suggest that the Thirdspace perspective is represented by sayings about "the new world" and the Kingdom. These references in 19:12, 14, 16, 23, 24, 28 are not part of an argumentation at the level of practice and ideology. The Kingdom seems both to integrate and to challenge the other dimensions and cannot easily be placed within First or Second space. I shall therefore attempt to analyse Matthew 19 by using these three different forms of space to locate the statements about masculinity.

Divorce as Firstspace Male Spatial Practice

The first issue under discussion in Matthew 19 concerns the male role in the most central aspect of masculinity: the husband's power and

14. Harvey, *Condition of Postmodernity*, 218–19.
15. Soja, *Thirdspace*, 53–82.
16. Ibid., 68.
17. Ibid., 34.

control over the household, especially his wife. The question from the Pharisees, "Is it lawful to divorce's one's wife for any cause" (19:3) emphasizes the unequal position between a husband and his wife. It is the man who has the right to divorce; it is only a question of whether there are any limits to this right. This position shows the male perspective of Matthew 19, since both Mark 10 and Paul in 1 Corinthians 7 take for granted that also women could initiate divorce.[18] This right to divorce practice represents a spatial separation; a divorce implies to "send away" his wife,[19] away from the house, back to her parental home. This is at the same time also a separation of families, of the social, economic and political alliances that had been established by the marriage.

Secondspace Legitimation of Divorce: Moses and Male Honor

The last part of the discussion between the Pharisees and Jesus (19:7–9) represents the ideological level of this spatial practice, that which gives it legitimacy and presents it as "natural."[20] The question from the Pharisees in defence of male rights to divorce is based on the authority of Moses, with a saying that corresponds directly to the question of practice: "Why then did Moses command one to give a certificate of divorce, and to put her away?" (19:7). Moses' saying represents a Secondspace legitimation of the spatial practice under discussion and although Jesus' response (19:8–9) in principle prohibits divorce, Matthew has an addition: "except for *porneia* ('unchastity')" that reduces the saying from one of principle to one of practical arrangements.[21] That is, it has the same logic as the original question about the practice of divorce, and therefore it represents a Secondspace regulation of male practice: divorce is illegal except for unchastity on the part of the wife. Most commentators hold that this does not go back to a word by Jesus,[22] but is an addi-

---

18. Martin, *Sex and the Single Saviour*, 130 n.15.

19. Bauer, *Lexicon*, 96.

20. Matthew has turned around the order of Mark 10, where the initial question about divorce procedures (10:2) is immediately followed by a discussion of the instructions by Moses (10:3–5).

21. Luz, *Matthew 8–20*, 492: "That the possibility of divorce is now granted runs contrary to the flow of the text."

22. Martin, *Sex and the Single Savior*, 232 n.16.

tion by Matthew, and it clearly presents the cultural presuppositions of Matthew's male world. As in the parable in 5:31–32 there is in 19:7–9 no indication of any concern for the woman, everything is seen from the man's perspective.[23]

The addition of "except for *porneia*" presents the fear of male dishonor, of being shamed by another man entering the sphere of his sexual rights as the underlying issue of the discussion of divorce. It is a man's honor and his power to protect his property and to secure a legitimate offspring that is at stake. This must have been an issue of great concern for Matthew's community, since he brings it up altogether three times, every time focusing on the sexual unfaithfulness of the wife. The first instance is in the story of Jesus' infancy, Matt 1:18–25. In Matthew the story is explicitly told from an androcentric perspective, describing the events with Joseph as the main protagonist.[24] When Mary, who was "betrothed" to Joseph, was found to be with child "before they came together," Joseph who is described as a "just man" who did not want to "put her to shame," decided to "send her away" quietly (1:18–19). It is the angel of the Lord who stops him from doing it, by proclaiming that it was not another man who had entered his wife (to be), but the Holy Spirit. But in the saying on divorce in the anti-theses in the Sermon on the Mount, 5:31–32, there is no such divine intervention. Thus, in a parallel to 19:9, a statement that in principle curtails the husband's right to divorce his wife,[25] and places the responsibility on him, is nevertheless undercut by the concessions to male reactions against the *porneia* of his wife that threatens his honor.[26] Thus, despite the protestations it is the spatial practice of divorce as a male prerogative that is protected against the threat of *porneia* as a female (ir)responsibility. Male honor and hegemony remains the last word in Matthew's discourse, in practice undercutting the troublesome use of the creation story in the words attributed to Jesus in the central section of the passage.

23. Luz, *Matthew 1–7*, 251–52; and Luz, *Matthew 8–20*, 492.

24. Moxnes, *Putting Jesus in His Place*, 34–36.

25. There is a discussion whether 5:32 and 19:9 refer (only or also) to the right to remarry after a divorce caused by unchastity of the wife; despite Martin (*Single Savior*, 135), it seems that the most plausible interpretation is that the unchastity clause refers only to divorce, Luz, *Matthew 1–7*, 255–56; *Matthew 8–20*, 493–94.

26. In the First Testament adultery is regarded as a pollution of the land of Israel, cf. Lev 18:25, 28 etc.; Luz, *Matthew 8–20*, 255.

Creation as a Third Space Category

The initial question from the Pharisee about the male practice of divorce (19:3) is followed up by the discussion in 19:7–9. In contrast, Jesus' response in 19:4–6 ignores the question about the right regulation of the spatial practice of divorce.[27] His response does not discuss regulations for divorce, but moves the discourse into a different place, into a Thirdspace imagination of the unity of man and woman. Jesus points to the Creation story and combines a saying about the creation of man and woman in the image of God (Gen 1:27) with the command to the man to leave parents and keep to his wife (Gen 2:24), and draws the conclusion that "they are not two, but one." This is a passage that seems to render itself to an argument about history (19:4), but this type of reading is challenged by Soja: "whenever you read or write a sentence that empowers history, historicality, or the historical narrative, substitute space, spatiality, or geography and think about the consequences."[28]

From a space perspective creation represents a different spatiality in the discussion of the husband's right over his wife within the household. The challenge it represents is not primarily one of time but of different organisations of space and the construction of the human. It is the spatial images of "the beginning" that Jesus presents – of the one body, the androgynous body of creation, that is used as a model metaphor for the transition of the man from his parental house into a new house with his wife, where the common dwelling and the sexual union of the couple is combined into the image of "one *body*" (19:5). The image of the one body and the union of the two bodies from creation challenge the patriarchal household at its most potent symbol, the man who can divorce his wife.

The type of union between man and woman the creation story points to the myth of the androgynous (man).[29] This use of the creation story has an innovative and destabilizing power as Wayne Meeks has pointed out in "The image of the Androgyne."[30] The myth of an androgynous or bisexual progenitor of the human race was widespread and came up in many different contexts. In early Christian texts of

---

27. Ibid., 489.
28. Soja, *Thirdspace*, 183.
29. Luz, *Matthew 8–20*, 489, n. 25.
30. Meeks, "Androgyne."

Gnostic providence, it forms the basis for rituals of spiritual marriage and the imagery of "the bridal chamber." Closer to Matthew is its use in the *Gospel of Thomas* and the encratic Thomas traditions of Syria which also speaks of "making the two one."[31] *Gospel of Thomas* 22 is especially illuminating; it combines the logion about the children and the Kingdom with a saying to the disciples that speaks about the identity of those who will enter the Kingdom. The list is characterised by the typical *Thomas* idea of making "two into one":

> Jesus said to them, "When you make the two into one, and when you make the inner like the outer and the outer like the inner, and the upper like the lower, and when you make male and female into a single one, so that the male will not be male nor the female be female, when you make eyes in place of an eye, a hand in place of a hand, a foot in place of a foot, an image in place of an image, then you will enter [the Kingdom]."[32]

Here we clearly see how making two into one is part of spatial metaphors, breaking the distinction of inner/outer, upper/lower. The use of the term "becoming one flesh" from Gen 2:24 in Matt 19:6 points to a real union that goes beyond regulations for marriage. This is the point also when Paul uses it in 1 Cor 6:16, when the union, "the new creation," comes into being by a sexual relation between a man and a woman, outside marriage.[33] Among the early Christians this idea of the new body that comes into existence became a metaphor for the relations between God and human beings, and especially for the relation between Christ and the believing man (1 Cor 6:16) or Christ and the *ekklesia* (Eph 5:32).[34] This metaphor of a union of the two, created by God, is in Matt 19:6b applied to the question of divorce raised in 19:6, but it represents more; it goes beyond the practicalities of marriage relations and the ideological rules regulating it. The metaphor represents a Thirdspace perspective.

Jesus' saying in 19:4–6 does not respond to the question in v.3 about divorce regulations in relations between husband and wife. The saying dislocates the understandings of identities that are taken for granted in that question, and replaces it with an understanding of the embodiment

---

31. Ibid., 17–18.
32. Translation by Patterson in *Gospel of Thomas*, 73.
33. Moxnes, "Asceticism," 21–23.
34. Satlow, *Jewish Marriage*, 44–50.

of the identities of husband and wife into one body.³⁵ The reference to Gen 1:27 and 2:24 locates this understanding in a new type of metaphor of creation, not just a model of the first marriage as in Jewish sources,³⁶ but as a metaphor for the union between God (Christ) and humans.

Moreover, Jesus' words about the two becoming one, even if applied to a context of marriage, does not support the male dominated household structure. This becomes apparent as the conversations moves on and shifts from a discussion with Pharisees to an exchange between the disciples and Jesus.

Third Space as the Kingdom for Eunuchs

The disciples follow up the male perspective from the question of the Pharisee in their reaction to Jesus' answer in 19:11: "If such is the case of a man with his wife, it is not expedient to marry?" The reaction from the disciples that it might be better not to marry may well be in keeping with a desire to preserve male power.³⁷ Even a mild mannered exegete as Ulrich Luz finds it necessary to say, "It is clear that the wife's perspective is no more a factor here than in the entire pericope" and goes on to characterize the disciples in the following way: "It is obvious from their masculine, human reaction that not every man is capable of making room for Jesus' marriage *halakah* in his own life."³⁸

Again Jesus does not respond to their question about marry or not to marry, but goes on to present one of the most unsettling ideals preserved in the Gospels of "eunuchs who have made themselves eunuchs for the sake of the Kingdom of heaven" (19:12). The sayings that bracket this response show an awareness that this reply was far removed from any normal discourse and insights, piling up warnings: "not all men can receive this saying, . . . he who is able to receive it, let him receive it" (19:11, 12d). Clearly, the saying moves away from Secondspace ideology of regulating a Firstspace practice into the Thirdspace image of the

---

35. Moxnes, *Putting Jesus in His Place*, 5–6.

36. Satlow (*Jewish Marriage*, 42–67) has pointed out the difference between Early Christian and Rabbinic use of Gen 1:27 and 2:24. The model for rabbinic interpretation was that of the first marriage, but the Rabbis were careful not to use it in the same way as the early Christians, as a metaphor for the relation between God and humanity, Christ and the believers as a union.

37. Conway, *Behold the Man*, 123–24.

38. Luz, *Matthew 8–20*, 500.

eunuch. But most ancient and modern interpreters try to make sense of the saying within an approach that does not make this move, but that stays within recognizable patterns.

Dale Martin points in this direction with his suggestions that Jesus' words of prohibition of divorce and remarriage "was interpreted along ascetic lines of self-control in expectation of the imminent Kingdom of God."[39] With the term "ascetic lines of self-control" Martin indicates the practice and ideology of sexual renunciation as expression of male self-control over body and environment. This was a form of constructing asceticism as a male place that we find both in antiquity and in modern periods. In an early Jewish context Philo and Josephus give a misogynistic description of ascetic, male communities.[40] It was also this form of interpretation that was given to the saying of Jesus about "eunuchs for the Kingdom of heaven" in antiquity. In *The Manly Eunuch*, Matthew Kuefler has convincingly shown how early Church fathers (*sic!*) interpreted the eunuch saying and other expressions of renunciation within the context of Roman masculinity.[41] Not surprisingly modern, male interpretations have followed the same lines.[42] The eunuch in Matt 19:12 is interpreted as an example of male self-control. As an ideal for Christian behaviour such interpretations look like attempts to regain male dominance, to recreate a male space as a privileged space, that women can only enter by "becoming male" (*Gos. Thom.* 114).

My argument is that this is an interpretation that belongs at the same level as the granting male privilege over women in divorce, where the context has domesticated a saying that was "out of place." The response from Jesus to the disciples' question is introduced in a way that shows that it does not follow the logic of Firstspace and Secondspace discussions of divorce and marriage practice. Instead his response is presented as something that cannot be grasped by "all men," but only by "those to whom it is given." This statement is similar to Jesus' introduction to the explanation of the parable of the Sower in 13:11. To the disciples it was given to understand "the mysteries of the Kingdom of heaven," but to outsiders it was not given. In 19:11 one can doubt that the disciples were included in the groups of those who were given

39. Martin, *Single Saviour*, 132.
40. Moxnes, *Putting Jesus in His Place*, 76–78.
41. Kuefler, *The Manly Eunuch*.
42. Moxnes, *Putting Jesus in His Place*, 75–76.

understanding. Not all, but only some are elected, who are given understanding, who can break away from the Firstspace and Secondspace existence, to the existence that is determined by the Kingdom of heaven.[43]

Jesus' response presents a figure that is "third gender,"[44] the eunuch, and who is determined by the goal of his existence, the Kingdom. The definition of a man as "third gender" corresponds spatially to a person who cannot fill the male space in the household. The third gender man is not fit for the household and its first space practice, he belongs to Third space. As I indicated above, the interpretation of the eunuch in terms of voluntary asceticism has been the dominant one. That is an interpretation in line with the male perspective of masculine control and self-control. But the figure of a eunuch was in itself singularly ill suited as a model of male control. Eunuchs were ambiguous and controversial figures in many societies in antiquity.[45] They are frequently described as "half-men," as "in between" men and women. They lacked the main indications of masculinity, the sexual power to regenerate, but they could still be suspected of sexual lust and activity.[46] They were persons in borderland, they had left the "male place" of household and fatherhood, and they lacked the authority of "real men." Whether "made themselves eunuchs" in the saying of Jesus actually implied self castration, a practice that was known among followers of some cults in the surroundings of Galilee, and also among some early Christians, is uncertain.[47] What is certain, however, is that in using this image, Jesus chose a picture that violated masculine identity. And even more controversial, this "unmanly" image was directly identified with "the Kingdom of heaven." Thus, it was associated with the central metaphor in the symbolic universe of Matthew.

There is a parallel between the creation myth of the androgynous "one flesh" in 19:6 and "eunuchs for the sake of the Kingdom of heaven" in 19:12. Seen together, they illustrate the saying in *Gos. Thom.* 22, where the new identity is expressed by the breaking with binary thought, that also underlies the Firstspace and Secondspace understanding of the

43. Patterson, *Gospel of Thomas*, 199–202.

44. See the discussion of third gender in relation to eunuchs in Ringrose, *The Perfect Servant*.

45. Moxnes, *Putting Jesus in His Place*, 72–90.

46. Martin, *Single Saviour*, 136.

47. Moxnes, *Putting Jesus in His Place*, 88–90.

world: "when you make the two into one, ... and when you make male and female into a single one, so that the male will not be male nor the female be female ... then you will enter [the Kingdom]." The identity of the Kingdom is not continuity with the household system, and therefore the eunuch does not represent a heightened male position but instead an ambiguous subjectivity where "the male will not be male." The best argument for this interpretation is that viewed from a perspective of ambiguity, of a break with male household dominance, the saying about the eunuch finds its continuation in the next pericope about Jesus and the little children.

Male Authority versus Children in the Kingdom of Heaven

Like in the previous section, the disciples represent the common sense and First- and Secondspace approach to a question of use of place. This time the issue is the place of children. The disciples who will hold back people who brought their children to Jesus so that he could pray for them, react within the patterns of a male paradigm of controlling household and space. Compared to adults, children were marginal in the household and were dependent upon adults, and thus had less power.[48] From this perspective, the words by Jesus "Let the children come to me, ... for to such belongs the Kingdom of heaven" (19:14) represents a *reversal* saying. In contrast to the saying in Mark, Luke and in Matthew 18, the saying does not have an exhortation linked to it, but it is simply a proclamation to the children without demand for reciprocity. This reversal makes it possible to speak of this statement as mirroring a Thirdspace context.

Again we may see the links to texts and combination of passages in the *Gospel of Thomas*. The link to the eunuch saying in Matt 19:12 brings this saying close to *Gos. Thom.* 22, which combines the "making the male and female into a single one" so that one shall enter into the Kingdom, with the logion about the children and the Kingdom. The idea seems to be that celibate asceticism negates sexual differentiation. The child serves as a metaphor for those entering the Kingdom, because

---

48. Carter, *Household and Discipleship*, 90–114.

it is considered asexual or presexual or nonsexual.[49] In the combination of sayings in *Gos. Thom.* 22 and Matt 19: 11–15, the element of chastity or blurring of gender lines is also present, so that there seems to be similarities between children and adults who do not any longer have their sex specific roles. In most instances we find the reversal motif; the infants are examples of God's reversal of status. Thus, the Kingdom is characterised by a reversal, in the Kingdom spatial hierarchies are turned upside down.

Gospel of Thomas 22: Transformations of Gender and Space

At several points I have compared parts of Matthew 19 with *Gos. Thom.* 22, and it is now time to make a fuller comparison. In New Testament studies, *Gos. Thom.* 22:1–3 has been used as one of the versions of the widespread narrative of Jesus and the children that is also found in Matt 19:13–15 (par. Mark 10:13–16, Luke 18:15–17; Matt 18:2);[50] but I suggest that *Gos. Thom.* 22:1–7 as a whole illuminates the underlying structure of transformation of male identity in Matt 19:3–15. A comparison with *Gos. Thom.* 22 suggests that Matt 19:3–15 participates not only in a discussion of household rules and divorce regulations (similar to Mark 10:2–16), but in a discourse of asceticism that is focused on creating new identities and on placing them within the symbolic universe of the Kingdom.

> *Gospel of Thomas* 22:
>
> 1 Jesus saw some babies nursing. 2 He said to his disciples, "These nursing babies are like those who enter the Kingdom." 3 They said to him, "Then shall we enter the Kingdom as babies?" 4 Jesus said to them, "When you make the two into one, and when you make the inner like the outer and the outer like the inner, and the upper like the lower, 5 and when you make male and female into a single one, so that the male will not be male nor the female be female, 6 when you make eyes in place of an eye, a hand in place of a hand, a foot in place of a foot, an im-

---

49. Meeks, "Androgyne," 17; see also *Gos. Thom.* 21, 37.

50. Luz, *Matthew 8–20*, 426. There is obviously a thematic relationship between *Gos. Thom.* 22:1–3 and the synoptic passage, but most likely not literary dependency, Patterson, *The Gospel of Thomas and Jesus*, 73–74.

age in place of an image, 7 then you will enter [the Kingdom]" (translation by Stephen Patterson and Marvin Meyer).

This logion combines a saying about the "babies" who are like those who enter the Kingdom (22:1–3), with the requirements to the disciples about what they must do to enter the Kingdom (22:7). The requirements represent a transformation of the body into a new body; the main point is the overcoming of the binary divisions of the body, from duplicity to singularity and the transformation of binary genders into a new and unitary gender. In spatial terms the same process is described as a transformation of inner/outer and upper/lower into one.

Richard Valantasis concludes that all people take on new meaning in the context of the Kingdom: "The new person, then, presents a totally integrated self who has worked through the binary opposites to create a fully harmonious self no longer regulated by binary distinctions and the hierarchies inherent in them. This new person in fact constitutes a third gender that supersedes previous gender categories while at the same time negating gender."[51]

Gospel of Thomas 22 speaks about transformations of the *body*, how breaking with the binary systems of distinctions and implied hierarchies creates a new body and a third gender. This corresponds to the transformation of male identity in Matt 19:3–15. The Jesus sayings about the androgynous man of creation in Matt 19:4–6 and about the eunuch in 19:12 illustrate a dislocation of identities from household to the original creation or to the Kingdom. The similarities with *Gos. Thom.* 22 may also explain the integration of the various sayings in 19:3–15 so that the eunuch saying in 19:10–12, which is lacking in Mark 10, is not "out of place in its context."[52]

What I have tried to express in spatial categories as a Thirdspace perspective is similar to the definition of asceticism that R. Valantasis gives in his discussion of the *Gospel of Thomas*: "performances within a dominant social environment intended to inaugurate a new subjectivity, different social relations, and an alternative social universe."[53] This definition does not focus on renunciation that is often understood as the central focus of asceticism, but rather on asceticism as a transforma-

---

51. Valantasis, *The Gospel of Thomas*, 96.
52. As Conway (*Behold the Man*, 123) suggests.
53. Valantasis, *The making of the self*, 194.

tive power. Valantasis finds that the saying in *Gos. Thom.* 22 is a central text that describes this new identity: singularity (two becoming one), consistency, a new gender ("that male be not male"), and bodily transformation. In *Gos. Thom.* 22, this is listed as something to be achieved in order to reach the goal "then you will enter (the Kingdom)."[54] It is the combination of the same themes in Matthew 19 that suggests that the Jesus sayings here are used as expressions of asceticism: the unity of the two (19:6), the eunuch for the Kingdom ("the male (who) will not be male") 19:12, and the babies who belong to the Kingdom (19:13–15).

Within a traditional definition of asceticism as a system of renunciation, it may seem farfetched to describe the Gospel of Matthew as an ascetic text.[55] Valantasis' definition may be so broad as to make it difficult to make asceticism a category that can be distinguished from anything else, but it does seem to catch the process of defining what it was to be(come) a Jesus follower.

In a general sense, all early Christian writings were concerned with the shaping of identities, since they all raise the question of what it means to one's identity to believe in Jesus. The main question is what specific aspects of identity are involved in a given text, and what modern theories and concepts we use in order to make these processes intelligible to modern readers. I read Matt 19:3–15 as responding to practical questions of the male role in divorce and remarriage, *not* with practical rules, but with attempts to change the understanding of gender roles and cosmology underlying the questions. The "dominant social environment" presupposed by Matthew 19 is that of male dominance of the household and that creation and the Kingdom represent an alternative symbolic space ("universe") within which a new male subjectivity can be inaugurated.

Queer Spaces for Queer People?

Read on its own, or in a synoptic context, Matt 19:3–9, 10–12, and 13–15 may seem like disparate texts, especially where the eunuch saying is difficult to fit into the context. In light of a reading of *Gos. Thom.* 22, we can

---

54. Ibid., 202.

55. See Saldarini, "Gospel of Matthew." But notice that Martin (*Single Saviour*, 132) finds that the most plausible reason why "the historical Jesus" prohibited divorce was to encourage asceticism.

see an underlying unity in the stories. The common theme is transformation of body, gender and space into a new identity that makes entry into the Kingdom possible. Body, gender, and space are different aspects of identity that undergo similar transformations, from duality and distinctions into oneness. Where *Gos. Thom.*22 is little specific, except for the story of the children ("babies"), Matthew 19 locates the question of transformation explicitly in the discussion of male authority in the household and of a husband's power over his wife. Using the lenses of First-, Second- and Thirdspace made it possible to see how the sayings of Jesus challenged the common sense discussions of divorce and marriage. Jesus' sayings spoke from a different place, not from within the household but from a place in creation and in the Kingdom.

In one sense this reading of Matt 19:3–15 seems to correspond to the conclusion of the studies of masculinity in Matthew by Anderson and Moore and Conway.[56] They found that in Matthew, we find both expressions of hegemonic masculinities as well as resistance to the hegemony in the form of "alternative masculinities." They recognize that these alternative masculinities represent an inversion of the household, of "leaving male place." I think this idea of "leaving male place" needs to be pushed further. To speak in terms of hegemonic and alternative masculinity is a terminology that may co-exist within the context of Firstspace and Secondspace. Typical for Thirdspace is that it breaks with binary categories; it represents an "otherness" which cannot be contained within known categories. The images of the "two shall become one flesh," the eunuch "for the Kingdom of heaven," children, to whom belong the Kingdom of heaven, are not defined alternatives to the social and spatial structures of divorce, marriage and household. Rather, they are unsettling images, they are dislocations of identities. They are not so much inverted household codes[57] as establishing a different space altogether; Kingdom and creation challenge household structures, but do not represent easy patterns to be copied.

Transformation of gender also influences space. In this respect we may ask what it means to speak of Kingdom as Thirdspace. It is easy to forget the strange character of the term Kingdom in the sayings of Jesus. It is used in a way that seems to take for granted that the hearers know

---

56. Anderson and Moore, "Matthew and Masculinity," 90–91; Conway, *Behold the Man*, 123–25.

57. Carter, *Household*, 216.

the term, but it is never defined, and it has proven notoriously difficult to interpret in modern categories. To see Kingdom as Thirdspace helps to see how it challenges the generally accepted order of things, of known spatial practices and ideological representations.[58] The implication is that we cannot easily categorize Kingdom; it is not a stable category. In some sense, it remains an unknown entity. This has consequences for how we think about the relations between gender and place. Jonathan Z. Smith has pointed out that the way we often think about place as a stable entity that influences and determines people is a misconception. Instead he suggests that there is much more of an interaction and in a pointed statement says that "people are not placed, they bring place into being."[59] This may give us ideas of how to think about the relationship between persons and the Kingdom, e.g., in relation to the discussions of who will enter the Kingdom. When the sayings of Jesus declare that eunuchs and children will enter the Kingdom, the Kingdom does not remain a stable entity. Its character as Kingdom associated with a certain image of God is challenged and changed and the concept of the Kingdom escapes easy definitions.

In modern terminology we may describe what happens in texts like Matt 19:3–15 and *Gos. Thom.* 22 as "dislocations of 'identity' (that) create . . . a zone of possibilities in which the embodiment of the subject may be experienced otherwise."[60] This statement from a modern literary critic points to where we can find a place for a hermeneutical discussion of the relevance of these texts. I suggest that we will find it in queer theory. I know that in U.S. terminology this is often associated with (and limited to) gay and lesbian theory, so I will emphasize that this is not what I am suggesting. I use queer as an epistemological term, for something that does not define a fixed category but rather is a protest against fixed categories that cross boundaries without setting up new boundaries.[61] It is a term that makes us aware that all categories are historically and socially constructed and that therefore makes us question these categories. It is here that we can see the parallels to Soja's use of "Thirdspace," which represents a queer perspective in space theory in that it breaks with the binary relationship between Firstspace and

---

58. Moxnes, *Putting Jesus in His Place*, 108–13.
59. Smith, *To Take Place*, 30.
60. Edelman, *Homographesis*, 114.
61. Turner, *Queer Theory*, 1–35, esp. 8–11, 35.

Secondspace. Soja speaks of it as "an–Otherness . . . a strategic and heretical space 'beyond' what is presently known and taken for granted."[62]

I think that Matt 19:3–15 opens a window into some unsettling aspects of Early Christian discussions of masculinity: male authority and household structures. The parallel in *Gos. Thom.* 22 may point to strands of philosophical, sometimes esoteric, ideas that were prevalent in many areas of earliest Christianity. These ideas questioned hegemonic masculinities as well as traditional household structures that also found much support in other texts in the gospel. It is therefore significant that such disturbing and problematic passages as the eunuch saying were not suppressed but were handed down in the Jesus tradition. This acceptance of sometimes contradictory positions is hermeneutically significant. Attempts to translate Thirdspace and third gender readings of passages like Matt 19:3–5 into modern categories may also challenge today's ideas of masculinities and "family values." Following the example of Carolyn Osiek,[63] I shall be happy to continue to do so.

---

62. Soja, *Thirdspace*, 34.
63. Osiek, "Family Values."

Bibliography

Anderson, Janice Capel, and Stephen D. Moore. "Matthew and Masculinity." In *New Testament Masculinities,* edited by Stephen D. Moore and Janice Capel Anderson, 67–91. Semeia Studies 45. Atlanta: Society of Biblical Literature, 2003.

Balch, David L., and Carolyn Osiek, editors. *Early Christian Families in Context.* Grand Rapids: Eerdmans, 2003.

Bauer, Walter. *A Greek-English Lexicon of the New Testament.* 2nd. rev. ed., by F. Wilbur Gingrich and Frederick W. Danker. Chicago: Chicago University Press, 1979.

Carter, Warren. *Household and Discipleship.* JSNTSup 103. Sheffield: Sheffield Academic, 1994.

Conway, Colleen M. *Behold the Man. Jesus and Greco-Roman Masculinity.* Oxford: Oxford University Press, 2008.

Crosby, Michael H. *House of Discipleship: Church, Economics, and Justice in Matthew.* 1988. Reprinted, Eugene, OR: Wipf & Stock, 2004.

Edelman, Lee. *Homographesis: Essays in Gay Literary and Cultural Theory.* New York: Routledge, 1994.

Foucault, Michel. *Power/Knowledge: Selected Interviews and Other Writings 1972–1977.* Edited by Colin Gordon. Brighton: Harvester, 1980.

Harvey, David. *The Condition of Postmodernity.* Oxford: Blackwell, 1989.

Kuefler, Matthew. *The Manly Eunuch: Masculinity, Gender Ambiguity, and Christian Ideology in Late Antiquity.* Chicago: University of Chicago Press, 2001.

Lefebvre, Henri. *The Production of Space.* Oxford: Blackwell, 1991.

Luz, Ulrich. *Matthew 1–7: A Commentary.* Translated by James E. Crouch. Hermeneia. Minneapolis: Fortress, 2007.

———. *Matthew 8–20: A Commentary.* Translated by James E. Crouch. Hermeneia. Minneapolis: Fortress, 2001.

Malina, Bruce J. "The Mediterranean Self." In *The Social World of Jesus and the Gospels,* 67–96. London: Routledge, 1996.

Martin, Dale B. *Sex and the Single Savior: Gender and Sexuality in Biblical Interpretation.* Louisville: Westminster John Knox, 2006.

Meeks, Wayne A. "The Image of the Androgyne." In *In Search of the Early Christians,* edited by Allen R. Hilton and H. Gregory Snyder, 3–54. New Haven: Yale University Press, 2002. (Original article, 1974.)

Moxnes, Halvor. "Asceticism and Christian Identity in Antiquity: A Dialogue with Foucault and Paul." *JSNT* 26 (2003) 3–29.

———. *Putting Jesus in His Place: A Radical Vision of Household and Kingdom.* Louisville: Westminster John Knox, 2003.

Neyrey, Jerome H. "Jesus, Gender and the Gospel of Matthew." In *New Testament Masculinities*, edited by Stephen D. Moore and Janice Capel Anderson, 43–66. Semeia Studies 45. Atlanta: SBL, 2003.

Osiek, Carolyn. "The Family in Early Christianity: Family Values Revisited." *CBQ* 58 (1996) 1–24.

Osiek, Carolyn, and David L. Balch. *Families in the New Testament World: Households and House Churches.* The Family, Religion, and Culture. Louisville: Westminster John Knox, 1997.

Osiek, Carolyn, and Margaret Y. MacDonald, with Janet H. Tullock. *Woman's Place: House churches in Earliest Christianity.* Minneapolis: Fortress, 2006.

Patterson, Stephen J. *The Gospel of Thomas and Jesus.* Sonoma, CA: Polebridge, 1993.

Ringrose, Kathryn M. *The Perfect Servant: Eunuchs and the Social Construction of Gender in Byzantium.* Chicago: University of Chicago Press, 2003.

Satlow, Michael L. *Jewish Marriage in Antiquity.* Princeton: Princeton University Press, 2001.

Saldarini, Anthony J. "Asceticism and the Gospel of Matthew." In *Asceticism and the New Testament,* edited by Leif E. Vaage and Vincent L. Wimbush, 11–27. New York: Routledge, 1999.

Smith, Jonathan Z. *To Take Place: Toward Theory in Ritual.* Chicago: Chicago University Press, 1987.

Soja, Edward W. *Thirdspace: Journeys to Los Angeles and Other Real-and-Imagined Places.* Oxford: Blackwell, 1996.

Turner, William B. *A Genealogy of Queer Theory.* Philadelphia: Temple University Press, 2000.

Uro, Risto. "Asceticism and Anti-Familial Language in the *Gospel of Thomas.*" In *Constructing Early Christian Families,* edited by Halvor Moxnes, 216–34. London: Routledge, 1997.

Valantasis, Richard. *The Gospel of Thomas.* London: Routledge, 1997.

———. *The Making of the Self: Ancient and Modern Asceticism.* Eugene, OR: Cascade Books, 2008.

5

"This Widow Keeps Bothering Me" (Luke 18:5)

Amy-Jill Levine

BIBLICAL WIDOWS ARE THE MOST UNCONVENTIONAL OF CONVENtional figures: expected to be weak, they move mountains; expected to be poor, they prove savvy stewards; expected to be exploited, they take advantage where they find it. Tamar, the Bible's first official "widow" (Gen 38:11), Naomi, Ruth, and Orpah, Abigail (1 Sam 27:3; 30:5; 2 Sam 2:2; 3:3), the guise of the wise woman of Tekoa (2 Sam 14:5), the widow of Zarephath (1 Kings 17; cf. Luke 4:26), Judith all manifest agency; all defy the convention. The so-called "importuning widow" of Luke 18 similarly shatters the stereotype of the poor, dependent, and weak woman, even as she epitomizes the strength, cleverness, and unclear, indeed problematic motives, of many of her predecessors.

 No wonder that Luke, the most conventional of the evangelists, domesticates this widow: for Luke, she exemplifies the "need to pray always and not to lose heart" (18:1) and stands for those "chosen ones" to whom G-d grants justice and who "cry to him day and night?" (18:7). Luke's concluding image is more "woman on her knees" than "woman with a fist." Thus Luke nicely tucks the widow of the parable within other conventional images of poor, dependent, or powerless widows: the widow of Zarephath and the "many widows in Israel" of Jesus' sermon (4:25–27), the widow of Nain (7:11–16), the widows preyed upon by venal scribes (20:47), the levirate widow of the Sadducees' question concerning resurrection (20:27–33); to this list we can add the conventional readings of both Anna (2:36–38) and the poor widow who puts her coins into the Temple treasury (21:2–3).

Luke is not the only one to domesticate the widow of the parable. Even readers who recognize her dismantling of the stereotype still conform her to a tidy theological or ethical message. In a profound study that reads the gospel in light of the struggles of the women in the diocese of San Cristóbal de las Casas in Chiapas, Barbara Reid describes our widow as "more like Ruth and Tamar, widows who take bold steps for their own wellbeing and who advance G-d's plan for good for the whole of the people ... [she] is an icon of godliness."[1] This is a helpful political reading. It may, however, be generous. Ruth and Tamar's motives are not expressed; it is the tradition, not the narrator, that ascribes to them the advancement of the divine plan. Similarly, Abigail manipulates her relationship with both Nabal and David, the wise woman of Tekoa plays the widow's role as a political ruse, Judith is also a lying, seductive assassin. Widows, like all women, like all humans, have complex personalities and not always transparent motives. We readers choose how to understand them. And we readers tend to give widows the benefit of the doubt.

Parables are designed to shake up one's worldview, to question the conventional. If a steward can be dishonest, a tax collector righteous, a landowner providing a living wage to everyone in the market place, and a judge neither fear G-d nor respect the population, surely a widow can be vengeful. For the parable to do its work, for it to challenge all our views rather than reinforce normative gender and class constructs, another look at our widow is necessary.

Initial Observations

Luke 18:1–8 has a long and intractable history of debates over tradition vs. redaction.[2] Rather than rehearse the various arguments, or interrogate the claims of religious bias—on various sides—that the rehearsal requires, I begin by looking at the verses needed to make a complete story: 18:2–5. I am not here making an historical argument that this is

1. Reid, *Taking Up the Cross*, 115–16. See also her "Beyond Petty Pursuits and Wearisome Widows, 284, where she finds in this parable "a bold portrait of the female face of God." For another homiletic social-location-based reading, see Zimmer, "A Fierce Mother and a Widow, 89–93.

2. Most commentaries detail the responses. For two helpful summaries among many, see Cotter, "The Parable of the Feisty Widow and the Threatened Judge (Luke 18:1–8)," 328–31; and Curkpatrick, "Dissonance in Luke 18:1–8," 107–21. For the best case for unity for 18:2–8, see Hicks, "The Parable of the Persistent Widow," 209–23.

the original parable, whether from Jesus himself or from the hypothetical L source (the argument has already been made). I am engaging in a thought-experiment: if this is the original parable, how then might it function?

This distinction between the widow of the parable and Luke's narrative frame creates (at least) three opportunities for exegetical creativity: (1) delineating the possible interpretations of the parable, detached from its Lucan domestication; (2) detailing how the recovered meaning provides a new lens for reading Luke's presentation of widows; and (3) interrogating the feminist implications of reading the parable from the moral to the Machiavellian.

How we identify this parable already determines how we understand it. The traditional designation, "the Parable of the Importuning Widow" is appropriate, for her case creates the reason for the story; her actions prompt the judge's reactions. But "importuning," aside from being antiquated, conveys weakness through its sense of "begging." Terms such as "persistent" or "tenacious" or even "nagging" provide her more agency. The "Parable of the Unjust Judge" is also popular: the story begins and ends with him, and his interior monologue takes up the majority of the words.[3]

However, he is only "unjust" in vs. 6, the narrator's comment. There is nothing in the parable proper (18:3–5) to prove that the judge is corrupt. I found no advocates for the "Parable of the Soon-to-be-Punished Opponent," although the opponent is also part of the story, and he, like the judge, will suffer because of the widow's demands. But he, and so his suffering, goes ignored, probably because most readers presume that the widow's case is just and that the opponent deserves whatever the court inflicts upon him.

I find most accurate the "Parable of the Vengeful (see below) Widow and the Co-opted Judge," but that doesn't preach as well. Perhaps that should be a starting point for understanding a parable: if the parable cannot be domesticated, if it cannot be turned into something that neatly fits our preconceived notions of religion or morality, if it shakes us up—then we may be on the right track.

---

3. Freed, "The Parable of the Judge and the Widow," 51, goes too far in his claim that "the unjust judge serves only as a foil to emphasize the persistence of the widow."

The Widow

Readers familiar with Scripture's convention of the widow in need of justice import her plight into Luke 18:2–5. Exodus 22:22 begins the convention: "You shall not abuse any widow or orphan." Because no one should abuse another, the mandate suggests that widows and orphans were especially vulnerable since they lacked the husband/father who, traditionally, would have cared for them. Deuteronomy 10:18 (cf. 24:19–21) provides the preferential option for the widow and orphan, and includes the stranger: G-d "executes justice for the orphan and the widow, and who loves the strangers, providing them food and clothing"; Deut 27:19 requires economic care for the "alien, the orphan, and the widow," and includes the threat: "Cursed be anyone who deprives the alien, the orphan, and the widow of justice." All the people shall say, "Amen!" Well, Amen.

The Torah's concern for the widow, presumed to be poor and exploited, extends to the Prophets and Writings. Isaiah 1:17 equates seeking justice with rescuing the oppressed, defending the orphan, and pleading for the widow (the widow does not plead on her own behalf). Jeremiah 22:3 (cf. 7:6) both connects oppressing the alien, orphan, and widow to the shedding of innocent blood and contrasts this oppression with the command that all "act with justice and righteousness, and deliver from the hand of the oppressor anyone who has been robbed." The same themes sound in Ezekiel (22:7; 44:22), Zechariah (7:9–10), Malachi (3:5), and elsewhere. Job (31:16–19) speaks of his care for the widow and the orphan along with the poor; the Psalms locate the widow together with the stranger and the orphan as individuals in vulnerable circumstances (94:6; 146:9).

In the Deuterocanonical texts, whereas Sirach (35:17) attributes to the widow some agency—"He will not ignore the supplication of the orphan or the widow when she pours out her complaint," he sees the widow less as demanding justice from her oppressors than as complaining to G-d about her circumstances. She is the pathetic figure about whom Sirach (35:18) insists, "Do not let the tears of the widow run down her cheek."

Consistent with this pathetic depiction are the scholarly claims about the status of widows in first-century Israel. Many commentaries insist—usually with no evidence—that because a widow had no legal rights to her dead husband's estate, she would be forced out of her house and on to the streets, where she'd have no choice but to beg. David Buttrick, for example, speaks of "frequent court cases in which a family contested a widow's right to inheritance because, after all, she was no longer 'family.'"[4] Family ties hardly prevent legal action (cf. Luke 12:13). Joel Green claims a "well-known topos of the widow who struggles with a corrupt judicial system for her rights,"[5] although I wonder if the topos is based on our parable, rather than a convention of the time; if the topos of the widow who obtains her case were so conventional, there'd be much less shock in our parable. Some posit that the widow is lacking a "nearest male relative" who would be "pleading her case, as would be his role," but also that "perhaps it is he who is bilking her of her rightful property."[6] Arland Hultgren suggests, "Possibly she has a lawsuit against one of the heirs of her husband's property, or perhaps she is being evicted from her home, as widows sometimes were (cf. 20:47).[7] Richard Ford has her as "almost resourceless . . . probably illiterate and clearly lacks political influence."[8] Luke Timothy Johnson invokes the image of the "enraged bag lady"[9] (the terminology is sexist: "bag man" has a much different connotation, and is better associated with Luke's "dishonest manager"). Luise Schottroff sees our widow as "the victim of a man who undermined the economic foundation of her life,"[10] for although "the parable gives no indication that the widow is an exception to the rule of social reality: the majority of the population was poor, and the majority of widows were extremely exploited and oppressed on account of their class *and* gender."[11] Brad Young goes as far as to call

---

4. Buttrick, *Speaking Parables*, 224. Snodgrass's *Stories with Intent*, 250–53 ("Helpful Primary Source Material"; see also the notes on 735), offers no cases of pleading widows; he does have a pleading woman who annoys Philip of Macedon to hear her case (Plutarch *Mor.* 179C-D), and a few papyrus records of widows seeking engaged in court cases.

5. Green, *The Gospel of Luke*, 640.

6. Reid, *Taking up the Cross*, 116.

7. Hultgren, *The Parables of Jesus*, 254.

8. Ford, *The Parables of Jesus*, 65, 67.

9. Johnson, *The Gospel of Luke*, 273.

10. Schottroff, *Lydia's Impatient Sisters*, 101.

11. Ibid., 277 n.197.

her an "outcast";[12] and Dorothy Jean Weaver sets her in the "ugly and oppressive socio-legal world of first century Palestine."[13]

How we would know that "the majority of widows" either in Jesus' purview or in Luke's were "extremely exploited and oppressed" remains an open question. No one mentioned any of this to Babatha of Maoza, the early second-century, twice-widowed woman whose personal papers, preserved in the Cave of Letters, attest, *inter alia*, that she seized her deceased second husband's property in Ein Gedi, petitioned the Roman courts to gain guardianship of her son by her first marriage, and was sued by Miriam, that second husband's co-wife over the estate.[14] Whereas the law may have prevented widows from inheriting (see e.g., *m. Baba Bathra* 8:1, "A woman bequeaths property to her sons, a wife to her husband and maternal uncles, but they do not inherit from them"),[15] the law could easily be circumvented by a deed of gift.[16] Moreover, Jewish widows would have had two means of receiving support: the marriage contract (*ketubah*) stipulations for her own finances, including her dowry, and her claim for alimentation (*mezonot*; see *m. Ketubot* 4:12, "[if he had not written for her], 'You shall dwell in my house and receive maintenance from my goods, so long as you remain a widow in my house,' he is still liable [thereto], since this is a condition enjoined by the court").[17] Certainly not all widows were rich or savvy, and Babatha as likely at a disadvatage vis-à-vis her male relatives. Nevertheless, the evidence does not show that widows were necessarily either helpless

---

12. Young, *The Parables*, 58.

13. Weaver, "Between Text & Sermon," 317.

14. Martin Goodman's comment that Babatha's willingness to enter into a bigamous relationship following the death of her first husband "may provide some indication of the helplessness of widows left with children" and that her "apparent lack of success in August A.D. 131 in compelling her son's guardians to pay more than two denarii a month for his upkeep . . . is testimony to her powerlessness after her second husband had died" ("Babatha's Story," 174) overstates the evidence. Babatha already owned property; her second marriage may have been as easily contracted for status, for her own desire to climb the economic ladder, or even for love. The date of 132 could indicate less powerlessness on Babatha's part and more indication of an increasingly difficult political situation.

15. For helpful comments on the relationship of rabbinic law to practices found in the Babatha archives, see Katzoff, "*P. Yadin* 21 and Rabbinic Law on Widows' Rights," 545–75.

16. See Cotton and Greenfield, "Babatha's Property."

17. Katzoff, "*P. Yadin* 21," 557.

or cast into the street. To the contrary, the church had problems with widows who, now independent of their husbands, took charge of their own finances, as 1 Timothy 5 shows.[18] As Carolyn Osiek has demonstrated, the churches sought to make widows dependent on bishops and deacons; they, like the altar, should stay in one place.[19]

The parable gives no indication of the widow's economic status. She may be poor and perhaps lacks money to bribe the judge;[20] on the other hand, she has access to the court, she does not invoke poverty as a reason for her appeal, she addresses the judge in the imperative, and she even manages a nice pun in insisting that she be avenged (ἐκδικέω) not against an exploiter or a thief, but an "adversary," "opponent," or "foe" (ἀντίδικος). The language is juridical, not personal.[21] Our widow sounds less like Ruth amid the alien corn and more like Leona Helmsley fighting a hostile take-over bid.

Another potential clue to her economic status might be her location: the parable is set in an unnamed "city" (ἔν τινι πόλει [18:2]). This setting evokes Luke 7:37, where a certain woman in the city (γυνὴ ἥτις ἦν ἐν τῇ πόλει) shows tenacity and achieves what she wants, to the distress of the man in charge of the setting. The woman in Luke 7:36–50, who gets the verdict she wants, is by no means poor, as her high-end ἀλάβαστρος indicates. But unlike the woman in Luke 7 "who loved much," the widow of the parable is not marked by love. She is marked instead by the desire that she be avenged.

A third clue might be her persistence. The woman "kept coming" (ἤρξετο the imperfect). Thus she had the time to be persistent. Time to continue to visit the judge is a luxury that those who work in a subsistence economy do not usually have.

The widow, finally, has voice. She makes no argument: she does not explain the justness of her case; she presents no evidence; and

---

18. See also Mary W. Matthews's contribution to Matthews, Shelley, and Scheele, "Proclaiming the Parable of the Persistent Widow (Lk. 18.2–5)," 49, on widows' independence. Contrast her sister author Scheele, who defines widows at the time as having "the legal status of property, and when their owners died, they had to be transferred to other proprietors" (64).

19. Osiek, "The Widow as Altar."

20. Reid, *Taking Up the Cross*, 116.

21. Johnson, *Gospel of Luke*, 269; Cotter, "Parable of the Feisty Widow," 336–37, notes that ἐκδικέω and ἀντίδικος are standard forensic terms, with the former having the connotation of "set things right" and the latter meaning "opponent" or "foe."

she omits any title of respect for the judge.²² The judge has no concern for honor; she shows him none. However, she does repeat, in the mild NRSV "'Grant me justice against my opponent,'" or in the harsher Greek, "Avenge me against my opponent" (Ἐκδίκησόν με ἀπὸ τοῦ ἀντιδίκου μου). There is a difference between the demand for justice (δικαιοσύνη) and the demand for vengeance (ἐκδίκησις). While her language is juridical, it is also colored by Septuagintal resonances. Her desire is comparable to the vengeance (ἐκδίκησις) executed upon Egypt's first-born sons (Exod 7:4; 12:12), by Israel against the Midianites (Num 31:2–3), by Samson against the Philistines (Judg 15:7; 16:28), and Judith against Holofernes (Jud 9:2). The ἀντιδίκος is the accuser (Matt 5:25/Luke 12:58) or the adversary (1 Pet 5:8).²³ The widow is not interested in coming to terms quickly with him (Matt 5:25//Luke 12:58), but in punishing him. Evidently she had not read Q.

We readers then typically root for this woman, because (a) she is a widow and therefore we see her as not only helpless and needy but also exploited and abused; our good natures prompt us to support her; (b) because we do not like the judge; not only does he lack appropriate religiosity and respect, but also Luke tells us that he is "unjust" (ἀδικίας, 18:6). We want him to lose, and for him to lose, the widow has to win. Our verdict is colored by our stereotypes, and those stereotypes allow us to paint a nice, tidy picture.

The aforementioned intertext from Sirach—not simply vv. 17–18 but all of 35:15b–25—offers an alternative, less comfortable reading that many commentators resist. Green, for example, claims that while this "instance of intertextuality solidly grounds Jesus' portrait of G-d within the Jewish tradition," Jesus offers an "innovation," namely, that "the passage from Sirach develops the notion of divine vengeance against the unrighteous, a motif absent from Jesus' parabolic teaching in 18:1–8."²⁴ Green's point requires nuance. First, there's a lot of divine vengeance in teachings assigned to Jesus (the "place of wailing and gnashing of teeth"

22. See Scott, *Hear Then the Parable*, 183, followed by Charles W. Hedrick, *Parables as Poetic Fictions*, 199, and especially Cotter, "Parable of the Feisty Widow," 335, who compares the widow's lack of polite, formal approach to legal papyri.

23. For similar nuances, see the sources collected in Freed, "Parable of the Judge," 46.

24. Green, *Gospel of Luke*, 638. See also, e.g., Hedrick, *Parables as Poetic Fictions*, 188 n.3; Manson, *The Sayings of Jesus*, 305; Scott, *Hear Then the Parable*, 186; Young, *Parables*, 55–56; Snodgrass, *Stories with Intent*, 356.

is hardly a vacation spot). Second, 18:8 literally reads, not "he will quickly grant justice to them" (so the NRSV) but "he will make vengeance against them swiftly" (ποιήσει τὴν ἐκδίκησιν αὐτῶν ἐν τάχει).

A third point regarding Sirach returns to the parable proper. Perhaps this widow, too, is seeking not (or not only) justice, but vengeance. The details of her request go unspoken: does she want money from her adversary? Access to property? Or does she want her opponent thrown into jail, or to suffer,[25] or to be executed? The parable, at the very least, does not preclude a motif of vengeance.[26] The good news is that vengeance belongs to the Lord, not to us (Deut 32:35; cf. Rom 12:19 [using the same verb as our parable]; Heb 10:30); the less attractive news is that vengeance is what the widow wants.

This is not the news the majority of commentators proclaim. Pheme Perkins reads the widow in light of Prov 25:15, "With patient persistence a high official may be persuaded, and a soft tongue can break stone."[27] I seem to have missed the widow's "soft tongue." Hultgren states, "The only decent figure [in the parable] is the woman."[28] But parables need not have a decent figure: there's no one in the "dishonest steward" or the "prodigal son" whom I would want my daughter to date. Bernard Brandon Scott finds that the widow's tenacity models the kingdom, which "keeps battering down regardless of honor or justice";[29] and Reid finds that the parable "asks one to leave behind stereotypes and wrestle with unfamiliar notions about what G-d is like and what justice in the realm of G-d looks like and how it is achieved."[30] Moving to divine justice and asking about the kingdom are standard, and usually admirable homiletic moves, but they are not necessary for the parable to work. The parable does not talk about the kingdom.[31] While the sermon based

---

25. Hedrick, *Parables as Poetic Fictions*, 199 (n. 48 offers papyrus details).

26. Green, *Gospel of Luke*, 640, proposes, based on (admittedly) no evidence, that "it is likely [her claim] had to do with material resources being withheld from her."

27. Perkins, *Hearing the Parables of Jesus*, 195

28. Hultgren, *Parables of Jesus*, 259.

29. Scott, *Hear Then the Parable*, 187. I do like the idea of justice (at least of some sort; preferably the kind I define myself). I am, after all, one of those politically aware academics who recognizes both the problem with defining the concept and the potentially greater problem of having "no regard" for it. As for honor: I'd rather redefine the concept than dump it entirely, and the same point holds for shame.

30. Reid, *Parables for Preachers*, 233.

31. See Curkpatrick, "Parable Metonymy and Luke's Kerygmatic Framing," 289–307

on these readings may well have a good message, it will also tame the parable, it will clip it of its sharp, disturbing edge.

Then there are readings that posit an evil Judaism over-against which the widow triumphs. Mary Matthews, for example, suggests, without primary source evidence, that Jesus' Galilean audience would have seen women, or widows, as "weak, foolish, silly, impotent, chattering, useless."[32] The widow may shatter conventions; there is no reason to offer a negative view of Jewish culture in order to describe the parable's provocation.

And while I agree with Reid and others that "this prophetic widow can help animate those who bemoan the fact that the systems of injustice are too big to take on,"[33] I am still discomforted by her motives. The more I listen to her, the more she reminds me of the judge; she acts toward him as he does toward her: without care for the needs or feelings of the other. Even if her ends are worthy (and that is an open question), I'm not sure her means are to be emulated. Crossan, on the other hand, may not be critical enough, "I look at the widow and I don't consider her right or good. Maybe her adversary is right, but more polite."[34]

With this more complicated picture of the widow, the parable's greater shock emerges. It is not the judge alone who is morally ambiguous (at best). So is his antagonist. To read the widow positively indicates, at least, that the end (her vengeance) justifies the means (her badgering, her threat). Worse, it can promote the idea that vengeance is ours, not G-d's. More work needs to be done.

The Judge

Just as the vengeance-seeking widow becomes the model supplicant in Luke's narrative frame and the justice-seeking exemplar in scholarly reception, so the judge receives separate roles in the parable proper, the frame, and the reception. In the parable proper he is not the epitome

(289 n.2: "Without kerygmatic framing, the L parables do not refer to the kingdom of G-d").

32. Matthews, "Persistent Widow," 50. Actually, this is a pretty accurate description of the disciples in most of Mark's Gospel.

33. Reid, *Taking Up the Cross*, 116.

34. Crossan, "Discussion," 58–59, cited by Curkpatrick, "Dissonance in Luke 18:1–8," 115 n. 24.

of righteousness, nor is he clearly corrupt. In the immediate narrative frame, Luke labels him "unjust." In the broader frame, he is the negative version of the deity; the *qal v'homer* argument suggests that if an unrighteous judge will grant justice, surely the Righteous Judge will do the same. In the progressive scholarly tradition, the judge represents systemic evil and institutional corruption.

According to the parable, the judge "did not fear God and had respect for anyone" (τὸν θεὸν μὴ φοβούμενος καὶ ἄνθρωπον μὴ ἐντρεπόμενος, 18:2). He confirms this description by interior monologue: "Though I have no fear of God nor respect for anyone . . ." (Εἰ καὶ τὸν θεὸν οὐ φοβοῦμαι οὐδὲ ἄνθρωπον ἐντρέπομαι, 18:4). He is exactly as described.

Questions concerning how this judge was appointed, where he sat, and whether his role corresponds to any known practice have no necessary bearing on the parable's meaning.[35] The parable itself establishes the relevant cultural expectations. For example, by stating that the judge neither fears G-d nor respects people, the parable suggests that these are unusual traits (otherwise, there would be no reason to mention them). Thus the judge is an odd judge at best: he does not fear or respect, when culturally (at least within a Jewish framework) he would be expected to do both.

Following Jill Harries's study of Roman court systems, Wendy Cotter proposes that the judge acts as he would be expected to act, for the "judicial system was a closed circle of ambitious elites whose attentions were trained on amassing greater wealth and increasing personal prestige."[36] The connection does not hold: the parable says nothing about money or wealth (a notable silence, given Luke's condemnation of the venal). That the parable describes him as not caring for his reputation suggests that judges generally do have such care: they would prefer to be thought just. He is an exceptional judge.

---

35. The commentaries frequently cite *m. Sanhedrin* 1:1, which mandates that property cases be heard by three judges, or follow Jeremias, *The Parables of Jesus*, 153, who suggests that behind the text is the ruling in *b. Sanhedrin* 4b that "An authorized scholar may decide money cases sitting alone," and thus concludes that the case is about finances, and/or follow J. Duncan M. Derrett's discussion of "customary" and "administrative" courts ("Law in the New Testament, 178–91).

36. Cotter, "Parable of the Feisty Widow," 332, following Harries, *Law and Empire in Late Antiquity*.

Whether he is unjust, as the narrative frame states, is also another question. To lack fear of the divine is not the same thing as to be unjust. It is unwise, given that "the fear of the Lord is the beginning of wisdom" (Ps 111:10; cf. Prov 1:7); it could signal lack of moral compass (cf. Gen 20:11, "Abraham said, 'I did it because I thought, There is no fear of God at all in this place, and they will kill me because of my wife'"), and it goes against Jehoshaphat's charge to the judges of Judah, "Let the fear of the Lord be upon you" (2 Chr 19:7). The judge is also not *halakhically* obedient (Lev 19:14, 32; Deut 4:10, etc.). But he is also not clearly initially corrupt.

The judge's lack of "respect" (μὴ ἐντρεπόμενος) can indicate a refusal to defer to a person of higher status; such lack of respect would put the judge outside the patron/client system. He is beholden to no one. Therefore, the proposal that the judge refused the widow justice because he accepted bribes from her opponent,[37] is not a necessary reading. A bribe would anticipate some degree of reciprocity, and this independent judge shows no interest in being in anyone's pocket. However, that his independence is a commendable trait, as Hedrick insists, with citations of Wis 6:7; Sir 4:22; 32:12; Job 32:21 (LXX); and Deut 1:17 (LXX) on the ideal impartiality of judges, remains unlikely.[38] More likely, the judge both lacks shame, as in the Pauline use of ἐντρέπω (1 Cor 4:14; 2 Thess 3:14; Tit 2:8) and has contempt for everyone.[39] Further, the combination of disregard for heaven and for community is nearly conventional; first-

---

37. See Manson, *Sayings of Jesus*, 305. Green, *Gospel of Luke*, 640, suggests that "she lacks the economic resources to offer the appropriate bribe necessary for a swift settlement." Amos 5:12 speaks of judges who afflict the righteous and take bribes; but the widow may not be righteous, and the judge need not be corrupt.

38. Hedrick, *Parables as Poetic Fictions*, 196. See also Derrett, "Law in the New Testament," 190–91.

39. Hultgren, *Parables of Jesus*, 254; for a fuller reading of the judge in light of honor/shame motifs, see Scott, *Hear Then the Parable*, 178–87. Malina and Neyrey, "Honor and Shame in Luke-Acts," 25–65, propose that the judge "came to the ... widow's assistance" (63), and thus the narrative demands "special sympathy for the precarious state of the 'shame' of the widow, the value worth more than gold" (64). Then again, economics can trump both honor/shame and gender systems. The judge's interest is not honor; the widow displays no honor for the court. Neither displays a concern for shame. Thus, Johnson, *Gospel of Luke*, 269, states that the middle voice of ἐντρεπόμενος "suggests someone incapable of shame."

century readers would have seen the judge as a negative figure.[40] He is unlikeable, dishonorable, and foolish.

Yet it may go too far to find the judge "ruthless by any human estimation."[41] Perhaps the best analogy is to the prodigal son, who expresses (whether sincerely or not) having sinned against heaven and against his father (Luke 15:18, 21) and thus showing disdain for both.[42] The judge may not be corrupt, but I would not want him to date my daughter either.

Thus the judge is a good match for the widow, who may not be corrupt but who is no moral exemplar herself. At least at the start, they are well matched, for her insistent pleas prompt his equally consistent refusal: "For a while he refused" (οὐκ ἤθελεν [18:4], an imperfect to match her "coming"). She does not respect his verdict, because it is not the verdict she wants; he does not respect her, and he does not care whether she respects him.

She, however, bests him. The NRSV, blandly, quotes the judge as saying to himself: "because this widow keeps bothering me, I will grant her justice, so that she may not wear me out by continually coming" (18:5). The Greek is sharper on three points. First, "Bothering me" is παρέχειν μοι κόπον, literally, "causing me labor," or, colloquially, "Giving me work." It is the same term that appears in Luke 11:7, where the householder initially refuses his friend's midnight plea for food: "Do not give me work (μή μοι κόπους πάρεχε); the door has already been locked, and my children are with me in bed; I cannot get up and give you anything."[43] The widow and the friend at midnight share annoying tenacity, but the widow is no friend of the judge. Whereas the friend sought food, the woman seeks vengeance.

Second, "wear me out" is ὑπωπιάζω, a boxing term, with the better English translation being "beat me up," "strike in the face," "doing vi-

---

40. Primary sources collected by, *inter alia*, Freed, "Parable of the Judge," 42; Cotter, "Parable of the Feisty Widow," 331–32; see also Hedrick, *Parables as Poetic Fictions*, 195 and nn. 29, 30.

41. Hultgren, *Parables of Jesus*, 253. Comparing the judge's description to Josephus's negative description of King Jehoiakim (*Ant.* 10.83): "He was neither reverent toward" (μήτε πρὸς θεὸν ὅσιος μήτε πρὸς ἀνθρώπους ἐπιεικής) are Hultgren; Scott, *Hear Then the Parable*, 180; Young, *Parables*, 57.

42. Bovon, "Apocalyptic Traditions," 386, draws this connection.

43. Hedrick, *Parables as Poetic Fictions*, 200; Hultgren, *Parables of Jesus*, 253; and Young, *Parables*, 41–65, develop the connections between 11:5–8 and 18:1–8.

olence to me,"[44] or "give a black eye."[45] Elsewhere in the New Testament, it appears only in 1 Cor 9:27 (the NRSV reads "punishing"), Paul's reference to the severe treatment he accords his own body. The cognate noun ὑπώπιον appears in Prov 20:30, which, as an ironic intertext to our parable, reads, "Blows (ὑπώπια) that wound cleanse away evil; beatings make clean the innermost parts." For our parable, the threat of the blow pushes the judge into a decision based on expedience, not justice.

Although I do not see the judge as "a tragic figure, a thoroughly honest man who permits himself to be corrupted for his personal convenience"[46]—his initially unattractive attitude prevents him from being tragic—he becomes corrupted. When the judge accedes to the woman's request, he facilitates her hatred of her neighbor. His fall is not because "he turns out to be vulnerable to embarrassment and to a threat to his privileged place in the society"[47] or because she will "defame" him[48] or "Although he is clear about his role as judge, he still has to wear the mantle of justice in public and keep the cover story alive."[49] His cover is already blown. Both the narrative voice and his interior monologue indicate his lack of concern for public honor. His motive is that he is tired and threatened, not that he is about to be dishonored.

Third, "grant her justice," ἐκδικήσω αὐτήν, literally means "avenge her." The widow will get what she wants: vengeance. The parable proper ends with the judge's decision and so it ends as a story about corruption, violence, and vengefulness. Stereotypes of judges and widows both fall. At best, our parable marches beside that of the unjust steward (Luke 16:1–8a): both tell of morally ambiguous figures, a steward and a widow, who get what they want by implicating others in their less-than-commendable plans.

If readers are not yet convinced that this judge is at least morally ambiguous, his thought process should confirm the point. The most the judge can muster in response to the woman is interior monologue; he does not speak with her directly, any more than Martha speaks to Mary,

---

44. Green, *Gospel of Luke*, 636.
45. See the general discussion by Weiss, "ὑπωπιάζω," in *TDNT* 8:590.
46. Hedrick, *Parables as Poetic Fictions*, 187, suggests that the phrase conveys a sense of physical debilitation, but this seems an overread given the parallel in Luke 11.
47. Ringe, *Luke*, 224.
48. Hultgren, *Parables of Jesus*, 255.
49. Herzog, *Parables as Subversive Speech*, 230.

or the elder brother to the Prodigal. The woman carries the verbal aspect of the parable. Further, the judge's interior monologue puts him in the same category as Luke's Rich Farmer (12:16–20), the Unfaithful Servant (12:42–46), the Prodigal Son (15:11–32), the Dishonest Steward (16:1–8a), and the Vineyard Owner (20:9–16).[50] The company is not complimentary.

Finally, comments both from Luke's own composition and words Luke attributes to Jesus indicate distaste for the role of judge, whether taken professionally or metaphorically. Luke 6:37 exhorts, "Do not judge" but rather "forgive" (two activities at which both characters in the parable fail: there is much judging, but no forgiving; the same observation holds true for most of the interpreters of the parable, as we have seen). In 12:14, Jesus refuses the role of judge; in 12:58 he describes the threat of being dragged before a judge. Like Jesus, Gallio the proconsul eschews the role of judge (Acts 18:15), and Paul, perhaps facetiously, speaks of Felix as "judge over this nation" (Acts 24:10). When judges in Luke-Acts do their jobs, the verdicts are harsh, as Luke 11:19; 19:22; and Acts 10:42 suggest. Luke may even be warning readers to avoid the courts. Whereas Matthew 5:40 states "if anyone wants to sue you and take your coat, give your cloak as well," Luke 6:29 simply reads, "If anyone strikes you on the cheek, offer the other also; and from anyone who takes away your coat do not withhold even your shirt." Judges are dangerous and to judge unadvisable. Our judge is no more appealing than the widow who bests him.

Luke's Narrative Frame: The Widows

Luke cannot abide a topsy-turvy world (*pace* Acts 17:6). Richard Ford, a clinical psychologist, diagnoses, "As an underwater swimmer breaks to the surface straining for air, so the editor reaches to grasp some other presence to overcome the suffocating exclusion locked into this parable."[51]

Luke's struggles begin with the lack of connection between 18:1 and 18:8. The opening focus on the "need to pray always and not to become discouraged," although reinforced by 18:7's insistence that "G-d . . . will grant vengeance (ποιήσῃ τὴν ἐκδίκησιν) to his elect who cry to

50. Sellew, "Interior Monologue," 239–53.
51. Ford, *Parables of Jesus*, 72.

him day and night," is compromised by bad theology. To "pray without ceasing" (1 Thess 1:3; 2:13; 5:17; 2 Tim 1:3) is to pray repeatedly, but as David Buttrick states, "The notion that, repeatedly, we must bang on the doors of heaven if we are to catch G-d's attention is hardly an appropriate theology of prayer."[52] Nor is praying for vengeance—*Schadenfreude* is not a theological category, despite its German origin—attractive.

Luke then shifts the focus from prayerful expectation to the concern that the "Son of Man" may not find faith on earth (18:8). The final verse sends the reader back to the apocalyptic materials in the previous chapter, with Jesus' comment, "The days are coming when you will long to see one of the days of the Son of Man, and you will not see it" (17:22). Delay and swift response clash, as do the focus on the worshiper not losing heart and the Son of Man's possible disappointment. The frame doesn't work externally, and it doesn't help the parable either.

Luke has more problems than basic continuity. True to Roman cultural values, Luke is no great friend of independent women. Aside from the infancy materials, which may be additions to a gospel that originally began with the preaching of John the Baptist,[53] Luke restricts women to ancillary roles. Simon's mother-in-law (perhaps a widow) requires Jesus' rescue (4:39) and responds with service. Luke 8:1–3 restricts women to patronage positions—they support Jesus and the apostles, who do the important work of preaching the word; the women respond to Jesus not because of their independent assessment of his message or a divine revelation, but in gratitude for his healing their bodies.[54] In Luke 8:19, Jesus' mother (here perhaps also a widow; Joseph goes unmentioned), not identified by name, seeks to see him, but he dismisses her concern, "My mother and my brothers are those who hear the word of God and do it" (8:21).

Although Martha (10:38–42) can be read in the same context as Simon the Pharisee (7:36–42) and other householders whom Jesus criticizes for inappropriate manifestations of hospitality,[55] she is nevertheless put down in favor of her silent sister Mary. Jesus also critiques or, at least, corrects, women who publicly express their admiration of

---

52. Buttrick, *Speaking Parables*, 186.

53. Tyson, *Marcion and Luke-Acts*.

54. For a more positive reading of the women in Luke 8:1–3, see DeBoer, "The Lukan Mary Magdalene and the Other Women Following Jesus," 140–60.

55. Carter, "Getting Martha Out of the Kitchen," 197–213.

him: to the woman who praises the womb that bore him and the breasts that nursed him, Jesus responds that more blessed are those who do the will of G-d (11:27–28). Women's biological gifts are fine, but they hold no comparison to Jesus' agenda. To the daughters of Jerusalem who weep for him, Jesus gives cold comfort in telling them rather to weep for themselves (23:28). That marvelous Canaanite/Syro-Phoenician woman, perhaps another widow (Matthew 15:21–28//Mark 7:24–30), has gone missing, and the Samaritan woman at the well (perhaps a five-time widow?) of John 4 makes no appearance.

The widows in Luke-Acts are similarly domesticated. They are, in order: Anna (2:36–38), the widow of Zarephath and her contemporaneous Israelite sisters (4:25–26), the widow of Nain (7:11–17), the multiply married Levirate widow (20:28–33), widows whose houses scribes devour (20:47), and the widow who puts her coins in the Temple treasury (21:1–4).[56] However, in light of the rereading of our active, probably vengeful, certainly morally ambiguous widow, these widows may have a different story to tell than that of the least, the lost, and the lachrymose.

Anna, the prophet in the Temple (2:37–38), anticipates the widow of 18:1–8 by praying always and not losing heart. According to Luke 2:36–37, "She was of a great age, having lived with her husband seven years after her marriage, then as a widow to the age of eighty-four. She never left the temple but worshiped there with fasting and prayer night and day." While Luke does grant that she is a prophet (2:36) and that she praised G-d and spoke about the child "to all who were looking for the redemption of Jerusalem" (2:38), he does not accord her direct discourse as he does with Simeon the prophet. By introducing her as "the daughter of Phanuel, of the tribe of Asher" (2:36), Luke could be understood as subtly infantilizing the prophet; although eighty-four, she is still a daughter.

And yet . . . Her tribal recognition means that she represents the Northern tribes taken into exile, and taken from history, in 722 BCE.[57] Her husband goes unnamed, and thus she, like Mary, emerges as the more important member of her spousal relationship. She is not simply

---

56. Acts includes the widows overlooked in the service (6:1–6) and the widows who mourn Dorcas (9:39–41). There may be other widows who are not designated as such, e.g., Mary the mother of John Mark, Lydia.

57. Bauckham, *Gospel Women*, 98–99; Bauckham also argues for her historicity.

identified by her father's name, but, unlike everyone else in the text save for Jesus via Joseph's genealogy, she receives an explicit connection to one of the tribes of Israel.

If her age is taken to be 105, then she will have lived two "week of years" (i.e., 14 years) prior to marriage, been married seven years, and then lived twelve "weeks of years" (i.e., 84 years) as a widow. Judith died at 105 years (16:22), and she too did not remarry.[58] With this intertextual connection, Anna is less comparably marginalized prophet and more echo of ancient warrior. Her interest in "the redemption of Israel" nicely follows from this observation, since the Hebrew version of the phrase appears on Bar Cochba's coinage.[59] Given these resonances, Anna is no quiet prophet but a vocal and visual symbol of Israel's hopes.

Luke next introduces widows in Jesus' synagogue sermon: "there were many widows in the days of Elijah, in Israel when the heaven was shut up three years and six months, and there was a great famine over all the earth; and to none of them was sent Elijah except to Zarephath in Sidon, to a widow woman" (4:25–26). In Luke's account, the widow is helpless and requires Elijah's aid. Again, Luke has domesticated a woman, for 1 Kings 17 depicts a feisty mother who first matches Elijah in verbal jousting and then demands that the prophet cure her son. The original story itself deconstructs: 1 Kgs 17:9 has G-d stating, "I have commanded a widow there to feed you," but the widow, apparently, has not heard the command; Elijah has to talk her into providing for him by promising that he will provide for her. This widow is not one who prays daily and has hope; instead, she states, with what may well be a note of sarcasm: "As the LORD your God lives, I have nothing baked, only a handful of meal in a jar, and a little oil in a jug; I am now gathering a couple of sticks, so that I may go home and prepare it for myself and my son, that we may eat it, and die" (1 Kings 17:12). The Lord of Elijah may live, but the widow is less optimistic about her own survival or that of her son.

She again criticizes Elijah when her son becomes ill. The NRSV offers: "What have you against me, O man of God? You have come to me to bring my sin to remembrance, and to cause the death of my son!" (17:18). However, the LXX does not read "sin" (ἁμαρτία) but "unrighteousness" (ἀδικίας), the same term Luke uses to describe the judge

---

58. Ibid., 99–100.
59. Ibid., 98–99 n. 83.

(Luke 18:6). In terms of gender and structural position (supplicant and grantor), the widow of the parable matches the widow of Zarephath. And if the widow of 1 Kings 17 is unrighteous, then the virtue of the parable's widow is again called into question. The judge of the parable in turn compares to the prophet Elijah, to the credit of neither. Elijah, seen in light of the judge, can easily be condemned for not aiding the widows in Israel.

The widow of Nain models the convention of widow: she is a pathetic figure, introduced in the funeral procession of her only son (Luke 7:12). Seeing her, Jesus has compassion for her (ἐσπλαγχνίσθη ἐπ᾽ αὐτῇ); the term evokes the "Good Samaritan," who "had compassion" (ἐσπλαγχνίσθη) for the man in the ditch (10:33), and the father of the "Prodigal Son," who was "filled with compassion" (ἐσπλαγχνίσθη) upon seeing the lad return (15:20). These are the only three times in Luke-Acts the term appears; each refers to the return of an individual from death to life. Thus the woman, not the son, is compared to the "half-dead" (10:30) injured traveler and the ignoble prodigal who "was dead and is lives again" (15:24); without her son, she too is dead.

To the widow of Nain, Jesus issues the negative command, "Do not weep" (7:13); she, unlike Anna, has given up hope. She, unlike the widow of Zarephath, did not demand that the prophet heal her only son. While the dead son, upon being raised, "began to speak" (Luke 7:15), the mother, like her foresisters in the Gospel, the widow Anna and the widow of Zarephath, speaks not a word.

The intertextual readings provide her a voice. First, the woman's weeping (κλαίω, 7:13) can register not simply as mourning, but also as protest; the same point holds for the weeping of the daughters of Jerusalem in 23:28 (μὴ κλαίετε ἐπ᾽ ἐμέ). Luke's beatitudes speak to the conditions of both the widow of Zarephath and the widow of Nain: "Blessed are you who are hungry now, for you will be filled" describes the former; "Blessed are you who weep now, for you will laugh" suggests the later (6:21). Since the beatitudes continue with the threats to those presently full and laughing, they also, but more subtly, anticipate the widow of our parable, who seeks vengeance. Her opponent will have no reason to laugh. Finally, the widow of Nain, unlike the man in the ditch or the prodigal, not only receives compassion but also receives the opportunity to act upon it. The final verse of her story indicates that Jesus gave the resuscitated son to his mother (καὶ ἔδωκεν αὐτὸν τῇ μητρὶ αὐτοῦ, 7:15). She will care for him, not he for her. Luke gives no indication that she is in need of additional help; she does not appear oppressed or exploited.

Luke retains the Sadducees' question concerning the widow married to seven brothers (20:28–33; cf. Matt 22:23–28; Mark 12:19–33). This woman, with no agency of her own, is property inherited from one brother to the next. The NRSV delicately states that "the seven had married her" (Luke 20:33); the Greek more bluntly states that "the seven had her as wife" (οἱ γὰρ ἑπτὰ ἔσχον αυτὴν γυναῖκα). "Had" is the operative term. However, the woman's agency is only removed in the Sadducees' question, not in Jesus' response: "but those who are considered worthy of a place in that age and in the resurrection from the dead neither marry nor are given in marriage" (20:35). The anticipated age rejects the idea not only that women need to marry, but also that they are "given" and thus can be "had."

Luke's next reference to widows is Jesus' warning: "beware of the scribes ... who devour widows' houses" (οἱ κατεσθίουσιν τὰς οἰκίας τῶν χηρῶν, 20:46–47; cf. Mark 12:40). Widows are, according to the conventional depiction, victims. On the other hand, these widows *have* houses. So much for all those claims about widows being tossed out onto the streets because they could not inherit. More intriguing, the widows are in the same position as the *father* of the prodigal, to whom his older son exclaims, "But when this son of yours came back, who has devoured your life ..." (ὁ καταφαγών σου τὸν βίον, 15:30). The connection to the father in the parable does not "rescue" these widows; it does, however, together with the other pericopae regarding widows, show that the scribal threat can be avoided. It presents the women as having agency, even agency perhaps to make the wrong choice, as did the prodigal son's prodigal father. The connection to 15:30, in which the older brother exaggerates the younger's fiscal situation, can even suggest that claim regarding the scribes is an exaggeration rather than, as some commentators would have it, a direct window into common Jewish legal practices.

Finally, immediately after the reference to the widow's houses, Luke retains from Mark the short account of the widow who puts her two coins in the Temple treasury (21:1–4). Of the "poor widow" Jesus states, she "has put in more than all of them; for all of them have contributed out of their abundance, but she out of her poverty has put in all she had to live on" (21:3–4). Despite tendencies to read the story as continuing the idea of Jewish leaders exploiting widows, and of the Temple as a "domination system" that sucks the last coins out of the hands of those on fixed incomes, the juxtaposition of the widow references in chapters 20 and 21 together with the material adduced above suggests an alternative reading. The widow of 21:1–4 retains her own income and chooses how to spend it; she has not had her house stripped from her by scribes. Unlike the rich ruler of 18:18–25 and the foolish rich men in parables (e.g., 12:16–21; 16:19–31), she is not attached to her coins; she gives generously, and Jesus praises her for it. The woman epitomizes what the Gospel exhorts. She is comparable to the disciples, who have left everything for a higher cause (Luke 5:11 [cf. Matt 19:27; Mark 10:28]; 5:28). Had she been exploited by the Temple system, Jesus might have advised her to save her money. If he finds her to be the model of generosity, it seems a bit ungenerous of the commentators to see in her an example of institutional exploitation.

Rereading Luke's widows in light of our parable reveals hints of agency and individualism where many have seen only abjection and convention. And these hints return us to the parable, where we can now be more confident in finding yet another atypical widow.

Feminist Observations

Klyne Snodgrass states of Luke 18:1–8, "I consider this one of the more difficult parables . . . The parable itself (vv. 2–5) is brief, and without its explanation (vv. 6–8) there is little indication of its intent."[60] Many readers choose to accept Luke's contextualization, regard the parable as about prayer, and take one or both of its main characters as exemplars (whether positive or negative); the parable then becomes a tidy story comprehensible only by allegory.

We choose how to read, and in doing so we harness the parable's ambiguity, and the ambiguity of the lives it depicts.[61] Rather than ask what the parable *means*, we might ask what it *does*. This parable disturbs. At the very least, it calls into question stereotypes of widows and

---

60. Snodgrass, *Stories with Intent*, 449.

61. On the ambivalence and contradictions of parabolic details, and Luke's framing of them to provide resolution, see Curkpatrick, "Parable Metonymy."

judges: widows may be powerful and vengeful and exploit their positions; judges may be unjust (nothing new here), but their lack of justice may be prompted not by greed or even a preferential option for one class or another, but by irascibility or self-protection. Once our stereotypes are shattered, we can begin to look at people as individuals, rather than as social roles. Despite the penchant in NT studies these days for matters of dyadic personality, or conforming to convention, stories, whether ancient or modern, hold our interest because people do what they are not expected to do. Sons show disrespect to parents, Samaritans show compassion, tax collectors recognize their sinful states, messianic figures die.

The parable also disturbs, or at least it disturbs me, by preventing positive assessments of either character. Neither judge nor widow is a moral exemplar; neither is even likeable. And yet many readers struggle to find their good qualities, with most readers, starting with Luke, rescuing the widow. Here is a lesson about our own cultural values: we resist the image of evil; we seek good qualities. Or we resist ambiguity: we force figures into opposites: good and bad, righteous and sinful, "us" and "them." I am more inclined to resist the stereotype, the dualistic categories, and the apologetic. This approach makes life messier, but it may also prevent the abuse that stereotype and dualism can prompt.

The parable disturbs again because the only form of closure it creates is that in which widow and judge—and so reader—become complicit in a plan to take vengeance. We may resist that complicity, and so opt out of the system that promotes it. We may decide that court cases are not worth our time; that compassion is less time consuming and less corrupting than vengeance. Our task may be to resist the parable, rather than rescue it.

Barbara Reid, critiquing the reading that sees the judge as the negative exemplar of the divine—if he can be worn down, how much more so can the deity?—offers a "far simpler" understanding, viz., "it is the widow who is cast in the image of G-d and who is presented to the disciples as a figure to emulate" for she represents, "godly power in seeming weakness."[62] The gender disruption, with the (male) disciples

---

62. Reid, *Parables for Preachers*, 234; see also Reid, "Beyond Petty Pursuits," 294, "When one doggedly resists injustice, faces it, names it, and denounces it until justice is achieved, then one is acting as God does. Moreover, the parable displays godly power revealed in seeming weakness." For others who read the widow as a divine image, see Scheele, "Persistent Widow," 69, and sources there.

prompted to see themselves as importuning widows, is an appealing reading, although it also strikes me as a bit anachronistic, at least for both Jesus and Luke. More, I'm not convinced that an allegorical leap, let alone to the divine, is needed for the parable to provide a helpful critique of a worldview, be that view based in the first or the twenty-first century. Luke wants the judge to be the negative image of the divine; Reid would have the widow be the positive image; I see no necessity for making either character the representative of heaven. Perhaps the judge and the widow are just that, judge and widow, and unpleasant ones at that.

Finally, I am wary of any reading that reinforces gender stereotypes, even in the attempt to dismantle them. The widow is not "weak," any more than Tamar or Ruth or Abigail or Judith is "weak." Widows in biblical narrative rarely are. To live in a patriarchal system is not the same thing as to be weak. The author of 1 Timothy knew that, which is why 1 Timothy 5 wants to control widows.

While Reid is correct that the widow achieves her goal without "resorting to violence,"[63] that widow nevertheless threatens the judge, or at least he perceives himself to be threatened. A punch thrown by a widow may be weaker than a punch thrown by Mohammed Ali, but a punch is still a punch, and a threat of violence is still a threat. The picture of the violent widow may be humorous, but it only works as humor if we again resort to stereotypes and reinforce gender roles: in the modern West, it's apparently O.K. for a widow to threaten violence, but not O.K. for a strapping young man to do the same. Or, we resist the idea that the widow would actually hit the judge, and thus find her humorous in her actual helplessness. This reading does her, and us, no good.

And yet, the threat creates a relationship. The judge had no relationships: no fear of G-d and no concern for humanity; had he at least the latter, he might have attended the widow rather than ignored her. His ignoring grates (cf. Matt 15:21–28; Jesus' initial silence is no less grating than his refusal to help the Canaanite woman or his calling her a dog). A negative response may be better than no response at all (I think, but cannot be sure, that Job would agree). The widow forces the judge to interact with humanity, and not by an objective stance; he has to interact with the widow because she has gotten to him. She has forced him into relationship. If there is a *qal v'homer* lesson here, perhaps it is

---

63. Reid, *Parables for Preachers*, 234.

that if interaction is to come—and it will—it is better to engage it than to be forced into it.

Luise Schottroff offers another appealing reading: for her, the widow is the symbol of resistance, a symbol that finds another signifier in Thecla. Further, the widow, as positive symbol, unmasks the sexism inherent in the "slander [of] women by accusing them of being violent."[64] Schottroff, like Reid, is more generous than I. Women can be violent, we can kill, we can rape, we can seek vengeance. This point cannot be ignored either; it would be sexist to do so.

And yet we learn from this depiction as well. The widow's behavior is consistent: a person who seeks to be avenged against her opponent is not a person who "loves her enemies." We readers resist the idea: we like to think of widows as both righteous and as needing our protection, for the stereotype of the weak widow reinforces the stereotype of the rescuing reader. At the very least, we readers can feel self-righteous, for we of course condemn the system that has trapped and exploited our widow. But if the widow is neither weak nor righteous, then the reader who supports her can represent neither the strong nor the virtuous. If we as readers question our roles—our stereotypes, our sense of justice, our desire for vengeance—the parable can begin to work on us.

William Herzog offers yet a third potentially appealing reading: he sees the parable as about systemic oppression and collusion of those trapped by it.[65] His general point about conscientization, a political interpretation wherein people recognize their entrapment in injustice and so can work to change the system, is helpful. On the other hand, telling people that judges can be corrupt, uninterested, or selfish is not news. Whether this reading leads to liberation is yet another issue: if the "good news" is that we collude in our own oppression, this is not news, and it is not good.

But Herzog's reading too opens to new possibilities. In the parable, vengeance rules. It is the desire for vengeance that drives the widow; this desire may be, especially in relation to law courts, more pressing than the desire for justice. I note this point as one who has taught almost every week for the past seven years in a maximum security prison in Nashville. My students at Riverbend—both from the divinity school and from the penal system—well understand the drive for vengeance;

---

64. Schottroff, *Lydia's Impatient Sisters*, 114.
65. Herzog, *Parables as Subversive Speech*, 231.

it is that drive that leads to the death penalty; it is that drive that leads to the refusal of parole despite every indication, especially after forty years, that the petitioner is not a societal threat. The widow's desire for vengeance will prompt her violent approach to the judge, and the judge, perpetuating the system of vengeance, will prompt violent action against the opponent.

The retributive system then continues: the widow's opponent may well counter-sue, and nothing is achieved. Indeed, ἀντίδικος appears in Luke (Q) 12:58 to show not only the problems of involvement in the courts at all, but the increasing violence that suits create: "For as you go with your opponent (ἀντίδικος) before a ruler (ἄρχοντα), on the way work to settle the case, lest you be dragged before the judge, and the judge hand you over to the officer, and the officer throw you in prison." The widow does not follow this advice, and everyone, including the reader attempting to make some sense out of the parable, suffers.

All have colluded in this system of oppression. The problem is not, however, the court. The court is only a system of the larger systemic concern: the human desire for vengeance, a desire that knows no gender or class boundaries, a desire that sucks everyone into its wake. Thus true systemic evil is revealed—and of course, readers seek to deny it.

The widow keeps bothering me. There is no easy closure to her story; there is no closure at all. I cannot root for the widow, or the judge, and I do not have enough information to speak about the opponent, but if he is tangled up with this widow, he may suffer guilt by association. Since I cannot find justice in the setting, I have to look elsewhere (the *qal v'homer* traditional reading is looking better and better). I also have to cross-examine myself: what are my stereotypes of widows and judges, of the legal system and its relationship to religious confession? Of human nature and the drive for vengeance? Why do I want one category of person to succeed and another to fail? What are my views of honor vs. personal preference? Of whether the end ever justifies the means (as it does in this story)?

Rather than look to the parable, or to the Bible, as a book of answers, perhaps the parable points us to the right questions, the ones we hesitate to ask. To paraphrase Lyn Osiek, and at the risk of unfortunate but parabolic grammar, here we have not "the widow as altar" but the "widow as alter."[66]

---

66. With gratitude to Richard Pervo and to the Greater Nashville Unitarian Universalist Congregation (GNUUC) for discussions of this paper, and for Carolyn Osiek, both for her contributions to the academy and for her friendship.

Bibliography

Bauckham, Richard, *Gospel Women: Studies of the Named Women in the Gospels*. Grand Rapids, MI: Eerdmans, 2002.

Bovon, François, "Apocalyptic Traditions in the Lukan Special Material: Reading Luke 18.1–8." *HTR* 90 (1997) 383–91

Buttrick, David. *Speaking Parables. A Homiletic Guide*. Louisville: Westminster John Knox Press, 2000.

Carter, Warren. "Getting Martha Out of the Kitchen: Luke 10.38–42 Again." In *A Feminist Companion to Luke*, edited by Amy-Jill Levine with Marianne Blickenstaff, 197–213. FCNT 3. London: Sheffield Academic, 2002.

Cotter, Wendy. "The Parable of the Feisty Widow and the Threatened Judge (Luke 18:1–8)." *NTS* 51 (2005) 328–42.

Cotton, Hannah M., and Jonas C. Greenfield, "Babatha's Property and the Law of Succession in the Babatha Archive." *Zeitschrift für Papyrologie und Epigraphik* 104 (1994) 211–24.

Crossan, John Dominic. "Discussion." In *Semiology and Parables: Exploration of the Possibilities Offered by Structuralism for Exegesis*, edited by Daniel Patte, 58–59. Pittsburgh: Pickwick, 1976.

Curkpatrick, Stephen. "Dissonance in Luke 18:1–8." *JBL* 121 (2002) 107–21.

———. "Parable Metonymy and Luke's Kerygmatic Framing." *JSNT* 25 (2003) 289–307.

DeBoer, Esther A. "The Lukan Mary Magdalene and the Other Women Following Jesus." In *A Feminist Companion to Luke*, edited by Amy-Jill Levine with Marianne Blickenstaff, 140–60. FCNT 3. London: Sheffield Academic, 2002.

Derrett, J. Duncan M. "Law in the New Testament: The Parable of the Unjust Judge." *NTS* 18 (1972) 178–91.

Ford, Richard Q. *The Parables of Jesus: Recovering the Art of Listening*. Minneapolis: Fortress, 1997.

Freed, Edwin D. "The Parable of the Judge and the Widow." *NTS* 33 (1987) 38–60.

Goodman, Martin. "Babatha's Story." *JRS* 81 (1991) 169–75.

Green, Joel B. *The Gospel of Luke*. NICNT. Grand Rapids: Eerdmans, 1997.

Harries, Jill. *Law and Empire in Late Antiquity*. Cambridge: Cambridge University Press, 1999.

Hedrick, Charles W. *Parables as Poetic Fictions: The Creative Voice of Jesus*. 1994. Reprinted, Eugene, OR: Wipf & Stock, 2005.

Herzog, William R. II. *Parables as Subversive Speech: Jesus as Pedagogue of the Oppressed*. Louisville: Westminster John Knox, 1994.

Hicks, John M., "The Parable of the Persistent Widow." *Restoration Quarterly* 33 (1991) 209–23.

Hultgren, Arland J. *The Parables of Jesus: A Commentary*. Grand Rapids: Eerdmans, 2000.

Jeremias, Joachim. *The Parables of Jesus*. 2nd rev. ed. Translated by S. H. Hooke. New York: Scribner, 1972.

Johnson, Luke Timothy. *The Gospel of Luke*. SacPag 3. Collegeville, MN: Liturgical, 1991.

Katzoff, Ranon, "*P. Yadin* 21 and Rabbinic Law on Widows' Rights." *Jewish Quarterly Review* 97 (2007) 545–75.

Malina, Bruce J., and Jerome H. Neyrey. "Honor and Shame in Luke-Acts: Pivotal Values of the Mediterranean World." In *The Social World of Luke-Acts: Models for Interpretation*, edited by Jerome H. Neyrey, 25–65. Peabody, MA: Hendrickson, 1991.

Manson, T. W. *The Sayings of Jesus*. London: SCM, 1957.

Matthews, Mary W., Carter Shelley, and Barbara Scheele. "Proclaiming the Parable of the Persistent Widow (Lk. 18.2–5)." In *The Lost Coin: Parables of Women, Work and Wisdom*, edited by Mary Ann Beavis, 46–70. London: Sheffield Academic, 2002.

Osiek, Carolyn. "The Widow as Altar: The Rise and Fall of a Symbol." *Second Century* 3 (1983) 159–69.

Perkins, Pheme. *Hearing the Parables of Jesus*. New York: Paulist, 1981.

Reid, Barbara E., "Beyond Petty Pursuits and Wearisome Widows: Three Lukan Parables." *Interpretation* 56 (2002) 284–94.

———. *Parables for Preachers: Year C*. Collegeville, MN: Liturgical, 2000.

———. *Taking Up the Cross: New Testament Interpretations through Latina and Feminist Eyes*. Minneapolis: Fortress, 2007.

Ringe, Sharon H. *Luke*. Westminster Bible Companion. Louisville: Westminster John Knox Press, 1995.

Schottroff, Luise, *Lydia's Impatient Sisters: A Feminist Social History of Early Christianity*. Louisville: Westminster John Knox, 1995.

Scott, Bernard Brandon. *Hear Then the Parable: A Commentary on the Parables of Jesus*. Minneapolis: Fortress, 1989.

Sellew, Philip. "Interior Monologue as a Narrative Device in the Parables of Luke." *JBL* 111 (1992) 239–53.

Snodgrass, Klyne R. *Stories with Intent: A Comprehensive Guide to the Parables of Jesus*. Grand Rapids: Eerdmans, 2008.

Tyson, Joseph B. *Marcion and Luke-Acts: A Defining Struggle*. Columbia: University of South Carolina Press, 2006.

Weaver, Dorothy Jean. "Between Text & Sermon: Luke 18:1–8." *Int* 56 (2002) 317–19.

Weiss, Konrad, "ὑπωπιάζω." In *TDNT* 8:590.

Young, Brad H. *The Parables: Jewish Tradition and Christian Interpretation*. Peabody, MA: Hendrickson, 1998.

Zimmer, Mary. "A Fierce Mother and a Widow: Models of Persistence." *Review & Expositor* 92 (1995) 89–93.

6

Symposiac Humor in Luke 14:1–24

Terri Bednarz, R.S.M

Introduction

AH, THE DINNER PARTIES WITH LYN! IN KEEPING WITH THE SPIRIT of the sisters of the Society of the Sacred Heart, Lyn always seems to enjoy a good dinner party. I cannot recall ever attending a feast with Lyn that she did not engage in some serious discussion of the biblical world in one moment and enjoy amusing anecdotes and teasing in the next moment. Even when Lyn travels abroad (which she loves to do!) to Turkey, Greece, Egypt, Palestine, Israel, Tunisia, and Malta, and a host of other places, she persistently situates herself at a table where intriguing questions, comic stories, quipped humor, and bantering often produce laughter, smiles and contorted facial expressions. And so, it seems fitting here to honor her with a discussion on ancient humor and its relevance for Lukan symposia. Unfortunately, however, symposiac humor is much more tendentious than the lighter forms of humor played out in those table feasts with Lyn!

So my aim here is to focus on the humor elements of symposia, which has garnered very little discussion in terms of the "modified symposium genus" present in the Gospel of Luke.[1] In developing the discussion on symposiac humor, I will focus on the following: 1) the fascination with symposia accounts; 2) the intermingling of seriousness and jesting indicative of Hellenistic symposia; 3) literary constructs of

---

1. Steele discusses in further detail the "modified symposium genus" of Luke 7:36–50; 11:37–54; and 14:1–24. See Steele, "Luke 11:37–54," 390–92.

symposium humor; 4) derisive forms of symposiac jesting and their effects; and 5) the presence of despised dinner guests at symposia. My intention is to explore the use and effects of humor in Greek symposia and its relevance for interpreting the possible presence of tendentious humor in Luke 14:1–24. My approach is a contextual one in which I situate a Lukan pericope within its Hellenistic literary context and within its cultural context of an honor-shame society. I will draw on the works of Greek philosophers and biographers and the Jewish historian, Josephus, as important sources for understanding the use of humor in symposium and symposium-like social settings. I will also turn to Roman rhetoricians to provide understanding on the effects of barbed humor in antagonistic exchanges.

Symposia in Luke

Luke's preference for depicting Jesus in table fellowship is commonly known. Three such meal scenes occur in Luke 7:36–50; 11:37–54; and 14:1–24.[2] A fourth meal scene occurs at Levi's house (5:29–39).[3] In three of these scenes, and in possibly the fourth, the Lukan Jesus dines with Lukan Pharisees.[4] During these table fellowships, the Pharisees experi-

---

2. Other meal scenes in Luke emphasize the Lukan Jesus' interactions with his disciples (22:14–38; 24:30–32; and 24:36–49). Only the scene with the woman and her ointment is similar in Luke 7:36–50; Mark 14:3–9; Matt 26:6–13. Most of 7:36–50 is L material, especially the placement of the meal at Simon, the Pharisee's house (rather than Simon, the leper's house), the subsequent parable of the creditor and the Lukan Jesus' post-parable comments. Regarding 11:37–54, Luke places Q material in the context of table fellowship. Luke 14:1–24 consists of four parts: 1) the healing of the man with dropsy (L material); 2) the teaching on table seating (L material); 3) the dictum on reversal (Q material); and 4) the parable of the great feast (Lukan redacted Q material). Luke explicitly shapes this parable as a dinner with strong allusions to a Hellenistic symposium.

3. The meal at Levi's house is found also in Matt 9:9–13 and Mark 2:13–17. Both Matthew and Mark distance the Pharisees from the table fellowship through their description that the Pharisees *saw* Jesus eating with tax collectors and sinners. Luke's version is ambiguous. The Pharisees could well be at the table as they grumbled against eating with tax collectors and sinners (5:30). In addition, we are told that ἄλλων οἳ ἦσαν μετ' αὐτῶν κατακείμενοι—"others were reclining at the table with them" (5:29). Unlike Matthew and Mark, Luke emphasizes that Levi provides a great feast (5:29). These Lukan additions suggest the Pharisees could well be present at the meal.

4. I use the designations, Lukan Jesus and Lukan Pharisees, in order to emphasize an awareness of the constructs of early Christian literature. Lukan Pharisees represent Pharisees constructed specifically for Luke's literary purposes.

ence less than congenial treatment as Jesus levels barbs at them. The intensity of these antagonistic barbs suggest witty Lukan constructions, which aim to de-legitimatize the Lukan Pharisees.[5]

There is little question that Luke reflects Hellenistic styles in the rendering of Jesus' discourses and anecdotes, and these styles are particularly evident in the symposia-type meal scenes (7:36–50; 11:37–54; and 14:1–24).[6] Dennis Smith has put forth a notable discussion comparing these meals with Hellenistic symposia.[7] He focuses particularly on table fellowship as a literary motif with special attention given to the following subthemes: table as symbol of status; table as a mode of teaching; meals as symbol of luxury; and table as symbol of service and community.[8] E. Springs Steele elaborates on the description of the symposium genre as a *genus litterarium* by discussing the key elements of a Hellenistic symposium: the *dramatis personae* (i.e., characters) and the structure (i.e., invitation, *fait divers*, discourse).[9] Steele details symposiac qualities in the exchanges between the host and the distinguished guest, especially noting the "wisdom, wit and perspicacity" of a distinguished guest's Socratic triumph over a host.[10] While Smith and Steele provide an extensive and favorable discussion on literary parallels between Hellenistic symposia and the Lukan Pharisaic meal scenes, neither of them explores the humorous elements of symposia and its relevance for the Lukan symposia.

---

5. For further discussion on de-legitimatizing effects of humor, see the following works: Gilhus, *Laughing Gods, Weeping Virgins*, 46–48; and Bednarz, "Humor-neutics," 71.

6. Johnson, *Gospel of Luke*, 3:3, 5–8, 12–14; and Smith, "Table Fellowship," 613–38.

7. For discussions on Luke and Hellenistic symposia as well as extensive bibliographical reference, see the following work: Smith, "Table Fellowship as a Literary Motif in the Gospel of Luke," 613–38. Other scholars who have discussed Luke's table fellowship and its relation to symposia include: X. de Meeûs, "Composition de Lc 14 et Genre Symposiaque," 847–70; and Steele, "Luke 11:37–54," 379–94.

8. Smith, "Table Fellowship," 616–17.

9. Steele, "Luke 11:37–54," 381. *Fait divers* refers to the catalyst that prompts the exchange between the distinguished guest and the targeted person.

10. Ibid.: 383.

Recollections of Symposia

Recollections of renowned dinner parties is a favorite topic of curiosity in Greek and Roman antiquity. We hear Timocrates ask Athenaeus in *Deipnophistae*, "Will you then share some of the fine talk you had over your cups with us?"[11] Athenaeus proceeds to describe an extensive dinner conversation held among famous attendees with particular attention given to food items and to the origins of words. His account of this renowned symposium depicts the dinner guests as quite curious about the symposia held by Persians, Egyptians, Arcadians, Celts, Thracians and many others.[12]

Accounts of symposia are often preceded by concerns for accuracy, although such accuracy is usually usurped by literary constructs. In Plato's *Symposium*, we hear Apollodorus respond to a request to provide an accurate and orderly report about a symposium that Socrates attended.[13] The Platonic account of this renowned symposium is a crafted composition that takes liberty in artistic expression.[14] Plutarch states that he seeks to give an accurate account of the symposium of the seven wise men that occurred at Delphi some centuries earlier.[15] He composes his literary and imaginative account of the dinner seemingly from a collection of sayings and proceeds to add four additional characters into his account of the dinner.[16] In the *Letter of Aristeas*, the concern for accuracy comes *immediately* at the conclusion of a series of symposia, even though Aristeas continues to write about other events.[17] Aristeas' work is arguably the work of Jewish apologetics, and therefore, consists of literary constructs as well.[18] Rather than precede or conclude his symposiac-meal accounts with a statement about accurate reporting, Luke precedes his whole gospel with a concern for accuracy (1:1–4). Strikingly, Luke's book consists of a series of table fellowships, which

---

11. Athenaeus *Deipn.* 3.9 (Olson, LCL).

12. Ibid., 4.128, 143–156; 5.193c-d.

13. Plato *Symp.* 172b, 174a.

14. Lamb discusses Plato's artistic composition. See Plato, *Lysis, Symposium, Gorgias*, trans. W. R. M. Lamb, LCL, 74–79.

15. Plutarch *Sept. sap. conv.* 2.146.

16. See Babbitt's introduction in Plutarch *Septem Sapientium Convivium* 346–47.

17. Shutt, "Letter of Aristeas," 2:32.

18. See the introduction in Shutt, "Letter of Aristeas," 2:10–11.

may be one explanation for the placing the words παρηκολουθηκότι ἄνωθεν πᾶσιν ἀκριβῶς—"having investigating everything accurately from the beginning" in the prologue of the gospel (1:3).[19] There is little doubt among scholars that Luke also employs literary constructs in his symposia accounts.[20]

On the Intermingling of Seriousness and Jesting

The intermingling of seriousness and jesting in Hellenistic symposia was a common practice with a long and rich tradition. Seriousness in solemn philosophical discussions surfaced with such topics as the administration of rulers, sycophants, squandered inheritance, love, justice, poverty, the expression of anger, hypocrisy, wealth, and the heavily favored topics of prudence and wisdom.[21] Jesting (sometimes called playfulness) was typically interspersed throughout serious discussions. Though it did not always consist of light-hearted bantering and witty applications of memorable verses from comic theater. Quite often jesting in symposia involved tendentious wit and barbed derision.

The intermingling of seriousness and jesting surfaces in several accounts of symposia. In Plato's *Symposium,* we find a number of instances of laughter, concerns about derision and facetiousness, amusement at the expense of others and allusions to comic humor. Through Plato's recollection of a dinner conversation, we hear various witty dicta interspersed within serious discourse. Of particular interest, Plato recalls how Agathon concluded his own speech by saying, "however I was able, I engaged playful jesting with a mix of seriousness."[22] Plato tells us that Agathon received a hearty applause from the dinner guests for this skill.[23] In *Deipnophistae,* Athenaeus recounts numerous exchanges

---

19. And quite like Athenaeus and Xenophon's report on symposia, which took place some 40–50 years previously, Luke's symposia accounts also take place some 40–50 years after the supposed events. Note: Luke does not state the concern for accuracy in his second volume, perhaps because it does not relate a series of symposia.

20. See discussion and bibliographic references, in Johnson, *The Gospel of Luke*, 3–26.

21. For examples of serious topics, see Plato *Symp.* 179a-b, 197b-e, 209a-b; Athenaeus *Deipn.* 3.74f–75a; 4.4.165–167; Xenophon *Symp.* 3.4–4.4; and *Letter of Aristeas* 187–294.

22. Plato *Symp.* 197e.

23. Ibid., 197e–198a.

of quick wit, humorous jesting, derisive wit, and sarcastic barbs. He records verbatim, albeit dubiously, the dinner attendees' creative weaving of hundreds of fragments of verses from both tragic and comic poets into their discourses. Nearly hundred and sixty years earlier, Xenophon in *Symposium* notes that it was commendable to reveal, not only the serious deeds of good and great persons, but also to relate how they engaged in amusement.[24] He provides a plethora of examples of the dinner attendees engaged in laughter, playfulness, and derision. Xenophon also notes quite explicitly that the dinner companions mixed raillery with seriousness.[25] In *Septem Sapientium Convivium*, Plutarch credits one of the wise philosophers (prob. Thales) with saying something in the vein of "a mindful person should not come to dinner to be filled up like a vessel; instead he should listen and speak . . . and be both serious and amusing."[26] These ancient Greek authors seem to agree on the intermingling of seriousness and jesting in symposia, but to what extent did they actually carry out raillery and other forms of derision? Did dinner guests really engage in biting, witty barbs that damaged the reputation and insulted the honor of their fellow dinner companions?

Literary Constructions of Symposium Humor

Literary constructions of symposia often include heavy-handed derision aimed at persons, who seem to be despised targets. These despised targets are generally hypocritical persons or persons whose character flaws typically expose them to ridicule (e.g., sycophants, flatterers, misers, etc.). Their inclusion in some symposia accounts may be explained as a sort of biased rhetorical device aimed at delegitimizing certain groups or persons.[27] Recollections of symposia, which depict extended bouts of mockery and scorn on despised targets, could hardly have happened in the way a Greek or Roman era author reconstructs it. The recipient of ridicule would not have taken the derisive barbs as lightly as the literary constructions of symposia often depict.

24. Xenophon *Symp.* 1.1.
25. Ibid., 4.28.
26. Plutarch *Sept. sap.conv.* 147f.
27. Desacralizing or delegitimatizing effects of humor requires a lengthy discussion beyond the bounds of this paper. See Gilhus, *Laughing Gods, Weeping Virgins*, 46–48; and Bednarz, "Humor-neutics," 71.

Athenaeus provides countless examples of humorous derision exchanged between dinner guests with particularly vicious barbs aimed at the Cynic, Cynulcus. In one such exchange, Ulpian directs a slur against the Cynics, telling them "to keep quiet, unless they want to gnaw on [bones in] which [case] they are welcome to enjoy their guise as dogs."[28] He then cites a line from Euripides' *Cretan Women,* saying "it is customary to throw the dinner leftovers to the dog (fr. 469)."[29] From there, he proceeds with a series of insults and an accusation that Cynics disrupt enjoyable conversations by their excessive drinking. Cynulcus has enough, and finally bites back with the epithet, "You glutton!"[30] He levels a host of ridicule upon Ulpian. Ulpian responds with a simple laugh and says, "Don't bark, my friend, or go wild and unleash your canine distemper . . . ! You should instead be fawning on your fellow guests, and wagging your tail at them to keep us from having a Dog-slaughter festival."[31] Athenaeus tells us that Cynulcus falls *silent* in response to Ulpian's relentless barrage of insults.[32] Aside from his silent response, we are not told how Cynulcus takes this abuse, but it is clear that he does not leave the banquet.[33] Later, we hear Cynulcus defend against derisions of lentil or bean soup (ridicule of bean soup encapsulated insults directed at Cynics). Twice, we are told, a burst of derisive laughter follows Cynulcus' praise of beans.[34] When one of the guests displays scornful disregard of his speech, Cynulcus reacts with barbed sarcasm.[35] Cynulcus then launches into a discourse on wealth, and gives humorous examples of how some greedy people ludicrously tried to take money with them when they died (e.g., one person swallowed gold coins and another sewed his money into his burial tunic).[36] Cynulcus, like the other dinner guests, cleverly weaves verses from comic and tragic plays

28. Athenaeus *Deipn.* 3.96–97 (Olson, LCL).

29. Ibid., 3.97a (Olson, LCL). This verse seems to be a popularized dictum. Its context in Athenaeus signals a riposte of barbed humor. A similar riposte is given by the Syrophoenician woman to the Markan Jesus (7:28) and by the Canaanite woman to the Matthean Jesus (Matt 15:27). Its use may signal a humorous barb.

30. Ibid., 3.97c.

31. Ibid., 3.99e (Olson, LCL).

32. Ibid., 3.100b.

33. Ibid., 4.156a.

34. Ibid., 4.157a-158d.

35. Ibid., 4.158d.

36. Ibid., 4.159a-b.

into his speech. He also includes an old Greek joke, "What do the Greeks use money for? They count it."[37] But with all of his efforts, he receives no applause and becomes quite *angry*.[38] It is remarkable that, in spite of the persistent barbs and the lack of congeniality, Cynulcus remains at the banquet, which suggests that his honor is either perpetually immune to the effects of shame, or else, we have a literary construct at work. It is reasonable that Cynulcus remains at the banquet so that Athenaeus may continue to make humor at his expense. In short, Cynulcus is probably a literary construct that Athenaeus uses to facilitate symposiac humor.

The modified symposium found in Luke 11:37–54 has the Lukan Jesus leveling a host of Ulpian-like derisive barbs, even a name-calling epithet, at the Lukan Pharisees. Most definitely, the Lukan Jesus insults his host and the other guests as well (11:45). He depicts them as fools, hypocrites, and unrighteous tyrants, and portrays them with despicable character flaws (11:39–44). The barbs are presented as pointed. They occur in rapid-fire succession, and are quite reminiscent of the tone of barbs aimed at the Cynic in Athenaeus' *Deipnophistae*. When one of the lawyers responds in a vocative voice, διδάσκαλε, ταῦτα λέγων καὶ ἡμᾶς ὑβρίζεις—"Teacher, saying these things, you insult us too" (11:45), the Lukan Jesus only thrusts out more barbs. These barbs can be characterized as intermittently tragic (vv. 42, 46, 47) and comic (vv. 43, 44, 48). Luke even has Jesus cite a tragic verse as a form of derisive barb—a common characteristic of symposia speeches.[39] Notably, the Lukan Pharisees and lawyers make no further riposte. They remain silent and fester in anger as the symposium concludes and Jesus departs. Their silence and anger is reminiscent of Cynulcus' response to the derisive barbs of Ulpian. We soon learn from Luke that the Pharisees are bitter in their antagonist exchanges with him. They ask him questions about all sorts of things, and plot how they might trap him in his speech (11:53–54).

---

37. Ibid., 4.159c.

38. Ibid., 4.159e.

39. This tragic dictum is from an unknown source. Διὰ τοῦτο καὶ ἡ σοφία τοῦ θεοῦ εἶπεν· ἀποστελῶ εἰς αὐτοὺς προφήτας καὶ ἀποστόλους, καὶ ἐξ αὐτῶν ἀποκτενοῦσιν καὶ διώξουσιν—"Therefore, the wisdom of God says, I will send them prophets and apostles to them, and some of them, they will kill and persecute" (Luke 11:49).

Humorous Barbs and Their Effects

While mockery and lighter forms of ridicule seem to be a customary practice in literary constructions of symposia, it is reasonable to doubt that harsh forms of ridicule were ever taken lightly. Simply put, the use of derisive barbs recounted in Greek symposia do not add up to the advice given by Greek philosophers and Roman rhetoricians, nor does it account for the dastardly effects of ridicule as recounted in Jewish literature (e.g., 2 Kgs 2:23–24; and Josephus *Ant.* 12.160–185).[40] Accounts of barbed ripostes quite often resulted in deadly serious matter whether they occurred in the assembly, court, theater or in symposia.

What follows are short excerpts from Greek and Roman works that admonish the inappropriate use of barbed wit and derision in symposia. In *De compotatione*, Dio Chrysostom denigrates those who give offense and insult other guests.[41] He praises the dinner guest, who does not quarrel so as to come to blows with others.[42] In *Lives*, Diogenes lists the following precepts of Chilon, "hold your tongue, especially in a symposium . . . do not let your tongue get ahead of your thoughts . . . hold your anger."[43] He also summons up Cleobulus' advice against laughing at those who are being ridiculed, and adds Cleobulus' admonition, "You will make them hostile toward you."[44] Plato writes that ill-natured jesting has its roots in anger.[45] He regards a lack of self-restraint, especially in matters regarding laughter and ridicule, as treacherous and foolish behavior.[46] While Aristotle writes in support of derision, he abhors its use, if it destroys a person's dignity or honor.[47] He views mockery as despicable when it serves only to agitate persons, and elicit violence from them.[48] Xenophon argues against the use of humor when it comes

---

40. For examples and discussions as well as biographical references on derision in Hebraic and early Jewish sources, see Bednarz, "Humor-neutics," 47–51, 59–72, 74–98.

41. Dio Chrysostom *Compot.* 27.3.

42. Ibid., 27.1–4; 30.33–36.

43. Diogenes Laertius *Lives* 1.69–70.

44. Ibid., 1.93.

45. Plato, *Leg.* 11.935. Grant, *The Ancient Rhetorical Theories of the Laughable*, 21–22.

46. Plato *Phileb.* 45d-e.

47. Aristotle *Poet.* 5.1449a.

48. Aristotle *Rhet.* 2.2.12.

at someone's expense.⁴⁹ Plutarch writes that ridiculing jests could sting like barbed arrows and cause hostility.⁵⁰

Roman rhetoricians also denounce derisive barbs in their treatises and letters. While Cicero himself had a reputation for the shrewd gibe and its shocking effect, he preferred its guarded application in defensive repartee.⁵¹ In *De oratore*, he cautions against the use of laughable invectives that insult.⁵² Friends, he says in *Orator*, should not be ridiculed with barbed wit.⁵³ Quintilian reiterates much of Cicero's views. He writes that a *ridiculum dictum* was often fallacious and mean-spirited.⁵⁴ For Quintilian, humorous wit held great potential to bring serious, if not deadly percussions.⁵⁵ He provides us with a memorable dictum: *a derisu non procul abest risus*—"laughter is not far from derision."⁵⁶

In *Antiquities*, Josephus, a Jewish historian, narrates several folkloric accounts in which laughter and derision produced dastardly effects. One of those accounts unfolds as follows. Powerful officials from Syria and Phoenicia had come to Alexandria to bid on taxes.⁵⁷ When Joseph, the high priest's nephew and an official from Jerusalem, arrived in the streets of Alexandria, they saw him and began to mock his simple and plain appearance. We are told by Josephus that Joseph went on to Memphis in search of Ptolemy. He found Ptolemy sitting beside his wife and Athenion in a chariot. Athenion, who had been befriended by Joseph while he was in Jerusalem, recognized Joseph on the road and sang his praises to Ptolemy. Ptolemy invited Joseph into his chariot and proceeded to complain about Onias, the high priest in Jerusalem and Joseph's miserly uncle. Joseph told Ptolemy how dimwitted his uncle was. He explained that Onias, like all old people, had lost his ability to reason. He assured Ptolemy that as a young person, he would fulfill Ptolemy's every request. Ptolemy laughed at Joseph's explanation for

---

49. Xenophon *Cyr.* 2.2.12–14. See Grant, *The Ancient Rhetorical Theories of the Laughable*, 23.

50. Plutarch *Quaest. conv.* 2.1.4.631.

51. Cicero *De or.* 2.58, 236.

52. Ibid., 2.60.244–245.

53. Cicero, *Or.* 89.

54. Quintilian, *Inst.* 6.3.6.

55. Ibid., 6.3.34.

56. Ibid., 6.3.7 (Russell, LCL).

57. Josephus *Ant.* 12.168–83.

Onias' miserly behavior. Now the officials from Syria happened upon the scene and were quiet unsettled by what they saw. Ptolemy was laughing with Joseph beside him in the chariot! When the day arrived for the bidding on taxes, Joseph outwitted the officials of Syria and Phoenicia. He also succeeded in securing from Ptolemy a small army. With his army, Joseph set out for Syria and Phoenicia![58]

Whether derisive humor occurs during symposia or in the streets, its effects could be quite serious. The deadly effects of humor certainly bring to mind the Neronian-ordered suicides of the satirists, Petronicus and Seneca.[59] It begs the question, would barbed wit or derision be taken as lightly as symposia accounts depict? Would contemptuous ripostes be brushed off in a quick fit of relatively controlled anger as in the case of Athenaeus' Cynulcus? Or would derisive barbs in symposia spill out into the streets as it seems to have done with the Lukan Jesus (11:53–54)?

Despised Dinner Guests

One construct of symposia needs further explanation—the construct of the despised dinner guest. In Plutarch's *Septem Sapientium Convivium*, we find an expressed aversion to guests who annoy and insult other guests.[60] Violent, difficult and overbearing, unmanageable and unpleasant guests, Thales claims, destroy the joy of a dinner party.[61] Such persons cause injury or inflicts indignities upon other guests.[62] He adds that some persons spoil a pleasant dinner by harboring resentment "like the dregs left in a wine vessel when someone insulted them or when someone got in a fit of anger brought about by [too much] wine."[63] We are told that Chilon even refuses to attend a dinner unless he knew the names of the other guests.[64] For Chilon, common sense dictated that one would not show up to dinner without knowing who one's dinner

---

58. Josephus *Ant.* 12.168–83.

59. See Plaza, *The Function of Humour in Roman Verse Satire*, 2; and Bednarz, "Humor-neutics," 92.

60. Plutarch *Sept. sap.conv.* 147f–148a.

61. Ibid., 147–148.

62. Ibid.

63. Ibid., 148a.

64. Ibid.

companions might be.⁶⁵ The despised dinner guest was enough to keep Chilon, perhaps others, from attending a symposium.

The Despised Guest in the Lukan Symposia

It is rather curious that the Lukan Jesus seems to fall into the category of the despised dinner guest. Luke presents three modified symposia, in which the Pharisees are repeatedly the recipients of Jesus' abusive and witty barbs (7:36–50; 11:37–54; and 14:1–24). Luke depicts the Pharisees as persistently placing themselves in situations where they will incur this abuse. In each case, they actually invite Jesus. This is somewhat tendentiously comic, in that, Luke constructs the Pharisees as less than wise regarding this matter. In spite of the Lukan Jesus' barbs, they keep inviting him to eat with them!

In Luke 7:36–50, the motif of the despised dinner guest surfaces after the *fait divers*, in which Simon (supposedly, but not conclusively, the host and a Pharisee) engages in *soliloquy* (a known comic device).⁶⁶ In short, Simon derides Jesus' status as a prophet (7:39). The Lukan Jesus responds by first telling Simon a parable about two debtors, and then poses a question to him (7:41–42). Simon's answer is correct (v. 43), and therefore, the question seems harmless. However, the Lukan Jesus' subsequent barbs directly mar Simon's reputation as a host (7:44–46). His final barb delivers a exceptional sting, ᾧ δὲ ὀλίγον ἀφίεται, ὀλίγον ἀγαπᾷ—"but the one whom is being forgiven little, loves little" (7:47). The Lukan Jesus seems to play the role of the despised dinner guest, but the lack of response from Simon suggests a Cynulcus-like silence. Simon's silence as well as his scornful soliloquy and failure to be a good host (14:44–46) align him with the barb being made in 7:47. In effect, Luke has subverted and constructed Simon, the Lukan Pharisee, as the despised one.

The modified symposia in Luke 11:37–54 carries the motif of the despised dinner guest to the utmost extreme. Here, the most dastardly barbs of the Lukan symposia surface. The *fait divers* surfaces when the

---

65. Ibid.

66. Steele discusses the *fait divers* of 7:36–50 as well as the Socratic questioning of Simon. See Steele, "Luke 11:37–54," 381, 83–84, 86–87. For discussion on soliloquy, see Sellew, "Interior Monologue," 239–53, Booth, *The Rhetoric of Fiction*; and Beavis, "Parable and Fable," 473–98.

Pharisee, the host, expresses *shock* (another comic device) that Jesus has not washed before eating.⁶⁷ The reaction of the Lukan Pharisee triggers a succession of barbs from the Lukan Jesus (11:39–44, 46–52). Luke, once again, silences the Pharisees, and we are told that they become infuriated. Again, the Lukan Jesus becomes the despised dinner guest, and yet again, Luke subverts and constructs the Pharisees and lawyers as despised tricksters, who harbor their hostile grudges and who lie in wait to entrap Jesus (11:53–54).

In the symposium of 14:1–24, the *fait divers* is the man with dropsy, who suddenly, and perhaps somewhat suspiciously, appears as if he is a purposely placed snare. We are told that Socratic questioning follows as the Lukan Jesus lays his own trap before the lawyers and the Pharisees. He asks them, ἔξεστιν τῷ σαββάτῳ θεραπεῦσαι ἢ οὔ—"Is it permitted to heal on the Sabbath or not?" (14:3). The lawyers and the Pharisees respond with silence (14:6). The Lukan Jesus heals the person (implying there was a correct answer to his question). He proceeds to ask a second question, τίνος ὑμῶν υἱὸς ἢ βοῦς εἰς φρέαρ πεσεῖται, καὶ οὐκ εὐθέως ἀνασπάσει αὐτὸν ἐν ἡμέρᾳ τοῦ σαββάτου—"If one of you has a son or an ox that should happen to fall into a well, would you not immediately draw him out on a Sabbath day (14:5)?" This time Luke stresses, not only silence of the lawyers and Pharisees, but their *inability* to answer (14:6). Once more the Lukan Jesus becomes the despised dinner guest as he makes the wise lawyers and the Pharisees appear ridiculous. And yet again, Luke depicts the lawyers and Pharisees as despised tricksters, whose attempts to *scrutinize* Jesus recoils back upon them.

Jesus' ripostes in each of the three Lukan symposia make him appear as the despised symposiac guest, yet this Lukan construct serves a comic function. When the Lukan Pharisees, in particular, invite the Lukan Jesus to their symposia, they become in the view of Chilon, οὐ νοῦν ἔχοντος ἀνδρός ἐστιν—"a person who possesses no sense."⁶⁸ They repeatedly subject themselves to the scorn and the ridicule of the Lukan Jesus' wit and perspicacity. Their lack of sense makes them appear somewhat comic, foolish, and absurd. Luke persistently subverts their honorable positions at symposia and constructs them as the woefully despised ones! This is Luke's tendentious symposiac humor at work and it is certainly unsettling for modern sensibilities!

67. Steele, "Luke 11:37–54," 389.
68. Plutarch *Sept. sap.conv.* 148a.

Symposiac Humor in Luke 14:1–24

What follows is a further elaboration on the symposiac humor of Luke 14:1–24. We have already seen the tendentious comic effect of the *despised dinner guest* on the lawyers and the Pharisees (14:2–6). Yet, the *despised dinner guest* motif and the degradation of the lawyers and Pharisees is only part of the symposiac humor of Luke 14:1–24. Several other aspects of symposiac humor surface. First, there is the presence of dreaded dinner companions, who hold a hostile grudge against the Lukan Jesus. Second, the Lukan Jesus, himself, stands out as the despised guest, whose exchanges with the dinner attendees involve clever Socratic-type questions, unsettling anecdotic ripostes, and derision. Third, comic elements such as ludicrous choices, sudden reversals of status, surprise, shock, an outburst, and disconcerting dicta are intermingled with serious discourse on Sabbath healing, symposiac customs (such as status recognition at banquets) and patron obligations to the poor.

> 14:1 Καὶ ἐγένετο ἐν τῷ ἐλθεῖν αὐτὸν εἰς οἶκόν τινος τῶν ἀρχόντων τῶν Φαρισαίων σαββάτῳ φαγεῖν ἄρτον καὶ αὐτοὶ ἦσαν παρατηρούμενοι αὐτόν.

The presence of the dreaded dinner companions is made known to us at the beginning of the symposium account (14:1–24). We are quickly told that the Lukan Pharisees are scrutinizing Jesus very closely (14:1). We have already been alerted that the Lukan Pharisees bear a grudge against him, a grudge that reverts back to an earlier Lukan symposium (11:53–54). And so, their observation of him here connotes hostility (11:53–54). Because of their animosity, the Pharisees (and the lawyers) have become the dreaded dinner companions that would have had the wise Chilon, himself, avoiding the dinner. Furthermore, this is the third Pharisaic invitation, that has been extended to the Lukan Jesus. Their prudence in extending yet another invitation to this despised dinner guest depicts them as lacking in sense. They have exposed themselves to further symposiac ridicule, thus demonstrating what Chilon calls οὐ νοῦν ἔχοντος ἀνδρός ἐστιν—"[one] who possesses no sense."[69]

> 14:2 Καὶ ἰδοὺ ἄνθρωπός τις ἦν ὑδρωπικὸς ἔμπροσθεν αὐτοῦ. 3 καὶ ἀποκριθεὶς ὁ Ἰησοῦς εἶπεν πρὸς τοὺς νομικοὺς καὶ Φαρισαίους λέγων ἔξεστιν τῷ σαββάτῳ θεραπεῦσαι ἢ οὔ; 4 οἱ δὲ ἡσύχασαν . . .

---

69. Plutarch *Sept. sap.conv.* 148a.

I have already explained the tendentious humor of the Socratic questions in this first exchange of the symposium (see above), but other types of symposiac humor are present here. When Luke presents the *fait divers*, a person with dropsy, there is a curious exclamation (14:2). The interjection ἰδού serves as a cue of humor in the comic plays of Aristophanes.[70] The sudden and unexpected appearance of the person with dropsy seems to signal a comic surprise, perhaps an act of trickery as well. As I noted above, it seems the person with dropsy is a purposely placed snare. Luke displays Jesus' perspicacity in responding to this act of trickery. The Lukan Jesus poses a Socratic question in such a way that he effectively silences the Lukan Pharisees and the lawyers. Their silent response, reminiscent of Cynulcus, signals that they have been out-maneuvered (14:4).

> 14:4 . . . καὶ ἐπιλαβόμενος ἰάσατο αὐτὸν καὶ ἀπέλυσεν. 5 καὶ πρὸς αὐτοὺς εἶπεν·τίνος ὑμῶν υἱὸς ἢ βοῦς εἰς φρέαρ πεσεῖται, καὶ οὐκ εὐθέως ἀνασπάσει αὐτὸν ἐν ἡμέρᾳ τοῦ σαββάτου; 6 καὶ οὐκ ἴσχυσαν ἀνταποκριθῆναι πρὸς ταῦτα . . .

The Lukan Jesus asks yet another question, which offers the ludicrous choice of pulling a son or ox to safety or leaving either one in a well for the duration of the Sabbath (14:5). The choice is comic, in that the correct answer is obvious to the Lukan audience, but we are told that the Lukan Pharisees and lawyers are, yet again, *unable* to answer (14:6). Their silent response, again signals that they have been outwitted.

> 7 Ἔλεγεν δὲ πρὸς τοὺς κεκλημένους παραβολήν, ἐπέχων πῶς τὰς πρωτοκλισίας ἐξελέγοντο, λέγων πρὸς αὐτούς·8 ὅταν κληθῇς ὑπό τινος εἰς γάμους, μὴ κατακλιθῇς εἰς τὴν πρωτοκλισίαν, μήποτε ἐντιμότερός σου ᾖ κεκλημένος ὑπ' αὐτοῦ, 9 καὶ ἐλθὼν ὁ σὲ καὶ αὐτὸν καλέσας ἐρεῖ σοι·δὸς τούτῳ τόπον, καὶ τότε ἄρξῃ μετὰ αἰσχύνης τὸν ἔσχατον τόπον κατέχειν.10 ἀλλ' ὅταν κληθῇς, πορευθεὶς ἀνάπεσε εἰς τὸν ἔσχατον τόπον, ἵνα ὅταν ἔλθῃ ὁ κεκληκώς σε ἐρεῖ σοι· φίλε, προσανάβηθι ἀνώτερον· τότε ἔσται σοι δόξα ἐνώπιον πάντων τῶν συνανακειμένων σοι. 11 ὅτι πᾶς ὁ ὑψῶν ἑαυτὸν ταπεινωθήσεται, καὶ ὁ ταπεινῶν ἑαυτὸν ὑψωθήσεται.

Next, we are told that the Lukan Jesus has noticed how the guests have their chosen places at the table (14:7). He proceeds to tell a parable that essentially exposes their lack of common sense (14:8–10), and

---

70. See Aristophanes *Eccl.* 136; *Eq.* 87, 157, 344; *Thesm.* 206; *Ach.* 366; and *Nub.* 825.

he concludes the parable with a somewhat disturbing didactic dictum (14:11).[71] In a similar account, Plutarch tells how Thales and his companions had just arrived at the dining hall, when they see Alexidemus stomping out in a fit of anger, talking to himself. Upon looking up and seeing Thales, Alexidemus ceases mumbling and exclaims to Thales, "What an insult!"[72] Alexidemus grumbles on, "[Periander] begged me to stay for dinner and then he assigned me to a *shameful couch*..."[73] Thales responds, "as the Egyptians say, the stars go higher (ὑψώματα) and lower (ταπεινώματα) in their place [so] that as they move they become better or worse. Is this so with you? Do you fear that you will become darkened (ἀμαύρωσις) or humiliated (ταπείνωσις) because of your place?"[74] Thales engages in delightful wordplay. He usurps an Egyptian maxim and turns it into a dictum with which to insult Alexidemus. Thales tells him that he will be viewed with contempt. He insinuates rather strongly that Alexidemus could have made it a place of honor, but instead of befriending his fellow table mates, he has stirred enmity.[75] Then Thales utters the unsettling dictum, "For indeed the one who displays scorn for his reclining place at the table, scorns the ones reclining with him, rather than the host. And he incurs the hatred of both."[76] Alexidemus rebuffs Thales' dictum with a barb, "Your words mean nothing... I see [how] you wise ones seek hard after honor!"[77] Alexidemus departs in agitation while Thales responds with shock at Alexidemus' absurdity.

---

71. Jónsson notes that the seating of guests at a feast has produced both tragic and comic scenes. He also recounts a rabbinic source in which Simon ben Azzai advises invited guests to take their places two or three seats farther down from where they think they should be, because it would be better to be told to move up rather than down (*Aboth de Rabbi Natan* 25, Strack & Billerbeck, 1:916). See Jónsson, *Humour and Irony in the New Testament*, 113.

72. Plutarch *Sept. sap.conv.* 148e. Smith discusses Thales' dictum in conjunction with Luke 14:7–11, but he does so from the philosophical perspective of ethics and friendship. See Smith, "Table Fellowship," 617–20. Steele also discusses Thales' response to Alexidemus with an emphasis on Thales' wisdom and compares this to the wisdom of Jesus in Luke 14:7–11. See Steele, "Luke 11:37–54," 384–85.

73. Plutarch *Sept. sap.conv.* 148–149.

74. Ibid., 149a. The reference to "darken (lit. blacken)" is a euphemism that connotes one's honor has been damaged or insulted.

75. Ibid., 149b.

76. Ibid.

77. Ibid.

He replies to his companions that Alexidemus is a senseless and hostile person.[78]

The similarity between the Lukan Jesus' parable with its disturbing didactic dictum (14:8–11) and Thales' exchange with Alexidemus is striking.[79] Noticeably, Plutarch conveys more explicit humor than Luke does. Plutarch recounts an assortment of comic typologies: Alexidemus' incoherent mumbling, Thales' barbed and belittling riposte, the delightful wordplay in Thales' riposte, and Alexidemus' agitated retort and departure. The Lukan parable only insinuates the comic in its element of surprise reversal (i.e., the guest must give up his seat and move to a lower place, vice versa). The Lukan Jesus' dictum, πᾶς ὁ ὑψῶν ἑαυτὸν ταπεινωθήσεται, καὶ ὁ ταπεινῶν ἑαυτὸν ὑψωθήσεται (14:11), is again similar to Thales' dictum, but it is not followed by the barbed Thaleslike insults. The Lukan audience, instead must supply the comic in the awkward, unsettling effect of dictum. They must imagine the sudden discomfort of those persons who had already chosen the seats of honor. Recognition of such an awkward situation might well have prompted at least some kind of pleasure from the hearers of the account. The *reversal of status* dictum also appears in 18:14 in the decisively comic parable of self-righteous Pharisee and the humble tax collector, which suggests that it may have been associated with comic anecdotes of unexpected and sudden reversals.

> 12 Ἔλεγεν δὲ καὶ τῷ κεκληκότι αὐτόν· ὅταν ποιῇς ἄριστον ἢ δεῖπνον, μὴ φώνει τοὺς φίλους σου μηδὲ τοὺς ἀδελφούς σου μηδὲ τοὺς συγγενεῖς σου μηδὲ γείτονας πλουσίους, μήποτε καὶ αὐτοὶ ἀντικαλέσωσίν σε καὶ γένηται ἀνταπόδομά σοι. 13 ἀλλ' ὅταν δοχὴν ποιῇς, κάλει πτωχούς, ἀναπείρους, χωλούς, τυφλούς· 14 καὶ μακάριος ἔσῃ, ὅτι οὐκ ἔχουσιν ἀνταποδοῦναί σοι, ἀνταποδοθήσεται γάρ σοι ἐν τῇ ἀναστάσει τῶν δικαίων. 15 Ἀκούσας δέ τις τῶν συνανακειμένων ταῦτα εἶπεν αὐτῷ· μακάριος ὅστις φάγεται ἄρτον ἐν τῇ βασιλείᾳ τοῦ θεοῦ.

Next the Lukan Jesus tells the Pharisee, a presumably well-to-do host, that he should invite the undesirables, the expendables and those of low status to his banquet. Sheer folly! Then we hear the sudden eruption of one of the guests, who says aloud, μακάριος ὅστις φάγεται ἄρτον ἐν τῇ βασιλείᾳ τοῦ θεοῦ—"Happy is anyone who will eat bread in the

---

78. Ibid.
79. Ibid., 148e–149a. See Steele, "Luke 11:37–54," 384–85.

Kingdom of G-d!" (14:15). This outburst in a symposiac setting would likely have drawn laughter or some kind of comic relief. One wonders if this is a sarcastic riposte to the Lukan Jesus' absurd dismissal of symposiac custom (i.e., inviting only one's friends to a symposium). The following parable of 14:16–24 suggests that it could be understood in this light.

> 16 Ὁ δὲ εἶπεν αὐτῷ· ἄνθρωπός τις ἐποίει δεῖπνον μέγα, καὶ ἐκάλεσεν πολλοὺς 17 καὶ ἀπέστειλεν τὸν δοῦλον αὐτοῦ τῇ ὥρᾳ τοῦ δείπνου εἰπεῖν τοῖς κεκλημένοις· ἔρχεσθε, ὅτι ἤδη ἕτοιμά ἐστιν. 18 καὶ ἤρξαντο ἀπὸ μιᾶς πάντες παραιτεῖσθαι. ὁ πρῶτος εἶπεν αὐτῷ· ἀγρὸν ἠγόρασα καὶ ἔχω ἀνάγκην ἐξελθὼν ἰδεῖν αὐτόν· ἐρωτῶ σε, ἔχε με παρῃτημένον. 19 καὶ ἕτερος εἶπεν· ζεύγη βοῶν ἠγόρασα πέντε καὶ πορεύομαι δοκιμάσαι αὐτά· ἐρωτῶ σε, ἔχε με παρῃτημένον. 20 καὶ ἕτερος εἶπεν, γυναῖκα ἔγημα καὶ διὰ τοῦτο οὐ δύναμαι ἐλθεῖν. 21 καὶ παραγενόμενος ὁ δοῦλος ἀπήγγειλεν τῷ κυρίῳ αὐτοῦ ταῦτα. τότε ὀργισθεὶς ὁ οἰκοδεσπότης εἶπεν τῷ δούλῳ αὐτοῦ· ἔξελθε ταχέως εἰς τὰς πλατείας καὶ ῥύμας τῆς πόλεως καὶ τοὺς πτωχοὺς καὶ ἀναπείρους καὶ τυφλοὺς καὶ χωλοὺς εἰσάγαγε ὧδε. 22 καὶ εἶπεν ὁ δοῦλος· κύριε, γέγονεν ὃ ἐπέταξας, καὶ ἔτι τόπος ἐστίν. 23 καὶ εἶπεν ὁ κύριος πρὸς τὸν δοῦλον· ἔξελθε εἰς τὰς ὁδοὺς καὶ φραγμοὺς καὶ ἀνάγκασον εἰσελθεῖν, ἵνα γεμισθῇ μου ὁ οἶκος. 24 λέγω γὰρ ὑμῖν ὅτι οὐδεὶς τῶν ἀνδρῶν ἐκείνων τῶν κεκλημένων γεύσεταί μου τοῦ δείπνου.

Next we are told that the Lukan Jesus *turns toward* the one who made the comic outburst and he proceeds to tells him the parable of a great dinner (14:16–24).[80] Note that the word, δεῖπνον in the parable is often used in conjunction with symposia. As the Lukan Jesus unfolds the story, it is clear that the invited guests have already accepted their invitations to dinner (14:17). Yet, they wait until after the preparation of food before they decline to come. At such a late hour, their excuses are ludicrous (14:18–19) and even comical (14:20).[81] Then the Lukan Jesus concludes the parable with a portentous and unsettling rebuke, λέγω γὰρ ὑμῖν ὅτι οὐδεὶς τῶν ἀνδρῶν ἐκείνων τῶν κεκλημένων γεύσεταί μου τοῦ δείπνου—"For I tell you, none of those who were invited will taste

---

80. For a discussion on the absurd excuses of the invitees, see Gary Webster, *Laughter in the Bible* (St. Louis: Bethany Press, 1960), 33, 115. For rabbinic discussions on similar anecdotes of invitations and feasts and their comic elements, see Jónsson, *Humour and Irony in the New Testament*, 131–33.

81. For a discussion on the humor of the Lukan Jesus in 14:21, see Longenecker, "A Humorous Jesus?" 179–204.

my dinner" (14:24). Here Luke abruptly ends the symposium. There is no riposte from the Pharisees, lawyers or any of the other guests—only Cynulcus-like silence.

Conclusion

Throughout the Lukan symposium of 14:1–24, we see an intermingling of seriousness and humor, which is characteristic of Hellenistic symposia. First, the Lukan Jesus outwits the Pharisees and lawyers with Socratic questions on the serious topics of healing and the Sabbath law. Then the silence of the Pharisees and lawyers gives way to an anecdote about the comic humor (horror) of being asked to give up one's honorable seat at a banquet. Then the Lukan Jesus' didactic dismissal of a symposiac custom (i.e., inviting only one's friends to a symposium) gives way to an exuberant (or sarcastic) outburst, which in turn gives way to the serious parable of a great symposium. The parable, itself, comprises an angry master, offensive friends (who say yes to an invitation and then refuse to come), ludicrous excuses, and the comic relief of a last minute wedding. The Lukan Jesus concludes the parable with an unsettling and shocking rebuke. Then symposium ends, as usual, with the silence of the Lukan Pharisees.

Bibliography

Beavis, Mary Ann. "Parable and Fable." *CBQ* 52 (1990) 473–98.
Bednarz, Terri. "Humor-Neutics: Analyzing Humor and Humor Functions in the Synoptic Gospels." PhD diss., Brite Divinity School, 2009.
Booth, Wayne C. *The Rhetoric of Fiction*. Chicago: University of Chicago, 1983.
Gilhus, Ingvild S. *Laughing Gods, Weeping Virgins: Laughter in the History of Religion*. London: Routledge, 1997.
Grant, Mary A. *The Ancient Rhetorical Theories of the Laughable: The Greek Rhetoricians and Cicero*. Madison: University of Wisconsin, 1924.
Johnson, Luke Timothy. *The Gospel of Luke*. SacPag 3. Collegeville, MN: Liturgical, 1991.
Jónsson, Jakob. *Humour and Irony in the New Testament: Illuminated by Parallels in Talmud and Midrash*. Leiden: Brill, 1985.
Longenecker, Bruce W. "A Humorous Jesus? Orality, Structure and Characterisation in Luke 14:15–24, and Beyond." *BibInt* 16 (2008) 179–204.
Meeûs, X. de. «Composition de Lc 14 et Genre Symposiaque.» *Ephemerides Theologicae Lovanienses* 37 (1961) 847–70.
Plato. *Lysis, Symposium, Gorgias*. Translated by W. R. M. Lamb. LCL. Cambridge: Harvard University Press, 1925.
Plaza, Maria. *The Function of Humour in Roman Verse Satire: Laughing and Lying*. Oxford: Oxford University Press, 2006.
Sellew, Philip. "Interior Monologue as a Narrative Device in the Parables of Luke." *Journal of Biblical Literature* 111 (1992) 239–53.
Shutt, R. J. H. "Letter of Aristeas." In *The Old Testament Pseudepigrapha*, edited by James H. Charlesworth, 12–34. New York: Doubleday, 1985.
Smith, Dennis. "Table Fellowship as a Literary Motif in the Gospel of Luke." *JBL* 106 (1987) 613–38.
Steele, E. Springs. "Luke 11:37–54: A Modified Hellenistic Symposium?" *JBL* 103 (1984) 379–94.
Webster, Gary. *Laughter in the Bible*. St. Louis: Bethany, 1960.

The Women Householders of Acts in Light of Recent Research on Families

Margaret Y. MacDonald

WITH THIS ESSAY, I CELEBRATE THE WORK OF CAROLYN OSIEK ON TWO overlapping topics where she has taught me a great deal: early church women and early Christian families. Since the publication of *A Woman's Place: Early Christian House Churches*, I have continued to ask questions about whether the now substantial work on early Christian families really makes a difference to the breadth and interpretation of our evidence concerning early Christian women. Here I will concentrate specifically on Acts, a New Testament work that has been the subject of intense analysis and debate with respect to its presentation of women.[1] The question that will guide my analysis is the following: Does recent scholarship on early Christian families and house churches challenge any common assumptions and conclusions about the women of Acts that have emerged especially from feminist analysis? In other words, does approaching the women of Acts with a focus on families and house churches simply confirm what we are already know or does it expand or complicate our vision?

Evidence for the lives of women in Acts is rich and varied, including evidence for women prophets, house-church leaders, widows, female slaves, wives, and virgins. All of the women are, in one way or another,

---

1. This essay is a revised version of a paper delivered in the Acts Section of the Society of Biblical Literature in November 2008. Carolyn Osiek and I were both invited to offer papers on Acts, families, and house churches. I am grateful to both Halvor Moxnes and Andrew D. Clarke for their responses. I am also grateful to the Social Sciences and Humanities Research Council of Canada for supporting my research leading to this essay.

connected to families and more often than not this is a crucial part of their identity in Acts. For none is this truer than the women leaders of households and/or house churches; Lydia, the mother of John Mark, and Prisc(ill)a (whose house-church leadership is exercised in conjunction with that of her husband), along with the women either directly associated with them (Rhoda, in the case of the mother of John Mark) or somehow connected to them by means of a textual commonality (the mantic slave girl in the case of Lydia), will be the main subject of this essay. It will be argued that the narratives concerning these three women are shaped by the author's idealized vision of household and community, but that this vision has a complicated and tangential relationship to the experience of women in the believing communities. One also detects a certain level of ambivalence in the author's presentation as there are features of the lives of the women that are on the margins of the author's idealized patterns and elements of their stories that do not seem to fit at all.

Women Leaders and Household Conversions

It has frequently been recognized that Acts—probably for apologetic purposes—seeks to link the rise of Christianity with familial institutions, including the influence of household heads, both male and female. Beginning with the story of Cornelius, Acts has four accounts of the conversion of a head-of-the-household, followed by the remainder of the household (Acts 10:1–11:18; cf. Acts 16:11–15; 16:25–34; 18:1–11). There is even a typical *oikos* formula, "and/with [all] his or her household," seemingly recalling the mission of evangelizing households given to the Seventy-Two in Luke 10:5–7, as noted by David Lertis Matson in his study of household conversions in Acts.[2] Roger Gehring reads the Acts conversion accounts as offering important confirmation of the recruitment of householders as an important Pauline missionary strategy.[3] Indeed, there is some corroborating evidence from Paul's letters, notably the reference to Paul baptizing the household of Stephanas in 1 Cor 1:16 (cf. 1 Cor 16:15), but it is remarkably scant. Outside of Acts, references to whole families turning their allegiance to early church groups are rare. Although there must have been cases where whole

2. See Matson, *Household Conversion Narratives in Acts*, 87–88.
3. Gehring, *House Church and Mission*, 185–87.

families turned to the Lord—especially given the traditional role of the *paterfamilias*—there is quite a lot of early evidence to suggest that more individualized conversion, including among women and slaves, was also prevalent (1 Cor 7:12–16; 1 Pet 3:1; 1 Tim 6:1–2).

Even the variety of pairings and individual women named in the Pauline corpus suggest that membership did not predictably follow the idealized "baptism of the whole family" model. There are many references which seem to imply that women such as Phoebe, or Euodia and Syntyche, have at least no believing husband or male authority in the house. Very often women who are presented as offering services to the church or acting independently have been understood to be widows and we do know that women, especially widows, did manage households for themselves in the Roman world. Nympha (Col 4:15), who hosts an *ekklēsia* in her house, is often understood to be a widow since it is difficult to imagine a woman hosting a house church with a believing husband in residence—but then her husband might frequently have been away, leaving her to manage the house; the ability to manage the affairs of the household while the husband was out of town was considered a wifely virtue, as Plutarch's *A Consolation to his Wife* demonstrates.[4] We should perhaps be more open than we often have been to understanding texts which describe independent women as referring to women living in a variety of circumstances, including with absentee and/or non-believing partners.

I would read the references to the conversion of householders in Acts in much the same way as I would read the harmonious image of believing families projected by the New Testament household codes— with one large grain of salt! While at face value the household codes appear to address the community in a manner assuming that all listeners will find their place within the categories, it is highly likely that some community members were living lives that departed from the ideal in significant ways. The instructions subsume groups without breaking down categories or considering overlapping categories such as parent and slave, or child and slave. Despite the fact that New Testament scholars continue to take the harmonious Christian image presented by the codes quite literally,[5] it is evident, especially in the case of Colossians,

---

4. See Osiek and MacDonald with Tulloch, *A Woman's Place*, 79. See Pomeroy, *Plutarch's Advice*.

5. In his 1998 commentary on Ephesians, for example, Ernst Best argued that the codes of Colossians and Ephesians "have in mind wholly Christian households." See

that the codes do not state that members belonging to the various pairs of relationships are all Christians.⁶ The question of whether the author viewed believers in familial relationships with nonbelievers as part of the audience needs to at least be left open.⁷ It is important to realize that the household code genre represents highly idealized familial ethics and simply does not tell the whole historical truth. The classical ideology of the subordinate household fully obedient to its head needs to be interrogated on the basis of a range of early Christian evidence and other comparative evidence from the ancient world concerning allegiance to religious groups and various voluntary associations.

Most importantly for this essay, the Acts accounts of the conversion of householders followed by the whole house might well have been shaped by a desire to paint early Christian groups as compatible with imperial family ideals. More obviously even than in the case of the household codes, when read in relation to new research on families in the Roman world, the descriptions of the conversion of the household heads lead us to confront the idealized and political dimensions of texts. Already a focus on women can help us to see the possible fictional dimensions of texts and their rhetorical strategies, but a focus on families sometimes brings this into sharper relief.

Lydia in Feminist Analysis

Concentrating especially on the figure of Lydia and the conversion of her household, scholars of Acts have examined the presentation of women within the broader framework of Luke's narrative structure. Shelley Matthews, for example, has explored parallels between Luke's narrative, Euripides' *Bacchae*, and Josephus' description of the conver-

---

Best, *Ephesians*, 524; see also Lincoln, *Ephesians*, 403.

6. With respect to Colossians, Jean-Noël Aletti has argued that the author of Colossians does not make the Christian allegiance of both partners explicit. See Aletti, *Colossiens*, 250: "Par exemple, il ne dit pas aux hommes: 'maries, aimez vos femmes car elles sont vos sœurs en Christ', 'maîtres, traitez vos esclaves avec justice, car se sont vos fréres en Christ à la suite de Col 3, 11.'"

7. The highly developed use of the marriage metaphor to speak of the relationship between Christ and the church reinforces the image of the Christian household in the Ephesians household code. But here I would agree with Turid Karlsen Seim that even the Ephesians code may well have spoken to women and slaves who were subject to non-believing heads of the household. See Seim, "A Superior Minority," 167–81.

sion of the royal house of Adiabene, including its women (*Ant.* 20.34–48). She highlights the ancient motif of the involvement of elite women in the initial reception of religions (while noting at the same time the ultimately, "marginal nature" of their contributions in what involves "the resolution of conflict between the male worthies of a locality and the male missionary/god").[8] Matthews responds to other feminist scholars, including the liberationist readings of Ivoni Richter Reimer and Luise Shottroff, who argue that Lydia is a woman of humble means involved in the manufacture of dye rather than only in its more lucrative trade, and that Lydia calls together a community which functions as a type of "contrast society" within the broader social order.[9]

While it is not possible to solve the issue of Lydia's status here, comparison of the different scholarly depictions of her identity offers a very interesting study into the variety of feminist readings of Acts and of the tension between historical and literary/rhetorical readings. Many scholars now view Lydia as a fictional character, while at the same time admitting, as does Matthews, that the author of Acts may well have known women like her.[10] For Dennis MacDonald, the parallels between Acts 16 and Euripides' *Bacchae* are so extensive that he feels confident that Lydia never existed. He warns feminist biblical interpreters not to "... lament the migration of women in this story from history to fiction," for it is important to recognize the symbolic significance of "Maenads in a Christian mode." He states: "Many Greeks and Romans considered Dionysian worship objectionable because of its irrationality, and Luke precludes such criticisms of Christian women by portraying Lydia and her sisters as altogether noble, sane, and faithful."[11] Along similar lines, Michael White questions the reality of Lydia's existence and views Acts 16 as conveying messages of respectability, though his emphasis is on

---

8. Matthews, "Elite Women," 124. Similarly, Judith Lieu argues that Acts shares the novelistic tendency of second-century Greek and Jewish novels, where the social influence of women seems to be exaggerated. See Lieu, "The 'Attraction of Women' in/to Early Judaism and Christianity," 16–17.

9. See especially Schottroff, "Lydia," 131–37; Reimer, *Women in the Acts of the Apostles*, 98–130.

10. Matthews, "Elite Women," 131. With particular focus on the work of Valerie A. Abrahamsen ("Women at Philippi"), see Reimer's response to theories concerning the fictional nature of Acts 16 in *Women in the Acts of the Apostles*, 128. For a recent detailed study of Lydia that emphasizes historical detail see Ascough, *Lydia*.

11. MacDonald, "Lydia and Her Sisters as Lukan Fictions," 110.

the convergence between the respectable, extended, household of antiquity and the locus of early Christian movement.[12]

In many respects, insights from Roman Family Studies further support the conclusions of these scholars. Historians of the Roman family have highlighted the socio-political impact of household and marriage ideals, where harmonious relations between husband and wife and the stability of families was communicated through a broad range of media, from imperial statues, to art, to funerary art, to inscriptions, to the speeches of emperors, political rhetoricians, and moralists.[13] By the end of the first century, Roman imperial household values had been widely disseminated from West to East.[14] Order, harmony, and convention—delivered via concepts the wider society would clearly recognize—were central to Josephus' answer to the question in *Against Apion*, "What are our marriage Laws?" (2.199), to the author of Ephesians' presentation of the idealized household and marriage in Eph 5:21–6:9, and to the repeated emphasis on the conversion of whole households headed by both men and women in Acts. Of particular interest is the use of household symbolism to convey a broad range of messages concerning civic harmony or even the appearance of civic harmony but actually encoding some elements of resistance, as Carolyn Osiek and I have argued with respect to Eph 5:21–33 in *A Woman's Place*.[15]

This last point—the encoding of elements of resistance—leads me to a discussion of how recent research on families not only supports apologetic readings of the presentation of the women of Acts, but also complicates our vision. On the one hand, the picture of Lydia fits with prominence of women in Philippi (though Paul's puzzling silence about Lydia has often been noted) and of evidence from the Roman world of women managing households for themselves. On one level, Lydia exudes the qualities of a more well-to-do matron—she is hospitable, independent, and capable of the household management responsibilities, which would include the management of the slaves, household goods, and even education of children and the arrangement of their affairs.[16]

---

12. White, "Visualizing the 'Real' World of Acts 16," 259.

13. See especially Dixon, "The Sentimental Ideal of the Roman Family," 99. See also discussion in Osiek and MacDonald with Tulloch, *A Woman's Place*, 120–21.

14. See Winter, *Roman Wives, Roman Widows*, 35.

15. See especially, 123–26.

16. See Nathan, *The Family in Late Antiquity*, 19, citing Pliny *Letters* 4.19. See also

Yet, as Beverly Gaventa has insightfully noted by means of her comparison of Acts to the *Roman Antiquities* of Dionysus of Halicarnassus, in his specific presentation of women, Luke is restrained when it comes to description of conventional female virtues. For example, there is no reference to Lydia's appearance, her devotion to children, husband—no male relatives are mentioned at all.[17] Emphasis is on independence and management. All the members of her household (ὁ οἶκος αὐτῆς) receive baptism with her. This is what one would expect with respect to a true head of a household. As noted previously, there are several examples among the elite classes of widows managing households independently, and it is not surprising that Lydia has been viewed as a widow.[18] In fact, the independent control of resources technically places Lydia on par with male householders. As the Roman historian Richard Saller has pointed out, legal discussions could even subsume female property owners within the purview of male terminology, casting them in terms of *paterfamilias*.[19] The status of Lydia as head of the household is made especially clear by her spoken invitation to Paul, "come to my house and stay" (Acts 16:15).

Virginia Burrus and Karen Torjesen have noted the rhetorical impact of the points of contact between Lydia's persona and elite female figures in ancient texts who were potentially "highly charged emblems of social power." According to Burrus and Torjesen, the role of female patron for Luke offers an opportunity "both to honor and (somewhat heavy-handedly) to instruct the women in his audience, while also serving his (undeniably androcentric) interests in buttressing the reputation of Christianity by enabling its men to go public under the influence of the right kind of women."[20] I would agree that

---

Dixon, *The Roman Mother*, 44, 62–63. Note that Ascough (*Lydia*, 99) has described Lydia as "well-off, but not elite."

17. Gaventa, "Whatever Happened to Those Prophesying Daughters," 55.

18. For evidence of widows managing their own households, see summary of the evidence in Osiek and MacDonald with Tulloch, *A Woman's Place*, 155–57.

19. Saller, "*Pater Familias, Mater Familias*," 184, 187. According to Saller *paterfamilias* is a term used in legal texts to refer essentially to the property ownership of men *sui iuris*, that is, not in the *potestas* of another male. In fact, the term *materfamilias* is rarely used to connote the property ownership of women and has more to do with maternity and female honor and virtue. See full discussion in Osiek and MacDonald with Tulloch, *A Woman's Place*, 154–55.

20. See Burrus and Torjesen, "Afterword," 173.

the presentation of Lydia in Acts is shaped by a desire to bolster the reputation of early Christianity. But some scholars go farther in suggesting that Lydia's offer of accommodation to Paul and his entourage is central to the agenda of the author of Acts to downplay Lydia's role as a missionary/leader in her own right.[21] As feminist interpreters have demonstrated, the author of Acts displays ambivalence towards female prophets,[22] but it is important not to overstate the distinction between traditional female responsibilities linked to domestic life and teaching roles in this ancient Mediterranean context. As Carolyn Osiek and I wrote in *A Woman's Place*:

> it can be established that women, probably for the most part widows who had autonomous administration of their own households, hosted house churches of the early Christian movement. This fact in itself does not necessarily mean that they had leadership in teaching or other spiritual responsibilities. That conclusion, however, might be inferred from several cultural patterns. First, it was normal procedure for the person in whose house a group met to dine, to preside, to select the menu and the entertainment that followed the meal, and to facilitate conversation, philosophical or otherwise. The entertainment could take a number of forms, and here an invited expert could be brought in, a philosopher or wisdom figure for the education of attendees.[23]

Lydia may well have been fictional—among other factors, the symbolic richness of the woman called Lydia from Thyatira, a city of Lydia suggests this—but the expectations of the audience of Acts probably included a woman in a speaking/teaching role with Paul as the *invited* expert.[24] Although she has been called, a "quiet convert"[25] (especially in relation to the noisy slave girl later in the text), her words, "come to my house and stay" are powerful indeed. Lydia is an example of a woman who administered her own property and had funds at her disposal. The

---

21. See, for example, Matthews, "Elite Women," 131–32. See also O'Day, "Acts," 310; Martin, "The Acts of the Apostles," 784–85.

22. See Matthews, "Elite Women," 128.

23. See Osiek and MacDonald with Tulloch, *A Woman's Place*, 162–63.

24. The ethnic appellation might also indicate that Lydia was a freed slave. But the inscriptional evidence for the use of the name is not conclusive. See Ascough, *Lydia*, 6–7.

25. See Burrus and Torjesen, "Afterword," 175.

series of events, which includes Paul's return visit before his departure from Philippi, implies that Lydia's house continues as the centre activity for encouragement of "the brothers and sisters" beyond the initial visit of the apostles. The presentation of Lydia as a true host, with all that it entails, needs to be acknowledged.[26]

Suspicious Circumstances: Lydia, the Mother of John Mark, and Unnamed Female Slaves

On the other hand, as the locus for the assembly of brothers and sisters, Lydia's space seems to fail to meet the ideals of respectability in some respects, located on the outskirts of the city and linked with a smelly trade, as Ivoni Richter Reimer has argued. When the author of Acts offers the scant details about Lydia's life he tells of a woman, a God-fearer (perhaps a sign of an ambiguous status) who deals (probably dyes and sells) purple cloth; her house appears to be located near a river likely because of the water required for her work and away from the more respectable inhabitants who did not want such a trade in their midst.[27] The buttressing of reputation through the figure of Lydia only goes so far, for one might reasonably ask the question, what is Paul doing going out there in the first place? The strange circumstances begin with the unusual reference to the synagogue (προσευχή is used instead of the typically Lukan συναγωγή) which is outside of the city gate at the riverside and seems to be attended only by women (or more accurately, only women are explicitly mentioned).[28] Dennis MacDonald, using Euripides' *Bacchae* as the basis for his interpretation and arguing

---

26. On the potential dangers of discrediting Lydia in some feminist scholarship, see Burrus and Torjesen, "Afterword," 175.

27. See evidence cited especially in Reimer, *Women in the Acts of the Apostles*, 106–7. She considers the relationship between the requirements of working with purple and the synagogue/place of prayer setting. But see also response to Reimer in Ascough, *Lydia*, 88–89. Ascough senses ambivalence in Luke's description of Lydia as a "worshipper of God" and of the "place of prayer" and questions the widely accepted view of Lydia as a worshipper of the God of Israel (83–90).

28. Matthews has argued that the visit to "the synagogue of women" along with the conversion of Lydia "resonate with Dionysiac propagandistic themes." See "Elite Women," 112. With reference to the work of Bernadette Brooten (*Women Leaders in the Ancient Synagogue*), Reimer has questioned the assumption that the presence of men was universally required for synagogue service. See *Women in the Acts of the Apostles*, 91–92.

against the interpretation of the word as a reference to a synagogue, goes so far as to say: "These women are outside the male-dominated city, in the wild, worshipping their god."[29] The relationship between this gathering and Lydia's house is intriguing even beyond the obvious fact that the gathering provides the vehicle of introduction for Paul's message to Lydia and to other women as well. After staying with Lydia for a time, the return trip to the place of prayer leads to Paul's entourage meeting a very different type of woman, a slave girl who had the spirit of divination (literally, a Pythonian spirit) and was the source of significant revenue for her owners. The expulsion of the spirit by Paul and subsequent loss of revenue result in Paul's imprisonment. Yet, despite all of this chaos, suspicion, and potential lack of respectability, Paul and Silas make a point of going back there, after escaping/being released from prison and before leaving Philippi.

It is interesting to note that similar tumultuous events involving imprisonment are part of the atmosphere surrounding the second woman in Acts who seems to manage her own household and host a house church: the mother of John Mark. The mother of John Mark (again usually understood to be a widow) has a house large enough in Jerusalem to host a good number of (ἱκανοὶ) of the believing community (Acts 12:12–17). Having escaped prison through miraculous intervention, Peter goes immediately to this house where the believers are gathered in night prayer and are awaiting news. The implication seems to be that this house is well known, a natural locus in a time of crisis and the obvious place for Peter to go.[30] But despite the fact that the audience is clearly meant to understand this woman as having considerable resources with the ability to provide security to the community, one cannot help but notice atmosphere of nocturnal prayer, anxiety, and, as in the account of Lydia's conversion, there is a reference to a female slave that believers find—for lack of a better word—annoying. The first reaction to Rhoda, the doorkeeper's announcement of Peter's miraculous appearance is that she is out of her mind. Like the anonymous prophesying slave girl of Acts 16 who keeps announcing over and over again that Paul and his entourage are slaves of the Most High, Rhoda is annoyingly insistent. The reaction of the group calls to mind Celsus' denunciation of Mary Magdalene's witness of the resurrection as that of

---

29. MacDonald, "Lydia and Her Sisters as Lukan Fictions," 105.
30. See discussion in Osiek and MacDonald with Tulloch, *A Woman's Place*, 157.

a "hysterical female" (Origen, *C. Cels.* 2.55). The dual image of deluded female and influential evangelist was central to both pagan reaction to early Christianity and to early Christianity's own fashioning of female characters and ethical directives concerning women.[31]

To return Acts 16, the juxtaposition of Lydia's identity with that of the slave girl has been of great interest to commentators, and they have differences of opinion on how to read the interwoven accounts. Dennis MacDonald sees a certain resolution and commonality between the messages communicated by the two accounts: "Lydia is not a wild woman in the hills in raving ecstasy. The mantic slave girl, exploited by her male owners, returns to her senses."[32] In contrast to MacDonald, Matthews views the slave girl as being portrayed as outside of the Christian community[33] and views Lydia as her idealized Christian counterpart: "The Christian Lydia is respectful and differential; the female speaking 'prophet' and sexual threat belongs to a defeated religion."[34] Paul's exorcism of the spirit from the slave girl despite the truth of her prophecy and with an attitude of extreme annoyance certainly supports the idea of the problematic nature of the slave girl's allegiance to the early church group, in line with Matthews' interpretation. But I would not go so far as to read the text as placing the mantic slave girl outside of the Christian community. Particularly telling here is the fact that the women's synagogue or place of prayer is presented as the occasion for Paul encountering both women—granted he meets Lydia there, but the slave girl only *on the way* there.

The relationship between the tales of the soothsaying slave girl and the conversion of Lydia is complex, containing somewhat contradictory and ambiguous elements. This has been highlighted with the help of post-colonial theory. According to Burrus and Torjesen, for example, the complexity of the doubled women, is reinforced by the figure of Paul himself who, both as an authoritative figure and as one who is himself beaten and imprisoned, is split "between the subjection of the colonized and the forces of (counter) colonization."

---

31. See MacDonald, *Early Christian Women and Pagan Women*, 5. Along similar lines, Seim has spoken of the liberating and constraining elements of Luke-Acts in *The Double Message*.

32. MacDonald, "Lydia and Her Sisters as Lukan Fictions," 110.

33. Matthews, "Elite Women," 132.

34. Ibid., 133.

They ask the following insightful questions about Paul's role: "If he has robbed the slave girl of her native gift of prophecy, has he also robbed the householder Lydia's of her right to leadership? On the other hand, if his exorcism functions effectively as a critique of the exploitation of the slave, does not that counter the possibility that he himself has simply exploited Lydia's hospitality and relative wealth?"[35] I would agree with Burrus and Torjesen that while Luke does not challenge the class-based authority of Lydia, his account contains "sly interrogations of slavery and imperial rule."[36]

A focus on "families" can lead to an enhanced appreciation of the complexity of domination and resistance as they surface in early Christian texts. A key aspect of this interpretive vision involves a heightened awareness of the diversity of community membership in terms of overlapping markers of identity such as class, gender, place/role in the household. While early Christian girls are the most underrepresented familial group in all of early Christian literature, the author of Acts provides intriguing evidence for the presence of young women of marriageable age, who in our culture would really only be adolescents. The four virgin and prophesying daughters (who actually never speak in the text) of Philip (Acts 21:8–9) are the most obvious example, but the mantic slave girl may offer another case in point. The Greek term for slave in this text (as in the reference to Rhoda in Acts 12:13) is παιδίσκη. Because of the overlap in terminology for slaves and children, we cannot be certain that this slave was actually young, but most commentators seem to have understood it to refer to a young female slave. While the daughters of Philip have a believing *paterfamilias*, the slave girl—now liberated at least spiritually—is the property of a pagan masters, her owners. They are represented as taking violent action against Paul and members of an ancient audience must surely have wondered what type of violence might befall the now useless girl. The difficult circumstances of believing slaves of non-believers leave a barely discernible trace in early Christian literature, but they come as a reminder of the diversity of early Christian membership and the ever so faint markers of slave resistance. Thus, another manner in which the story of Lydia and the story of the mantic slave girl are juxtaposed is

---

35. Burrus and Torjesen, "Afterword," 175. They are influenced especially by Stanley, "Changing Woman," 113–35.

36. Burrus and Torjesen, "Afterword," 176.

that while the conversion of Lydia's whole household is presented as the ideal, the very next account tells of Paul's impact on subordinate members of the household leading to conflict with the imperial order of house, city, and state.

If the slave is an adolescent girl, I would argue that she finds a male counterpart in the youth mentioned in Acts 20:7–12 (cf. Acts 23:16–19). Once again, the terminology is ambiguous (νεανίας, παῖς), with the setting suggesting a slave boy who is at the meeting waiting for his master. Eutychus was present at the church gathering in an upper room dwelling in Troas. He had been listening to Paul, but had fallen asleep "while [the Apostle] talked still longer." Sitting in the window, he accidently fell to the ground only to be miraculously healed by Paul. Challenging previous scholarship that has understood peristyled *domus* as the primary setting for house churches, David Horrell has drawn a connection between the kind of space envisioned here and the simple dwellings uncovered in the buildings east of the Theatre in Corinth. These buildings seem to have been comprised of butchery kitchens with families residing in second (or possibly third) storey one or two-room dwellings.[37] Acts does offer a window into a variety of spaces for church meeting. For example, on the one hand, we find references to the *oikos* of the mother of John Mark, which presupposes a certain economic and social level. On the other hand, the Troas scene suggests an apartment house or rented meeting place, or what Robert Jewett has called a "tenement church."[38] This scene underscores the vulnerability of children in non-elite urban neighborhoods, but also an atmosphere where the presence of children was taken for granted and where children might simply come into meetings by chance; as Beryl Rawson has argued, the neighborhood for non-elite children was essentially the playground of non-elite children in the Roman world.[39] The account in Acts does not

---

37. Horrell has drawn a connection between the kind of domestic space described in Acts and the buildings east of the Theatre in Corinth, but has not drawn attention to the fact that this is an episode involving a child. See Horrell, "Domestic Space and Christian Meetings at Corinth," 368–69. Horrell critiques the influential work of Jerome Murphy-O'Connor which associates house church life with the Roman villa. See Murphy-O'Connor, *St. Paul's Corinth*.

38. Jewett, "Tenement Churches and Communal Meals in the Early Church," 23–43. Osiek and Balch link such a setting to "those who belong to Chloe" (1 Cor 1:11). See Osiek and Balch, *Families in the New Testament*, 98.

39. Rawson, *Children and Childhood in Roman Italy*, 211.

elaborate the future of the mantic slave girl, beyond the fact that she no longer represents a source of income for her owners. It is a blank we can't fill in. But we may cautiously ask the question of whether slaves who came into contact with church groups and were somehow rendered useless by their new allegiance were ever acquired by believers? Women like Lydia, having modest resources, crossed paths with such slaves, were probably slave owners themselves, and were capable of acting as pseudo-mothers, masters, and managing households/house churches.[40]

Priscilla: Wifely Influence and Conventional Appearances

Consideration of space, movement, and the crossing of paths leads me to a brief consideration of Prisc(ill)a. Prisc(ill)a has been of great interest to feminist interpreters of the New Testament for a variety of reason, ranging from the persistent memory of her influence, to the fact that her name frequently appears before that of her husband Aquila (e.g., Acts 18:18, 26; Rom 16:3), to her teaching of Apollos along with her partner, to the possible attempt to emphasize her legitimately married status in Acts—for in Acts she is clearly a wife. Paul's letters indicate that Prisc(ill)a and Aquila were hosts to house churches in Ephesus and Rome (1 Cor 16:19 and Rom 16:3–5), but the reference in Acts to them offering hospitality to Paul in Corinth suggests that this might have been the case in Corinth as well (Acts 18:2–3; 18:18—9:1).[41] In fact, David Horrell has argued that the dwellings uncovered in the buildings east of the theatre, with quarters of approximately 10 X 5 meters, "was the kind of space that might well have been occupied by small traders

---

40. On slaves being cared for by masters who acted as pseudo-parents, see Rawson, *Children and Childhood in Roman Italy*, 260–261. For a slave child being raised/adopted by a believer, we might consider the description of the daughter of Felicitas, born in prison before Felicitas' martyrdom in the *Martyrdom of Perpetua and Felicitas*. She is explicitly said to have been raised by one of the "sisters." On the fate of the slave girl see also suggestions by Reimer in *Women in the Acts of the Apostles*, 182–83.

41. There is comparatively little difficulty in harmonizing the material from Acts with material from Paul's letters on Prisc(ill)a and Aquila with respect to geographical locations and the movement of the couple from place to place. In his study of the situation of foreigners at Rome, Noy has observed that the couple ". . . has one of the most complete surviving migration histories of any individuals of similar status" in the Roman world. See Noy, *Foreigners at Rome*, 259.

and business folk, not too different in social level, perhaps, from artisans like Prisca and Aquila, and Paul himself."[42]

Unlike Lydia and the mother of John Mark, Prisc(ill)a is not presented as being at the head of a household and, as stated previously, in Acts she is very clearly a wife. As with the presentation of these other women, however, her persona is complicated by the use of "families" as a category of analysis. Unlike the other women, she is explicitly presented as having a teaching/missionary role and the mention of her name first might imply not only that she was of higher status, but possibly also that she was a more successful missioner than her husband. Moreover, if we remember that the work of Pris(ill)a and Aquila involved literally moving and setting up house, we are reminded that Pric(ill)a's missionary opportunities may have taken full advantage of conventional expectations with respect to women's activities and responsibilities. Prisc(ill)a and Aquila clearly match the author of Acts' ideal of the believing household, but as a wife (and probably also a mother, though this is never stated), artisan, missionary, and house church co-host, Prisc(ill)a must have participated in a broad range of activities that could support the less respectable members, the slaves, the children, the needy widows, and the wives who found themselves at church meetings out of need or in active defiance of familial authorities.[43] While it is beyond the scope of this essay to examine the intriguing references to widows in Luke-Acts, Tabitha's ministry of good works, including the gift of clothing to widows, fits with this picture (Acts 9:39–41).[44]

Conclusion

The descriptions of the conversion of whole households in Acts, including Lydia's household, have sometimes been viewed as highly problematic for their role in reinforcing the forced conversion of slaves and children.[45] From a feminist perspective, Luke's idealized vision is indisputably problematic for it marries early Christian expansion with patriarchal power—power exercised by men and women alike. In addition,

---

42. Horrell, "Domestic Space and Christian Meetings," 367.

43. See full discussion in Osiek and MacDonald with Tulloch, *A Woman's Place*, 29–35.

44. See Reid, "Power of Widows," 86–87.

45. See Matthews, "Elite Women," 125, citing Glancy, *Slavery in Early Christianity*.

the author of Acts generally denies or plays down women's presence in the public forum. But when informed by knowledge of ancient families, coupled with a strong awareness of the scope of a domestically-based movement, I would argue that this idealized vision has a complicated and tangential relationship to the experience of the first communities. I have argued that there is plenty of counter-evidence to suggest that the conversion of whole households, uniformly obedient to their head, was comparatively rare. It is part of the problematic legacy of the Luke that he finds this embarrassing, or at best such an explosive situation in the society of the day that apologetic interests sometimes dominate. Yet, one of the most fascinating features of Acts is that the work introduces us to characters that cannot fit or are on the margins of the author's idealized patterns. Concerning the women of Acts, a focus on families both expands and complicates our vision, certainly with respect to relationship between ministerial and domestic roles and responsibilities. A familial perspective sharpens our awareness of what feminist scholars have now said for decades, that "on women" Acts is a complicated, even dangerous text. But in my opinion, it can also offer new appreciation for what some interpreters have also noted, as revealed perhaps most clearly in the boldness and persistence of the two slave girls, Rhoda and the unnamed mantic slave: surprising insight into the lives of the marginalized.

Bibliography

Abrahamsen, Valerie A. "Women at Philippi: The Pagan and Christian Evidence." *JFSR* 3 (1987) 17–30.

Aletti, Jean-Noël. *Saint Paul: Épitre aux Colossiens*. Paris: Galbalda, 1993.

Ascough, Richard S. *Lydia: Paul's Cosmopolitan Hostess*. Paul's Social Networks: Brothers and Sisters in Faith, edited by Bruce J. Malina. Collegeville, MN: Liturgical, 2009.

Best, E. *A Critical and Exegetical Commentary on Ephesians*. ICC. Edinburgh: T. & T. Clark, 1998.

Brooten, Bernadette. *Women Leaders in the Ancient Synagogue: Inscriptional Issues and Background Issues*. BJS 36. Chico, CA: Scholars, 1982.

Burrus, Virginia, and Karen Jo Torjesen. "Afterword to 'Household Management and Women's Authority.'" In *A Feminist Companion to the Acts of the Apostles*, edited by Amy-Jill Levine with Marianne Bickenstaff, 171–76. FCNT 9. London: T. & T. Clark, 2004.

Dixon, Suzanne. *The Roman Mother*. London: Croom Helm, 1988.

———. "The Sentimental Ideal of the Roman Family." In *Marriage, Divorce, and Children in Ancient Rome*, edited by Beryl Rawson, 99–113. Oxford: Clarendon, 1991.

Gaventa, Beverly Roberts. "Whatever Happened to Those Prophesying Daughters." In *A Feminist Companion to the Acts of the Apostles*, edited by Amy-Jill Levine with Marianne Bickenstaff, 49–60. FCNT 9. London: T. & T. Clark, 2004.

Gehring, Roger W. *House Church and Mission: The Importance of Household Structures in Early Christianity*. Peabody, MA: Hendrickson, 2004.

Glancy, Jennifer A. *Slavery in Early Christianity*. Oxford: Oxford University Press, 2002.

Horrell, David G. "Domestic Space and Christian Meetings at Corinth: Imagining New Contexts and the Buildings East of the Theatre." *NTS* 50 (2004) 349–69.

Jewett, Robert. "Tenement Churches and Communal Meals in the Early Church: The Implications of a Form-Critical Analysis of 2 Thess 3:10." *BR* 38 (1993): 23–43.

Lieu, Judith. "The 'Attraction of Women' in/to Early Judaism and Christianity: Gender and the Politics of Conversion." *JSNT* 72 (1998) 5–22.

Lincoln, Andrew T. *Ephesians*. WBC 42. Dallas: Word, 1990.

MacDonald, Dennis R. "Lydia and her Sisters as Lukan Fictions." In *A Feminist Companion to the Acts of the Apostles,* edited by Amy-Jill Levine with Marianne Bickenstaff, 105–110. FCNT 9. London: T. & T. Clark, 2004.

MacDonald, Margaret Y. *Early Christian Women and Pagan Women: the Power of the Hysterical Woman*. Cambridge: Cambridge University Press, 1996.

Martin, Clarice J. "The Acts of the Apostles." In *Searching the Scriptures II: A Feminist Commentary*, edited by Elisabeth Schüssler Fiorenza, 763–99. New York: Crossroad, 1994.

Matthews, Shelley. "Elite Women, Public Religion, and Christian Propaganda in Acts 16." In *A Feminist Companion to the Acts of the Apostles,* edited by Amy-Jill Levine with Marianne Bickenstaff, 111–23. FCNT 9. London: T. & T. Clark, 2004.

Matson, David Lertis. *Household Conversion Narratives in Acts: Patterns and Interpretation*. JSNTSup 123. Sheffield: Sheffield Academic, 1996.

Nathan, Geoffrey S. *The Family in Late Antiquity: The Rise of Christianity and the Endurance of Tradition.* London: Routledge, 2000.

Noy, David. *Foreigners at Rome: Citizens and Strangers.* London: Duckworth with the Classical Press of Wales, 2000.

Murphy-O'Connor, Jerome. *St. Paul's Corinth: Texts and Archaeology.* 3rd rev. and expanded ed. Collegeville, MN: Liturgical, 2002.

O'Day, Gail R. "Acts." In *The Women's Bible Commentary* edited by Carol A. Newsom and Sharon H. Ringe, 305–12. Louisville: Westminster John Knox, 1992.

Osiek, Carolyn, and David Balch. *Families in the New Testament: Households and House Churches.* Louisville: Westminster John Knox, 1997.

Osiek, Carolyn, and Margaret Y. MacDonald, with Janet H. Tulloch. *A Woman's Place: House Churches in Earliest Christianity.* Minneapolis: Fortress, 2006.

Pomeroy, Sarah B. *Plutarch's Advice to the Bride and Groom and A Consolation to His Wife.* Oxford: Oxford University Press, 1999.

Rawson, Beryl. *Children and Childhood in Roman Italy.* Oxford: Oxford University Press, 2003.

Reid, Barbara E. "The Power of Widows and How to Suppress It." In *A Feminist Companion to the Acts of the Apostles,* edited by Amy-Jill Levine with Marianne Bickenstaff, 71–88. FCNT 9. London: T. & T. Clark, 2004.

Reimer, Ivoni Richter. *Women in the Acts of the Apostles: A Feminist Liberationist Perspective.* Translated by Linda M. Maloney. Minneapolis: Fortress, 1995.

Saller, Richard. "*Pater Familias, Mater Familias,* and the Gendered Semantics of the Roman Household." *Classical Philology* 94 (1999) 182–97.

Schottroff, Luise. "Lydia: A New Quality of Power." In *Let the Oppressed Go Free: Feminist Perspectives on the New Testament,* 131–37. Translated by Annemarie S. Kidder. Louisville: Westminster John Knox, 1993.

Seim, Turid Karlsen. *The Double Message: Patterns of Gender in Luke-Acts.* Studies of the New Testament and Its World. Edinburgh: T. & T. Clark, 1994.

———. "A Superior Minority: The Problem of Men's Headship in Ephesians 5." In *Mighty Minorities? Minorities in Early Christianity—Positions and Strategies,* edited by David Hellholm et al., 167–81. Oslo: Scandinavian University Press, 1995.

Stanley, Jeffrey L. "Changing Woman: Post-colonial Reflections on Acts 16:6–40." *JSNT* 73 (1999) 113–35.

White, Michael L. "Visualizing the 'Real' World of Acts 16: Toward Construction of a Social Index." In *The Social World of the First Christians,* edited by. L. Michael White and O. Larry Yarbrough, 234–61. Minneapolis: Fortress, 1995.

Winter, Bruce W. *Roman Wives, Roman Widows: The Appearance of the New Women and Pauline Communities.* Grand Rapids: Eerdmans, 2003.

PART THREE

Johannine Documents

8

Birthed from the Side of Jesus (John 19:34)

Barbara E. Reid, O.P.

It is with great pleasure that I join in honoring Carolyn Osiek, who was my colleague at Catholic Theological Union until 2004. Lyn was assigned to be my mentor when I joined the faculty of CTU in 1988 as a newly minted PhD. I was privileged to be accompanied by such a wise woman who had already paved the way as a feminist biblical scholar, and who would help me find my own voice. With deep gratitude for more than two decades of friendship and companionship, I offer this modest contribution.[1]

The uniqueness of the Fourth Gospel is nowhere more evident than in the Passion Narrative. One of the singular details is found in John 19:34, where a soldier pierces the side of Jesus, from which flow blood and water. From earliest times commentators have seen profound symbolism in this verse. Not a few have noted that blood and water are the same liquids that accompany the birthing process and have understood the death of Jesus as the portal of new life for the church. In this essay, I will show that the evangelist has woven birthing imagery throughout the whole gospel, beginning with the Prologue, so that the hearer is well prepared to understand how the image functions in 19:34. By interpreting the death of Jesus as a birthing of new life, the Fourth Evangelist offers a strong antidote to atonement theologies.

---

1. This essay relies in part on chapter 5 of my book, *Taking up the Cross*, 155–80.

"All things were born through him" (John 1:3)

From the very opening lines of the Prologue, the Fourth Evangelist plants the theme of birthing. In the first stanza, which elaborates the relationship of the *Logos* (Word) with *Theos* (God), is the assertion, πάντα δι' αὐτοῦ ἐγένετο, καὶ χωρὶς αὐτοῦ ἐγένετο οὐδὲ ἕν. ὃ γέγονεν (1:3). The *NRSV* renders this verse, "all things came into being through him."[2] This translation, while accurate, does not capture the full range of meaning of the verb γίνομαι, whose primary definition is "to come into being through process of birth or natural production, be born, be produced."[3] In Gal 4:4, for example, γίνομαι is translated "born": "God sent his son, born (γενόμενον) of a woman, born (γενόμενον) under the law." Another possible rendering of John 1:3 is "all things *were birthed* through him."

The theme of birthing is reprised in verses 12 and 13 of the Prologue, "But to all who received him, who believed in his name, he gave power to become (γενέσθαι) children of God, who were born (ἐγεννήθησαν), not of blood or of the will of the flesh or of the will of man, but of God." Here both the verbs γίνομαι and γεννάω occur. The latter is defined: (1) "become the parent of, beget;" (2) "to give birth to, bear."[4] While both verbs can connote both male begetting and female birthing, the former tends to be used more frequently for male begetting (e.g., Matt 1:2–20), and the latter for female birthing. Clearly birth from the mother's womb is the meaning of γεννάω in John 3:4 and 16:21.[5] John 1:13 emphasizes that the birthing of God's children comes about through divine action, and contrasts with human procreation, which

---

2. Similarly, NAB translates: "all things came to be through him," NJB renders it: "through him all things came into being." All biblical citations in English are taken from the NRSV unless otherwise noted.

3. According to BDAG, 196–99, other nuances include (2) "to come into existence, be made, be created, be manufactured, be performed; (3) come into being as an event or phenomenon from a point of origin, arise, come about, develop; (4) to occur as process or result, happen, turn out, take place; (5) to experience a change in nature, and so indicate entry into a new condition, become something; (6) to make a change of location in space, move; (7) to come into a certain state or possess certain characteristics, to be, prove to be, turn out to be; (8) to be present at a given time, be there; (9) to be closely related to someone or something, belong to; (10) to be in or at a place, be in, be there."

4. One other connotation is "to cause something to happen, bring forth, produce, cause." BDAG, 193–94.

5. The verb γεννάω occurs also in John 3:3, 5, 6, 7, 8; 8:41; 9:2, 19, 20, 32, 34; 18:37.

originates in human desire ("will of the flesh"), more precisely, that of males ("the will of man").⁶ "Not of blood" likely refers to the belief in antiquity that conception occurred through the mingling of woman's blood with male seed.⁷ It is also notable that in John 1:13 "blood," αἱμάτων, is plural. In Hebrew, the plural דָּמִים means "bloodshed." Taken in this sense, there is a link between 1:13 and 19:34, where the blood shed at the death of Jesus is a new act of divine birthing.

The Prologue sets the stage for an understanding of discipleship that entails acceptance of one's birth as a child of God, and empowerment to engender life in others through faith in the *Logos*. There is an intriguing blurring of gender boundaries: the male *Logos* births all things (1:3) and *Theos* births the children of God (1:12–13). Moreover, in the final verse of the Prologue the Son is at the breast (εἰς τὸν κόλπον) of the Father (1:18). The word κόλπος means "bosom, chest, breast,"⁸ and can refer to either a man's chest or a woman's breast. In Luke 16:23, for example, the rich man, looking up from the netherworld, sees Lazarus ἐν τοῖς κόλποις, "in the bosom" of Abraham. In the book of Ruth, however, κόλπος refers to a woman's breast, where Naomi takes Ruth's child "and held him to her breast" (*NJB*, εἰς τὸν κόλπον αὐτης), "and became his nurse" (4:16). This same phrase reappears in John 13:23, where, at the Last Supper, the Beloved Disciple is reclining ἐν τῷ κόλπῳ τοῦ Ἰησοῦ, "in the bosom of Jesus."⁹ The intimacy between the Father and Jesus and between Jesus and the Beloved Disciple is like that of a nursing mother with her child at her breast.

---

6. The Greek word in John 1:13 is ἀνδρός, which refers specifically to males, unlike ἄνθρωπος, which connotes both women and men. "The will of man" refers to the notion in antiquity that the male was the primary agent in human procreation. Sexual activity was by his initiative and woman was thought to be only the vessel for the embryo.

7. Ford, *Redeemer, Friend, and Mother*, 193. Another interpretation is that blood and water symbolize true humanity, so that John 19:34 can be understood as having an anti-docetic thrust. See ibid., 194, for references from patristic writings.

8. BDAG, 556.

9. Author's translation. The NRSV and NAB mask the connection with 1:18 when they translate 13:23: "was reclining next to him" and "was reclining at Jesus' side."

The Birthing of Jesus' Public Ministry (John 2:1–11)

The symbols of water and blood do not appear for the first time in John 19:34; they recur again and again in the Fourth Gospel.[10] The first time that water is mentioned is when John the Baptist contrasts his baptism with water to that of the Coming One who will baptize with the Holy Spirit (1:26–34). There is further elaboration on the meaning of water and Spirit in John 3, in Jesus' dialogue with Nicodemus, but in the intervening chapter, there is the episode of the wedding feast at Cana where Jesus turns the six stone jars of water into wine.

This episode is the inauguration of Jesus' public ministry and culminates in the revelation of Jesus' glory and the initial response of belief on the part of his disciples (2:11). Critical to the account is that it is the mother of Jesus who initiates the whole process. It is she who recognizes "the hour" for the birthing of his public ministry (2:3). Jesus, however, initially responds, "My hour has not yet come" (2:4). Throughout the Fourth Gospel, the "hour" primarily refers to the hour of Jesus' return to the Father, accomplished in his passion, death, resurrection, ascension, and glorification.[11] Thus, at 12:23, shortly after the chief priests and Pharisees have resolved to arrest Jesus (11:57), Jesus announces "The hour has come for the Son of Man to be glorified." The Last Supper scene opens with the assertion, "Jesus knew that his hour had come to depart from this world and go to the Father" (13:1). Previously, the evangelist twice noted that the attempts to arrest Jesus failed because "his hour had not yet come" (7:30; 8:20). In the farewell discourse to his disciples, Jesus interprets his "hour" in terms of birthing. He likens his coming passion to the pains of a woman in labor, and assures his followers of the ensuing joy at the new birth (16:20–22).

The Cana scene is intimately tied to the crucifixion of Jesus by the figure of Jesus' mother. There are a number of verbal and thematic links: in both scenes Jesus addresses his mother as γύναι, "woman" (2:4; 19:26), there is reference to "the hour" (2:4; 19:27), and to belief (2:11; 19:35), and water plays an important symbolic role. These two scenes, unique to the Fourth Gospel, are the only two in which the mother

---

10. On the symbol of water in the Fourth Gospel, see Jones, *The Symbol of Water in the Gospel of John*; Koester, *Symbolism in the Fourth Gospel,* 175–206; Lee, *Flesh and Glory,* 65–87.

11. See Brown, *The Gospel According to John,* 517–18.

of Jesus is present. They serve as bookends, bracketing the story, and bringing to the fore the interpretation that rests on birthing images. The one who gave Jesus physical birth draws him forth in the Cana episode, assisting in the birth of his public mission as would a midwife in the birth of a child. In the crucifixion scene, she witnesses the completion of his earthly life and ministry, and is midwife to the birth of the next phase to be carried on by his disciples.

Born Anew/From Above in Water and the Spirit (John 3:3–8)

In Jesus' conversation with Nicodemus, the verb γεννάω, "to be born," occurs seven times, making the theme of birth most explicit. Jesus says to Nicodemus, "No one can see the kingdom of God without being born from above (γεννηθῇ ἄνωθεν)," (3:3). Nicodemus is puzzled, "How can one be born (γεννηθῆναι) after having grown old? Can one enter a second time into the mother's womb and be born (γεννηθῆναι)?" (3:4). Jesus explains, "Very truly I tell you, no one can enter the kingdom of God without being born (γεννηθῇ) of water and the Spirit . . . Do not be astonished that I said to you, 'you must be born from above (γεννηθῆναι)'" (3:5, 7). There is a play on words as ἄνωθεν denotes both "again" and "from above." While Nicodemus understands Jesus to say "born again," Jesus explains that being born "from above" means birth in water and the Spirit.

It is in the crucifixion scene that the meaning of birth in water and Spirit comes clearer. At Jesus' death, he hands over the Spirit (19:30),[12] which is juxtaposed with flowing water from the pierced side of Jesus (19:34). Just as in Ezek 36:25–27, where the prophet proclaims, "I will sprinkle clean water upon you . . . and a new spirit I will put within you," the symbols of water and spirit signal a rebirth accomplished by divine action.[13]

---

12. See Schneiders, *Written That You May Believe*, 179 and Swetnam, "Bestowal of the Spirit in the Fourth Gospel," 556–76, for reasons why the expression παρέδωκεν τὸ πνεῦμα, "he handed over the Spirit," (19:30) should be understood as the giving of the Spirit rather than a euphemism for death.

13. Schneiders, *Written That You May Believe*, 121, notes that juxtaposing water and spirit should have alerted Nicodemus to the true meaning of spiritual birth, since the two are found in the promise of renewal in Ezekiel 36:25–27.

Gift of Living Water (John 4:10)

The episode of Jesus' encounter with the woman of Samaria (4:4–42) also advances the theme of birthing. After Jesus' initial request for a drink, and the woman's query, "How is it that you, a Jew, ask a drink of me, a woman of Samaria?" (4:9), the dialogue shifts to a deeper plane, as Jesus offers her the gift of "living water" (4:10). Like the scene with Nicodemus, the ensuing dialogue is rife with double entendre, misunderstanding, and irony, as Jesus and the woman reveal themselves to one another, and the meaning of the metaphor unfolds.

There are marital overtones in the scene, as biblical stories of a man meeting a woman at a well typically end in marriage. It was at a well that Abraham's servant found Rebekah, the future wife of Isaac (Gen 24:10-61), where Jacob met Rachel (Gen 29:1-20), and where Moses met Zipporah (Exod 2:16–22).[14] Accordingly, Jesus, who was identified by John the Baptist as the bridegroom (3:29), seeks to wed Samaria, represented by the woman.[15] The result of their encounter will be a birthing of faith in the Samaritan townspeople (4:39).

Jesus offers the woman "living water" (4:10), and elaborates, "Those who drink of the water I give them will never be thirsty. The water that I will give will become in them a spring of water gushing up to eternal life" (4:14). It is notable that "living water" or "flowing water" occurs several times in the Hebrew Scriptures where the expression has sexual overtones. In the Song of Songs, the lover says: "a garden locked is my sister, my bride, a garden locked, a fountain sealed . . . a garden fountain, a well of living water, and flowing streams from Lebanon" (4:12, 15). Similarly, the author of Proverbs advises that a man should take pleasure in his own wife, saying, "Drink water from your own cistern, flowing water from your own well" (5:15). The water Jesus promises the Samaritan woman can also be read against the backdrop of Old Testament writers and others of the period who used "water" to refer to "the processes of human reproduction and particularly to the actual coming forth from the womb after the breaking of the mother's water."[16]

---

14. Ibid., 135.

15. On the Fourth Evangelist's technique of using single characters in a representative role, see Raymond F. Collins, "Representative Figures."

16. Schneiders, *Written That You May Believe*, 120. See further Witherington, "The Waters of Birth, 155–60.

Jesus' offer to the woman of Samaria points toward the water of birth at the cross (19:34).

Living Water from the Womb (John 7:37–39)

The meaning of the expression "living water" is further developed in the scene during the Feast of Dedication, when Jesus cries out, "Let anyone who is thirsty come to me, and let the one who believes in me drink. As the Scripture has said, 'Out of the believer's heart (κοιλία) shall flow rivers of living water.' Now he said this about the Spirit, which believers in him were to receive; for as yet there was no Spirit, because Jesus was not yet glorified" (7:37–39). In v. 38 the word κοιλία, often translated in this passage as "heart,"[17] is actually the word for "womb, uterus,"[18] once again evoking a birthing image, and pointing ahead to the water that flows from the pierced side of Jesus in 19:34.

There is ambiguity in 7:38 with regard to the referent of the possessive pronoun. Is it the womb of Jesus or that of the believer from which the rivers of living water flow?[19] The expression κοιλίας αυτοῦ, "his womb," could refer to either the believer or Jesus. When read in light of 19:34, both referents can be understood to be in view. The life-giving mission birthed by Jesus is carried forward by believers, who are not mere receptacles for living water, but are themselves conduits of it.[20]

---

17. The phrase ἐκ τῆς κοιλίας αὐτοῦ is translated variously: "from the believer's heart." (NRSV), "from his heart" (NJB), "from within." (NAB), "out of his belly" (KJV).

18. This is clearly the meaning in John 3:4, where Nicodemus puzzles over how a person can "enter a second time into the mother's womb and be born." So also Luke 1:41, 44; 2:21; 11:27; 23:29. κοιλία can also mean "belly, stomach," as in Matt 15:17; Mark 7:19; Luke 15:16; 1 Cor 6:13; Rev 10:9. It can also be understood as the seat of inward life, of feelings and desires, thus the rendering of it in English as "heart." See BDAG, 550.

19. See Brown, *John*, 1.320–24 for a fuller discussion of the range of interpretive possibilities. The NAB footnote at 7:38 points out that if the referent is Jesus, it continues the Jesus-Moses motif, with an allusion to the water Moses drew from the rock (Exod 17:6; Num 20:11) or the theme of Jesus as the new Temple, alluding to the water flowing from the new temple (Ezek 47:1). The NAB editors judge that grammatically, αὐτοῦ goes better with the believer. BDAG notes however, that here κοιλία "has often been taken to be that of the believer, but there is an increasing tendency to punctuate with a period after ἐμέ in vs. 38 rather than after πινέτω at the end of vs. 37 [s. mg. and text] and understand κοιλία of Jesus" (p. 551).

20. Moore, "Are There Impurities in the Living Water," 87.

Labor Pangs in Birthing a Renewed People of God (John 16:21–22)

The use of the metaphor of birthing is nowhere more explicit than in the Farewell Discourse where Jesus speaks to his disciples about his impending passion, "Very truly, I tell you, you will weep and mourn, but the world will rejoice; you will have pain, but your pain will turn into joy. When a woman is in labor, she has pain, because her hour has come. But when her child is born, she no longer remembers the anguish because of the joy of having brought a human being into the world. So you have pain now; but I will see you again, and your hearts will rejoice, and no one can take your joy from you" (16:20–22).

With these verses, the Johannine author portrays Jesus' travail in parallel terms to the divine anguish in bringing forth the renewed Israel. Isaiah, voices God's struggle to rebirth Israel after the exile thus: "For a long time I have held my peace, I have kept still and restrained myself; now I will cry out like a woman in labor, I will gasp and pant" (Isa 42:14). Israel's own anguish over the longed-for peace and restoration is expressed similarly: "Like a woman with child, who writhes and cries out in her pangs when she is near her time, so were we because of you, O LORD; we were with child, we writhed, but we gave birth only to wind. We have won no victories on earth, and no one is born to inhabit the world." (Isa 26:17–18). This lament over the failure to give birth is followed with an assurance of hope in the ensuing verse: "Your dead shall live, their corpses shall rise. O dwellers in the dust, awake and sing for joy!" (Isa 26:19). Isaiah 66:7–8 assures speediness and effortlessness in Zion's birthing of a renewed people, "Before she was in labor she gave birth; before her pain came upon her she delivered a son. Who has heard of such a thing? Who has seen such things? Shall a land be born in one day? Shall a nation be delivered in one moment? Yet as soon as Zion was in labor she delivered her children."

There are other places in the Hebrew Scriptures where God is portrayed as a birthing mother. In his farewell before his death, Moses combines two powerful images as he admonishes the Israelites to be faithful: "You were unmindful of the Rock that bore you; you forgot the God who gave you birth" (Deut 32:18). In another text, the Psalmist acclaims: "You are my son; today I have begotten[21] you" (Ps 2:7). In

---

21. The LXX renders the Hebrew יְלִדְתִּיךָ as γεγέννηκα, the verb more often associated with female birthing than male begetting.

speaking of the divine work in creation, Job offers both images of a begetting father and a birthing mother: "Has the rain a father, or who has begotten the drops of dew? From whose womb did the ice come forth, and who has given birth to the hoarfrost of heaven?" (Job 38:28–29). In one instance Isaiah juxtaposes images of God as both nursing mother and birth mother: "Can a woman forget her nursing child, or show no compassion for the child of her womb? Even these may forget, yet I will not forget you" (49:15). Isaiah also portrays God as a comforting mother: "you shall nurse and be carried on her arm, and dandled on her knees. As a mother comforts her child, so I will comfort you; you shall be comforted in Jerusalem" (Isa 66:12–13).

There are also texts that portray God as a midwife. Isaiah reassures the successful rebirth of the people: "Shall I open the womb and not deliver? says the LORD; shall I, the one who delivers, shut the womb? says your God" (Isa 66:9). Similarly the Psalmist says, "Yet it was you who took me from the womb; you kept me safe on my mother's breast. On you I was cast from my birth, and since my mother bore me you have been my God" (Ps 22:9–10). It is notable that it is the opening verse of this same psalm, "My God, my God, why have you forsaken me?" that Mark and Matthew place on the lips of the dying Jesus (Mark 15:34; Matt 27:45). Virginia Ramey Mollenkott observes that the psalm "contains many harrowing details that well describe crucifixion" juxtaposed with the midwife image. She proposes, "We may imagine that in the hour of his own anguished 'birth contractions' on the cross, Jesus tried to comfort himself by remembering that God had been the midwife drawing him out of the womb of his own mother. Since God had been with him 'from my mother's womb,' Jesus, like the Psalmist, may have felt justified in hoping that God would not 'stand aside' now, when 'I have no one to help me.'"[22]

There is also an image of God as a midwife assisting the community through its afflictions in one of the hymns from Qumran. It is of note that twice birthing is said to be deathly.

> And I was in distress,
> As a woman in travail brings forth her first child;
> For her birth pangs wrench,
> And sharp pain, upon her birth canal
> (or, with her birth throes),

22. Mollenkott, *The Divine Feminine*, 33.

To cause writhing in the crucible of the pregnant one.
For sons have come to the deathly birth canal,
And she who is pregnant with a man is distressed by her pains;
For through deathly contractions she brings forth a male child,
And through infernal pains, there burst forth from the crucible of the pregnant one,
A Wonderful Counselor with his might,
And a man is delivered from the birth canal by the pregnant one. (1QH 3:7–18)[23]

An important observation is that images of birthing occur in two of the most crucial and painful times in Israel's history: the slavery in Egypt and the exile in Babylon.[24] The Fourth Evangelist employs this same metaphor so that the crucifixion of Jesus can be understood as a similar experience of death that God will use to open the way for new life. Just as in Isaiah, where the birth pangs are experienced by both God and Israel, so in John 16:20–22 Jesus speaks of the labor pains that both he and his disciples will undergo in his impending passion. The focus is on the ensuing joy at the new life that will result, not on the suffering as an end in itself. This promise of joy is fulfilled in the Johannine resurrection appearance stories. In John 20:1–2, 11–18, Mary Magdalene embodies the grieving community,[25] as she weeps inconsolably at the empty tomb. The weeping turns to joy for the gathered community when Jesus appears to the disciples gathered behind locked doors in the upper room. After greeting them "Peace be with you" and showing them his hands and side "the disciples rejoiced when they saw the Lord" (20:20).

---

23. Ford. *Redeemer, Friend and Mother*, 165. Ford quotes the text from Brownlee, "Messianic Motifs of Qumran and the New Testament," 23–24. See also Judith Lieu's comments on this text ("The Mother of the Son in the Fourth Gospel," 61–77, esp. 73–74), who notes that "waves of death" (1QH 3:8–9) may be a play on "mouth of the womb." She comments, "The womb can sometimes be viewed as a grave, and the woman as the mediator of birth through death, birth and death, provides the proper context for the Johannine passage" (74).

24. Ford, *Redeemer, Friend, and Mother*, 43.

25. Just as the Samaritan woman is a representative character for her people, so Mary Magdalene embodies the community of disciples. She speaks in the plural, "we do not know where they have laid him" (20:2).

Birthed from the Side of Jesus (John 19:34)

The theme of birthing, so carefully woven throughout the gospel, climaxes in the crucifixion scene, where, following Jesus' death, "one of the soldiers pierced his side with a spear, and at once blood and water came out" (19:34).[26] The birthing of a renewed people of God is symbolized by the breaking of the amniotic fluid, accompanied by uterine blood.[27] The "power to become children of God" that was assured in the Prologue (1:12) is accomplished. The mother of Jesus, who gave him physical birth and who mediated the birth of his public ministry (2:1–11), is present again (19:25), as witness of the fulfillment of his earthly life and mission, and as midwife to the rebirth of the people who will continue his mission. Nicodemus, who struggled to understand what "born again/from above" could mean in 3:1–21, returns with Joseph of Arimathea, with a hundred pounds of myrrh and aloe with which to embalm Jesus' body (19:39). As they wrap Jesus' body with the spices in linen cloths (19:40), images of death and birth meld. They swaddle him with bands of cloth, as with a newborn (Luke 2:7).[28] The presence of Nicodemus also recalls Jesus' words to him about being born by water and the Spirit (3:5), which is now accomplished.[29] Jesus' offer of "living water" (4:10) and his promise that from his womb and that of the believer would flow "rivers of living water" (7:38), is brought to fulfillment as he hands over the spirit (19:30). Jesus' final declaration, "It is finished" (19:30) can be heard as the declaration of a mother who cries out in joy when the birthpangs are over and her child is born.[30]

---

26. For a discussion and further references on those who attempt to explain this phenomenon historically and medically, rather than symbolically, see Brown, *John*, 2.946–48; Brown, *Death of the Messiah*, 2.1088–92; Edwards, Gabel, and Hosmer, "On the Physical Death of Jesus Christ," 1455–63. For a sampling of the enormous body of literature on the spiritual meaning of the pierced side of Jesus, see Brown, *Death of the Messiah*, 2.1178–79, n. 95.

27. Ford, *Redeemer, Friend, and Mother*, 195. The author of Hebrews uses a similar image: "we have courage to enter the sanctuary by the blood of Jesus, by the new and living way that he opened for us through the curtain (that is, through his flesh)" (Heb 10:19–20).

28. Kitzberger, "Transcending Gender Boundaries in John," 204.

29. See Brown, *John*, 2.950, for comments on 1 John 5:6–8, which has the same confluence of water, blood, spirit, testimony as John 19:34–35.

30. Ford, *Redeemer, Friend, and Mother*, 196.

Insufflation with the Breath of Life (John 20:19–23)

One final image associated with birth is found in the resurrection appearance scene in which the disciples' grief turns to joy (20:19–23). After a two-fold blessing of peace, and after entrusting his mission to the disciples, Jesus then breathes on them and says, "Receive the holy Spirit" (20:22). Just as a midwife may blow breath into the nostrils of a newborn to help it to breathe on its own, so Jesus breathes the breath of the Spirit upon the rebirthed community.[31] There is an echo of the action of the Creator, who birthed the first human creature by breathing into its nostrils "the breath of life" and it became a "living being" (Gen 2:7). Ezekiel also used this image in prophesying the rebirth of Israel, as he proclaimed over the valley of dry bones, "I will cause breath to enter you and you shall live" (Ezek 37:5). The Book of Wisdom calls on this image while lamenting the foolishness of those who worship clay idols, who "failed to know the one who formed them and inspired them with active souls and breathed a living spirit into them" (Wis 15:11).

A Long History of Interpreting Jesus' Death as Birth

It is not a modern feminist invention to interpret Jesus' passion as labor pangs through which new life is birthed.[32] As early as the turn of the third century, Clement of Alexandria (153–217) wrote about "the body of Christ, which nourishes by the Word the young brood, which the Lord Himself brought forth in throes of flesh, which the Lord Himself swathed in his precious blood." He then exclaims, "O amazing birth!" (*The Instructor* 1.6).[33] Similarly, Ambrose, bishop of Milan (d. 397) refers to Christ as the "Virgin who bare us, Who fed us with her own milk" (*On Virgins* 1:5).[34] In Syriac tradition there is a comparison made between Adam's side that gave birth to Eve and the pierced side of Jesus that gave birth to the church. In the sixth century, Jacob of Serugh wrote:

---

31. Ibid., 200.

32. The following references and quotations are taken from Ford, *Redeemer, Friend, and Mother*, 196–97.

33. For an English translation of the text, see http://www.ccel.org/ccel/schaff/anf02.vi.iii.i.vi.html.

34. For the English translation of the text see: http://www.ccel.org/ccel/schaff/npnf210.iv.vii.ii.v.html.

> For from the beginning God knew and depicted
> Adam and Eve in the likeness of the image of his Only-begotten;
> He slept on the cross as Adam had slept his deep sleep,
> his side was pierced and from it there came forth the Daughter of Light,
> water and blood as an image of divine children
> to be heirs to the Father who loves his Only-begotten ...
>
> Adam's side gave birth to a woman who gives birth to immortals.
> In the crucifixion he completed the types that had been depicted,
> and the hidden mystery that had been covered revealed itself.[35]

In another place Jacob writes:

> His side was pierced in his sleep,
> he gave birth to the Bride, as happened with Eve...
> And from him came forth the Mother who gives birth to all spiritual beings:
> ...water and blood for the fashioning of spiritual babes
> flowed from the side of that Living One who died, in order to bring life to Adam.[36]

Maternal images of Jesus were most prevalent in the Middle Ages.[37] Carthusian prioress Marguerite Oingt (d. 1310), for example, speaks of mother Jesus, "Ah, my sweet and lovely Lord, with what love you labored for me and bore me through your whole life ... when the hour of your delivery came you were placed on the hard bed of the cross ... and your nerves and all your veins were broken. And truly it is no surprise that your veins burst when in one day you gave birth to the whole world."[38] Julian of Norwich (mid-fourteenth century), says that Jesus "our savior is our true Mother in whom we are endlessly born and out of whom—

---

35. Ford, *Redeemer, Friend, and Mother*, 196.

36. Ibid., 197.

37. See Bynum, *Jesus as Mother*.

38. Quoted in Bynum, *Jesus as Mother*, 153. Another image associated with the pierced side of Jesus is that of an "open door" by which a believer "may enter whole," into the heart of Jesus, "the sure seat" of his mercy (William of St. Thierry, quoted in Bynum, *Jesus as Mother*, 120). In addition to speaking of "the holes in the wall of his [Jesus'] body, in which, like a dove, you may hide," Aelred of Rievaulx (d. 1167), among others, thinks of the blood and water from the side of Christ as offering nourishment: "Then one of the soldiers opened his side with a lance and there came forth blood and water. Hasten, linger not, eat the honeycomb with your honey, drink your wine with your milk. The blood is changed into wine to gladden you, the water into milk to nourish you" (from *De institutione,* chap. 31, *Opera omnia* 1:671, quoted in Bynum, *Jesus as Mother*, 123).

we shall come."[39] And further, "all the lovely works, all the sweet and loving offices of beloved motherhood are appropriated to the second person for in him we have this godly will, whole and safe forever, both in nature and grace, from his own goodness proper to him."[40] In a similar vein, the German Dominican mystic and scholar Meister Eckhart (1260–1328) mused, "What does God do all day long?" His answer was, "God lies on a maternity bed giving birth all day long."

An Antidote to Atonement

Almost all Christians, when asked why Jesus died, respond quickly and simply: "to save me from my sins." Atonement for sin, while only one of myriad theological explanations for the death of Jesus found in the New Testament, has had the greatest staying power in the minds and spiritualities of Christians. Many theologians have recently engaged in discussions about the pitfalls inherent in this theology, pointing out the ways in which it can foment violence and victimization.[41] Dangerous images of an offended God who needed to be appeased or paid off for human sinfulness have had frightening consequences, especially in the lives of women who are abused. Countless women think of themselves as deserving of punishment for their sinfulness and they submit mutely to violence directed at them. Many make meaning of their suffering by understanding it as the way to follow Jesus by "taking up their cross." Metaphors of ransom, scapegoat, or silent suffering servant likewise pose problematic images of a divine Father who sends his son to be tortured and executed in exchange for human liberation. Such formulations obscure the gratuitous love of God, placing sin and guilt center stage. In addition, they promote meek compliance in persons oppressed

---

39. Julian of Norwich, *Showings*, 292.

40. Ibid., 296–97. For a different interpretation of the Johannine crucifixion scene, see Fehribach, *The Women in the Life of the Bridegroom*, 115–42. Fehribach sees the death of Jesus as a blood sacrifice that establishes a patrilineal kinship group. With Jesus portrayed as giving birth to the children of God, women's roles and powers are co-opted and the birthing role of his mother obliterated.

41. A short sample includes: Brock and Parker, *Proverbs of Ashes*; Callahan, *Created for Joy*; Finlan, *Problems With Atonement*; Grey, *Redeeming the Dream*; *Feminism, Redemption and the Christian Tradition*; Heim, *Saved from Sacrifice*; Heyward, *The Redemption of God*; Chung, *Struggle to be the Sun Again*; Johnson, *She Who Is*; Schüssler Fiorenza, *Jesus: Miriam's Son, Sophia's Prophet*; Thomsen, *Christ Crucified*; Trelstad, ed., *Cross Examinations*.

by violence and systems of injustice, rather than stir them to action to do what they can to confront and dismantle these systems.

The image of Jesus' death as birth offers rich theological and pastoral possibilities and avoids some of the pitfalls of other metaphors. As with every metaphor, there are both positive and negative aspects. One of the positive contributions that the birth metaphor offers is that it opens the way for female disciples to identify more fully with Christ, the Creator, and the Spirit. Gender boundaries are blurred and transcended in the images presented in the Fourth Gospel of the person of Jesus,[42] who gives birth to a renewed people, of God who births believers (1:13), and of the Spirit, through whom believers are born again/from above (3:5).[43] As all three members of the Trinity are spoken of in birthing terms, a helpful insight is that it is not one single member that is the "female face" of God; the whole of the divine being and divine activity is expressed in female form and action. Taking this to heart can lead to a transformed reality. Guatemalan Nobel prize-winner Julia Esquivel articulates what will be the effect when women and men are both equally recognized as the image and likeness of God: there will be "equality in difference, flourishing in a creative, fruitful harmony, in the couple and in the relationships of all peoples and societies."[44]

In addition, the metaphor of birthing gives dignity to the bodily experience of women and sees it as a locus for the holy.[45] This image helps break down the dualism between what is bodily and what is spiritual, helping believers to encounter God in all aspects of life. It feeds an incarnational faith that rejoices in the Word having become flesh (1:14) and that finds the divine in what is bodily, not in spite of it.

From such an image of God's action in Jesus and the Spirit, comes liberation and empowerment. As María Clara Bingemer describes:

---

42. See further Kitzberger, "Transcending Gender Boundaries," 193; María Clara Bingemer, "Mujer y Cristología. Jesucristo y la salvación de la mujer," 89–90. See also Johnson, "The Maleness of Christ," 307–15.

43. See Aquino, "The God of Life and the *Rachamim* of the Trinity," and "Speaking of God in the Feminine," 130–38; Bingemer, "Reflections on the Trinity," 56–80.

44. Esquivel, "Conquered and Violated Women," 113.

45. For a more extensive exploration of this theme and of the image of all creation coming from the womb of God, see McFague, *Body of God*.

> The poor who are discovering themselves as active makers of history and are organizing for liberation are experiencing God as the God of life, as embodying the very fullness of life, as the only source from which it is possible to derive hope and promise in the situation of death they live every day. God's female entrails—maternal *rahamin*, fertile, in labor and compassionate—enable this liberation to come about with force and firmness, but also with creativity and gentleness, without violence. Once God is experienced, not only as Father, Lord, strong warrior, but also as Mother, protection, greater love, struggle is tempered with festivity and celebration of life, permanent and gentle firmness ensures the ability 'to be tough without losing tenderness,' and uncompromising resistance can be carried on with joy, without excessive tension and sterile strain. God's compassion, flowing from female and maternal entrails, takes on itself the hurts and wounds of all the oppressed, and a woman who does theology is called to bear witness to this God with her body, her actions, her life.[46]

Such female imagery of God also opens up new possibilities for women who have survived incest or sexual abuse by a male relative. For many such survivors, relating to a male image of God is impossible. As Shirley Gillett observes, "Depictions of God as a loving Father wanting a close relationship with his children may be comforting to those who have had loving earthly fathers, but for women whose fathers approached them looking for close relationships that involved pain and humiliation, these depictions are both terrifying and distancing."[47]

Finally, the birthing metaphor gives value to suffering, as part of a natural process, but not as deserved or desirable. Suffering is seen as the consequence of a choice to entrust oneself to love. This metaphor enables us to understand Jesus' self-gift as similar to that of lovers who choose to make painful sacrifices out of love for the other, able to be endured because of that love, and because of the new life that will result. Unlike the kinds of economic transactions between God and humanity that are implied in sacrificial and ransom metaphors, the birthing image evokes an exchange of love that is mutual and self-replicating.

---

46. Bingemer, "Women in the Future of the Theology of Liberation," 485.
47. Gillett, "No Church to Call Home," 108–09.

Dangerous Directions

As empowering as is the image of Jesus' death as birth, there are also dangerous aspects. First, birthing and motherhood are easily romanticized, especially by those committed to celibacy![48] The reality that not all children are conceived in love, that some are unwanted, and that some are the product of rape,[49] can become obscured in a romantic aura painted around motherhood. In addition, not all birth pangs give way to joy. As Kathleen Rushton points out, "particularly for young women, childbirth may be the result of lack of information and choice, poverty, exploitation, sexual and cultural violence. Hazards arise from fertility control, or lack of it, and the low priority given to diseases affecting women."[50] There can be increased anxiety about the ability to economically support more children and the impact of pregnancy and childrearing on one's ability to work.[51] In addition, childbirth can result in death, for the mother, the child, or both. In antiquity approximately one in three women died in childbirth.[52] Today in the developing world,

---

48. Johnson, *She Who Is*, 177–78. See Bynum, *Jesus as Mother*, 133, for remarks on the how the sentimentalizing of maternal images by medieval monks and mystics functioned. She notes, "It was peculiarly appropriate to a theological emphasis on an accessible and tender God, a God who bleeds and suffers less as a sacrifice or restoration of cosmic order than as a stimulus to human love." McFague, "Mother God," 138–43, here 139, observes that we should "not suppose that mothers are 'naturally' loving, comforting, or self-sacrificing. Our society has a stake in making women think that they are biologically programmed to be these things, when, in fact, a good case can be made that the so-called qualities or stereotypes of mothers are social constructions—women are not born, but become, mothers through education and imitation."

49. In the U.S.A. it is estimated that one woman is beaten every 15 seconds; one woman is raped every three to six minutes. See "Get the Facts: The Facts on Domestic, Dating, and Sexual Violence," http://www.endabuse.org/content/action_center/detail/754. See also AARDVARC, An Abuse, Rape and Domestic Violence Aid and Resource Collection: http://www.aardvarc.org/dv/statistics.shtml. For global information see the UNICEF report on Domestic Violence Against Women and Girls: http://www.unicef-icdc.org/publications/pdf/digest6e.pdf.

50. Rushton, "The (Pro)creative Parables," 208.

51. Ibid., 223.

52. Ford, *Redeemer, Friend, and Mother*, 38, does not provide the evidence on which she bases this assertion. Osiek and MacDonald, *A Woman's Place*, 20, note that "in antiquity giving birth was by far the greatest threat to a young woman's life." See also their discussion of "Giving Birth, Labor, Nursing, and the Care of Infants in House-Church Communities," ibid., 50–67. Ilan, *Jewish Women in Greco-Roman Palestine*, 116–19, examines literary and inscriptional evidence. She contests the estimate of Mayer, *Die*

sixty-one percent of women receive no pre-natal care, fifty percent of women give birth without professional medical assistance, and one in forty-eight die in childbirth.[53] Consider, too, the anguish of a mother who endures agonizing labor, only to have her child stillborn or live only a brief time. Currently, in Bolivia, for example, which is the poorest country in Latin America, four hundred and twenty women per one thousand die in childbirth; sixty-eight of every one thousand children born die as infants; 93 of every one thousand die before they reach five years of age.[54] There is also the danger that is posed by the idealized image of mothers who die to themselves to give life to their children, which can all too easily render women sacrificial victims to others' desires.

Another problematic aspect is when motherhood is seen as the epitome of woman's calling and "mother" is the only female image offered for God. Other images than mother, such as "sister," "midwife," "friend," are needed to speak of the ways that single women, vowed celibate women, childless married women and widows incarnate divine being.[55] Another danger is the use of parental metaphors at all for God. Thinking of the divine in either maternal or paternal images can narrow our ways of relating to God, keeping us in perpetual childhood. As Sallie McFague remarks, "At a time when we need desperately to be 'adults,' to take responsibility for our world and its well-being, we cannot support a model that suggests that the 'great mother' or 'great father'

---

jüdische Frau in der hellenistisch-römischen Antike, 93, that about 50 percent of women die in childbirth, and advances that the figure was closer to 5 percent, based on the number of ossuaries of women buried with their children.

53. United Nations State of the World Population Report, 2000.

54. United Nations State of the World Population Report 2005. The maternal mortality figure is from 2000. The statistics measuring infant mortality are from 1993–2003. http://www.un.org/esa/population/publications/worldmortality/WMR2005.pdf. By contrast, in the U.S.A. the maternal mortality rate is only 17 per 1000; only 7 children per one thousand die as infants; 8 children per thousand die before their fifth birthday.

55. McFague, "Mother God," 139, remarks on how dangerous and oppressive maternal language can be when it suggests that women who are not mothers are not true or fulfilled women, and when it gives power to an image that has been used to oppress women over the centuries. She cautions that we must be careful to see the maternal model of God as only *one* model; we must also speak of God as sister, midwife, and in other female terms. See also her chapter "God as Mother" in *Models of God*, 97–123; and Johnson, *She Who Is*, 177–78.

will take care of our crises of poverty, discrimination, damage to the ecosystem, and so forth."[56]

One other problematic aspect is that this image that is particular to women has been co-opted by men to give voice to their experience, thus obliterating specifically female embodiment of the divine. Whereas the transcendence of gender boundaries in the depiction of a male Jesus who gives birth can help work toward dissolving hierarchies and inequities based on gender differences, it can also obscure the ability of women to fully image the divine. From as early as the apostle Paul, male spiritual writers have appropriated to themselves the images of birthing and mothering. Paul addresses the Galatians, "My little children, for whom I am again in the pain of childbirth until Christ is formed in you" (Gal 4:19). In another instance, he uses the image of a nursing mother, saying to the Thessalonians, "we were gentle among you like a nurse tenderly caring for her own children" (1 Thess 2:7). While it is important for men and women to collaborate in advancing ways in which female bodies and experience are seen as fully expressive of divine being and action, it is not always helpful to have female experience appropriated by men.

Mother Jesus and the Mother of Jesus

The role that the mother of Jesus plays in the Fourth Gospel in relation to Jesus' death has much potential for opening new liberative avenues. While traditionally the image of Jesus' mother at the foot of the cross has provided comfort, accompaniment, and strength to endure suffering, there is also potential in the Johannine figure of Jesus' mother for confronting patriarchal attitudes and for opening out other horizons for women. At Cana, Jesus' mother is not resigned and accepting of the plight in which the hosts and guests find themselves. She takes initiative toward resolving the distress, and insists that her son alleviate the situation. Despite his protest, she recognizes it is the correct time for the birthing of his public ministry. She does not back down from her expectations. On a human level, a lack of wine at a wedding is not exactly a situation of injustice that needs to be confronted. But on a theological level, the necessity for Jesus to manifest himself so as to begin the birthing process of bringing disciples to belief in him was a matter of

56. McFague, "Mother God," 139.

life and death. The fortitude and perceptiveness of Jesus' mother are qualities that are essential for contemporary women as they recognize the opportune moments for initiating change and gather their strength to act as midwife to justice and new life.

Likewise, the image of Jesus' mother at the foot of the cross can be seen not only as a dolorous mother who is helpless to stop her son's execution, and who can only offer her pain up to God, but she can also be viewed as a witness to the injustice of Jesus' execution, who protests it by her presence and her testimony. She refuses to let the death-dealing of the empire have the upper hand, as she once again mediates the birth of new life, acquiring new children in the community of the Beloved Disciple, and nurturing their mission, as she first did with her biological son. She refuses to be defeated by the powers of domination and death, and, empowered by the Spirit, she accompanies the fledgling community of disciples into their mission for life.[57]

For Mexican and Mexican-American women the image of Our Lady of Guadalupe can also be an emancipatory image. Guadalupe presents a strong symbol of God's solidarity with and care for the poorest and the least powerful. Appearing as an india, with dark skin, and adorned with symbols of Aztec divinity, she embodies God's presence with, and predilection for, the conquered native peoples. Like Jesus, who became one with humanity by taking on flesh (John 1:14), so Guadalupe takes on the appearance of an indigenous woman, incarnating God's presence with those who suffer most. And like Jesus, she is not simply present with people who suffer, but she embodies God's power to alleviate suffering, through her embrace of tender motherly love, and through transformation of unjust structures. When Guadalupe appears to Juan Diego, she births in him the courage to confront the Spanish Archbishop Zumárraga with her liberating message. By wrapping Juan Diego in her tenacious motherly protection and treating him with dignity and respect, Guadalupe emboldens him to move from his dejection and submission as a conquered person, to one who takes action for the restoration and dignity of his people. Like Jesus whose death is a birth

---

57. The Fourth Evangelist does not tell any more of the story of Jesus' mother beyond the scene of the cross. It is Luke who names Mary as present with the eleven, the other women, and with Jesus' siblings when the Spirit descends on them at Pentecost (Acts 1:14). Ancient legends continue the story, saying that she traveled to Ephesus, in the companionship of the Beloved Disciple, where she is said to have died.

to new life, Guadalupe appears as pregnant, heralding hope of new life for a victimized people. She opens the way to envision and take action toward a different World.[58]

Conclusion

The Fourth Gospel provides us with depictions of Jesus and his mother that provide potent images of God's power to birth new life out of death. Such portrayals give us an antidote to theologies that focus on God's wrath or human sinfulness. God's love, freely given, life-giving and productive, evokes from us a response in kind, transforming even the most hopeless of situations. As Ivone Gebara says,

> To be birthed anew is to return to our roots, to re-enter the maternal uterus, the breast of the earth, and so rediscover who we are. The image of a Father God, who exists independently from its child, who causes all to submit to himself—this is not our true origin. This image is . . . not capable of uniting humanity, respecting differences. We have to return to the matrix, earth, suck primal energy from her. This entails a spiritual-ethical-political movement, which does not accept that we can just contemplate passively the mystery of life. It enters constantly into the work of birthing, so that women and men passionate for life and for a unifying anthropological vision, can overcome deadly dualisms.[59]

It takes risk and courage to give birth to new ways of thinking, understanding, relating, and living. For Carolyn Osiek's intrepid spirit that engendered feminist hope in me while committed to ministry in a church deeply entrenched in patriarchy, I am profoundly grateful.

---

58. Rodríguez, *Our Lady of Guadalupe*, 139.
59. Gebara, *Teología a ritmo de mujer*, 136.

Bibliography

Aquino, María Pilar, "The God of Life and the *Rachamim* of the Trinity," and "Speaking of God in the Feminine." In *Our Cry for Life: Feminist Theology from Latin America*, 130–38. Maryknoll, NY: Orbis, 1993.

Bingemer, María Clara, "Mujer y Cristología. Jesucristo y la salvación de la mujer." In *Aportes para una Teología desde la Mujer*, edited by María Pilar Aquino, 89–90. Nuevo Exodo 5. Madrid: Biblia y Fe, 1988.

———. "Women in the Future of the Theology of Liberation." In *The Future of Liberation Theology. Essays in Honor of Gustavo Gutiérrez*, edited by Marc H. Ellis and Otto Maduro, 473–90. Maryknoll, NY: Orbis, 1989.

Brock, Rita Nakashima, and Rebecca Ann Parker. *Proverbs of Ashes: Violence, Redemptive Suffering, and the Search for What Saves Us*. Boston: Beacon, 2001.

Brown, Raymond E. *The Death of the Messiah: From Gethsemane to the Grave. A Commentary on the Passion Narratives in the Four Gospels*. 2 vols. ABRL. Garden City, NY: Doubleday, 1994.

———. *The Gospel according to John*. 2 vols. AB 29, 29A. Garden City, NY: Doubleday, 1966, 1970.

Bynum, Caroline Walker. *Jesus as Mother: Studies in the Spirituality of the High Middle Ages*. Berkeley: University of California Press, 1982.

Callahan, Sidney. *Created for Joy. A Christian View of Suffering*. New York: Crossroad, 2007.

Collins, Raymond F. "The Representative Figures in the Fourth Gospel." *Downside Review* 94 (1976) 26–46, 118–32.

Edwards, W. D., W. J. Gabel, and F. E. Hosmer. "On the Physical Death of Jesus Christ." *Journal of the American Medical Association* 255 (1986) 1455–63.

Esquivel, Julia. "Conquered and Violated Women." In *The Power of Naming. A Concilium Reader in Feminist Liberation Theology*, edited by Elisabeth Schüssler Fiorenza, 105–14. Maryknoll, NY: Orbis, 1996.

Fehribach, Adeline. *The Women in the Life of the Bridegroom: A Feminist Historical-Literary Analysis of the Female Characters in the Fourth Gospel*. Collegeville, MN: Liturgical, 1998.

Finlan, Stephen. *Problems with Atonement: The Origins of, and Controversy about, the Atonement Doctrine*. Collegeville, MN: Liturgical, 2005.

Ford, Josephine Massyngbaerde. *Redeemer, Friend, and Mother: Salvation in Antiquity and in the Gospel of John*. Minneapolis: Fortress, 1997.

Gebara, Ivone. *Teología a ritmo de mujer*. Translated by José Ma. Hernández. Mexico: Dabar, 1995.

Gillett, Shirley. "No Church to Call Home." In *Women, Abuse, and the Bible: How Scripture Can Be Used to Hurt or to Heal*, edited by Catherine Clark Kroeger and James R. Beck, 108–9 Grand Rapids: Baker, 1996.

Grey, Mary. *Feminism, Redemption and the Christian Tradition*. Mystic, CT: Twenty-Third Publications, 1990.

———. *Redeeming the Dream: Feminism, Redemption and Christian Tradition*. London: SPCK, 1989.

Heim, Mark S. *Saved from Sacrifice. A Theology of the Cross*. Grand Rapids: Eerdmans, 2006.

Heyward, Carter. *The Redemption of God: A Theology of Mutual Relation*. 1982. Reprinted, Eugene, OR: Wipf & Stock, 2010.

Ilan, Tal. *Jewish Women in Greco-Roman Palestine*. Peabody, MA: Hendrickson, 1996.

Johnson, Elizabeth A. "The Maleness of Christ." In *The Power of Naming: A Concilium Reader in Feminist Liberation Theology*, edited by Elisabeth Schüssler Fiorenza, 307–15. Maryknoll, NY: Orbis, 1996.

———. *She Who Is: The Mystery of God in Feminist Theological Discourse*. New York: Crossroad, 1994.

Jones, Larry Paul. *The Symbol of Water in the Gospel of John*. JSNTSup 145. Sheffield: Sheffield Academic, 1997.

Julian of Norwich. *Showings*. New York: Paulist, 1978.

Kitzberger, Ingrid Rosa. "Transcending Gender Boundaries in John." In *A Feminist Companion to John. Vol. 1*, edited by Amy-Jill Levine with Marianne Blickenstaff, 173–207. FCNT 4. Cleveland: Pilgrim, 2003.

Koester, Craig R. *Symbolism in the Fourth Gospel: Meaning, Mystery, Community*. 2nd ed. Minneapolis: Fortress, 2003.

Kyung, Chung Hyun. *Struggle to Be the Sun Again: Introducing Asian Women's Theology*. London: SCM, 1990.

Lee, Dorothy. *Flesh and Glory: Symbolism, Gender, and Theology in the Gospel of John*. New York: Crossroad, 2002.

Lieu, Judith, "The Mother of the Son in the Fourth Gospel." *JBL* 117 (1998) 61–77.

McFague, Sallie. *The Body of God: An Ecological Theology*. Minneapolis: Fortress, 1993.

———. "Mother God." In *Motherhood: Experience, Institution, Theology*, edited by Anne Carr and Elisabeth Schüssler Fiorenza, 138–43. Concilium 206. Religion in the Eighties. Edinburgh: T. & T. Clark, 1989.

Mollenkott, Virginia Ramey. *The Divine Feminine: The Biblical Imagery of God as Female*. New York: Crossroad, 1983.

Moore, Stephen D. "Are There Impurities in the Living Water That the Johannine Jesus Dispenses?" In *A Feminist Companion to John*, vol. 1, edited by Amy-Jill Levine with Marianne Blickenstaff, 78–97. FCNT 4. New York: Sheffield Academic, 2003.

Osiek, Carolyn. *Beyond Anger: On Being a Feminist in the Church*. New York: Paulist, 1986.

Osiek, Carolyn, and Margaret Y. MacDonald, with Janet H. Tulloch. *A Woman's Place: House Churches in Earliest Christianity*. Minneapolis: Fortress, 2006.

Reid, Barbara. *Taking up the Cross: New Testament Interpretations through Latina and Feminist Eyes*. Minneapolis: Fortress, 2007.

Rodríguez, Jeannette. *Our Lady of Guadalupe: Faith and Empowerment among Mexican-American Women*. Austin: University of Texas Press, 1994.

Rushton, Kathleen. "The (Pro)creative Parables of Labour and Childbirth (John 3:1–10 and 16:21–22)." In *The Lost Coin: Parables of Women, Work, and Wisdom*, edited by Mary Ann Beavis, 206–29. BibSem 86. Sheffield: Sheffield Academic, 2002.

Schneiders, Sandra M. *Written That You May Believe. Encountering Jesus in the Fourth Gospel*. Rev. ed. New York: Crossroad, 2003.

Schüssler Fiorenza, Elisabeth. *Jesus: Miriam's Son, Sophia's Prophet.* New York: Continuum, 1994.

Swetnam, James. "Bestowal of the Spirit in the Fourth Gospel," *Bib* 74 (1993) 556–76.

Támez, Elsa, editor. *Through Her Eyes. Women's Theology from Latin America.* Maryknoll, NY: Orbis, 1989.

Thomsen, Mark W. *Christ Crucified: A 21st Century Missiology of the Cross.* Minneapolis: Lutheran University Press, 2004.

Trelstad, Marit, editor. *Cross Examinations: Readings on the Meaning of the Cross Today.* Minneapolis: Fortress, 2006.

Witherington, Ben III. "The Waters of Birth: John 3.5 and 1 John 5.6–8." *NTS* 35 (1989) 155–60.

History and Theology in the Johannine Presentation of the Causes for the Death of Jesus

John 11:45–53 as Convergence Point

Donald Senior

IT IS AN HONOR FOR ME TO CONTRIBUTE TO THIS VOLUME IN HONOR OF Carolyn Osiek, RSCJ. She has been a long-time friend and a colleague in the biblical department at Catholic Theological Union for twenty-five years. I am pleased to dedicate this probe into the historical context of John's Gospel in her honor.[1] Her own distinguished work focused on the social context of early Christianity, particularly its interaction with the Greco-Roman world. The interface of the Johannine community is a topic of growing interest for biblical scholarship and this study of a unique Johannine passage is intended to be a modest contribution to that perspective.

A Review of the Passage and Its Literary Context

The Johannine account of the deliberations of the "council" in 11:45–53 is an interesting example of the convergence of historical, literary, ethical and theological dimensions of the causes and meaning of Jesus' death in the Fourth Gospel.

This scene is a key transition point between the climax of the public ministry of Jesus in the story of the raising of Lazarus in chapter 11 and the unfolding of the passion story that begins in chapter 13. It is commonplace to consider the Lazarus story as the climax of the so-called

---

1. This is an adaptation of a paper presented at the Society of Biblical Literature seminar on John, Jesus, and History in November, 2008.

"Book of Signs" and of Jesus' public ministry as presented by John. The meeting of the Sanhedrin is triggered by concern over public reaction to Jesus' raising of Lazarus but, as will be noted below, this reaction is also part of a larger pattern of reactions to Jesus' public ministry earlier in the gospel story. Likewise, the determination of the council to seek Jesus' death at the conclusion of their deliberations provides immediate preparation for the passion story itself (see 11:53).

There is relatively little debate about the essential contents of the passage. The immediate result of the raising of Lazarus is that "many of the Jews" who had witnessed this spectacular sign "believed in him [Jesus]" while "some of them" reported to the "Pharisees" what Jesus had done (11:45–46). The Pharisees, together with the "chief priests," convene the "a meeting of the council" (συνέδριον 11:47). The role of the Pharisees in this pivotal episode is noteworthy. In the Synoptic Gospels, once the passion story begins, the Pharisees cede ground to the priests and elders as the chief opponents of Jesus. John, on the other hand, identifies them as the drivers of this scene and as participating in the deliberations of the council or Sanhedrin and also, along with the chief priests, initiating the arrest of Jesus on the eve of his death (18:3).[2]

The precise meaning of the term συνέδριον, or "council", is a subject of debate. The term could refer to a formal deliberative body. Since most historians consider it unlikely that such a formal juridical body with this make-up existed during Jesus' lifetime that would make John's assertion anachronistic.[3] However, the term could simply mean a more

---

2. The Pharisees play a decisively negative role in John's Gospel; with the exception of 3:1 which simply identifies Nicodemus as a member of the Pharisees, John portrays this group of religious leaders as standing in opposition to Jesus (and seemingly to John the Baptist in 1:24). As in 11:47 they are often concerned about the reactions to Jesus: for example: in 7:32 the response of the crowds to Jesus prompts them to join the other leaders in attempting to arrest Jesus, in 7:45–52 when the attempt to arrest Jesus fails, and in the episode of the man born blind where the Pharisees are hostile to the man and his parents because of their reaction to Jesus (9:13, 15, 16, 40). Concern about the crowd's favorable reaction to Jesus continues in 12:19 and 12:42 (where the crowds themselves are afraid to openly confess their belief in Jesus because the Pharisees might expel them from the synagogue). In several of these passages, the Pharisees join with the "chief priests" as in meeting of the council: see 7:32, 45; 11:57; 18:3.

3. Bammel, for example, considers the fact that Pharisees participate in the council in John's account more typical of the period from Agrippa to the Jewish War than at the time of Jesus. However, he states that the inclusion of Pharisees at this earlier period cannot be ruled out (Bammel, "Ex Illa Itaque Die Consilium Fecerunt . . . ," 20–21); Brown has a similar view (Brown, *John*, 440).

informal gathering of the elite decision makers trying to come to some strategic decision about the threat posed by Jesus.[4]

The translation of the plaint of the leaders in v. 47 could either be deliberative, "What are we to do?" (see NRSV, NAB, etc.) or an exasperated declaration, "What are we doing?" with the implication that nothing is being done.[5] The specific problem is that "this man is performing many signs. And if we let him go on like this, everyone will believe in him, and the Romans will come and destroy both our holy place (literally, τὸν τόπον) and our nation (literally τὸ ἔθνος)" (v. 48).

The precise meaning of the term τόπος is somewhat ambiguous. It could refer to "land," as in the NAB ("both our land and our nation") but John's Gospel never uses the word elsewhere in this sense. It might also refer to the temple as a sacred place (see NRSV "holy place"), although John does not oblige by adding the word "holy" as, for example, in Matthew 21:15 (ἐν τόπῳ ἁγίῳ). However, out of 17 uses of the word (all referring to a specific place or location) one other instance of the term's use in John might justify translating the word as "temple" and that is John 4:20 where the Samaritan woman tells Jesus "but you say that in Jerusalem is the place where one must worship" (καὶ ὑμεῖς λέγετε ὅτι ἐν Ἱεροσολύμοις ἐστὶν ὁ τόπος ὅπου προσκυνεῖν δει). The "place" in Jerusalem where Jews worshipped was obviously the temple and so here "place" is equivalent to "temple." If that is the case, this would support a parallel between 11:45–53 and John 2:13–25, especially with 2:18–25 where there is a convergence of a connection of the temple action with the death of Jesus, a reference to his many "signs," as well as a reference to the reactions of many to Jesus' signs and mention of the approaching Passover. The temple reference would also be a potential link to the Synoptic traditions which make Jesus' prophetic action in the temple area the trigger for the culminating hostility of the leaders against Jesus.

The term ἔθνος occurs only in this passage in John's Gospel (11:48, 50, 51, 52) and in the passion narrative (18:35). In all instances, the contexts suppose that it means the Jewish "people" or "nation" (see

---

4. See, for example, Koestenberger, *John*, 348–49.

5. See Barrett, *John*, 405: "'What are we now doing?' and implies the answer 'Nothing.'" Brown, on the other hand, prefers the deliberative subjunctive: "What are we going to do?" (Brown, *John*, 439).

especially, Pilate's words in 18:35: "Am I a Jew? Your own nation (ἔθνος) and the chief priests have handed you over to me").

The statement of Caiaphas, the reigning High Priest, is the center point of the passage. The text does not suggest that Caiaphas is presiding over the Sanhedrin (perhaps further indication it is a more informal council) but that he is "one of them" (11:49). The gospel notes that Caiaphas was High Priest "that year"—leading some to conclude that the composer of the text is unaware of the fact that the High Priest did not have a yearly term. However, most commentators agree that the composer of the Fourth Gospel seems well-acquainted with Jewish customs in other instances and here may simply mean equivalently "in that momentous year of Jesus' death" (a solution already proposed by Origen).[6] John is consistent in his references to Caiaphas, noting that those who arrest Jesus bring him first to Annas, "the father- in-law of Caiaphas, the High Priest that year" (18:13) and later that "Caiaphas was the one who had advised the Jews that it was better to have one person die for the people" (18:14). After deliberations before Annas, Jesus is sent by Annas to "Caiaphas the high priest" (18:24), and then is brought to Pilate "from Caiaphas to Pilate's headquarters" (18:28).[7]

Caiaphas' statement provides the rationale for deliberating against Jesus. His comments begin somewhat harshly: "You do not understand . . ." and goes on to provide a pragmatic reason for condemning Jesus: "you do not understand that it is better to have one man die for the people (ὑπὲρ τοῦ λαοῦ) than to have the whole nation (ὅλον τὸ ἔθνος, parallel to the term in 18:14) destroyed" (v. 49–50).[8]

The statement provides an opening for the Fourth Gospel's characteristic use of irony or double meaning.[9] On one level, Caiaphas

---

6. See the discussion in Brown, *John*, 439–40; also Keener, *John*, 853–54.

7. On the respective roles of Annas and Caiaphas, see VanderKam, *From Joshua to Caiaphas*, 394–490; also Brown *Death of the Messiah*, 404–11.

8. It is difficult to determine what nuance of meaning, if any, there is between these two words. John uses the word *laos* only here in 11:50 and in another reference to Caiaphas' statement in 18:14 (ἦν δὲ Καιάφας ὁ συμβουλεύσας τοῖς Ἰουδαίοις ὅτι συμφέρει ἕνα ἄνθρωπον ἀποθανεῖν ὑπὲρ τοῦ λαοῦ). Based in part on the use of the word "people" rather than consistently "nation" (*ethnos*), both Brown 1966, 440 and Lindars, *John*, 406, conclude that "for the sake of the people" in 11:50 is a gloss (as is 18:14) to align the High Priest's words with Johannine theology. However, as Barrett notes, this is a supreme example of Johannine irony and fits well into the evangelist's style: see Barrett, *John*, 406–7.

9. See Duke, *Irony*, 144–45.

expresses a pragmatic political wager: it is better to have one person sacrificed to quell the public reaction to his activities which, if unchecked, could trigger a disastrous Roman response that might sweep away the temple and the entire nation—a calamitous prospect that the leaders wanted to avoid. But the gospel sees a far more profound purpose at work. Unwittingly, Caiaphas is not speaking "on his own" but "being high priest for that year" was prophesying that "Jesus was about to die for the nation (ὑπὲρ τοῦ ἔθνους)" (vs. 51). And, the text goes on, "And not for the nation only, but to gather into one the dispersed children of God" (v. 52).

The notion of Jesus' dying as the "one for the many" has several echoes in John's theology of the death of Jesus, as does the ultimate consequence of the mission of Jesus as gathering together the scattered children of God.[10] The "gathering into one" that Jesus' death will cause (11:52) stands in contrast to the "gathering" of the leaders to plot Jesus' death (11:47).[11]

The ominous concluding verse of the passage projects the action forward. "So from that day on, they planned to kill him" (11:53). Likewise the remaining verses before the transition of 12:1 ("Six days before Passover...") continue the brooding atmosphere. Jesus no longer walks around in public among the Jews but instead leaves for Ephraim and remains there with his disciples (11:54). Meanwhile the reader is told that the Passover is approaching and that many pilgrims who had come up to Jerusalem for the festival were looking for Jesus (i.e., confirming the public impact of his signs feared by the leaders), speculating where he might be and whether he will come up for the Passover feast. At the same time the leaders have given orders that anyone who knows Jesus' location should report it so he could be arrested. (11:57).

---

10. The notion of Jesus' giving his life for the many goes deep into Johannine theology: see, for example, 3:16; 6:51; 10:11, 15. Also the motif of the gathering of the scattered "children of God" also has strong resonance with Johannine theology; e.g., 10:15–16; 17:20–22. On this see, Smith, *John*, 231; Lincoln, *John*, 330–31; also van de Sandt "Purpose of Jesus' Death," 635–46, who links John's motif of gathering to a similar theme in the Didache.

11. On this see Beutler "Two Ways of Gathering," 399–406.

Summary

In effect, this dramatic scene recapitulates Jesus' public ministry and its impact—seen from the vantage point of his opponents. Triggered by the raising of Lazarus, the last and most dramatic of Jesus' signs, the Pharisees and chief priests gather because they are troubled by the impact of Jesus' signs, fearing that the public sensation they cause will ignite a disastrous response from the Romans and lead to the destruction of the temple and a calamity for the people themselves. But the reigning high priest Caiaphas brings a decisive conclusion to the council's deliberation, declaring that it is expedient for one man to die instead of the people. The Gospel, however, recognizes another, more profound level of truth beyond this political expediency, namely that the High Priest unwittingly utters a prophecy of divine truth. Jesus would die, not only for his own nation but in order to gather into one the scattered children of God (11:51–52). The decision of the Sanhedrin sets in motion the chain of events that would lead to the arrest and execution of Jesus but also to the fulfillment of his God-given mission to reveal God's love for the world and to be the source of life and communion for the children of God.[12] Thus the "sign" of the raising of Lazarus and its consequences lead to the Gospel's ultimate "sign," the death of Jesus.[13]

Resonance within the Johannine Narrative

The content and tone of 11:45–53 has resonance throughout the gospel. The Fourth Gospel asserts several interconnected levels of causality for the death of Jesus, including:

   a. The most profound reason is the God-given mission of Jesus, the Word Incarnate, to reveal God's redemptive love for the world which paradoxically is expressed most definitively in his dying on the cross for those he loves (e.g., 3:16–17; 13:1; 15:12–13).

---

12. Thatcher considers this a prime example of how Rome and its agents are ultimately powerless before Jesus and his mission—thus signaling the inherent opposition between the Christology of the Fourth Gospel and Roman imperial power; see Thatcher, *Greater Than Caesar*, 60–61.

13. Dodd eloquently describes the death of Jesus as the ultimate "sign" in John's Gospel; see Dodd, *Interpretation*, 438–39; also Senior, "Death of Jesus as Sign."

b. Another level of causality is the hostile response of the religious leaders to Jesus' words which assert that he is the definitive revealer of God and seems to claim equality with God, thus presenting himself as one who is greater than Moses or Abraham (e.g., 5:18; 10:33).

c. Another type of causality is the impact of Jesus' "signs" or "works" which cause the crowds to be stirred and to believe in Jesus and which is perceived to be a threat to public order and propriety by the religious leaders.

It is this last motif that has the most immediate connection to 11:45–53. Several passages in the body of the Gospel fall into this category of causality:

- 2:13–25 *The Cleansing of the Temple.* While severe threats against Jesus do not yet appear in this scene, as noted earlier, there are several elements that relate to the thematic of 11:45–53: the scene takes place in Jerusalem at Passover (2:13, 23); there is the prospect of the destruction of the temple (2:19–20); reference to Jesus' "signs" (2:18, 23); the latent hostility of the religious leaders (2:18; here designated as the "the Jews" although in the following scene Nicodemus, a "Pharisee," refers to Jesus' "signs"; see 3:1–2); an allusion to Jesus' death (2:21–22); and the reaction of the crowds to Jesus because of his signs (2:23).

- 4:1 Reaction of the Pharisees to Jesus' alleged baptizing. At the beginning of chapter 4, Jesus decides to leave Judea and go back to Galilee after he learned that "the Pharisees had heard 'Jesus is making and baptizing more disciples than John.'" Although there is no explicit threat to Jesus, the text implies that Jesus withdraws from Judea because of the reaction of the Pharisees to the public stir his mission is making (even though, as the text notes, it was the disciples and not Jesus who had been baptizing; 4:2).

- 5:16–18 Reaction to the cure of the man at Bethzatha. The gospel notes that "the Jews" begin "to persecute Jesus" because he had done "such things" (i.e., the cure of the man at the pool). In 5:18, the threat escalates as the "Jews were seeking all the more to kill" Jesus not only because of his doing signs on the Sabbath but also because he "called God his own Father, thereby making himself equal to God."

- 6:14–15. Reaction to the multiplication of the loaves. The crowds seek to make Jesus king because they "saw the sign that he had done" (6:14). Their reaction continues in the discourse that follows (see 6:30).

- 7:1 Threat to Jesus' life. No specific reason is given for this threat but, presumably, it follows upon the previous reactions to Jesus' works of healing and the multiplication of the loaves. As in 4:1, Jesus remains in Galilee rather than risk going to Judea.

- 7:19–31 Threats to kill Jesus. The crowds react to Jesus' claim that some are looking for an opportunity to kill him (7:19); they accuse him of having a "demon" and question whether anyone wants to kill him (7:20). Yet Jesus responds that they "marvel" at his "one work" ("Ἐν ἔργον ἐποίησα καὶ πάντες θαυμάζετε) Here "work" may refer to his teaching (which also causes the crowd to "marvel"; see 7:15) or may refer more generically to his ministry of teaching and healing. The threats against Jesus' life are alluded to again in 7:25–26 and in 7:30 where "they" (the crowds? or, more likely, the temple authorities) try to arrest him. A significant passage is 7:31 where "many" react favorably to Jesus and the signs he performs, indicating that he is the messiah.

- 7:32–52. The reactions of the Pharisees and the chief priests. This segment has particular resonance with 11:45–53. As in the later scene, here the Pharisees join with the "chief priests" (7:32, 45) to plot against Jesus. The impact of Jesus' signs and the persuasion of many that Jesus was the messiah lead the authorities to attempt to arrest him. But the division in the response to Jesus—some favorable, others not—frustrates the attempt to arrest Jesus (7:43–44), leading in turn to an inconclusive debate among a gathering of the Pharisees and chief priests (7:45–52). At the end of the session, the narrator simply says "each of them went home" (7:53).

- 9:16 Reactions of the Pharisees to Jesus' healing of the man born blind. Here again a dramatic sign of Jesus leads to a hostile reaction and division on the part of the authorities, in this instance the Pharisees. Disapproval of Jesus' healing on the Sabbath is seen as proof for some that Jesus is "not from God" but others ask, "How can a man who is a sinner perform such signs?"

- 10:31–39 Reactions to Jesus' works and to his apparent blasphemy. Threats to stone Jesus and another futile attempt to arrest him on the part of "the Jews" are triggered both by his works (10:31) and by his claim to be "God's Son" and therefore equal to God (10:33). Jesus escapes the attempt to arrest him (10:39) and many believe in Jesus because of the signs he performs (10:41–42).

This rapid survey demonstrates that the drama of 11:45–53 is not isolated in the Johannine narrative but is the culmination of a series of hostile reactions throughout the public ministry of Jesus. Although the reactions of the authorities represent concern about his teaching—particularly his claim to be God's son which is viewed as blasphemous (e.g., 5:18; 10:33–39)—and about his alleged violation of the Sabbath (e.g., 5:16; 9:16), in several instances hostile reactions are directly linked to the impact of Jesus' works or signs on an individual or the crowds, as in 11:45–53 (e.g., 4:1–3; 7:25–31; 7:32; 7:37–52; 10:39–42). The authorities' judgment that Jesus' messianic claims are illegitimate only adds to their hostility to Jesus and their determination to arrest and even kill him. Note that this type of reaction continues after the deliberations of the council in 11:45–53. Because the crowds desire to see not only Jesus but also the risen Lazarus, the "chief priests" determine to kill both Lazarus and Jesus precisely because of the reaction that the "signs" were creating (12:9–11). The continuing response of the crowds to this great sign leads the Pharisees to lament that, "You see, you can do nothing. Look, the whole world has gone after him"—a despairing verdict that echoes their frustration in 11:47–48. Jesus himself hides from the authorities (12:36), realizing that although he had "performed so many signs in their presence" yet they do not believe in him (12:37). Yet "many"—including even some of the authorities—believed in him but did not express it publicly because they feared being expelled from the synagogue by the Pharisees (12:42–43; as in 9:22).

What is new and unique to 11:45–53, compared to the earlier expressions of hostility on the part of the Jewish authorities, is the explicit link of their concern to the threat of Roman intervention. Only in this scene do the authorities express the fear that, if reaction to Jesus is unchecked, the consequence may be Rome's retaliation.

This line of reasoning on the part of the authorities is ironically expressed in the Johannine passion story. The threat of Roman intervention is not mentioned in the hearings before Annas (18:12–24) or Caiaphas (18:25–28).[14] However, the motif of kingship plays a major role in the trial before Pilate (18:33, 36, 37, 39; 19:14–16), in the mockery by the soldiers (19:1–3), and in the fixing of the placard over the cross of Jesus (19:19–22). Jesus' supposed pretensions to be a king do coincide with the fear of Roman intervention to the extent that a pretension to kingship and public support for this would be reason for stirring the Roman response to such supposed treason. The issue of sedition comes to the fore, ironically, not on the part of Pilate but from the religious leaders themselves. When Pilate appears on the brink of releasing Jesus, the "Jews" warn him, "If you release this man, you are no friend of the emperor. Everyone who claims to be a king sets himself against the emperor" (19:12). This irony is reaffirmed in 19:15 when the "chief priests" declare: "We have no king but the emperor"—leading to Pilate's reluctant condemnation of Jesus (19:16).

An initial probe of the content of the council scene in 11:45–53 and of the Johannine narrative as a whole indicates that on one level John affirms a plausible set of "historical" circumstances that ultimately lead to the death of Jesus. The sensational "signs" or "works" that Jesus performs win over many of the crowds and lead them to believe he is the Messiah or promised deliverer of Israel. His healings and extraordi-

---

14. It may be that John implies Roman soldiers join in the detail that arrests Jesus in the garden (see 18:3, ὁ οὖν Ἰούδας λαβὼν τὴν σπεῖραν καὶ ἐκ τῶν ἀρχιερέων καὶ ἐκ τῶν Φαρισαίων ὑπηρέτας ἔρχεται ἐκεῖ μετὰ φανῶν καὶ λαμπάδων καὶ ὅπλων). The term *speira* or "cohort" is a Roman military term referring to 600 men or a tenth part of a legion. However, the evangelist does not elaborate on this although in 18:12 he is consistent in referring to the officer in charge of the soldiers as a *chiliarchos* which was the proper title for the commander of a cohort (Ἡ οὖν σπεῖρα καὶ ὁ χιλίαρχος) and for distinguishing this group from the Jewish group who had joined Judas in arresting Judas (καὶ οἱ ὑπηρέται τῶν Ἰουδαίων). See the discussion in R. Brown who speculates that these may have been Roman mercenary troops at the disposal of the Jewish authorities to maintain order or that John is simply using without any particular accuracy or historical data a common way of referring to a military group; Brown, *Death of the Messiah*, 248–52. See also Piper, "Characterisation of Pilate," esp. 142–45.

nary works such as the miraculous multiplication of the loaves and the raising of Lazarus create a dramatic public response, with many flocking to Jesus and even to Lazarus.

The reaction of the Jewish authorities to Jesus in the gospel narrative is multi-faceted. Some, for example, are opposed to his apparent violations of the Sabbath and skeptical of his messianic claims and consider him a "sinner" or worse, a demonic (e.g., 7:20; 8:48). Entwined with this are Jesus' own claims to be God's own Son which in the view of his opponents is interpreted as claiming to be equal with God and therefore blasphemous (e.g., 5:18; 10:38–42). But one public consequence of all these claims and activities is the widespread stirring of the crowds by Jesus' mission, leading the authorities who are concerned about the hostile reaction of the Roman authorities to fear that the disruption of public order caused by Jesus' public works or signs, and their potential interpretation as treasonous because of Jesus' supposed messianic claims, will spell disaster for their people.

In the setting of John's Gospel this doomsday scenario is particularly true in Judea, as distinct from Galilee. The Pharisees and the chief priests (and the temple guards they employ) move against Jesus in Jerusalem, attempting to arrest him on more than one occasion (e.g. 5:18; 7:32; 8:37; 10:39; 11:57) and perhaps even threatening to stone him on the spot (e.g., 8:59; 10:31). Galilee, on the other hand, is the place to which Jesus withdraws in the face of threat in Judea and where he can apparently go about in public without immediate fear of arrest (see especially, 7:1, but also 3:22; 6:1; 10:40 [Transjordan]; 11:54). While the gospel assumes rather than explicitly explains the reason for this distinction, in fact it is in Judea and especially in the temple area of Jerusalem that the plausibility of Roman intervention would be most acute. As is well known, during the lifetime of Jesus the Romans ruled directly over Judea and Samaria, but used Herodians as surrogates in upper and lower Galilee and in the Transjordan.

Causality for Jesus' death on the level of right order or political expediency is, as we have noted, only one level that the Gospel of John identifies. Of greater significance for the theological perspective of the Gospel is Jesus' carrying out of his God-given mission to reveal God's redemptive love for the world, a love most eloquently and unimpeachably revealed through the act of friendship love that, from the gospel's point of view, is the true significance of Jesus' death on the cross (see, especially 15:12–13 and the "completion" of Jesus' mission at the moment of death: 13:1 and 19:30). Thus while the authorities might plot against Jesus and ultimately succeed in arresting him and leading him to his death, the Jesus of John's Gospel can truly say that "no one takes it (my life) from me but I lay it down of my own accord. I have power to lay it down, and I have power to take it up again. I have received this command from my Father" (10:18). Also on the theological level, the paradigmatic act of Jesus' laying down his life for others out of love defines the core of Jesus' teaching, sets the pattern for authentic discipleship, and reveals the destiny of all who believe in Jesus and his teaching and therefore will be one with him and with the Father.[15] At the same time, the scenario of fearing the disruption of public order and the disaster of Roman intervention provides an apparent historical grounding or plausible human narrative for why Jesus would be in danger and ultimately be arrested and executed. Thus within John's Gospel, theological, ethical, and historical perspectives converge at the moment of Jesus' death as they do by anticipation in the deliberations of the Sanhedrin in 11:45–53.

Assessing the Historical Grounding of John's Gospel

How are we to assess what we are calling the "apparent historical grounding" of the causes that lead to Jesus' death in John? Did the Johannine tradition have access to historical information originating from Jesus' lifetime that in fact the Jewish authorities feared the public impact of Jesus' ministry and determined to put a stop to it in order to avoid a far greater danger? Or did the Fourth Gospel present his scenario for the causes of Jesus' death drawing in some fashion on source material from the Synoptic Gospels and their reflections on the reasons for Jesus' death? Or did the gospel writer, aware of the tragedy of the suppression of the Jewish revolt in 70 AD and the *de facto* siege of Jerusalem and the destruction of the temple that took place at this time, read this future tragedy back into the supposed circumstances of Jesus' passion as he composed his narrative?

    This is the nub of the question that is the focus of the seminar and remains a set of questions difficult, if not impossible, to answer definitively. Let me begin with considering the possibility of some contact

---

15. See Senior, "Death of Jesus as Sign," esp. 290–91.

with the Synoptic Gospels, aware that this is a long debated question far exceeding the limits of this paper.

We should note at the outset that the overall Johannine narrative scenario tracing the cause of the opposition to Jesus, stated most explicitly in 11:45–53 but with echoes throughout the gospel, has several characteristic elements:

1. The impact of Jesus' ministry on the crowds.

2. The religious authorities' (including the Pharisees and the chief priests) hostile reaction to this sensation.

3. The concern that the ultimate consequence of this public sensation might be a destructive intervention by Roman authorities.

4. The location of the most intense concern in Judea, Jerusalem, and the temple area.

5. The role of the Sanhedrin and Caiaphas.

6. The decision to arrest and kill Jesus in order to spare a more tragic consequence of a violent Roman intervention.

A comparison with the Synoptic Gospels reveals a significant difference in content and tone in references to the hostility of Jesus' opponents leading up to the passion story itself. As has often been noted, John refers more frequently and with more intensity to the threats against Jesus in the body of the Gospel than either Mark, Matthew, or Luke do.[16] Most of the conflicts between Jesus and the religious authorities in the Synoptic Gospels concern supposed violations of purity or Sabbath laws: e.g., working on the Sabbath, eating with unwashed hands, associating with sinners, and so on. John's Gospel includes many of these same conflicts (although the accusation of associating with sinners is not among them).

Certainly in the Synoptic Gospels the religious authorities recognize that Jesus had an impact on the crowds (see, for example, Mark 11:18) but in most instances fear of the crowds' reactions plays a deterrent role for the authorities, preventing them from arresting Jesus outright and having to resort to "stealth" (e.g., Mark 14:1–2 and parallels). In John's Gospel, however, in several instances Jesus' impact on the crowd

---

16. See Zumstein, "L'interpretation johannique," 2119–38; also van Belle, "Death of Jesus," 3–64; Senior, *Passion of Jesus*, 15–44.

is a cause of consternation and opposition on the part of the authorities in its own right (see particularly, 7:40–52; 9:16; 11:42–43; 12:19). And John's portrayal of the Sanhedrin's deliberations in 11:45–53 offers a further rationale for the authorities' negative reaction: namely, the enthusiasm of the crowds for Jesus as the supposed Messiah can lead to the calamity of Roman intervention.

With one exception, this distinction between the Gospel of John and the Synoptics carries over into the passion story itself. For Mark, Matthew and Luke the key reasons for the condemnation of Jesus by the religious authorities include his alleged threats against the temple and his supposedly blasphemous confession that he is the "Christ" and the "Son of God" (e.g., Mark 14:61–64). In John's account of Jesus' encounter with Annas and then Caiaphas these specific charges are not explicit; Annas questions him "about his disciples and his teaching" (18:19).[17] However, earlier in John's Gospel Jesus had been in conflict with the authorities about the temple (2:13–22). And if 11:45–53 is to be considered the Johannine equivalent of the meeting of the Sanhedrin presented within the Synoptic passion stories, the accusation against Jesus now becomes his stirring up the crowds—an accusation that does not occur in the Synoptic accounts of the hearing before the Sanhedrin.

The one exception to this is in Luke's account of the trial before Pilate. The entire group of leaders accuse Jesus (which according to Luke 22:66 includes the elders, chief priests and scribes): "We found this man perverting our nation, forbidding us to pay taxes to the emperor, and saying that he himself is the Messiah, a king" (23:2). When Pilate balks, the assembly adds to their list of accusations Jesus' impact on the crowds: "He stirs up the people by teaching throughout all Judea, from Galilee where he began even to this place" (23:5). As in John's account, ironically the Jewish leaders themselves express concern about treasonous behavior on the part of Jesus and its impact on the people while the Roman Governor remains unconvinced and reluctant to condemn Jesus.

---

17. Brown, however, surmises that Annas' question about "his disciples" in fact refers to the many who were believing in Jesus and therefore constitutes a link to 11:48. The question about "his teaching" would refer to Jesus' controversial assertions about his identity as Son of God or Messiah (see 10:24–25, 36). Brown, *Death of the Messiah*, 413–14.

Conclusion

How are we to assess this interesting narrative strand in the John's portrayal of the events and dynamics leading to Jesus' death? There is no doubt that John's scenario contains historical verisimilitude:

- Although revolutionary tensions would increase after 44 AD, the threat of violent Roman retaliation for perceived rebellion was also a real danger at the time of Jesus and under Pilate's regime.[18]
- John alone is aware of the historical fact of the distinctive roles of Annas and Caiaphas as High Priests and as influential leaders of the Jewish community at the time of Jesus.
- The Fourth Gospel is also aware of the direct role played by the Roman authorities in the governance of Judea, in distinction to Galilee (e.g., 18:28–31).
- While intra-Jewish conflicts between Jesus and his contemporaries over law observance and even messianic claims are also part of the Synoptic narrative, John alone ascribes to the Jewish authorities the concern about public order, particularly in Jerusalem—a concern that is historically plausible given the relationship between Roman authority and the local community. While the claim to kingship, which is a motif in all four passion stories, also has some resonance with John's motif, the concern for Roman retaliation for such a claim is not exploited by the gospel writers other than John. The motif of Jesus' kingship is used for theological purposes, contrasting the kingship of Jesus with the secular power of Pilate.[19]

Only Luke's passion story has a motif somewhat similar to John's rationale but it is limited to the accusations made by the religious lead-

---

18. Josephus, for example, refers several times to crisis points during the reign of Pilate: see *Ant.* 18.3.1 (rioting and subsequent massacre triggered by the posting of images in Jerusalem); also in *J.W.* 2.9.2; as well as the incident of using temple funds to build an aqueduct also led to rioting and retaliation (*J.W.* 2.9.4). Josephus asserts that Pilate was removed from office by Tiberius because Pilate had also slaughtered Samaritans in retaliation for an uprising (see *Ant.* 18.4.1–2).

19. "Theological" does not mean without political significance however; see the recent works of Carter, *John and Empire*; and Thatcher, *Greater Than Caesar*.

ers in the Roman trial scene, accusations which in the narrative seem patently false. John, however, provides a much more nuanced and believable rationale for the behavior of the Jewish authorities; in John's narrative Jesus had in fact stirred up the crowds and they did seek to declare him Messiah and king.

Could the gospel writer have constructed his rationale based on later knowledge of the actual intervention of Rome in AD 66 and the ultimate destruction of Jerusalem and its temple in AD 70? This cannot be ruled out; however, there is nothing in the Johannine account that could not be considered a reflection of actual circumstances at the time of Jesus' death. The accurate details about the relationship of Annas and Caiaphas is one such indication. Even the specific threat that the Romans could come and destroy the temple and the people need not depend on later post-70 knowledge, given known examples of Roman response to acts of sedition.[20]

Could John have been influenced by the synoptic passion tradition (or independent versions of it) which included an accusatory role for the religious authorities, concern about Jesus' messianic identity, and the role of Pilate and the Romans in ultimately condemning and executing Jesus? Here again this cannot be ruled out. From the general synoptic portrayal of the opposition of the religious authorities to Jesus' ministry (e.g., healings on the Sabbath, purity laws, association with sinners, messianic claims, etc.), from the passion accounts dealing with the arrest of Jesus, his arraignment before the Sanhedrin, and the trial before Pilate with its emphasis on the motif of kingship, the Johannine tradition itself could have developed a scene such as 11:45–53 and the echoes of this in other parts of the Johannine narrative. As noted above, Luke's Gospel injects a similar note into the Roman trial when the leaders accuse Jesus before Pilate of seditious behavior that is stirring up the masses.[21]

Could theological motivations alone explain the origin of this characteristic Johannine theme of political expediency? Here, again, it cannot be ruled out. The motif of "one for the many" which was not unfamiliar to the Greco-Roman world also fits well into the overall theol-

---

20. See the references to Josephus, above n. 18.

21. In Luke's case, his overall apologetic concerns to portray the Christian movement as not incompatible with Roman rule could well explain this insertion in the passion narrative. In Luke's account both Pilate and Herod testify to Jesus' innocence.

ogy of John's Gospel which interprets Jesus' death as an act of friendship love, as a "laying down of one's life" (10:15), as the giving of Jesus' "flesh for the life of the world" (6:51). The unwitting prophetic statement of Caiaphas in 11:50 confirms that the concept of political expediency in allowing the death of one man to avoid greater calamity provides an excellent opening for John's understanding of the meaning of Jesus' death as a revelation of God's redeeming love for the world, as a model for the love command that defines authentic discipleship, and as the source of ultimate gathering and communion among the children of God.[22]

In fact, any of these options might work and one could not exclude the presence of all three at once as converging factors leading to the inclusion of 11:45–53 and its accompanying materials in the Fourth Gospel. John's Gospel could have had contact with the synoptic tradition about the nature of the opposition to Jesus and the motifs of the passion story, either on a literary or oral level or through mutual influence. At the same time John could have also had access to independent historical traditions about the reasons that prompted the Jewish authorities to turn Jesus over to Roman authority which gave a more specific focus to the reasons for the opposition to Jesus.[23] And, lastly, the nature of the authorities' opposition and their decision to hand Jesus over for the sake of the good of the wider community served well the theological perspective of the Fourth Gospel about the ultimate meaning of the death of Jesus.

One's decisions about these options no doubt depends in large measure on one's convictions about the nature of the Fourth Gospel's overall relationship to early Christian tradition and to the Synoptic Gospels. For my part, I believe that this passage concerning fear of Roman intervention on the part of the Jewish authorities as a trigger for the arrest of Jesus takes its place alongside other intriguing historical information found in John's Gospel, such as his knowledge of Jerusalem, aspects of Jewish liturgy, and topography, which suggest that this most "theological" of the Gospels also had historical groundings in the circumstances of Palestinian Judaism during the period of Jesus' lifetime.

---

22. See, for example, Barrett, *John*, 404; Lincoln, *John*, 331–35.

23. Keener suggests that Joseph of Arimathea, a member of the Jewish elite whom the gospel portrays as ultimately becoming an ally of Jesus and who could have known of the council's deliberations, may have been a historical source of information for the Johannine community; see Keener, *John*, 852.

Bibliography

Bammel, Ernst. "Ex Illa Itaque Die Consilium Fecerunt . . ." In *The Trial of Jesus: Cambridge Studies in Honour of C. F. D. Moule*, edited by Ernst Bammel, 11–40. SBT 2/13. London: SCM, 1970.

Barrett, C. K. *The Gospel according to St. John*. 2nd ed. Philadelphia: Westminster, 1978.

Belle, G. van. "The Death of Jesus and the Literary Unity of the Fourth Gospel." In *The Death of Jesus in the Fourth Gospel*, edited by G. van Belle, 3–64. BETL 200. Leuven: Peeters, 2007.

Beutler, Johannes. "Two Ways of Gathering: The Plot to Kill Jesus in John 11.47–53." *NTS* 40 (1994) 399–406.

Brown, Raymond E. *The Death of the Messiah: From Gethsemane to the Grave*. Vol. 1. New York: Doubleday, 1994.

———. *The Gospel according to John I–XII*. AB 29. Garden City, NY: Doubleday, 1966.

Carter, Warren. *John and Empire: Initial Explorations*. New York: T. & T. Clark, 2008.

Dodd, C. H. *The Interpretation of the Fourth Gospel*. Cambridge: Cambridge University Press, 1953.

Duke, Paul D. *Irony in the Fourth Gospel*. Atlanta: John Knox, 1985.

Keener, Craig S. *The Gospel of John: A Commentary*. Vol. 2. Peabody MA: Hendrickson, 2003.

Köstenberger, Andreas J. *John*. Baker Exegetical Commentary on the New Testament. Grand Rapids: Baker Academic, 2004.

Lincoln, Andrew T. *The Gospel according to Saint John*. Black's New Testament Commentaries 4. Peabody, MA: Hendrickson, 2005.

Lindars, Barnabas. *The Gospel of John*. New Century Bible. Greenwood, SC: Attic, 1977.

Piper, R. A. "The Characterisation of Pilate and the Death of Jesus in the Fourth Gospel." In *The Death of Jesus in the Fourth Gospel*, edited by G. van Belle, 123–62. BETL 200. Leuven: Peeters, 2007.

Sandt, Huub van de. "The Purpose of Jesus' Death: John 11,51–52 in the Perspective of Did 9,4." In *The Death of Jesus in the Fourth Gospel*, edited by G. van Belle, 635–46. BETL 200. Leuven: Peeters, 2007.

Senior, Donald. "The Death of Jesus as Sign: A Fundamental Johannine Ethic." In *The Death of Jesus in the Fourth Gospel*, edited by G. van Belle, 271–91. BETL 200. Leuven: Peeters, 2007.

———. *The Passion of Jesus in the Gospel of John*. Passion Series 4. Collegeville, MN: Liturgical, 1991.

Smith, D. Moody. *John*. Abingdon New Testament Commentaries. Nashville: Abingdon, 1999.

Thatcher, Tom. *Greater than Caesar: Christology and Empire in the Fourth Gospel*. Minneapolis: Fortress, 2009.

VanderKam, James. *From Joshua to Caiaphas: High Priests after the Exile*. Minneapolis: Fortress, 2004.

Zumstein, Jean. "L'interpretation johannique de la mort du Christ." In *The Four Gospels 1992: Festschrift Frans Neirynck*, edited by F. van Segbroeck et al., 2119–38. BETL 100. Leuven University Press, 1992.

10

Til Death Do Us Part

Uniting Social-Scientific and Narrative Criticisms in Johannine Exegesis

Jason L. Merritt

BOTH DR. CAROLYN OSIEK AND I CAME TO BRITE DIVINITY SCHOOL IN the fall of 2003, she as a new faculty member and I as an incoming master's student. Coincidentally, we both departed at the close of the spring 2009 semester, she having retired from her professorial position at Brite and I having completed my PhD. During those six years it was my distinct honor and privilege to learn from her vast knowledge and expertise.

I must confess that I was sometimes an odd fit in the New Testament PhD program at Brite given that my own interests were primarily Johannine and narrative critical while Dr. Osiek's were Pauline and social-scientific. However, Mark Allen Powell argues that understanding a narrative in its social setting ("setting" here being used in the narrative critical sense of the various contexts in which the story occurs) is "intrinstic to narrative criticism, properly understood."[1] It would seem to me that a fitting way for me to honor the scholar who has contributed so much to my own scholarly formation would be to bring our own respective methodological concerns into dialogue with one another in examining two discrete but connected stories in the Gospel of John: the

---

1. Powell, *What is Narrative Criticism?*, 75.

miracle at the wedding in Cana (2.1–11), and Jesus' committing of his Mother[2] into the care of the Beloved Disciple (19.25–27).[3]

My goal in writing is not to break new ground in either methodology. Indeed, I will draw heavily on work done previously by major scholars in each area. Rather, the goal is to put into dialogue two methodologies that often remain segregated from one another. The scope of my inquiry must be limited given the restraints of time and space for this essay, so I will focus most closely on the way that John's Gospel characterizes both Jesus and his Mother in these two stories, the narrative connections between the stories, and the implications of those connections for the overall structure of the narrative of John's Gospel.

The focus of scholarly inquiry into the story of the miracle at Cana has tended primarily toward the theological meaning of the sign, but interest in the exchange between Jesus and his Mother has been a point of significant secondary interest. Interpretive approaches are quite varied. Questions regarding the historicity of the miracle itself are often posed, with a variety of conclusions being drawn.[4] On the negative side, Bultmann (not surprisingly) sees the story as having been inspired by pagan myths of Dionysus,[5] and on the positive side, Carson (perhaps as unsurprisingly) argues for the historicity of the story.[6] Lindars takes

---

2. Johannine scholarship has virtually turned "the Beloved Disciple" into a proper name of sorts, and that does not seem to me to be out of keeping with Johannine usage. The Fourth Evangelist seems to use this appellation as a way of honoring a character of significance both to the story and the community that produced it. It strikes me that "the mother of Jesus" is used in a similar way in the Fourth Gospel, i.e., a character of significance in the story is left unnamed and her identity is developed through her relationship to Jesus. To refer to her as "Mary" is foreign to the thought world of the story, but to refer to her as "the Mother of Jesus" is more in keeping with Johannine parlance and a means of elevating her status, though it may seem patriarchal to modern ears. For this reason, I have chosen to treat "Jesus' Mother" or its equivalent as a proper title, just as many Johannine scholars similarly treat "the Beloved Disciple."

3. The choice of these two stories from John's Gospel has the added benefit of allowing me to touch upon the role of women in early Christianity, which has long been one of the primary areas of concern in Dr. Osiek's research.

4. See Keener, *John*, 2:492–93, for a concise treatment of the question of the historicity of the Cana miracle and the accompanying methodological problems surrounding the discussion.

5. Bultmann, *John*, 118–19.

6. Carson, *John*, 166–67. See also Blomberg, *Historical Reliability*, 85–87, for a less lengthy, and somewhat less pointed, but still positive evaluation of the essential historicity of the story.

something of a mediating position, arguing that the story is a Johannine expansion of a brief but authentic parable.[7] Form criticism continues to make contributions to our understanding of the story, with Berenson MacLean recently arguing that the story should be understood as a trickster story that is part of the larger "Jacob cycle" in John 1–4.[8]

Interpretations of Jesus' entrusting his Mother to the Beloved Disciple in 19:25–27 have also tended to fall along the lines of historical and theological inquiry. Bultmann dismisses the scene as an ahistorical redactional addition to the Gospel that symbolizes Jewish Christianity (Jesus' Mother) and Gentile Christianity (the Beloved Disciple) being joined together.[9] Brown sees the historical question as "insoluble,"[10] and formulates a rather lengthy argument that Jesus' Mother here represents a new Eve who helps to bring about a new people of God.[11]

Scholarship that can generally be described as narrative-critical has tended to see the Mother of Jesus as having highly symbolic value in both stories. Indeed, narrative critics tend to recognize a connection between the two stories based on the presence of the mother of Jesus in both stories and the repetition of the theme of Jesus' "hour." Moloney understands Jesus' response to his mother's request at the wedding in Cana as one that creates distance between the two of them, seeing it even as "some form of rebuke."[12] Likewise, Koester sees Jesus' response to his mother as creating distance: "Jesus responded by calling her 'woman' (2:4a), a term that could be used for other women without disrespect, but not one that a son would use for his mother."[13] Culpepper departs from a more typical interpretation of the exchange between Jesus and his mother by following McHugh, who translates

---

7. Lindars, *John*, 126–28. Specifically, Lindars argues that the words of the ἀρχιτρίκλινος in v. 10 constitute the remnant of the authentic parable around which the Johannine expansion was developed. Lindars notes that Dodd, *Historical Tradition*, 227, comes to a similar conclusion.

8. Berenson MacLean, "The Divine Trickster."

9. Bultmann, *Gospel of John*, 671–73. This line of interpretation still exists in various forms. Lincoln, *John*, 477, argues that Jesus' Mother "represents all who are receptive to salvation from Jesus, perhaps believing Jews in particular ..."

10. Brown, *John XIII–XXI*, 922.

11. Ibid., 924–26.

12. Moloney, *Belief in the Word*, 80–83.

13. Koester, *Symbolism*, 82.

Jesus' response as "What is that to me and to thee, woman?"[14] Seen in this light, Jesus' response creates closeness rather than distance; Jesus and his mother are allied together by their mutual concerns, which are not shared by the rest of the wedding party. The problem with this interpretation is that the parallels for this phrase in LXX and NT uniformly express some sort of distance between the two parties involved in the exchange.[15] Indeed, all of its uses in the Synoptics are between demons and Jesus and the tone is clearly one of hostility (Mark 11:24; Luke 4:34; Matt 8:29). The preponderance of evidence suggests that Jesus' reply to his mother is, as Moloney and Koester have described it, a rebuff that places distance between himself and his Mother. But why does Jesus respond in this way, especially given that his next act in the narrative is to perform a miracle that meets the need presented to him by his Mother? A common answer is that Jesus rebuffs his Mother, a human authority, because he will only receive directives from his heavenly father.[16]

Jesus' Mother appears again in 19:25–27, and this particular pericope has proven to be fodder for a wide variety of interpretations, though Culpepper notes that very little has been done from a narrative-critical perspective.[17] Culpepper has very helpfully summarized some of the most important narrative-critical work done on this pericope by Stibbe, Zumstein, and Coloe.[18] These three scholars, as Culpepper summarizes their arguments, are generally agreed that a symbolic interpretation of the episode is best, and all three tend to understand the

---

14. Culpepper, *Anatomy*, 134; and McHugh, *Mother of Jesus*, 403. However, see also McHugh, *John 1–4*, 181–82. Here, McHugh changes course and argues that Jesus' response has the force of asking "What relationship is there between you and me?" The theological import of the question is that Jesus is effectively dissolving obligations of blood kinship while opening the doors for the kinship birthed by belief.

15. See Judg 11:12; 2 Chr 35:21; 1 Kgs 17:18; 1 Kgs 3:13; and Hos 14:8.

16. Implied in Culpepper, *Anatomy*, 133, and spelled out more explicitly in Moloney, *Belief in the Word*, 82–83, and Talbert, *Reading John*, 85. Koester, *Symbolism*, 83, takes a somewhat different approach, arguing: "This peculiar interchange enables readers to see that Jesus' actions cannot be understood on the level of typical relations between mother and son, but must be interpreted retrospectively in light of his death and resurrection."

17. Culpepper, "Symbolism and History," 45. On 40–44, Culpepper provides a concise but very helpful summary of the work conducted on this pericope by five significant Johannine scholars of the mid-twentieth century (Bultmann, Barrett, Dodd, Brown, and Schnackenburg).

18. Ibid., 44–51.

Mother of Jesus and the Beloved Disciple as a "family" that symbolizes the Johannine community.[19] Culpepper himself comments only briefly on this pericope, but his understanding of its meaning comes very close to that of Stibbe, Zumstein, and Coloe: "His act of 'filial piety' is much more than that; it constitutes the believing community which can now receive the Spirit.... What Jesus does and says to his disciples in chapter 20 is based on the constitution of the new family of faith at the cross."[20]

The narrative critics have made a compelling case for understanding the constitution of the new family of Beloved Disciple and Mother of Jesus as symbolizing the institution of the new community of faith, and I would not dispute their findings. However, while their treatment of this particular aspect of the pericope is rather detailed, they have neglected other important aspects. There is, for instance, very little evident concern for connecting the Cana miracle with the scene at the cross. The Mother of Jesus is obviously present in both, and the theme of "the hour" that finds its culmination in 19:25–27 is first mentioned in 2:4, yet little concern is expressed for exploring the implications of this fact for the overall narrative of John's Gospel. While much has been accomplished on the narrative critical side of scholarship, much remains to be done.

Social-sciences critics have contributed to the discussion of the miracle story and have tended to focus more on the implications of the shortage of wine for the newly married couple and their families, Jesus' Mother's apparent request that Jesus do something about the shortage, and Jesus' curt refusal to act. Malina and Rohrbaugh note the potential loss of honor incurred by the newly-weds and their families due to the shortage of wine (a position taken even by most commentators

---

19. Culpepper's presentation of the "familial" interpretation is certainly legitimate with regard to Stibbe and Zumstein. See Stibbe, *John as Storyteller*, 153–54, 160–67; and Zumstein, "Johannes 19,25–27." However, it ought to be noted that Coloe understands "family" in strongly ecclesiological terms and she in fact deals equally in the symbolism of new temple. See Coloe, *God Dwells with Us*, 187–90, 210.

20. Culpepper, *Anatomy*, 134. So also briefly Moloney, *Glory not Dishonor*, 145: "Because of the cross, and from the moment of the cross, a new family of Jesus has been created . . . the reader of the Johannine story concludes that at the cross and because of the cross the lifted up Son of Man has established a new family." While Culpepper and Moloney are in essential agreement with Stibbe, Zumstein, and Coloe regarding the symbolic imagery of family in this pericope, their arguments are far briefer and less well-developed.

with methodological approaches other than a social-scientific one).²¹ Several noteworthy points are made in regard to the exchange between Jesus and his Mother. Since the managing of the food and drink for the wedding would have been handled by women in the more private spaces of the home²² in which the wedding feast was held, Jesus' Mother would have been privy to the shortage while Jesus, who would have occupied a more public space in the home, would have been unaware. Jesus' Mother's petition would have arisen out of the particularly close relationship shared between mothers and sons in the ancient Middle East and Mediterranean.²³ However, her petition is seemingly rebuffed. Malina and Rohrbaugh argue that the apparently curt address γύναι may actually have been a customary way for Jesus to address females. They further argue that the reason for Jesus' dismissal of Mary's request could have stemmed from her making it in public, which would have constituted a challenge to Jesus' honor.²⁴ The real crux of the analysis conducted by Malina and Rohrbaugh, however, comes in their argument that the pattern of request-refusal-fulfillment in John is actually typical of Jesus' dealings with petitions made by natural in-group members.

In analyzing the exchange between Mary and Jesus according to this pattern, Malina and Rohrbaugh draw heavily upon the work of

---

21. Malina and Rohrbaugh, *John*, 66.

22. Malina and Rohrbaugh assume a single house as the setting for the miracle story, in which case the demarcations of public and private spaces at the wedding would not have been significantly different from day-to-day usage. Other scholars have imagined a setting in which the main banquet would have occurred in a courtyard central to a plurality of dwellings, in which case a sharp change may have occurred in perceptions regarding public and private space at the wedding. Spaces that might normally have been considered public space in a home may have been temporarily viewed as private in order to accommodate the preparations being made by women for the banquet. Whether John had the former or latter (or some other) setting in mind, the general social principle still holds true: Mary has probably spent most of her time at the wedding in private spaces while Jesus has occupied a public space.

23. Malina and Rohrbaugh, *John*, 272–73. See also Plutarch *Advice to the Bride and Groom* 35, who urges newly-wed brides to forge bonds of personal affection with their husbands in such a way that they do not threaten the bonds of affection that already exist between mother and son.

24. Malina and Rohrbaugh, *John*, 66–67. Brown, *John I–XII*, 99, makes a very similar observation regarding the use of τί ἐμοὶ καὶ σοι: "(a) when one party is unjustly bothering another, the injured party may say, 'What to me and to you?'... (b) when someone is asked to get involved in a matter which he feels is no business of his, he may say to the petitioner, 'What to me and to you?'"

Giblin.²⁵ Giblin notes four instances in John's Gospel where someone makes a request of Jesus, only to be rebuffed in some way by him. However, after an initial refusal to grant the request, Jesus reverses course and grants the request, with his actions then leading to conflict with the Judeans.²⁶ Malina and Rohrbaugh interpret this pattern through their understanding of the Johannine community as an anti-society that employs anti-language.²⁷ They define an anti-society as "a society that is set up within another society as a conscious alternative to it. It is a mode of resistance, resistance which may take the form either of passive symbiosis or of active hostility and even destruction."²⁸ Malina and Rohrbaugh join Giblin's analysis with their anti-society reading by arguing that the petitioners in the four episodes cited by Giblin represent those who would be considered in-group members by "straight" society. "In 'straight' society, as opposed to antisociety, these in-group persons all deserve and receive immediate compliance . . . Perhaps John uses this pattern to inform members of his group about how to deal with their relatives and other natural in-group persons."²⁹ Neyrey, on the other hand, argues that the key to understanding Giblin's pattern is to recognize that each request represents some form of challenge to Jesus' honor; Jesus both preserves his honor and grants the request in dealing with these honor challenges by first declining to act but then acting "voluntarily."³⁰

These solutions are creative and have merit, but they are not without their problems. First, the four petitioners or groups of petitioners cited by Giblin can be further subdivided into family members (the

25. Ibid., 68. See also Giblin, "Suggestion, Negative Response, and Positive Action," 197–211.

26. I here reflect on the term employed by Malina and Rohrbaugh, and indeed the overwhelming majority of social-sciences critics, to translate John's much-discussed use of οἱ Ἰουδαῖοι. I am well aware that this translation is not universally accepted by New Testament scholars. Indeed, this translation has met with a rather vigorous resistance in some quarters. My own position is that we should not limit our translation of this term to one shade of meaning, but should acknowledge that such a term could be used with nuance to express geographical, political, religious, and/or ethnic backgrounds.

27. See particularly Malina and Rohrbaugh, *John*, 7–15 of the introduction of their commentary for a thorough discussion of the model employed.

28. Ibid., 7, quoting Halliday, *Language as Social Semiotic*, 171.

29. Ibid., 68.

30. Neyrey, *Gospel of John*, 66–67.

Mother and brothers[31] of Jesus) and non-family members (the official, and Mary and Martha). All of these petitioners, including non-family members, are understood by Malina and Rohrbaugh as "natural" in-group members by virtue of their shared ethnic identity but out-group members by the standard of the Johannine community.[32] However, Philip Esler and Ronald Piper use social identity theory to argue persuasively that Mary and Martha are actually in-group members by the community's standard.[33] In fact, they are not merely in-group members, but *ideal* in-group members, models for all members of the Johannine community to emulate. A further problem is encountered in Jesus' treatment of his brothers in 7:1–9. Giblin treats Jesus' attending Sukkoth as a fulfillment of his brothers' request. However, Malina and Rohrbaugh essentially make the case that Jesus had intended to attend Sukkoth all along and actually hid his intentions from his brothers.[34] In this scenario, Malina and Rohrbaugh understand Jesus and his brothers as treating one another as out-group members, which is consistent with their application of Giblin's pattern to the Cana story. However, in this instance the pattern is broken. Jesus' brothers do in fact make a request of him, but the fact that he goes to Sukkoth does not mean that he has fulfilled their request. Rather, he had intended all along to go, but kept this fact hidden from his brothers since they did not believe in him. Neyrey recognizes the tension created by Jesus' brothers' "request" that he attend Sukkoth and Jesus' subsequent supposed fulfillment, attempting to explain it by arguing that Jesus' brothers have made their request in order to gain honor for themselves through their brother when he gains honor for himself by acting publicly.[35] The problem here is that

31. I am, of course, aware of the difficulties in referring to "the brothers of Jesus" in an article written for my Roman Catholic mentor. For thorough treatments of the question of the "brothers" of the historical Jesus, see Meier, *A Marginal Jew,* 1:318–32; and Brashler, "Jesus, Brothers and Sisters of," 819–20.

32. Malina and Rohrbaugh leave this standard undefined, though one may presume that it is belief in Jesus as the Messiah. Additionally, it should be noted that Malina and Rohrbaugh create a tension within their own interpretive framework. On *John*, 270, commenting on Jesus' committing his mother to the care of the Beloved Disciple, they write: "At Cana the mother of Jesus is a type of the faithful Israelite community that believes in Jesus. She therefore stands for the membership of John's antisociety."

33. Esler and Piper, *Lazarus, Mary, and Martha,* 75–103.

34. Malina and Rohrbaugh, *John,* 141–42.

35. Ibid., 136–37. Barrett, *John,* 256–57, seems to have something similar in mind (although, of course, he does not employ the same social-scientific categories and

7:5 states that Jesus' brothers make their request because *they do not believe in him*. Both Moloney and Bernard rightly point out the conditional nature of the brothers' evaluation of Jesus' ability to perform the miracles they "request" of him: εἰ ταῦτα ποιεῖς.[36] How could Jesus' brothers expect to gain honor through Jesus by making a request of him they believe he cannot fulfill? Again we are led to conclude that Jesus' subsequent trip to Sukkoth should not be seen as a fulfillment of the brothers' petition, but as the acting out of plans made prior to his brothers' negative challenge. Thus we have two fundamental difficulties in the readings proposed by Malina and Rohrbaugh and Neyrey: (1) the proposed insider/outsider framework of the exchanges is not as clear-cut as it first appears, and (2) the "fulfillment" stage of the pattern as proposed by Giblin is also dubious.

Social-scientific commentary on the entrusting of Jesus' Mother to the Beloved Disciple at the crucifixion is rather brief, with a high degree of uniformity exhibited in the interpretations offered. The strength and significance of the mother/son relationship in ancient Mediterranean societies is noted, as is the responsibility of the eldest son to ensure for the care of his mother should he precede her in death.[37] Malina and Rohrbaugh attempt to connect the story of the miracle at Cana to Jesus' entrusting his Mother to the Beloved Disciple by arguing for a variation of the interpretation offered by the narrative critics, namely, that the Mother of Jesus is a representative figure who symbolizes the Johannine community. Therefore, Jesus' entrusting his Mother to the Beloved Disciple in the Gospel narrative is actually a way of reinforcing the community's acceptance of the Beloved Disciple as their leader and authoritative interpreter of the person and work of Jesus.[38] Neyrey's comments are brief and limited to strictly social-scientific observations.[39] While he notes that Jesus' entrusting his Mother to the Beloved Disciple effectively creates a fictive kinship, he avoids interpreting this act theologically and/or symbolically.

---

methods used by Neyrey), arguing that the brothers want Jesus to regain the disciples who deserted him in chapter 6 by performing miracles publicly at Sukkoth. Beasley-Murray, *John*, 106–7, follows Barrett's interpretation very closely.

36. Maloney, *John*, 237; and Bernard, *John*, 1:267.
37. Malina and Rohrbaugh, *John*, 272–73; Neyrey, *Gospel of John*, 309–10.
38. Malina and Rohrbaugh, *Gospel of John*, 270.
39. Neyrey, *Gospel of John*, 309–10.

Both narrative critical and social-scientific approaches to these pericopae have yielded beneficial interpretations which sometimes complement or mutually reinforce one another. However, as I have noted, each approach leaves gaps that need to be filled in. It would seem to me that, as Powell has noted, an approach that combines both methodologies may yield additional results that could advance our understanding of these two stories individually and in relation to one another. This is an initial exploration of an intentional blending of these two methodologies and, it would seem to me, a seamless combination of the two is neither attainable nor desirable. For this reason, I will focus more on each individual methodology as seems most appropriate to the immediate question being addressed, with a summary of findings at the end of each story. I will begin with the story of the miracle at Cana.[40]

Three aspects of this story strike me as significant for understanding the story as a whole and for understanding its relationship to the scene at the foot of the cross: (1) Jesus' Mother's appeal to Jesus, (2) Jesus' rebuff, and (3) Jesus' "granting" his Mother's request. Certain aspects of Jesus' Mother's appeal have been covered quite thoroughly and I will not attempt to rehearse that information here.[41] My primary concern when examining this particular aspect of the story is this: Given that Jesus' rebuffs his Mother's request, is his Mother's request one that is socially acceptable or not? To put it in social-scientific terms, who is deviating from their social script, Jesus or his Mother? To put it in narrative critical terms, which character is acting out of character?

Neyrey, I believe, correctly observes that John's Gospel presents Jesus' Mother as a widow.[42] In that case, her appeal to Jesus is understandable: He is the eldest son and, after the death of the father, it has fallen to him to provide for his Mother. The exact concern of Jesus'

40. More could be said about both pericopae than space allows in this essay. For this reason, my remarks will focus most closely on the particularities rather than generalities of each story. So, for example, commonly accepted scholarly conclusions regarding the general nature of weddings and crucifixions will form the background of my interpretation though I will not go into explicit and lengthy rehearsals of those conclusions in my study.

41. For example, was Jesus' Mother asking in faith for Jesus to perform a miracle? If so, how did she know that Jesus was capable for such an act given that Jesus had performed no prior miracles in the course of the narrative? Does Jesus' Mother make her appeal because the shortage has occurred as a direct result of Jesus and his disciples "crashing" the wedding?

42. Neyrey, *Gospel of John*, 309.

mother, the shortage of wine, is also within the scope of a woman's responsibilities in ancient Mediterranean society. Xenophon[43] notes that males have the responsibility of bringing goods into the household, while females have the responsibility of overseeing what leaves the household,[44] and Xenophon goes on to state that the greatest responsibility of both husband and wife is "to be discreet" (εἶναι σωφρονεῖν).[45] He then defines "discretion" for both men and women as "acting in such a manner that their possessions shall be in the best condition possible, and that as much as possible shall be added to them by fair and honourable means."[46] Further, Plutarch illustrates the sympathy of the marital relationship with the contemporary medical belief that pain on one side of the body also registers on the other side.[47] While Xenophon and Plutarch speak specifically of the relationship between husband and wife, I have noted above the closeness of the mother-son relationship in ancient Mediterranean societies, and Jesus has, in some respects, taken the place of his Mother's husband. It would stand to reason, therefore, that the type of marital duties and sympathies of which these writers speak would be applicable to the mother-son relationship, especially after the death of the mother's husband. Finally, Plutarch tells us that "Mothers appear to have a greater love for their sons because of a feeling that their sons are able to help them. . . ."[48] All of this information would indicate that Jesus' Mother has acted in accordance with social expectations. She has helped in the "discreet" distribution of goods to the wedding guests and has resorted to her eldest son when necessity dictates that additional goods be brought in to the wedding banquet.

43. I here make reference to a Greco-Roman author when commenting on a story with a Palestinian Jewish setting, and some might object to such a cross-cultural usage of texts. However, Kraemer, "Typical and Atypical Jewish Family Dynamics," 130–56, has ably demonstrated that Jewish family dynamics in the ancient world did not differ substantially from that of Roman and Greek families. Therefore, in my opinion, the use of Greco-Roman authors for illuminating family dynamics in a Jewish setting is justified.

44. *Oeconomicus* III.15.

45. Ibid, VII.14–15. Ischomachus' wife tells him that her mother informed her that this is her greatest obligation, to which Ischomachus replies that his father informed him of the same.

46. Ibid. Plutarch also holds discretion in high estimation. See *Advice to the Bride and Groom*, 17.

47. Plutarch, *Advice to the Bride and Groom*, 20.

48. Ibid., 36.

She has a reasonable and socially validated expectation that her eldest son will give her aid in this situation based upon expectations of familial sympathy and the close emotional relationship enjoyed between mother and son in the ancient Mediterranean world. From this it can be concluded that Jesus' Mother did not deviate from her social script or act out of character.[49] Given the social expectations and values of her culture, her request is valid and ancient readers[50] would have expected her request to be met. It is Jesus and his rebuff of his Mother's request that should come as a surprise.

Jesus' reply to his mother has usually been broken down into two parts for examination: (1) τί ἐμοὶ καὶ σοί and (2) γύναι. Despite the alternative understanding of τί ἐμοὶ καὶ σοί proposed by McHugh and Culpepper, there can be little doubt that Jesus' response to his Mother is intended to create distance between the two of them. For a typical 1st century reader in the ancient Mediterranean, this would come as quite a surprise, for all the reasons listed above. Jesus, in this situation, does not act as a son should. Compounding the surprising nature of Jesus' reaction to his Mother's request is the title he uses to address her: "woman." It has been widely noted in the literature that this is not an uncommon or even rude form of address between males and females, and indeed it was common and not derogatory in classical usage for a husband to address his wife as "woman," just as it was common for a wife to address her husband as "man." However, there is no known precedent for a son

---

49. Malina and Rohrbaugh, as noted above, have concluded that Jesus' Mother must have made her request in public, thus making the request something of an honor challenge. However, this is nowhere stated in the narrative; all the information that is given in the narrative points toward "discreet" actions on the part of Jesus' Mother.

50. I here introduce the term "reader" into the discussion and some word of explanation ought to be offered regarding my use of this term. I do not use it to the exclusion of hearers since studies of literacy rates in the Roman empire indicate that the overwhelming majority of people would have been illiterate and in need of someone to read the Gospel to them. (For a very brief discussion of the issue of literacy in the Roman empire, see Duling, *The New Testament: History, Literature, and Social Context*, 24–25.) Nor would I limit the reader to the "ideal" or "intended" reader in this particular instance, though I believe that the reaction of a general 1st century Mediterranean reader and the "ideal" reader would be more or less the same in this instance. The "ideal" reader would, I presume, be a member of the Johannine community, but describing that reader would be a highly speculative task that would introduce an unnecessary amount of controversy into the present study. Therefore, I do not have in mind a reader as narrowly defined as a member of the Johannine community, but a reader (or hearer) who held to the general social conventions of 1st century Mediterranean culture.

referring to his mother as "woman." Again, Jesus' response creates distance, this time by using a generic rather than familial form of address when speaking to his Mother.

Jesus' surprising rebuff to his Mother's seemingly appropriate request is then followed by yet another surprise: Having seemingly declined to help, Jesus immediately grants his Mother's request! How is this reversal to be explained? I have noted above the common interpretation that Jesus refuses to take his cue from his earthly Mother and instead awaits instruction from his heavenly Father. Social-scientific critics take their cue from Giblin, with Malina and Rohrbaugh arguing that the Fourth Evangelist is here illustrating how members of the Johannine community should treat natural in-group members and Neyrey arguing that each request presents a challenge to Jesus' honor. Giblin himself argues that Jesus' rebuff is meant "to establish a dominant, personal concern on the part of Jesus himself."[51] In other words, Jesus is not taking his cue from his earthly Mother or heavenly Father, but from himself.[52] However, as noted above, there are problems with all of these interpretations. A strong note of tension has been introduced into the story: Jesus declines to act, but then acts as soon as his Mother exits the scene. The narrator does not resolve this tension by explaining Jesus' action, but instead allows the tension to stand. The reader is left to puzzle over these events as the narrative moves on to Jesus' visit to Jerusalem for Passover.

Using social-scientific criticism to create a context for reading this story of Jesus' first miracle in John's Gospel should help us to see that a 1st century reader may very well have experienced conflicting reactions to the events that unfold in the narrative. Jesus' Mother's request seems perfectly in keeping with the social scripts and expectations of the culture, but Jesus' brusque reply disorients the reader. His reason for declining his Mother's invitation to help is equally perplexing. What is this hour of which he speaks and how does the fact that it

---

51. Giblin, "Suggestion and Action," 203.

52. Ridderbos, *The Gospel of John,* 106, posits something of a combination of Giblin's "personal concern" approach and the more common "cue from God" approach: "This is not to say that for every deed Jesus had to wait, as it were, for a certain cue from God; rather, that he was conscious that the great moment at which the Father called him to this revelation of glory had not yet come. Hence what comes sharply to the fore here, precisely at the beginning of Jesus' ministry, is his awareness that his life was subject to a certain calling that he had to fulfill at God's direction . . ."

has not yet arrived prevent him from acting? Then Jesus immediately seems to fulfill his Mother's request by miraculously providing wine that is better than that which was placed before the wedding guests earlier on in the banquet. Here a typical first-century reader would have experienced conflicting reactions. On the one hand, the reader regains some degree of orientation because Jesus has now behaved as he should have at first; he has met the need presented by his Mother. On the other hand, some disorientation on the reader's part remains because there is no indication that Jesus' hour has suddenly come, making it possible for Jesus to act. A tension remains that will not be resolved until the reader arrives at the scene at the foot of the cross in chapter 19, to which we now turn.

This second episode is striking inasmuch as it recalls the story of the miracle at Cana through notable points of continuity while reversing several key elements found in the miracle story. The first and most obvious point of continuity is the presence of Jesus' Mother, the only other scene in John's Gospel in which she is a significant character (passing mention is made of her in John 6:42). Significantly, Jesus again refers to his Mother as γύναι. However, this point of continuity is also the first reversal, for the context of Jesus' reference to his Mother as γύναι seems to indicate affection rather than distance. The reversals in the story do not end there. While Jesus occupies public space in this episode, the space is anything but honorable. In fact, Jesus has been subjected to the most shameful form of death to be meted out by the Roman Empire.[53] The setting, of course, is far more somber, and Jesus, affixed to the cross, is in no position to dole out any miracles and his Mother comes asking for none. Yet this time, Jesus voluntarily acts on his Mother's behalf, committing her to the care of the Beloved Disciple. Not only is his act voluntary, but it is also in keeping with the expectations of ancient Mediterranean society regarding the care that a son would render for

---

53. For a thorough treatment of the subject of crucifixion and its function within the Roman imperial system, see Hengel, *Crucifixion, passim*, but particularly 38: "Crucifixion was widespread and frequent, above all in Roman times, but the cultured literary world wanted to have nothing to do with it, and as a rule kept quiet about it." This quote concludes a chapter on crucifixion as the supreme Roman penalty and makes much of the fact that Roman authors tended to avoid discussion of the subject. In social-scientific terms, this aversion stems from the highly shameful nature of the act.

his widowed mother.⁵⁴ But Jesus' concern is not only that his Mother's physical needs be met; the act of entrusting his Mother to the care of the Beloved Disciple also indicates that Jesus was concerned for her social well-being. While in the first story Jesus' Mother comes hoping to save the wedding party from the shame of running out of wine at the wedding banquet, Jesus here attempts to minimize the shame incurred by the mother of a crucified man.⁵⁵

These continuities and reversals serve to resolve the tensions felt by the reader at the conclusion of the miracle story. Jesus seems to fulfill his Mother's request but only after rebuffing her in a seemingly curt manner. Ultimately, however, Jesus shows himself to be an honorable male, providing for the care of his mother and attempting to alleviate the shame brought upon her by his crucifixion. Further, the reader is reassured that Jesus' Mother is not treated as an outsider, as it might have seemed from Jesus' earlier exchange with her. Hanging from the cross, Jesus ensures for the care and honor of his Mother by entrusting her to the care of the Beloved Disciple, exchanging the family of human relations for the family of faith. Finally, the ambiguity over the question of Jesus' "hour" is resolved.⁵⁶ Now that Jesus has been "exalted" on the cross, he is able to meet the most profound spiritual need of his Mother,

54. See particularly Keener, *Gospel of John*, 2:1144, nn. 679, 681, and 682, for sources regarding the care of one's aged parents. Keener notes that Seneca, *Controv.* 7.7.12, seems to describe a scenario not unlike that envisioned here in John wherein a crucified man is allowed to give instructions regarding the care of women for whom he is responsible. The only possible surprise in this scene is that Jesus arranges for a non-relative to care for his Mother. However, given the tension between Jesus and his brothers exhibited in chap. 7 and discussed above, a 1st century reader may very well have been prepared for the brothers to be excluded from Jesus' final instructions regarding the care of his Mother.

55. As an aside, this scene also impacts the characterization of Jesus in John's Gospel. Jesus' reaction to his Mother in the Cana story seems almost callous, and much of the remainder of John's portrayal of Jesus focuses on his divine nature. Though there are flashes of a vulnerable Jesus (such as his weeping over Lazarus' death and the sorrow of Mary and Martha at Bethany) the overall image tends to be elevated. The scene of Jesus' committing his mother to the care of the Beloved Disciple is still one that depicts Jesus as in control of the circumstances, but it also introduces a note of poignancy. A very human side of Jesus is brought to the forefront as he displays concern for the welfare of his Mother even as he suffers and dies on the cross.

56. I am here indebted to Haenchen, *John 1*, 178–79. Here Haenchen argues that all of the signs in John's Gospel anticipate the ultimate sign of Jesus' death on the cross. Therefore, Jesus' fulfillment of his Mother's request at Cana is really no fulfillment at all.

as well as that of the rest of the world.⁵⁷ In that regard, the two stories work together as a sort of inclusio for the entire Gospel. The Cana story begins 52 verses into the narrative and the scene at the foot of the cross occurs approximately 46 verses from what was probably the original ending of the Gospel.⁵⁸ All of the social and narratival peculiarities of the two individual stories help to tie the two together in the mind of the reader, but it is the common theme of the hour that is most significant for the unfolding of the plot. It is in the miracle story that Jesus first mentions his hour and it is in the crucifixion that his hour arrives. The first story provides the telos toward which the narrative is working and the second story signals to the reader that the *telos* has been reached.

This brief examination of these two pericopae by no means exhausts the possibilities open to us when we bring social sciences and narrative criticism together. However, I do believe that the results of this examination have been fruitful enough to promote further explorations along the same methodological path. More importantly, it is my hope that this small contribution to scholarship has in some way honored a wise mentor and trusted friend. May she enjoy to the fullest her well-deserved retirement.

---

57. Eucharistic symbolism is a highly contested element of Johannine theology, so I tread carefully when making this suggestion, but it may very well be that the flow of blood and water from Jesus' side in v. 34 also recalls the miracle story. Jesus' Mother asks for wine and he rebuffs her by claiming that his hour has not yet come. However, when his hour does come, the sacramental wine of his blood pours forth.

58. Though unresolved disputes persist regarding common authorship of the two, the majority of Johannine scholars would argue that the whole of chapter 21 is a later addition to the Gospel, and I would agree with that basic conclusion.

Bibliography

Barrett, C. K. *The Gospel according to St. John: An Introduction with Commentary and Notes on the Greek Text*. London: SPCK, 1965.
Beasley-Murray, George R. *John*. 2nd ed. WBC 36. Nashville: Nelson, 1999.
Berenson MacLean, Jennifer K. "The Divine Trickster: A Tale of Two Weddings in John." In *A Feminist Companion to John: Volume 1*, edited by Amy-Jill Levine with Marianne Blickenstaff, 48–77. FCNT 4. Cleveland: Pilgrim, 2003.
Bernard, J. H. *A Critical and Exegetical Commentary on the Gospel according to St. John*. 2 vols. ICC. Edinburgh: T. & T. Clark, 1928.
Blomberg, Craig L. *The Historical Reliability of John's Gospel: Issues and Commentary*. Downers Grove, IL: InterVarsity, 2002.
Brashler, James A. "Jesus, Brothers and Sisters of." In *Anchor Bible Dictionary*, edited by David Noel Freedman, 3:819–20. New York: Doubleday, 1992.
Brown, Raymond E. *The Gospel according to John I–XII*. AB 29. New York: Doubleday, 1966.
———. *The Gospel according to John XIII–XXI*. AB 29A. New York: Doubleday, 1970.
Bultmann, Rudolf. *The Gospel of John: A Commentary*. Translated by George W. Beasley-Murray et al. Philadelphia: Westminster, 1971.
Carson, D. A. *The Gospel according to John*. Pillar New Testament Commentary. Grand Rapids: Eerdmans, 1991.
Coloe, Coloe. *God Dwells with Us: Temple Symbolism in the Fourth Gospel*. Collegeville, MN: Liturgical, 2001.
Culpepper, R. Alan. *Anatomy of the Fourth Gospel: A Study in Literary Design*. Minneapolis: Fortress, 1983.
———. "Symbolism and History in John's Account of Jesus' Death." In *Anatomies of Narrative Criticism: The Past, Present, and Futures of the Fourth Gospel as Literature*, edited by Tom Thatcher and Stephen D. Moore, 39–54. SBL Resources for Biblical Study 55. Atlanta: Society of Biblical Literature, 2008.
Dodd, C. H. *Historical Tradition in the Fourth Gospel*. Cambridge: Cambridge University Press, 1965.
Duling, Dennis C. *The New Testament: History, Literature, and Social Context*. 4th ed. Belmont, CA: Wadsworth, 2003.
Esler, Philip F., and Ronald Piper. *Lazarus, Mary, and Martha: Social-Scientific Approaches to the Gospel of John*. Minneapolis: Fortress, 2006.
Giblin, C. H. "Suggestion, Negative Response, and Positive Action in St. John's Portrayal of Jesus (2:1–11; 4:46–54; 7:2–14; 11:1–44)." *NTS* 26 (1979–80) 197–211.
Haenchen, Ernst. *John 1: A Commentary on the Gospel of John 1–6*. Hermeneia. Translated by Robert W. Funk. Minneapolis: Fortress, 1984.
Halliday, M. A. K. *Language as Social Semiotic: The Social Interpretation of Language and Meaning*. Baltimore: University Park Press, 1978.
Hengel, Martin. *Crucifixion: In the Ancient World and the Folly of the Message of the Cross*. Translated by John Bowden. Philadelphia: Fortress, 1977.
Keener, Craig S. *The Gospel of John: A Commentary*. 2 vols. Peabody, MA: Hendrickson, 2003.
Kraemer, Ross Shepard. "Typical and Atypical Jewish Family Dynamics: The Cases of Babatha and Berenica." In *Early Christian Families in Context: An Interdisciplinary*

Dialogue, edited by David L. Balch and Carolyn Osiek, 130–56. Grand Rapids: Eerdmans, 2003.

Koester, Craig R. *Symbolism in the Fourth Gospel: Meaning, Mystery, Community*. 2nd ed. Minneapolis: Fortress, 2003.

Lincoln, Andrew T. *The Gospel according to St. John*. Black's New Testament Commentary 4. Peabody, MA: Hendrickson, 2005.

Lindars, Barnabas. *The Gospel of John*. New Century Bible. London: Oliphants, 1972.

Malina, Bruce J., and Richard L. Rohrbaugh, *Social-Science Commentary on the Gospel of John*. Minneapolis: Fortress, 1998.

McHugh, John. *The Mother of Jesus in the New Testament*. London: Darton, Longman & Todd, 1975.

———. *A Critical and Exegetical Commentary on John 1–4*. ICC. London: T. & T. Clark, 2009.

Meier, John P. *A Marginal Jew, Rethinking the Historical Jesus, Volume One: The Roots of the Problem and the Person*. Anchor Bible Reference Library. New Haven: Yale University Press, 1991.

Moloney, Francis J., SDB. *Belief in the Word: Reading the Fourth Gospel, 1–4*. Minneapolis: Fortress, 1993.

———. *Glory not Dishonor: Reading John 13–21*. Minneapolis: Fortress, 1998.

———. *The Gospel of John*. SacPag 4. Collegeville, MN: Liturgical, 1998.

Neyrey, Jerome H. *The Gospel of John*. New Cambridge Bible Commentary. Cambridge: Cambridge University Press, 2007.

Powell, Mark Allen. *What Is Narrative Criticism?* Guides to Biblical Scholarship. Minneapolis: Fortress, 1990.

Ridderbos, Herman. *The Gospel of John: A Theological Commentary*. Translated by John Vriend. Grand Rapids: Eerdmans, 1997.

Stibbe, Mark W. G. *John as Storyteller: Narrative Criticism and the Fourth Gospel*. SNTSMS 73. Cambridge: Cambridge University Press, 1992.

Talbert, Charles H. *Reading John: A Literary and Theological Commentary on the Fourth Gospel and the Johannine Epistles*. New York: Crossroad, 1992.

Zumstein, Jean. "Johannes 19,25–27." *Zeitschrift für Theologie und Kirche* 94 (1997) 131–54.

PART FOUR

Pauline Documents

11

Seen but not Heard
Women Prophets in Caesarea[1]

Laurie Brink, O.P.

TO PARAPHRASE THE LUCAN PAUL, I WAS EDUCATED AT THE FEET OF Carolyn Osiek on the relevance of ancient realia for the interpretation of the New Testament. At her suggestion, I worked on the archaeological team excavating Herod's city on the Mediterranean, so I am particularly interested in the place of Caesarea in the development of the early Church. By the third century, Origen would relocate to Caesarea Maritima and here establish a school of theology. His work on Scripture would have influence on successive generations. Less than a century later, Eusebius composed his *Ecclesiastical History* while residing in Caesarea. Archaeological efforts have uncovered discernible Christian structures from the fifth century. But of the primitive Church of Caesarea, Acts of the Apostles provides our sole textual evidence.[2]

Surely, a city that is mentioned 15 times in Acts,[3] one of only three places noted to have hosted both Peter and Paul[4] and the locale for the first unequivocally Gentile convert (Acts 10) held a significant pride of

---

1. I am grateful to Barbara Bowe, RSCJ, for her careful reading and suggestions on earlier drafts of this chapter and to Catherine Meyering, OP, for her assistance in research and translation.

2. Josephus describes the building of Caesarea and its early history, but does not make mention of any Christian community. See *Ant.* 15.8.5 and *J.W.* 1.4.2. Josephus also recounts the conflicts arising among the Syrian and Jewish residents (*Ant.* 20.173–78).

3. Caesarea Maritima is mentioned in Acts 8:40; 9:30; 10:1, 24; 11:11; 12:19; 18:22; 21:8, 16; 23:23, 33; 25:1, 4, 6, 13.

4. According Gal 2:11, Paul confronted Cephas (Peter) in Antioch. Acts 15 places both Peter and Paul in Jerusalem.

place in the Lucan geography.[5] If, as Barrett and Harnack propose, the stories set in Caesarea derive from a local source,[6] then perhaps we have a shadow of evidence indicating something of that community, at least as it might have been remembered in Luke's day. Further, those who hope to find stories of women in ministry in the early Church are often pleased with the multiple female characters peppered throughout Luke-Acts,[7] because they presume that the presence of women in the narratives may indicate a place and public role for them in the primitive church. Could it be then that the odd little insertion that Philip had four virgin daughters who prophesized might hint at the presence of oracular women in the Caesarean community?

Of greater curiosity is not the mention of the four prophesying daughters, but their silence. Why identify the daughters as those who prophesy but not include evidence of their gifts? What function do they serve in the narrative? The works of Reid and others have already demonstrated that visible women do not mean vocal women.[8] In fact, the following assessment seems accurate: "Although it is indisputable that there are women disciples in Luke and Acts, a closer study reveals that they do not participate in the mission of Jesus in the same way that the men disciples do. If we are looking to Luke's narrative to show that women and men shared equally in Jesus' mission in the first century, we will be disappointed."[9]

In this sobering light, the mention of the four daughters of Philip may simply be an interesting addition, meant to more fully describe the character of Philip, whom the author has called an evangelist and one of the seven. Perhaps we are meant to see him also as a family man.

---

5. Barrett concurs, adding "There is no doubt that Luke was interested in Caesarea" (*Acts*, 1.51 n. 3).

6. "Whatever we make of the historical value of 21.8, the verse claims, on the author's part, some contact with Philip the Evangelist. Even if the contact was less direct than a surface reading of the verse suggests, the author had access to traditions about, perhaps emanating from, Philip—we may again add, so as not to claim too much, whatever their historical value" (Barrett, *Acts*, 1.51). Harnack suggested that the daughters of Philip were Luke's source for the stories about women (*Luke the Physician*, 153–55).

7. Alfred Plummer called the Gospel of Luke "the gospel for women . . . All through this gospel [women] are allowed a prominent place, and many types of womanhood are placed before us" (*Luke*, xlii–xliii).

8. Reid, *Choosing the Better Part*. Also D'Angelo, "Women in Luke-Acts," 441–61; Schaberg, "Luke"; Seim, *Double Message*.

9. Reid, *Choosing the Better Part*, 4.

In the larger narrative, the four virgin daughters known to prophesy may function as a theological fulfillment of Joel's prophecy (Joel 3:1), quoted by Peter in his Pentecost address (Acts 2:16–21). From the perspective of the story, verse 9 serves both purposes—it adds to the characterization of Philip and it is a verification of prophecy. But how would Luke's authorial audience[10] hear the acknowledgment that Philip had four girls, each gifted with prophesy? Wouldn't they anticipate some evidence of the oracular gift? Why is it that an outsider gets the speaking part? Is the authorial audience to conclude that women, despite their giftedness, should be seen and not heard?

Perhaps as Loisy once noted, in the original source, the daughters did utter a prophecy, which under Luke's editorial hand has been transferred to another.[11] This chapter examines the four prophesying daughters in light of the portrayal of women prophets in Scripture and finds that, like their male counterparts, women can be both true and false prophets. Only the presence of the Holy Spirit validates one's prophetic abilities. Anything other is magic—a practice often the purview of women.[12] Luke may have seen the oracles of ecstatic women as too close a parallel to the contemporary magical practices from which he was trying to distance the Christian community.

10. An analysis of the author's literary efforts, use of imagery, vocabulary, and rhetoric produces a portrait of the audience that the author presumes would understand his literary genius. The horizon of expectations—the authorial audience's knowledge of other literature, history, culture, etc.—permits the author to leave unspoken what he could readily expect his authorial auditors to know. The Lucan authorial auditor was a culturally literate member of the late-first- or early-second-century Mediterranean world who knew basic facts about the Roman Empire, including its history, politics, and geography and the way it functioned politically and militarily. Luke presumes his authorial audience possessed a knowledge of major cities and ethnic groups. The authorial audience was also familiar with popular Greco-Roman literature and some of its literary features including miraculous prison breaks (Acts 12:4–10; 16:23–29) and harrowing shipwrecks (Acts 27:13–44). The unusual aspect of this contextualized auditor was his or her knowledge of the Greek Bible, which Luke engages through his use of Septuagintalisms, and biblical allusions throughout the two-volume work. Members of this audience belonged to the wide social network of Theophilus, which included men and women, slave and free, patrons and clients, Jew and Gentile, Roman citizens and noncitizens. The authorial auditor resided within a Hellenistic urban setting and may have been an artisan or small-business owner (Acts 16:14; 18:2; 19:24, 38). The audience was likely composed of both Christians and God-fearers and was aware of Greco-Roman religious beliefs and practices (Acts 14:11–13; 19:27; 28:4–6).

11. Loisy, *Actes*, 785.

12. Ilan, "It's Magic," 166.

Hospitality and Prophecy in Caesarea

In Acts 21:7–18, Paul arrives first in Caesarea and subsequently travels to Jerusalem. The verses include a substantial portion of "we passages," perhaps written by a companion of Paul.[13] While in Caesarea, Paul and the others reside with Philip who is doubly identified: he is Philip the evangelist and one of the seven. Verse 9 adds to the description of Philip. He also has daughters who prophesy. Perhaps the acknowledgment of their spiritual gifts is meant to ascribe honor to Philip as their father. As 1 Tim 3:11 states, deacons are to manage their children and households well. That one of the seven who is known as an evangelist also has children who display prophetic gifts testifies to Philip's worthiness.

The narrator is in Caesarea, staying at the home of Philip, so we presume his daughters are located there as well. We learn that these daughters are four in number and are παρθένοι, as was Mary in Luke 1:27. Witherington sees no Lucan insistence on virginity as a necessary requirement for prophesy,[14] and Eusebius reported that one of the daughters was married (*Hist. Eccl.* 3.30.1). Yet, Luke could simply have identified them as the daughters of Philip who prophesy without describing them as παρθένοι. The "unmarried" or "virginal" status may be meant to assure their credibility.[15] The participle προφητεύουσαι is ambivalent. Luke could mean either prophesying in the sense of inspired preaching or spirit-given charismatic speech.[16] The very use of the participle rather than the nominative προφῆτις could indicate that the daughters engaged in occasional acts of prophecy and did not hold

---

13. Robbins argues that the use of the first person plural is a literary convention of sea journeys ("We-Passages," 5–18). Brown counters, "If 'we' is purely conventional, why does this pronominal usage not appear throughout all the sea-journeying in Acts instead of in only a few sections separated by years in the narrative?" (*Introduction*, 323). The second century tradition that Luke, the occasional companion of Paul, was the author of the "we" passages is not "impossible," according to Brown (327). More recently, William S. Campbell has analyzed the "we" passages through the lens of reader-response theory, identifying the enigmatic figure as a narrative character who replaces Barnabas as the verifying witness to Paul's activities (*"We" Passages*).

14. Witherington, *Acts*, 633.

15. "When women's prophetic status is positively valued, their sexual purity is emphasized, often by pointing out that they were virgins, chaste widows, or even occasionally devoted wives." See King, "Prophetic Power," 28).

16. Fitzmyer, *Acts*, 689.

the office of prophet.¹⁷ We are told nothing else, nor do they appear again in the text. They are not named, nor does the audience know if they are even present in the scene.

Perhaps their absence explains why it is an out-of-town prophet—who is named—who predicts what awaits Paul in Jerusalem. The authorial audience is introduced to Agabus (whom they have actually met in Acts 11:28 when he predicted the famine under Claudius). The presence of an introductory phrase (τις), place of origin (Ἰουδαίας), and two attributes—his occupation and his name (προφήτης ὀνόματι Ἄγαβος)—show that Luke intends his authorial audience to recognize Agabus as a character, if only a minor one.¹⁸ The unnamed daughters of Philip who were purported to prophesy are upstaged by Agabus whom Reimer presumes has firsthand information about the situation in Jerusalem.¹⁹ If insider information prompted Agabus' pronouncement there would be little need for the prophet to credit his words to the Holy Spirit (Acts 21:11). In Acts 11:28, Agabus, again coming from Jerusalem under the direction of the Holy Spirit, announced the worldwide famine. In both cases, Luke stresses that it is the presence of the Spirit and not the origin of the prophet that validates the prophecy.

While residing in Caesarea for some days, Paul and his companions are beset by Agabus. He seizes Paul's ζώνη, wrapping it around his feet and hands (Acts 21:11). The prophet then announces τάδε λέγει τὸ πνεῦμα τὸ ἅγιον· τὸν ἄνδρα οὗ ἐστιν ἡ ζώνη αὕτη, οὕτως δή σουσιν ἐν Ἰερουσαλὴμ οἱ Ἰουδαῖοι καὶ παραδώσουσιν εἰς χεῖρας

---

17. Barrett, *Acts*, 2.994.

18 Luke introduces a character, offers description, and then proceeds with the story, a narrative device that Dickerson names, "New Character Narrative." See Dickerson, "New Character Narrative," 295. The introductory formula contains an introduction (ἰδοὺ ἀνδορ τις) and at least three forms of identification, including the character's place of origin and various attributes. Thirty characters appear to evidence this formula. They are Zechariah and Elizabeth (Luke 1:5–6), Simeon (Luke 2:25), Anna (Luke 2:36–37), the son of Nain (Luke 7:11–15), the woman who loved much (Luke 7:37–50), the Gerasene demoniac (Luke 8:26–39), Jairus (Luke 8:41–56), Martha (Luke 10:38), Zacchaeus (Luke 19:2), Joseph (Luke 23:50–51), the cripple at the Beautiful Gate (Acts 3:2–8), Ananias and Sapphira (Acts 5:1–6), Gamaliel (Acts 5:34), Simon (Acts 8:9), Ethiopian official (Acts 8:27), Ananias (Acts 9:10–17); Aeneas (Acts 9:33), Tabitha/Dorcas (Acts 9:36), Cornelius (Acts 10:1–2), Bar-Jesus/Elymas (Acts 13:6), the cripple at Lystra (Acts 14:8–10), Timothy (Acts 16:1–2), Lydia (Acts 16:14–15), Aquila and Priscilla (Acts 18:2–4), Apollos (Acts 18:21), Demetrius (Acts 19:24), and Eutychus (Acts 20:9–12).

19. Reimer, *Women in the Acts of the Apostles*, 249.

ἐθνῶν. Like the Old Testament prophets, Agabus appears to be engaging in a prophetic action,[20] but as Witherington recognized "Paul will indeed be put in a bind by Jews in Jerusalem, and he will indeed be actually bound by Gentile authorities . . . , but he is not literally bound by the Jews nor is he handed over by them to the Gentiles."[21] Barrett excuses the incomplete correspondence between the prophecy and its fulfillment suggesting that as a writer Luke was not concerned with "neat correspondences (witness his three accounts of Paul's conversion);" rather, Luke means for the action awaiting Paul in Jerusalem to resemble the arrest and trial of Jesus.[22]

The plural narrator responds by joining the chorus of the others who are present begging Paul not to continue his journey. Paul's response echoes that of Jesus who rebukes Peter for wanting to prevent his death, an incident which Luke has left out of his Gospel (Mark 8:32–33//Matt 16:22–23). After their reprimand from Paul, "we" and the others consent that the Lord's will should be done. The travelogue continues, departing Caesarea and moving toward Jerusalem. An overnight stay is assumed since the group lodges at the house of Mnason of Cyprus, identified as an early disciple. The next scene occurs in Jerusalem where Paul and the group meet with James and the elders, and the first person narrator ends his travelogue.

The prophesying daughters function theologically to confirm that the Spirit has been poured out, but as F. Scott Spencer recognizes despite Peter's citation of Joel in Acts 2, the prophecies of neither daughters nor slave girls herald the coming day of the Lord.[23] The praises of Anna the daughter of Phanuel may be recorded indirectly in the Gospel of Luke, but the voices of the four daughters of Philip are mute (Acts 21:9). Slave girls fare somewhat better. In the gospel, as Jesus is dragged before the high priest, his slave girl recognizes Peter and announces, "This one was with him" (Luke 22:56). In Acts, a slave girl responds with amazement when she hears Peter's voice (Acts 12:13). In her joy, she leaves him knocking on the outside gate and runs to announce his presence. Just as Peter denies the truth of the high priest's slave girl, those gathered in the

---

20. Barrett, *Acts*, 2.995.

21. Witherington, *Acts*, 634.

22. Barrett, *Acts*, 2.996. For Paul's Damascus road experience see Acts 9; 22:6–16; and 26:12–18.

23. Spencer, "Out of Mind," 133–55.

house of Mary silence Rhoda (Acts 12:15). The last slave girl to appear in Acts is possessed of a Pythian spirit (Acts 16:16–18). She proclaims that Paul and those with him are slaves of the most high God and that they have come to announce a way of salvation. Rather than rejoicing in her astute proclamation, Paul is annoyed (διαπονέομαι) and casts the spirit out of her. Spencer concludes: "While the infancy narrative in Luke 1–2 and especially the Joel citation in Acts 2 provide radical-idealistic support for prophetic women in general and servant-women in particular, their vision is ultimately overwhelmed by conventional-pragmatic considerations. Women may have the right and gift to speak, but few audiences—even in the church—are willing to hear them."[24]

Whether historically accurate or not, the mention of Philip's prophesying daughters would not have occurred odd or out of place to Luke's authorial audience. Male and female prophets appeared throughout the Greco-Roman world. A woman sat upon the tripod at Delphi and Cumae, uttering oracles sought after by kings and commoners alike. Protected in the Capitoline Temple, the Sibylline Oracles were the refuge of wisdom when Rome and its leaders desperately needed direction. Luke could assume that his authorial audience had also encountered portrayals of prophetic women in the bible.

Prophetic Women in the Old Testament and Early Christian Literature

Though infrequent women prophets are not unheard of in the Scriptures. Miriam is called a prophet (Exod 15:20), as is Hulda (2 Kgs 22:14; 2 Chr 34:22) and Noadiah (Neh 6:14). Deborah is both prophet and judge (Judg 4:4). Not all women prophets were equally revered. Miriam challenges Moses' authority and his marriage to a non-Hebrew. As a result she is punished by God who inflicts her with leprosy (Num 12:1–15). Nehemiah accuses Noadiah of trying to frighten him and to thwart his building plans (Neh 6:12–15). The woman prophet in Isaiah 8:1 is not named though she may be the wife of Isaiah. At the direction of God, Isaiah and this woman prophet conceive a son who is given the name "Maher-shalal-hash-baz," meant to depict the coming destruction of Judah. Gafney sees this as "a joint prophetic undertaking," and agrees

---

24. Ibid., 150.

with Blenkinsopp that the woman is not to be understood as Mrs. Isaiah Prophet, but as a prophet in her own right.[25]

Ezekiel's scolding of false prophets is particularly vituperative in Chapter 13. Both male and female prophets incur his ire. The men lie and falsify their prophecies (13:7–9). Daughters who prophesy out of their own imagination are taken to task. God promises to rescue the people from the clutches of these false female prophets who use magical bands to ensnare their victims and practice divination (13:17–23).

Evidently the test of prophecy among one's children—sons and daughters—is the presence of the Spirit (Joel 3:1), which God pours out upon all humanity when the Day of Lord comes. Joel's vision is one of "radical universality."[26] Peter recognizes the experience of Pentecost as the heralding of the Day of the Lord when he readily quotes Joel in Acts 2:17–20.

In the New Testament, the genuine Pauline epistles appear to affirm that prophets were a legitimate group within the early ecclesia and that women were part of that group, though Paul recommends that they cover their head when prophesying (1 Cor 11:5). The admonition that women should keep silent in the churches (1 Cor 14:34) can be explained as an interpolation from a later community who sought to harmonize 1 Tim 2:11f.[27] Or if the verse is genuinely from Paul, it may not refer to spirit-inspired speech.

Luke is the only Gospel writer to mention women prophets. The elderly widow Anna is identified as the daughter of Phanuel of the tribe of Asher (Luke 2:36). Her continual prayer and fasting in the temple demonstrate her piety (Luke 2:37). She begins to speak about the child Jesus to all who awaited the redemption of Jerusalem (Luke 2:38). Simeon is said to possess the Holy Spirit (Luke 2:25), but Anna is given no such acknowledgment. Elizabeth and Mary may perform acts that resemble that of prophets, but they are not so designated.[28]

---

25. Gafney, *Daughters of Miriam*, 238.

26. Ibid., 111.

27. Wire, *Corinthian Women Prophets*, 229–32.

28. Barbara Reid demonstrates that both Elizabeth and Mary engage in prophetic actions and are filled with the Holy Spirit (*Taking up the Cross*, 101–2). Gafney also identifies women in the Hebrew Scriptures who, though not named as prophets, engage in activities that could be labeled prophetic (*Daughters of Miriam*, 151–65).

In Acts, Luke distinguishes between the prophets of old (3:18, 21, 24, 25; 7:42, 52; 10:43; 13:15, 27, 40; 15:15; 24:14; 26:22, 27; 28:23) and current prophets like those who traveled from Jerusalem (11:27; 21:10), the prophets and teachers of Antioch (13:1), Judas and Silas (15:32); Bar-Jesus, the false prophet (13:6), and Agabus (21:10). Only in two settings are female prophets mentioned: Luke 2:36–38 where the aged and widow Anna is in the Temple and in Acts 21:9 where Philip's virgin daughters are part of the household. We discover that Anna spoke, but Luke does not narrate what she said. The contemporary male prophets fare somewhat better. We learn of Agabus' two pronouncements (Acts 11:28; 21:10). Luke confirms that the famine predicted by Agabus occurred during the reign of Claudius (Acts 11:28) and the authorial audience learns what awaits Paul in Jerusalem. In Acts 13, the Holy Spirit speaks but we are not told through which of the Antiochene prophets. According to the Spirit, Barnabas and Saul are to be set apart for the work for which they have been called. Indeed, they are sent off to proclaim the word of God. Judas and Silas are sent by the Jerusalem assembly to relay the message to the Gentiles of Antioch (Acts 15:27). Being prophets themselves, they exhort and strengthen the believers and after a time are sent back to Jerusalem with greetings of peace. For those whom Luke designates as prophets or those who prophesy, the narrator states directly or indirectly the content of their message, with the exception of Philip's daughters. They are silent.

The Book of Revelation depicts prophets who work against God. The visionary criticizes the self-proclaimed prophet from Thyatira whom he calls Jezebel. She leads the people astray and encourages them to turn to adultery and to eat foods sacrificed to idols (Rev 2:20). Associated with the beast and the devil, the false male prophet uses signs to deceive people. He will be cast into the fire and sulfur (Rev 16:13, 19:20 and 20:10).

Distinguishing between true and false prophets continued to be a challenge for the developing church. By the end of the first century, traveling Christian prophets required some regulation, as evidenced by the Didache. While both a true and false prophet may claim inspiration from the Spirit, only the one who holds τοὺς τρόπους κυρίου is to be judged rightly (11.8). *The Shepherd of Hermas* also delineates the differences between a true and false prophet (*Man.* 11.8–12). A true prophet displays a quiet disposition, avoids evil and does not utter a prophecy simply when asked to do so (*Man.* 11.8). A false prophet, on the other hand, exalts himself, is arrogant and shameless, and enjoys the money he receives for his prophecies (Man. 11.12). The double-minded seek out the false prophet as a fortune teller (μάντις, 11.2). The devils fills him with his own spirit (τῷ αὐτοῦ πνεύματι), in order to beat down the righteous (11.3).

Throughout the Scriptures the test of the true prophet is not the verifiability of his or her message, but the source of inspiration. One does not consult the Spirit of God, as Hermas reports:

πᾶν γὰρ πνεῦμα ἀπὸ θεοῦ δοθὲν οὐκ ἐπερωτᾶται ἀλλὰ ἔχον τὴν δύναμιν τῆς θεότητος ἀφ' ἑαυτοῦ λαλεῖ πάντα ὅτι ἄνωθέν ἐστιν ἀπὸ τῆς δυνάμεως τοῦ θείου πνεύματος. (*Man.* 11.5)[29]

True prophets do not initiate their pronouncements or their prophetic acts. They do not rely on external devices to entice or provoke the Spirit's presence, nor do they accept remuneration in response to their prophecy. Prophecy as presented in the biblical texts and the Apostolic Fathers is divinely-initiated. Anything else is filled with empty falsehoods and comes from the devil (*Hermas, Man.*11.17).

Divining the Difference between Magic and Prophecy

This discussion of true and false prophets depicts an on-going dilemma in Jewish and Christian communities. One's personal comportment and the presence of the Holy Spirit were the true validators. Any use of divining instruments surely indicated self-initiated—and hence false—prophecies. This invocation/provocation of the divine is often associated with the use of magical devices or garments as seen in Ezekiel.

The women prophets in Ezekiel sew bands, tying them around the wrist of their clients. They make head coverings or veils of various sizes and use them in their hunt for souls (Ezek 13:18). Through Ezekiel, God vows to tear the bands from the wrists of those ensnared and set them free from the power of these daughters who prophesy falsely.

---

29. "For no spirit given by God needs to be consulted; instead, having the divine power, it speaks everything on its own initiative, because it is from above, from the power of the divine spirit" (*Man.* 11.5; translation from Holmes, *Apostolic Fathers*, 541).

We see a similar use of divining devices in the Testament of Job. Unlike the canonical Book of Job, the apocryphal Testament of Job develops the role and place of women in the life of the patriarch. His maid servant (6–7) and first wife (21–26) are portrayed as dutifully concerned with his honor and well-being, but they nonetheless become unwitting tools for Satan. Though not called prophets, Job's daughters by his second wife, are given exemplary inheritances—three multicolored cords which provide them with prophetic abilities (46–52). When Hemera wraps her cord around herself, she is no longer focused on earthly concerns but turns towards matters of the heart (48.2). She speaks in an angelic language and offers hymns to God (48.3). While she chants, she permits the spirit to be inscribed on her stole (48.4). Likewise, after wrapping the cord around herself, her sister, Kasia speaks in the dialect of the ancients (49.2). The last daughter, Amaltheias-keras, girds herself and speaks in the dialect of those on high (50.1). In Chapter 51, Job's brother Nereos, adds a epilogue. After the three daughters had ceased singing their hymns, and while the Lord and the holy angel were present (51.1), Nereos writes down the notations for the hymns, so as to serve as a safeguard, since these were great things from God (51.3). When Job senses that his death nears, he gives each daughter an instrument so that they might praise God. The daughters then glimpse a vision of heaven and witness their father's ascent.

The garment of Job is called a "cord" (48:1), "cincture" (52:1) and "phylactery" (47:11). Spittler notes that the more common "girdle" is not found.[30] The variety of vocabulary used to describe the girdle or belt may indicate that actual objects were part of the story's background.[31] Cords or girdles were used to hold up loincloths or to gather in garments. Purses and weapons could also be attached to external belts. On women, they also served as a primitive bra and were worn under the garments.[32] According to Omerzu, girdles have symbolic meaning and have been related to magic and cultic practices.[33] Retaining some of the power of its wearer, the belt or clothing can thus transfer that power. Likely this is the understanding in Luke 6:19 where people sought to touch Jesus, and in Luke 8:44 where the woman hopes to be healed if

30. Spittler, "Testament of Job," 1.864, n. 46d.
31. Omerzu, "Women, Magic and Angels," 95.
32. Ibid., 90.
33. Ibid.

she but touches the edge of Jesus' garment. In Acts 19:12, clothes of Paul have healing effects.

Does the characterization of the prophetic daughters in the Testament of Job indicate a positive portrayal of women in religious roles to which Luke's portrait stands in judgment? Certainly, the Testament of Job demonstrates that women participated in cultic activities, sanctioned by the male head of the household. Van der Horst argues that chapters 46–53 in *Testament of Job* originated from a Jewish ecstatic group "in which women played a leading role by their greater ecstatic gifts and their superior spiritual insight into heavenly reality."[34] But despite the multiple female characters and their cultic roles, Garrett concluded that the women in the *Testament of Job* are stereotyped along ancient gender lines. "A fundamentally negative view of females as preoccupied with that which is earthly and corruptible underlies the [*Testament of Job*] from beginning to end . . . Job's second set of daughters do not display such preoccupation with earthly affairs—but only because they have been given 'different' or 'changed' hearts. The implication is that otherwise the mundane realm would have been the focal point of their existence, as it had been for Sitidos."[35]

Though van der Horst views the portraits of the daughters as positive, Garrett posits that like the Therapeutae of Philo who have "spurned the pleasures of the body," Job's daughters are approved of by the author precisely because they have let go of earthly (read: womanly) concerns.[36]

Then there are the daughters of Philip. Though noted for their ability to prophesy, they do not speak. The authorial audience is not even certain if the daughters are present in the scene in which they are mentioned. There is a magical belt of sorts, but this did not belong to Philip but to Paul. And it is when Agabus takes Paul's belt and girds his feet and hands that the Holy Spirit is said to endow his prophecy. "The girding before the reception of a revelation probably depends on the

---

34. Van der Horst, "Images of Women," 113. Though the strong emphasis on the challenging speech and the role of the daughters may led some to suggest a woman or circle of women penned the Testament of Job, Garrett argues that "authorship by a woman is possible, inasmuch as most women probably accepted without question the ideological construction of their own gender offered by contemporary males" (Garrett, "The 'Weaker Sex,'" 70 n. 45).

35. Garrett, "The 'Weaker Sex,'" 57, 70.

36. Ibid., 58.

magical or mystical idea of transmission of heavenly-spiritual qualities to humans by means of a girdle."[37]

What if Luke's source included the prophetic speech of the daughters, who themselves took up Paul's belt and received power in the spirit? As Loisy once proposed, the redactor may have then transposed the daughters' prophecy and placed it on the lips of Agabus (21:4).[38] Similar to Loisy, Boismard and LaMouille propose that the daughters' prophecy was given to the disciples in Tyre. They have reconstructed how the original may have read:[39]

9	Il (Philippe) avait quatre filles prophé tisant,
4b	[qui] disaient à Paul ( ) de ne pas monter à Jérusalem.
12	Quand nous eûmes entendu cela, nous le priâmes, nous et ceux de l'endroit de ne pas monter ( ).
14	Comme il ne se laissait pas convaincre, nous restâmes cois en disant: "Que la volonté du Seigneur arrive."

The reconstructed scene would then more closely parallel the presentation of Anna and Simeon in Luke 2:22–38. The speech of the daughters who are known to prophesy and Anna the prophet are indirectly stated, while Agabus and Simeon are quoted directly. It would seem that a woman may prophesy but her words are not stated, and therefore are not given the same narrative weight as those of the male speakers.[40] But since Luke has already set a precedent with Anna and Simeon, why aren't the daughters' words mentioned? If, indeed, Loisy, Boismard and LaMouille are correct, Luke has gone to some length to silence them.

Perhaps in the original source, the daughters not only utter a prophecy but also engaged in a prophetic act, which has now been given to Agabus. Such a proposal attempts to reconstruct a source only available via its redacted version and would take quite a slight of hand

---

37. Omerzu., "Women, Magic and Angels," 95.
38. Loisy, *Les Actes des Apôtres*, 785.
39. Boismard and LaMouille, *Les Actes des Deux Apôtres*. 3.254.
40. Alter develops the difference between the credibility of direct and indirect speech in his discussion of characterization (Alter, *Art of Biblical Narrative*, 116–17).

to prove. But since our concern is the narrative silence of the prophesying daughters, a possible transposition of prophecy and act might explain the text as we now have it. The question becomes why would Luke find it necessary to mollify Philip's daughters? Scriptural warrants confirm the presence of women prophets. But in almost equal measure these women can be praised and criticized. Miriam is a case in point. Ezekiel reserves the most vehement censure for those women who use objects in their divination, providing false prophecies. The apocryphal *Testament of Job* positively portrays daughters who utter prophecies via the mediation of an object. Might Luke be concerned with how his own authorial audience might perceive or misperceive Philip's daughters? Is there something inherently dangerous about belt-wielding women?

Luke's Critique of Magic

The relationship between prophecy and magic has a long history and has often been used by societies to deal with deviant minority movements.[41] Likewise, the association of women with sorcery is a reoccurring theme. 1 Enoch traces the origins to the fallen angels who taught the magical arts of healing and sorcery to the women whom they seduced (*1 Enoch* 7:1). According to rabbinic sources, most women practiced some form of witchcraft (*y. Sanhedrin* 7:9, 25d). "The issue of exorcism, possession, and prophecy . . . is slightly mixed up in the Hebrew Bible and thoroughly confused in the New Testament."[42]

In the Greco-Roman world, the determination of whether a miraculous event occurred by "magic" or the power of the god(s) depended on the perspective of the observer.[43] For the Christian disciple, the actions of Jesus and the Apostles were clearly by means of the Holy Spirit. But according to unbelievers, the miracles were wrought by magic at the hands of a sorcerer (*Contra Celsus* 1.38, 71; 2.32, 48) inspired by Beelzebul (Luke 11:15). For the uninitiated, the cult looked more like an *exitiabilis superstitio* than anything resembling bona fide religion in the Roman context (Tacitus *Ann.* 15.44). As Klauck has demonstrated, Luke used the polemic himself.[44] The difficulty facing the early Christian

---

41. Wilson, *Prophecy and Society in Ancient Israel*, 73–74.
42. Ilan, "It's Magic," 171.
43. See Aune, "Magic in Early Christianity," 1506–57.
44. Klauck, *Magic and Paganism*, 48. Stratton further develops the polemical use

missionaries preaching in a syncretistic religious world was distinguishing the words and deeds of Jesus from those of so many other wonder workers. Acts of the Apostles presents no "heavily aggressive polemic" against magicians, according to Klauck.[45] Rather, the author has demonstrated that the power of the apostles not only supersedes that of the magicians (Acts 8:9–13) but becomes a prize they wish to buy (Acts 8:18–19) and a power they attempt to emulate (Acts 19:13–16).

The problem Luke faced is depicted in Acts 14: 8–18. Paul and Barnabas appear to the astonished people of Lystra as gods in human form. "Luke develops a variety of strategies: he orientates and subordinates the miracles of the Christian messengers to the proclamation of the word; he also attempts to the best of his ability, on the basis of the biblical faith in creation, to exclude every confusion between God and human beings and every transgression of the boundary between the divine and the human spheres..."[46]

Luke disparages rivals through the derogatory use of the term "magic" and clearly attempts to distinguish the human actor from the divine source of power. But what to do when a woman prophet of another god acknowledges your own messengers? The slave girl with a Pythian spirit seemingly errs not in her theology but in her insistent delivery. She followed Paul for several days, announcing that he and those with him were servants of the most high God (δοῦλοι τοῦ θεοῦ τοῦ ὑψίστου v. 17). We may wonder why this woman whom the authorial audience knows is speaking truthfully is not given the same consideration as is the person in Luke 9:49 who is casting out demons in Jesus' name though he is not of their company.[47] Paul is annoyed and casts out the spirit in the name of Jesus Christ. "Exorcism becomes a

---

of the label of "magic" in the early Christian writings. See Stratton, "The Rhetoric of 'Magic.'"

45. Klauck, *Magic and Paganism*, 119.

46. Ibid., 120.

47. The problem is the possible confusion with the use of the term "most high god," which could have various referents. Additionally, she claims these servants preach "a" way of salvation. Her pronouncement could be understood as echoing that of the Christian messengers. But, as Klauck notes, "a syncretistic misunderstanding would be equally possible: a new higher god is announced, a competitor to those who already exist, and a new offer of salvation with a new redeemer-figure aims merely at widening the existing spectrum, without being fundamentally different from other offers" (*Magic and Paganism*, 69).

means of getting rid of those (especially prophets) one does not want . . . Not only Acts' Paul, but also the early church found exorcism of demons an effective way of dispiriting women who were a problem."[48] When we come to the four daughters of Philip, Luke may have feared that the association of women with sorcery and false prophecy would taint their words or actions.[49] Indeed, no commentary mentions that Agabus' employment of Paul's belt could resemble the use of magical garments, despite the earlier episodes involving the handkerchiefs and aprons that had touched Paul's skin (Acts 19:2). Instead, Agabus' actions are consistently compared to those of the Old Testament prophets.[50]

Conclusion: The Presence of the Spirit in the Church at Caesarea

If the original audience for Luke-Acts knew of Philip's daughters, the author would be hard pressed to leave them out of his account, particularly since Paul is residing in Philip's home. With their mention, the authorial audience would likely anticipate some indication of the daughters' ecstatic ability. But Luke may fear such evidence might be misconstrued. He refashions his source so that on the narrative level, Philip's daughters serve as further description of their father and may even confirm that Peter's invocation of Joel (Acts 2:16–21) is accurate. If we have not unduly "salted the trench"[51] in our attempt to reconstruct the original source, we may propose that the daughters did speak, after having taken up Paul's belt. Wrapping it around themselves as did the daughters of Job, they receive the Holy Spirit and utter a pronouncement that warned of what awaited Paul in Jerusalem. In this scenario, the actions of the local folks make sense. Would not the words of their own prophets convince them more quickly than those of a stranger from Judea. Paul speaks to their emotional response before comment-

---

48. Kolenkow, "Miracle and Prophecy," 1499.

49. Gaventa disagrees that Luke deliberately silences women, because "he fears repercussion from outsiders who will associate female leadership with exotic cults from the East" ("What Ever Happened?" 60). My concern is not the view of outsiders, but that of Luke's authorial audience.

50. Barrett, *Acts*, 2.995.

51. In archaeological circles, this means placing artifacts in a trench that do not belong there so that they can be found often by unwitting volunteers.

ing on the prophecy itself: τί ποιεῖτε κλαίοντες καὶ συνθρύπτοντές μου τὴν καρδίαν; (Acts 21:13).

Despite their silence in Acts of the Apostles, the four daughters make quite an impact in the emerging church both in Caesarea and beyond. Papias claims some of his information about early Christian origins came directly from Philip's daughters, two of whom lived out their days in Hierapolis (Eusebius *Hist. Eccl.* 3.39.9).[52] By the end of the second century, Origen had determined that Philip's daughters must have prophesied privately since Luke did not include their speech and it was inappropriate for women to speak publicly.[53] "His rhetorical strategy is to reduce prophecy to public speaking in which the orator speaks in his own voice and claims the authority the podium conveys . . . But for Origen, because the Greco-Roman gender system did not authorize women's public speech, neither did God."[54] By the time Origen is writing, he is countering the women prophets of the Montanist movement, who claimed descent from Philip's daughters.[55] Jerome reports that Paula visited Caesarea and saw the room in Philip's house in which the prophesying daughters resided (*Ep.* 108.8).

The four virgin daughters of Philip who prophesy may be seen and not heard, but their narrative presence and their memory hint at the existence of an emerging Christian community in Caesarea—a church that acknowledged that the Holy Spirit resided in both its men and its women.

---

52. Bauckham seems not to share Eusebius' suspicions about Papias' intellectual ability. "There is no reason why we should adopt this prejudiced attitude to Papias, who seems to have been in a good position to know some interesting facts about the origins of the Gospels" (Bauckham, *Jesus and the Eyewitnesses*, 13).

53. Jenkins, "Origen on I Corinthians. IV," 41–42.

54. Torjesen, "The Early Christian *Orans*," 52.

55. Hopkins, "The Epiphany of the Dove," 305.

Bibliography

Alter, Robert. *The Art of Biblical Narrative*. New York: Basic Books, 1981.
Aune, David E. "Magic in Early Christianity." In *ANRW* 2.23.2, 1506–57.
Bauckham, Richard. *Jesus and the Eyewitnesses: The Gospels as Eyewitness Testimony*. Grand Rapids: Eerdmans, 2006.
Barrett, C. K. *A Critical and Exegetical Commentary on the Acts of the Apostles*. ICC. Edinburgh: T. & T. Clark, 1994–98.
Blankinsopp, Joseph. *Isaiah 1–39*. AB 19. New York: Doubleday, 2000.
Boismard, M.-É, and A. LaMouille. *Les Actes des Deux Apôtres. Vol 3. Analyses Littéraires*. Paris: LeCoffre, 1990.
Brown, Raymond E. *An Introduction to the New Testament*. ABRL. New York: Doubleday, 1997.
Campbell, William S. *The "We" Passages in the Acts of the Apostles: The Narrator as Narrative Character*. Studies in Biblical Literature 14. Atlanta: Society of Biblical Literature, 2007.
Darr, John. *On Character Building: The Reader and the Rhetoric of Characterization in Luke-Acts*. Literary Currents in Biblical Interpretation. Louisville: Westminster John Knox, 1992.
Dickerson, Patrick L. "The New Character Narrative in Luke-Acts and the Synoptic Problem." *JBL* 116 (1997) 291–312.
Fitzmyer, Joseph. *The Acts of the Apostles*. AB 31. New York: Doubleday, 1998.
Gafney, Wilda. *Daughters of Miriam: Women Prophets in Ancient Israel*. Minneapolis: Fortress, 2008.
Garrett, Susan R. "The 'Weaker Sex' in the Testament of Job." *JBL* 112 (1993) 55–70.
Gaventa, Beverly Roberts. "What Ever Happened to Those Prophesying Daughters?" In *A Feminist Companion to the Acts of the Apostles*, edited by Amy-Jill Levine, 49–60. FCNT 9. New York: T. & T. Clark, 2004.
Gowler, David B. *Host, Guest, Enemy, and Friend: Portraits of the Pharisees in Luke and Acts*. Emory Studies in Early Christianity 2. New York: Lang, 1991.
Harnack, Adolf. *New Testament Studies I: Luke the Physician*. Translated by John Richard Wilkinson. New York: Putnam, 1907.
Holmes Michael W. *The Apostolic Fathers: Greek Texts and English Translations*. Grand Rapids: Baker, 2007.
Hopkins, Julie. "The Epiphany of the Dove: Healing and Prophecy in Mark's Gospel (New Approaches in Women's Studies)." In *Biblical Interpretation: The Meaning of Scripture—Past and Present,* edited by John M. Court, 284–309. New York: T. & T. Clark, 2003.
Horst, Pieter W. van der. "Images of Women in the Testament of Job." In *Studies on the Testament of Job*, edited by Michael A. Knibb and Pieter W. van der Horst, 93–116. SNTSMS 66. Cambridge: Cambridge University Press, 1989.
Ilan, Tal. "It's Magic: Jewish Women in the Jesus Movement." In *The Beginnings of Christianity: A Collection of Articles*, edited by Jack Pastor and Menachem Mor, pp. 161–72. Jerusalem: Yad Ben-Zvi Press, 2005.
Jenkins, Claude "Origen on I Corinthians. IV." *JTS* 10 (1909) 41–42.
King, Karen L. "Prophetic Power and Women's Authority: The Case of the Gospel of Mary (Magdalene)." In *Women Preachers and Prophets through Two Millennia*

of Christianity, Beverly Mayne Kienzle and Pamela J. Walker, 21–41. Berkeley: University of California Press, 1998.
Klauck, Hans-Josef. *Magic and Paganism in Early Christianity: The World of the Acts of the Apostles*. Edinburgh: T. & T. Clark, 2000.
Kolenkow, Anitra Bingham. "Relationships between Miracle and Prophecy in the Graeco-Roman World and Early Christianity." In *ANRW* 2.23.2: 1470–506.
Kurz, William S. *Reading Luke-Acts: Dynamics of Biblical Narrative*. Louisville: Westminster John Knox, 1993.
Loisy, Alfred. *Les Actes des Apôtres*. Paris: Nourry, 1920.
Omerzu, Heike. "Women, Magic and Angels: On the Empancipation of Job's Daughters in the Apocryphal Testament of Job." In *Bodies in Question: Gender, Religion, Text*, edited by Darlene Bird and Yvonne Sherword, 85–103. Burlington, VT: Ashgate, 2005.
Parsons, Mikeal. *Luke: Storyteller, Interpreter, Evangelist*. Peabody, MA: Hendrickson, 2007.
Pervo, Richard I. *Profit with Delight: The Literary Genre of the Acts of the Apostles*. Philadelphia: Fortress, 1987.
Reid, Barbara. *Choosing the Better Part: Women in the Gospel of Luke*. Collegeville, MN: Liturgical, 1996.
———. *Taking up the Cross: New Testament Interpretations through Latina and Feminist Eyes*. Minneapolis: Fortress, 2007.
Reimer, Ivoni Richter. *Women in the Acts of the Apostles: A Feminist Liberation Perspective*. Minneapolis: Fortress, 1995.
Robbins, Vernon. "By Land and By Sea: The We-Passages and Ancient Sea Voyages." In *Perspectives on Luke-Acts*, edited by Charles H. Talbert, 215–42. Danville, VA: Association of Baptist Professors of Religion, 1978.
Schaberg, Jane. "Luke." In *The Women's Bible Commentary*, edited by Carol A. Newsom and Sharon H. Ringe, 363–380. Louisville: Westminster John Knox, 1992; rev. ed. 1998.
Spencer, F. Scott. "Out of Mind, Out of Voice: Slave-girls and Prophetic Daughters in Luke-Acts." *BibInt* 7 (1999) 133–55.
Spencer, Patrick E. *Rhetorical Texture and Narrative: Trajectories of the Lukan Galilean Ministry Speeches*. LNTS 341. New York: T. & T. Clark, 2007.
Spittler, R. P. "Testament of Job." In *The Old Testament Pseudepigrapha*. Vol 1, edited by James H. Charlesworth, 829–68. New York: Doubleday, 1983.
Stratton, Kimberly B. "The Rhetoric of 'Magic' in Early Christian Discourse." In *Mapping Gender in Ancient Religious Discourses*, edited by Todd Penner and Caroline Vander Stichele, 89–115. Leiden: Brill, 2007.
Torjesen Karen Jo. "The Early Christian *Orans*: An Artistic Representation of Women's Liturgical Prayer and Prophecy." In *Women Preachers and Prophets through Two Millennia of Christianity*, edited by Beverly Mayne Kienzle and Pamela J. Walker, 42–56. Berkeley: University of California Press, 1998.
Wilson, Robert R. *Prophecy and Society in Ancient Israel*. Philadelphia: Fortress, 1980.
Wire, Antoinette Clark. *The Corinthian Women Prophets: A Reconstruction through Paul's Rhetoric*. Rev. ed. 1995. Reprinted, Eugene, OR: Wipf & Stock, 2003.
Witherington, Ben III. *Acts of the Apostles. A Socio-Rhetorical Commentary*. Grand Rapids, MI: Eerdmans, 1998.

12

Two Visions of the Lord

A Comparison of Paul's Revelation to His Opponents' Revelation in 2 Corinthians 12:1–10[1]

Jeremy W. Barrier

THE TWO VISIONARY EXPERIENCES FOUND IN 2 COR 12:1–10, HAVE been the subject of much discussion and speculation.[2] In 2 Cor 12:2–4, Paul relates a revelatory experience using an ascension motif, followed by revelatory oracle in 12:7–10 that is regarded as a Greco-Roman *Heilungsorakel* ("healing oracle").[3] It is within this pericope that Paul plays the fool and makes a strong boast (in his weakness) against his opponents in Corinth.[4] The text of 2 Cor 12:1–10 reads as follows:

---

1. This essay is a revision of the paper that I presented on Saturday, March 6, 2004 at 1:30 P.M. at the Society of Biblical Literature Southwestern Region meeting, held at the Harvey Hotel in Irving, Texas. Credit is due to Laurence L. Welborn, who first encouraged me to work on this area of 2 Corinthians for my master's thesis during the years 2000–2002. It was subsequently published as "Visions of Weakness," 33–42. The motivation for revising this article in a Festschrift for Carolyn Osiek is due to the fact that she approached me immediately after attending my lecture in Irving, Texas, and encouraged me to continue to develop this essay for publication. In her honor, I present several more thoughts on the issue of identifying characteristics of Paul's opponents that have previously been ascribed to Paul.

2. See Gooder, *Only the Third Heaven?*, for a recent comprehensive treatment of this passage. See also Baird, "Visions, Revelations, and Ministry," 651–62; Betz, *Apostel Paulus*; Dassmann, "Paulus in der Visio sancti Pauli," 117–29; Lincoln, "Paul the Visionary," 204–20. Morray-Jones, "Paradise Revisited," 262–92; Welborn, "The Runaway Paul," 115–63.

3. Aune, *Prophecy*, 250–51. According to Aune, from a Jewish perspective it would have been considered a *Heilsorakel*. Aune ultimately gives Betz credit for arguing this case most conclusively in "Eine Christus-Aretologie," 288–305.

4. Furnish, *2 Corinthians*, 498.

It is necessary to boast; nothing is to be gained by it, but I will go on to visions and revelations (ὀπτασίας καὶ ἀποκαλύψεις) of the Lord. I know a person in Christ who fourteen years ago was caught up to the third heaven-whether in the body or out of the body I do not know; God knows. And I know that such a person-whether in the body, or out of the body I do not know; God knows- was caught up into Paradise and heard things that are not to be told (ἄρρητα ῥήματα), that no mortal is permitted to repeat. On behalf of such a one I will boast, but on my own behalf I will not boast, except of my weaknesses. But if I wish to boast, I will not be a fool, for I will be speaking the truth. But I refrain from it, so that no one may think better of me than what is seen in me or heard from me, even considering the exceptional character of the revelations. Therefore, to keep me from being too elated, a thorn was given me in the flesh, a messenger of Satan to torment me, to keep me from being too elated. Three times I appealed to the Lord about this, that it would leave me, but he said to me, "My grace is sufficient for you, for power is made perfect in weakness." So, I will boast all the more gladly of my weaknesses, so that the power of Christ may dwell in me. Therefore I am content with weaknesses, insults, hardships, persecutions, and calamities for the sake of Christ; for whenever I am weak, then I am strong. (NRSV)

What does a journey into paradise have to do with boasting, and why is Paul using an apocalyptic motif in this passage? These questions and many others have been asked in an attempt to explain this difficult text in the Corinthian correspondence. Some scholars have suggested that this passage is dealing with Hekhaloth Literature, i.e. Jewish Mysticism.[5] To be more specific, descriptive elements in the story, such as "the third heaven" and "paradise," have been interpreted as coming from Merkabah texts. On the other hand, Hans Dieter Betz set forth a second possible interpretation by suggesting this passage is a parody; however, his interpretation has been widely rejected.[6] From Betz' perspective, Paul is attempting to make a mockery of his opponents for telling incredulous stories of journeys to heaven. If one accepts this interpretation, then it becomes clear that Paul is using standard Greco-Roman rhetorical

---

5. See Morray-Jones, "Paradise Revisited: Part 1," 177–217; and "Paradise Revisited: Part 2," 262–92; Scholem, *Jewish Gnosticism, Merkabah Mysticism, and Talmudic Tradition*.

6. Betz, *Apostel*, 84; see also the "Excursus: 2 Corinthians 12.1ff. as a Parody of Heavenly Ascent, 192–94."

skills to argue his case.[7] Betz has been interpreted by scholars to mean that 2 Cor 12:1–10 cannot be autobiographical, thus dismissing the passage as non-historical in relation to any event in Paul's life.[8]

While the autobiographical interpretation is the most widely accepted interpretation, it cannot be accepted without several serious reservations. First, Paul never makes a direct statement to suggest that he is the individual who experienced these revelations. Paul addresses the "Man in Christ" in the third person. Due to this fact, scholars have suggested that Paul is using irony to subtly boast in himself and refute his opponents. While it is possible that Paul is using irony, it is difficult to prove this claim. Is it possible that there is another explanation for this text that somehow links the two interpretations together, suggesting that Paul is speaking in the form of a parody and speaking autobiographically? I think this is accomplished best by seeing 12:2–4 as a separate account than what we read in 12:7–10. In this essay, I intend to show that the opponents of Paul have been identified in 2 Corinthians 12:1–6, thus recreating a description of the opponent's claims to authority in the form of a parody common to Greco-Roman readers. Paul mocks the opponents through a parody in 12:1–6, and offers an antithesis in 12:7–10 that records a second visionary experience which demonstrates his own weakness. According to Paul, the true sign of an apostle is found in weakness and subjection to Christ, not in self exaltation.

Margaret Thrall, in the midst of publishing the two volumes of her "magisterial" commentary on 2 Corinthians, also published an article entitled "Paul's Journey to Paradise: Some Exegetical Issues in 2 Corinthians 12.2–4."[9] Within this article she provides a good overview of the issues pertaining to 2 Cor 12:1–10. I will briefly summarize some of her thoughts. In regard to the identification of the ἄνθρωπον ἐν Χριστῷ, if it is not Paul, then who is he? This article is not the first place that someone has suggested that this person is someone other than

---

7. Ibid.; For information on this subject see Kennedy, *Classical Rhetoric*. See also Kennedy, *New Testament Interpretation*. For the opposing view consider Betz, *Galatians*, 14–25.

8. Ibid., 89.

9. Betz calls it a "magisterial work" in his review of her commentary; see Betz review of Thrall, *A Critical and Exegetical Commentary on the Second Epistle to the Corinthians*, 108–9. The commentary that I am referring to is Thrall, *A Critical and Exegetical Commentary on the Second Epistle to the Corinthians*; and the other article is "Paul's Journey to Paradise," 347–63.

Paul. In particular, over a quarter of a century ago, Léon Herrmann suggested that the ἄνθρωπον ἐν Χριστῷ was none other than Apollos.[10] This is based upon Herrmann suggesting that Apollos authored *2 Enoch* and subsequently is the object of discussion in 2 Cor 12:2–10.[11] Thrall dismisses this suggestion as "extraordinarily unconvincing, needless to say."[12] Morton Smith proposed another unconvincing theory that suggests that Jesus is the ἄνθρωπον mentioned in 2 Cor 12:2.[13] Thrall dismisses this on several levels based upon weak foundational arguments. For instance, why would Christ be called an ἄνθρωπον ἐν Χριστῷ, since he *is* the Christ? Smith argues for translating Οἶδα ἄνθρωπον ἐν χριστῷ πρὸ ἐτῶν δεκατεσσάρων as "I knew in Christ, fourteen years ago, a man . . ."[14] While neither of these two individuals provide a satisfactory identification of the "man in Christ," I do think that there is one other alternative that makes better sense than suggesting that Paul is speaking of his own personal experience in the third person. It may be likely that Paul is contrasting an account claimed by his opponents (12:2–4) to his own visionary experience (12:7–10).

In order to make my case, I would like to begin by looking at the internal evidence that can be seen through a closer analysis of the text of 2 Corinthians 10–13. In particular, I am speaking of Paul's use of demonstrative pronouns in the third person to refer to the individual who made the journey to heaven. In 12:2–3, Paul speaks of "such a person" (τὸν τοιοῦτον ἄνθρωπον) as if he has no relationship with this person, other than being able to boast of similar apocalyptic experiences. Initially, Paul's use of τοιοῦτον does not draw attention to itself. This demonstrative pronoun appears to be referring back to the previous sentence, identifying the person whom Paul is addressing. A closer examination reveals that this explanation is not sufficient. This pronoun refers back to ἄνθρωπον ἐν χριστῷ, but this does not identify the individual any more than the pronoun. One would think that Paul would be more specific, considering that this pronoun occurs three times in four verses, with the noun, ἄνθρωπον, occurring three times in these same four verses. The identity of the "person in Christ" is apparently

10. See also Furnish, *2 Corinthians*, 524.
11. Herrmann, "Apollos," 330–36.
12. Thrall, "Exegetical Issues," 348.
13. Smith, "Ascent to the Heavens," 403–29.
14. Thrall, "Exegetical Issues," 348.

important and familiar to Paul, although he does not explicitly state the individual's name. I would even go so far as to say that the identity of the person mentioned in this revelation would have been familiar by name to the Corinthians.

The key to unlock this door is found in verse five, where Paul steps outside of the fool's speech (in the same way he does in 11:1, 12, and 17) and articulates the purpose of speaking as a "fool." To be more specific, he provides a summary of the importance of boasting, and how boasting is to be accomplished. In this verse, Paul says "on behalf of such a one (τοῦ τοιούτου) I will boast, but on my own behalf I will not boast, except of my weaknesses." If one is to take Paul literally, then within this passage Paul identifies this man as someone other than himself.

Who is the τοῦ τοιούτου? Paul uses this pronoun ten times within 2 Corinthians, and seven of these references are used to identify certain people in Corinth who have opposed Paul (2 Cor 2:6, 7; 10:1; 11:13; 12:2, 3, 5). Paul uses this demonstrative pronoun six times within the context of 2 Corinthians 10–13 (10.11 [twice]; 11:13; 12:2, 3, and 5). Consider each of these references one at a time. The first passage in 10.9–11 reads:

> I do not want to seem as though I am trying to frighten you with my letters. For they say, "His letters are weighty and strong, but his bodily presence is weak, and his speech contemptible." Let such people understand (Τοῦτο λογιζέσθω ὁ τοιοῦτος) that what we say by letter when absent, we (τοιοῦτοι) will also do when present. (NRSV)

Following this passage in 11:12–13, Paul states:

> And what I do I will also continue to do, in order to deny an opportunity to those who want an opportunity to be recognized as our equals in what they boast about. For such boasters (Οἱ γὰρ τοιοῦτοι) are false apostles, deceitful workers, disguising themselves as apostles of Christ. (NRSV)

In both passages, Paul makes an effort to identify those "of such a kind" with the opponents. In the first instance, Paul quotes from the opponents to identify the accusations they had been making against him. They accused him of having strong letters, while being weak in appearance. The context also clarifies that the verb λογιζέσθω (which means "to understand/account") is also a technical mathematics/accounting term used metaphorically within the context of Paul's arguments in chapters 10–13.[15] The verb, λογίζομαι, already appears in 10:2, 7, 11, and 11:5, while also the appearing in the form of a noun in 10:4. This confrontation juxtaposes "what Paul 'has in mind' in relation to what they should 'account' to his ministry."[16] The implicit dialogue filled with numerous subtle arguments is what characterizes the entire text. This provides all the more reason to suspect Paul's use of τοιοῦτος in a subtle, yet specific way. Paul then makes the point, τοιοῦτος, namely those who made the accusation (i.e. the opponents), should beware for Paul can be weighty in person, in similar fashion to his letters and similar to the opponents. The next step is to ask whether or not Paul is doing the same thing in 12:2, 3, and 5?

It is only reasonable to connect these earlier references with the ones that follow in chapter twelve for several reasons. First, Paul's use of this demonstrative pronoun in 10:11 and 11:13 explicitly points the Corinthian church to look at his opponents when he makes accusations against them. Second, Paul over-emphasized the "person in Christ," but never makes an explicit identification of the person. At the same time, Paul makes a strong indirect identification in 12:5, by contrasting "such a person" with himself. The only way to get around Paul's clear contrast in 12:5 is to either conclude that Paul is using irony, or Paul is identifying someone else. If Paul was identifying the opponents by his use of τοιοῦτος, then this would mean that 12:2–4 is serving the function of a mockery of the opponents by ridiculing their apocalyptic claim.

To take this issue one step further, *A Greek Grammar of the New Testament and Other Early Christian Literature* (BDF) devotes an entire paragraph (§274) to the article when it appears before the demonstrative pronoun.[17] The grammar states "τοιοῦτος occasionally takes the article (*when pointing to individuals* or embracing a class): e.g. Mt 19:14 τῶν τοιούτων (referring to τὰ παιδία above); but rarely with a substantive following: 2 Cor 12:3, Mk 9:37 ..."[18] In the case of 2 Cor 12:2–3 the substantive appears in 12:3, but not in 12:2, thus demonstrating both examples described in BDF. A similar case would be represented in Gal 6:1, where the text reads "My friends, if anyone (ἄνθρω–

---

15. BDAG, 597.
16. Furnish, *2 Corinthians*, 469.
17. Blass, Debrunner, and Funk, *Greek Grammar*, 143, emphasis added.
18. Blass, Debrunner, and Funk, *Greek Grammar*, 143 (§274).

πος) is detected in a transgression, you who have received the Spirit should restore such a one (τοιοῦτον) in a spirit of gentleness." Now, in this case τοιοῦτον points back to ἄνθρωπος just as is the case in 2 Corinthians 12. However, one would be mistaken to assume that in Gal 6:1, it is merely providing generic advice. Obviously, Paul considers some of the Galatians to be blinded and bewitched (Gal 3:1ff.) and filled with the evil Spirit (i.e., evil eye).[19] This issue is further reinforced by Paul's warning that anyone who received a different Gospel will be accursed/bewitched (Gal 1:6–9). As a practical litmus test, Paul provides a few clear markers in 5:16–26 that will help the Galatians to tell the difference between those filled with the Spirit of God and those who are "opposed to the Spirit" (Gal 5:17). In light of this, in Gal 6:1, τοιοῦτον syntactically may be limited to ἄνθρωπος, however it is obvious that this is referring to a specific group or person within the Galatian community. The evidence seems all the stronger in 2 Corinthians 10–13, especially in the "fool's speech," where Paul is attempting to draw out the contrasts between himself and his opponents. The text explicitly states, as reinforced by Lincoln and others that the opponents of Paul are claiming to be able to demonstrate τὰ σημεῖα τοῦ ἀποστόλου.[20] This revelatory experience should be interpreted as one more attribute ascribed to *the such* who are opposing Paul.

It is my conclusion, concerning τοιοῦτος, that Paul is making an identification of his opponents through his implicit language. If one interprets the text in this manner, then several key questions must be addressed. How does one make sense of Paul's argument, rhetorically speaking? How would boasting in the credentials of the opponents help Paul's case? To answer this question, one must keep in mind Paul's conclusion to all of his boasting. Paul is not truly boasting, but mentioning different areas within his resume that ultimately make him look weak. In 12:10, at the conclusion to the fool's speech, Paul clearly says that he wishes to boast only in those things that demonstrate his weakness. Consider several of Paul's boasts: his connection to Judaism, his sufferings and hardships, fleeing from Damascus, and then finally a visionary experience. Ultimately, Paul is hoping to demonstrate his weakness in Christ as his grounds for boasting. Hardships and fleeing from govern-

19. See Esler, *First Christians*, 19–21.

20. Lincoln, "Paul the Visionary," 210; Georgi, *Opponents of Paul*, 446 which states "[m]iracles played a role in the weekly worship of the church . . ."

ment officials demonstrates nothing to boast about but rather demonstrates his limited power and insufficient resources. For instance, in the case of Paul having to be lowered out of the window by means of a basket in Damascus essentially reaffirms that Paul was doing the opposite of brave Roman soldiers storming the walls of cities as they sought the *corona muralis*.[21] But the last example, the visionary experience is not as easily interpreted. To answer this question, more background information is needed concerning Greco-Roman apocalyptic literature to demonstrate how Paul's last example in 12:1–10 demonstrates his weakness.

The way that Greco-Roman apocalyptical experiences influenced Paul has been addressed with much less detail in comparison to Paul's possible Jewish apocalyptic influences.[22] Betz presents several examples that pose as possible parallels for Paul utilizing the apocalyptic genre as found in Greek and Hellenistic literature.[23] He takes several examples and provides a light treatment of the material, while admitting that he is only scratching the surface.[24] In addition to this, Collins made a study of "The Genre Apocalypse in Hellenistic Judaism" while admitting near his conclusion that "The relation of this material [Greek tradition] to the Jewish heavenly journeys has not yet been adequately explored." It is possible that the Greek apocalyptic tradition might have a stronger affinity to Paul than is typically thought. If one considers that Paul spent years in Achaia, Macedonia, and Asia working with these churches, then the plausibility of using examples familiar to the audience would be expected in his writings.

Looking at this issue from the broadest sense, scholars readily admit to a strong tradition within Greco-Roman society to dreams, visions, and out of body experiences.[25] Aune makes reference to the common understanding that the apostles (namely Paul) were considered prophets, thus the connections to Paul as a visionary would be expected, whether the Corinthians audience had a strong Jewish or

---

21. Lincoln, "Paul the Visionary," 208; Furnish, *2 Corinthians*, 542.

22. Once again, see Gooder, *Only the Third Heaven?*, which deals primarily with the Jewish apocalyptic experiences, while devoting a few pages to Betz work on 192–94.

23. Betz, "Problem of Apocalyptic Genre," 577.

24. Collins, "Genre Apocalypse," 596.

25. Hanson, "Dreams and Visions," 1396.

Hellenistic background.²⁶ To be more specific, 2 Cor 12:1–10 has been considered the earliest evidence of an apocalyptic visionary experience within early Christianity. In Hanson's study of dreams and visions in the Greco-Roman World and early Christian literature, he identifies several examples of a *terminus technicus* that indicate that a writer is entering into an apocalyptic genre. He mentions the words "revelation" (ἀποκάλυψις) and "vision" (ὀπτασία) as two specific examples for this genre.²⁷ The significance of these two words being considered technical terms automatically makes the Greco-Roman connections to 2 Cor 12:1–10 much greater than ever thought previously. It is important to note that these two terms are found in Paul's introductory remarks, rather than within the actual ascension story itself. Paul is defining the events he is about to tell by preceding it with the technical road signs for the reader to follow in the midst of his rhetorical discourse. This definition places upon the text a specific genre for interpreting what follows in light of other apocalyptic experiences. It would have been difficult for a citizen living in Corinth to have missed such a signifier provided by Paul.

Several examples of the apocalyptic vision experience within other Greco-Roman writers can be examined in order to see how well the experience that Paul mentions in 2 Cor 12:1–10 fits within this framework. The first example, Lucian's *Icaromenippus,* relates a parody concerning a man flying into the heavens. The story begins by Menippus trying to play the part of an "astronomer" (ἀστρονομενεῖς) by determining the distance from the earth to the moon, from the moon to the sun, and finally the sun to the heavens.²⁸ Menippus' friend quickly responds in astonishment that he is curious as to what Menippus is talking about. Menippus then tells his friend that he has just come back from making a journey into the heavens.²⁹

As their discussion continues, the friend points out that it must have been a long dream for Menippus to have slept for "leagues and leagues." Menippus promptly responds that it was not a dream, but that he is just finished visiting with Zeus.³⁰ Λανθάνω or "to escape notice"

26. Aune, *Prophecy in Early Christianity*, 248.
27. Hanson, "Dreams and Visions," 1408.
28. Lucian *Icaromennipus*, 2.267–323, LCL.
29. Ibid., 1.1, LCL.
30. Ibid.

is the first verb used in this text to portray Menippus "loosing himself."[31] The satire within the text seems to revolve around people who "loose themselves" and go into visions and revelations. Next, Menippus gives several different measurements for the length of his journey. His friend immediately interprets it in the context of time, as in how long the sleep must have lasted. Following this, Menippus responds in turn that he has just come back from this journey that is fresh upon his mind.[32] This type of language is also found in Diogenes Laertius mockery of visionaries when he writes: "someone was discoursing on celestial phenomena, 'How many days,' asked Diogenes, 'were you in coming from the sky?'"[33] In both Diogenes and Lucian, the context suggests that these writers were mocking people who had claimed to have made heavenly journeys. The context of the example presented by Diogenes expresses the common feeling in antiquity that the authenticity of such a prominent claim (such as going into the heavens) must be proven before one is allowed to expound about "celestial phenomena." Whether an individual is skeptical or sincerely wanting to know when one has returned from their journey, such a claim must have some authentic proof. It is similar within 2 Cor 12:2–4 that the "person in Christ" locates the time of his occasion fourteen years before. Such a journey is without a doubt a memorable occasion and the necessary proof of authenticity is being presented.

A second example is found in the story of Bellerophon,[34] a mythological character who was considered to be part of the royal family of Corinth, and was later deified as one of the gods and heroes of Corinth and Lycia.[35] While this example does not demonstrate the use of parody in apocalyptic experiences, it does demonstrate other features of the apocalyptic genre that are also found in Paul's account in 2 Cor 12:1–10. The key features of Bellerophon's story are his relationship to Pegasus, the winged horse, and the latter part of his life when Bellerophon at-

31. DBAG, 466.

32. Lucian *Icaromennipus* 1.1, LCL.

33. Diogenes Laertius, 6.39, LCL.

34. In order to gain a complete picture of Bellerophon one has to investigate several sources to grasp the life of this divine-man. A good place to begin is the article by March, *OCD*, 237–38.

35. Grimal, *Dictionary of Classical Mythology*, which is a translation of *Dictionnaire de la Mythologie Grecque et Romaine*, 74.

tempted to fly to the heavens. In this story, Athena entrusts Bellerophon with Pegasus, in order to fight the Chimera. Eventually, he flies higher and higher, and Pegasus angered and enraged, throws him off his back so that Bellerophon falls back down to the earth.[36] Pindar writes, "But, if any man lifteth up his eyes to things afar, he is too short to attain unto the brass-paved floor of heaven; for the winged Pegasus threw Bellerophon, his rider, who would fain have gone to the homes of heaven and the goodly company of Zeus."[37] Homer is able to grasp the pride of Bellerophon when he speaks of this attempted journey to heaven in a comparison to unattainable love.[38] It is interesting to see how Bellerophon is compared in this verse to Phaëthon. Phaëthon was the son of the god Helios. After he grew up to be a man he asked his father if he might drive his chariot that carried the sun across the sky. Helios gave him his permission and allowed this to take place. After driving the chariot for some time Phaëthon became afraid and came too close to the earth, almost scorching the surface. Following this he went too close to the stars, and the stars complained to Zeus. To resolve the conflict, Zeus struck him down with a thunderbolt of lightning, thus killing him.[39] After comparing unattainable love to Phaëthon, Horace then compares it to Bellerophon by stating: "Scorched Phaëthon serves as a warning to ambitious hopes; and winged Pegasus, who brooked not Bellerophon, his earth-born rider, affords a weighty lesson, to follow ever what befits thee, and to shun an ill-assorted mate, deeming it wrong to hope for more than is permitted."[40] The story of Bellerophon ends in shame and disrepute from the gods as he walks the Aleian fields. It was indeed his own grandson, Glaucus, who saved him from death, not from the fall, but at the hand of Megapenthes, the son of Proetus, who almost killed him.[41]

---

36. Nonnos writes of this occasion in light of Pegasus being in a rage and angrily disposing of Bellerophon. See Nonnos *Dionysiaca* 38.390–415, LCL. On another occasion a horse is compared to Pegasus who, "flying high in the air as swift in his course as the wandering wind, threw Bellerophontes" (Nonnos *Dionysiaca* 28.164–7, LCL). In yet another instance, Pegasus is compared to the angry horses who threw Bellerophon's father Glaucus to the ground just before his death (Nonnos *Dionysiaca* 11.140-46, LCL).

37. Pindar *Isthmian Odes* 7.43–8, LCL.

38. Homer *Iliad* 6.154–206, LCL.

39. Grimal, *Dictionary*, 363.

40. Horace *Odes* 4.21–28, LCL; Pindar *Olympian Odes* 13.83–94, LCL.

41. *Greek Anthology*, 102–3, LCL.

There are several key features to be remembered concerning the mythology surrounding Bellerophon. First of all, it is important to recognize the tradition in Greco-Roman literature (also in Lucian *Icaromennipus*)[42] of journeys to heaven as a forbidden act. In the same way that Mennipus was allowed into the heavens with some resistance (this is part of the humor of *Icaromennipus*), so also the tradition exists where mortals are simply not allowed to go there.[43] It is a common thread running throughout the culture that such a visit is limited to the divine or to the dead. It was forbidden territory. Such is the explanation given for Paul's hearing "things that are not to be told, that no mortal is permitted to repeat" (2 Cor 12:4). Laurence Welborn convincingly argues this point using similar examples from Lucian.[44] Another example is found in Tantalus, who lived on Mount Sipylus. He was highly favored of the gods. The gods frequently allowed him to come dine with them, and he allowed his pride to become too great. He lost his favor with the gods, because he began divulging the secrets of the heavens to other mortal friends.[45] As a result, his punishment in the Underworld was to have his head wedged underneath a "monstrous stone."[46] It appears that the stone was perpetually under the influence of gravity, yet suspended in that one spot to maintain the punishment for Tantalus.

Secondly, the fall of Bellerophon is without a doubt rooted in his pride of thinking that such a journey for a mortal is possible. Seeing how Horace interpreted this journey (as mentioned above) leaves little room for misunderstanding. The similarities to Paul are very interesting, because Paul is trying to make the point clear that all such boasting is foolishness.

Third, one must take notice of the fascination of the ancient world of humans making journeys into the heavens. Making a journey into

---

42. In *Icaromennipus* 1.22–23, upon his arrival to heaven he knocks at the door and startles the gods who were not expecting a man in Heaven. When Menippus comes before Zeus to give account of himself, Zeus speaks (quoting the *Odyssey* 1.170) in a "terrible voice: 'What is your name, sir, whence do you come, and where is your city and hearth-stone?'" Upon hearing this he "nearly dropped dead of fright," his "jaw was hanging", and he was overwhelmed by "the loudness of his voice" It is evident from the passage that gods were not pleased for a man to be there.

43. Ibid., 1.22, LCL.

44. Welborn, "Runaway Paul," 149.

45. Grimal, *Dictionary*, 431.

46. Pindar *Olympian Odes* 1.55–63, LCL.

heaven was a very impressive feat for any individual. These texts demonstrate the evidence for extensive traditions concerning the heavens in Greco-Roman Literature and popular culture. It also illuminates the strongly divided line between heaven and earth, and the difficulty for humanity to attempt to go from one to the other.

The most probable conclusion is that Paul was aware of these prominent apocalyptic, heavenly stories of the Greco-Roman world. It is highly possible that Paul and the Corinthian church would have been aware of Bellerophon, who was a local god and hero of Corinth. By the time of the early second century, a statue of Bellerophon and Pegasus could be found standing over a prominent fountain in the city.[47] Euripides devoted an entire play to him entitled *Bellerophontes*.[48] It is also possible that paintings of the events recorded in the literature were within some of the homes of the Christians in Corinth in the form of wall paintings that celebrated the hero.[49] These traditions could have had a significant influence upon what Paul chose to write to the Corinthians. Stories such as *Icaromennipus* attest that telling of journeys into heaven was popular in the first century. Diogenes Laertius accounts for this fact also. In addition, the parody presented by Lucian and the skeptical humor by Diogenes Laertius also attests to the practice of making mockeries of such journeys. In the case of Paul, it is not a stretch of the imagination to see Paul as parodying a journey to heaven in 12:1–6, followed by another revelatory experience (12:7–10) that Paul claims as true. In fact, it makes even better sense for Paul to make use of this genre considering that the opponents were making claims to their authority over the Corinthian church based upon such journeys. This opens them up to the possibility of Paul making full use of the Greco-Roman apocalyptic tradition to attack the opponents using their own claims.

---

47. Pausanias *Description of Greece* 2.3.5, LCL.

48. Euripides *Opera Omnia* 584–91, LCL; see also the fragment of Euripides' *Stheneboea* in *Select Papyri*, 126–29.

49. Paintings and sculptures have been recovered in Pompeii and other cities that depict Bellerophon. A sketch of Bellerophon's departure, as found in Pompeii, is reproduced in Seyffert's *A Dictionary of Classical Antiquities*, 95. See also the mural in the atrium of the house in Pompeii found at domus IX.2.16, where Bellerophon is represented as standing before Proteus and Sthenoboea (circa 50 CE). Last, but not least is the image in the triclinium in the thermopolium of domus I.8.8 in Pompeii.

With these examples in mind, it is possible that in 2 Cor 12:2–4 Paul could have Hekhaloth literature in mind also, but this should not take away from the effectiveness of a broader genre in which Paul places his argument. This interpretation accounts for the species of Paul's rhetoric (Judicial[50] [2 Corinthians 10–13]); the general structure and genre for each argument within the species (fool's speech[51] [2 Cor 11:1—12:18]); the specific genre (apocalypse [2 Cor 12:1–10]); and the details within the specific genre (examples familiar to Hellenistic Jews and Greeks in Corinth[52] [2 Cor 12:2–4]). Such a mixture explains how Paul is able to use typical heuristics (invention) of Greco-Roman rhetoric for the purpose of combating his opponents.

If this assessment is true, then notice how it changes the interpretation of the whole passage. First, Paul never identifies himself with the person he has mentioned within the context of the apocalyptic story. Second, Paul has now identified the story of a journey to the third heaven with the opponents. This suggests that the whole story is biographical of the opponents. This explains why Paul is using terminology familiar within Judaism for the heavenly realm. More importantly, this answers Thrall's main opposition to Betz's theory that this is a parody. Namely, she cannot come to terms with Paul "using the name of Christ" in both accounts in 12:2–4 and 12:7–10. If Paul is recounting the opponents own story, then it must be concluded that they are claiming to be ἄνθρωπους ἐν Χριστῷ, and Paul is simply mentioning the details that they claim for themselves. By contrast, the second story in 12:7–10

---

50. Kennedy, *New Testament Interpretation*, 92.

51. Welborn has put forward the most specific identification of the genre of 2 Cor 11.1—12.18. He makes the argument that the fool's speech, being referred to in this passage, has to do with the first century mime, a hypothesis previously mentioned by Windisch (Welborn, "Runaway Paul," 122; Windisch, *Der Zweite Korintherbrief*, 316). This genre is used to categorize the whole discourse from 11:1 to 12:10. The stock fools set forth by Welborn are, "the 'leading slave' in 11:21b–23, acting the braggart warrior" in 11:24–27, evoking the 'anxious old man' in 11.28-29, and portraying the 'learned impostor' in 12:1b–4 and 12:7–9" ("Runaway Paul," 137). Afterwards, Welborn gives a short description of what is known of the satire surrounding the "learned imposter" or quack doctor. It is shown in antiquity that the philosophers were a point of satire, and were often represented by the mimes in the comical skits being performed at many of the street corners in the ancient cities of the Roman Empire ("Runaway Paul," 124, 135; Lucian *Icaromennipus* 5).

52. This is where the parallels from Hekhaloth and Jewish Apocalyptic Literature are incorporated into the text.

is about Paul. This would answer the reservation of Thrall (who also draws upon Christian Wolff for support) who questions whether or not Paul would use "the grace-proclamation fundamental to his whole understanding of his existence" recorded in 2 Cor 12:9a within a comical parody of his opponents.[53] In short, the grace-proclamation *is* about Paul and not the opponents as it is found in the second oracle. The interpretation that Paul is making a parody in 12:2–4 seems all the more appropriate since Paul is making a mockery of their story, while contrasting it to his own story in 12:7–10. When Paul states in 12:5, "On behalf of such a one I will boast, but on my own behalf I will not boast, except of my weaknesses," he is evidently making the conclusion that such boasting performed where self-commendation is the end result is foolishness. On the other hand, boasting in weakness is most important.

In addition to the foolishness of the claim to journey to heaven, one must also consider the difficulty in verifying apocalyptic experiences. In the words of Lincoln:

> In the context Paul's ironic boasting of his experience of the third heaven is extremely significant, for it is meant to show that outward success and visionary experiences cannot count as proof of the truth of claims. In fact this sort of evidence easily leads to deception, and Paul not only hints at this in xii. 6 but says so explicitly in xi. 13–15. It is his opponents who are deceitful, who disguise themselves as servants of righteousness...Paul refrains from reciting further visions and revelations because they can only provide evidence of a sort that cannot be verified and that is removed from the realm of that which others can perceive, through seeing or hearing ...[54]

While Lincoln believes the vision to be Paul's own, if one looks closely, Lincoln's argument is actually stronger if the vision experience was indeed that of the opponents. The deception of the opponents is most translucent in their claim that cannon be verified. This way of evaluating truth and deception is also reinforced in 1 Cor 14:19 when Paul makes clear that "in church I would rather speak five words with my mind, in order to instruct others also, than ten thousand words in a tongue."

---

53. Thrall, "Exegetical Issues," 350; Wolff, *Der zweite Brief des Paulus an die Korinther*, 241.

54. Lincoln, "Paul the Visionary," 210.

A tongue without interpretation had no more value to the Corinthian church than unutterable words.

In conclusion, the evidence suggests that it may be appropriate to draw a stronger distinction through the middle of 2 Cor 12:1–10, realizing that as Paul has done at other places within this strong defense in chapters 10–13, Paul is further making identification of the ὑπερλίαν ἀποστόλος (11:5; 12:11) who have been attacking his apostolic authority and character. If one accepts this interpretation, then what we have is Paul moving on to their claims about ὀπτασίας καὶ ἀποκαλύψεις κυρίου. Paul then compares one of their accounts filled with glorious detail, but it culminates in "unutterable words," which is laughable. This mockery of a journey to heaven is comical, especially contrasted to Paul's sober *Heilungsorakel* that results in Paul's humiliation in weakness and Christ's exaltation. The comparison could not be more effective for Paul's intended result of boasting in his weakness, while mocking his opponents claim at the same time. Such a conclusion is supported in several ways. First, this interpretation makes rhetorical sense, and accounts for the primary reluctance of Thrall and others to accept Betz explanation of a parody. Second, this essentially embraces part of Betz theory, while reversing his interpretation of 12:7–10, which makes his explanation more possible. In addition to make better rhetorical sense, this also makes better theological sense of understanding Paul. Previous to this passage, Paul never provides any visual details of any of his visionary experiences. Between Paul's own accounts and the Acts of the Apostles, Paul's visions of Christ are predominantly auditory.[55] If Paul did not have an experience taking him to the third heaven, then this simplifies Paul's theology and appears to be more consistent with other texts that inform us of Paul's experiences.

Beyond the theological consistency, the literary structure of the text suggests a dualistic comparison of Paul to his opponents. In particular, I am referring to the chiastic structure that is found in both apocalyptic

---

55. In addition to 2 Cor 12:7–10 for visions of Christ by Paul, see Gal 1:12ff.; Acts 9:1–9, 12; 22:3–16, 17–21; 18:9–11; 23:11; 26:9–18. In all of the instances, it is safe to say that Paul tells nothing of any details of significance that Paul had visual revelations, but on the contrary had strong auditory visionary experiences. It would seem that the λεπίδες are best understood to reinforce the dominance of Paul's oratorical revelations. It is even possible that the opponents of Paul could have been mocking Paul's visionary ability based on the fact that he was consistently restricted from having any significant visual revelations.

stories.⁵⁶ The texts appear to be carefully selected as examples to contrast one with the other. In addition, this structure fits well with what Aune identifies as the Jewish *Heilsorakel* ("oracle of assurance").⁵⁷ In short, the structure serves to emphasize the response of the deity (hence providing assurance). In short, in the first oracle in 12:2–4, we have no word from the deity, and from the second (superior) oracular story, we learn from the deity that ἀρκεῖ σοι ἡ χάρις μου (12:9a).

In sum, the evidence for reinterpreting this passage as Paul providing a quotation or detailed description of the opponents has sufficient evidence. In addition to the rhetorical, theological, and literary reasons mentioned above, the exegetical connotations of τοιοῦτος as an indicator of Paul's opponents are extensive enough to warrant a reinterpretation of the passage. The correct interpretation appears to be that Paul has found a way to mock his opponents by providing a parody of a journey into heaven filled with their own descriptions of the event. Finally, this serves Paul in his final argument that personal weakness and submission to the Lord are what truly counts when it comes to authority, not arrogant and superfluous claims of glory.

---

56. Aune, *Prophecy in Early Christianity*, 250.
57. Ibid., 249–50.

Bibliography

Aune, David E. *Prophecy in Early Christianity and the Ancient Mediterranean World.* 1983. Reprinted, Eugene, OR: Wipf & Stock, 2003.
Baird, William. "Visions, Revelations, and Ministry. Reflections on 2 Cor 12:1–5 and Gal 1:11–17." *JBL* 104 (1985) 651–62.
Barrier, Jeremy W. "Visions of Weakness: Apocalyptic Genre and the Identification of Paul's Opponents in 2 Corinthians 12:1–6." *Restoration Quarterly* 47 (2005) 33–42.
Bauer, Walter. *A Greek-English Lexicon of the New Testament and Other Early Christian Literature.* Edited by William F. Arndt, F. Wilbur Gingrich. Edited and Revised by Frederick William Danker. 3rd ed. Chicago: University of Chicago Press, 2000.
Betz, Hans Dieter. *Der Apostel Paulus und die sokratische Tradition: Eine exegetische Untersuchung zu seiner "Apologie" 2 Kor 10–13.* Tübingen: Mohr/Siebeck, 1973.
———. "Eine Christus-Aretologie bei Paulus (2 Kor 12,7–10)." *Zeitschrift für Theologie und Kirche* 66 (1969) 288–305.
———. *Galatians: A Commentary on Paul's Letter to the Churches in Galatia.* Hermeneia. Philadelphia: Fortress, 1979.
———. "The Problem of Apocalyptic Genre in Greek and Hellenistic Literature: The Case of the Oracle of Trophonius." In *Apocalypticism in the Mediterranean World and the Near East: Proceedings of the International Colloquium on Apocalypticism Uppsala, August 12–17, 1979,* edited by David Hellholm, 577–98. Tübingen: Mohr/Siebeck, 1983.
———. Review of Margaret E. Thrall, *A Critical and Exegetical Commentary on the Second Epistle to the Corinthians. Journal of Religion* 83 (2003) 108–9.
Blass, Friedrich, and Albert Debrunner. *A Greek Grammar of the New Testament and Other Early Christian Literature.* Translated and Edited version of the 9th-10th edition of the German edition by Robert W. Funk. Chicago: University of Chicago Press, 1961.
Collins, John J. "The Genre Apocalypse in Hellenistic Judaism," in *Apocalypticism in the Mediterranean World and the Near East: Proceedings of the International Colloquium on Apocalypticism Uppsala, August 12–17, 1979,* edited by David Hellholm, 531–48. Tübingen: Mohr/Siebeck, 1983.
Dassmann, Ernst. "Paulus in der Visio sancti Pauli (or Apocalypse of Paul; II Corinthians 12.2–4)." In *Jenseitsvorstellungen in Antike und Christentum: Gedankbuch for Alfred Stuiber,* 117–29. Jahrbuch für Antike und Christentum Ergänzungband 9. Munster: Aschendorff, 1982.
Esler, Philip F. *The First Christians in Their Social Worlds: Social-scientific Approaches to New Testament Interpretation.* London: Routledge, 1994.
Euripides. *Opera Omnia.* Edited by Samuel Musgrave. 7 vols. Glasgow: Duncan, 1821.
Furnish, Victor Paul. *2 Corinthians.* AB 32A. Garden City, NY: Doubleday, 1984.
Georgi, Dieter. *The Opponents of Paul in 2 Corinthians.* Philadelphia: Fortress, 1986.
Gooder, Paula. *Only the Third Heaven? 2 Corinthians 12.1–10 and Heavenly Ascent.* LNTS 313. Sheffield: T. & T. Clark, 2006.
Grimal, Pierre. *The Dictionary of Classical Mythology.* Translated by A. R. Maxwell-Hyslop. Oxford: Blackwell, 1996

Hanson, John S. "Dreams and Visions in the Graeco-Roman World and Early Christianity." In *ANRW* II.23.2 (1980) 1395–427.

Herrmann, Léon. "Apollos." *Revue des sciences religieuses* 50.4 (1976) 330–36.

Kennedy, George A. *Classical Rhetoric and Its Christian and Secular Tradition from Ancient to Modern Times.* Chapel Hill: University of North Carolina Press, 1980.

———. *New Testament Interpretation through Rhetorical Criticism.* Chapel Hill: University of North Carolina Press, 1984.

Lincoln, Andrew T. "Paul the Visionary: The Setting and Significance of the Rapture to Paradise in II Corinthians 12.1–10." *NTS* 25 (1979) 204–20.

March, Jennifer R. *Oxford Classical Dictionary.* Edited by Simon Hornblower and Antony Spawforth. 3rd rev. ed. Oxford: Oxford University Press, 2003, 237–38.

Morray-Jones, C. R. A. "Paradise Revisited (2 Cor 12.1–12): The Jewish Mystical Background of Paul's Apostolate. Part 1: The Jewish Sources." *HTR* 86 (1993) 177–217.

———. "Paradise Revisited (2 Cor 12.1–12): The Jewish Mystical Background of Paul's Apostolate. Part 2: Paul's Heavenly Ascent and its Significance." *HTR* 86 (1993) 262–92.

Scholem, Gershom G. *Jewish Gnosticism, Merkabah Mysticism, and Talmudic Tradition: Based on the Israel Goldstein Lectures, Delivered at the Jewish Theological Seminary of America, New York.* New York: Jewish Theological Seminary of America, 1965.

Seyffert, Oskar. *A Dictionary of Classical Antiquities, Mythology, Religion, Literature, and Art.* Revised and Edited by John Edwin Sandys and Henry Nettleship. 6th ed. London: Swan Sonnenschein, 1901.

Smith, Morton. "Ascent to the Heavens and the Beginning of Christianity." In *Aufstieg und Abstieg,* edited by Adolf Portmann and Rudolf Ritsema, 403–29. Frankfurt: Insel, 1981.

Thrall, Margaret E. *A Critical and Exegetical Commentary on the Second Epistle to the Corinthians.* 2 vols. ICC. Edinburgh: T. & T. Clark, 1994–2000.

———. "Paul's Journey to Paradise. Some Exegetical Issues in 2 Cor 12,2–4." In *The Corinthian Correspondence*, edited by R. Bieringer, 347–63. BETL 125. Leuven: Peeters, 199.

Welborn, Laurence L. "The Runaway Paul." *HTR* 92 (1999) 115–63.

Windisch, Hans. *Der Zweite Korintherbrief.* Edited by Georg Strecker. 9th ed. Göttingen: Vandenhoeck & Ruprecht, 1970.

Wolff, Christian. *Der zweite Brief des Paulus an die Korinther.* Theologisches Handkommentar zum Neuen Testament 8. Berlin: Evangelische Verlagsanstalt, 1989.

PART FIVE

Early Church Documents

13

Tertullian's Reception of Paul's Instructions about Women[1]

Adela Yarbro Collins

IN 1986 OUR HONOREE PUBLISHED A BOOK ENTITLED *BEYOND ANGER* on how a feminist can remain in the institutional church and construct a viable ministry and spirituality.[2] For many of us, ancient Christian texts that define women as inferior or subordinate and restrict their activities in the church have also evoked anger.[3] In this essay I follow her encouragement to move beyond anger by attempting to interpret Tertullian's work *On the Veiling of Virgins* without anger and without partiality (*sine ira et studio*).[4]

As all of Tertullian's works did, *On the Veiling of Virgins* had a particular rhetorical purpose. In order to appreciate that purpose, it is necessary to have some idea of the symbolic universe constructed by this work and to situate, at least briefly, that system of symbols in his life as a member of the Christian community in Carthage. There is no compelling reason to conclude that he was born before 170 CE.[5]

---

1. I am happy to present this essay in honor of Lyn Osiek, who has been my friend and colleague since our days as graduate students at Harvard.

2. Osiek, *Beyond Anger*.

3. See the trenchant critique of the establishment and theological rationalization of patriarchal order in North African Christianity by Miles, "Patriarchy as Political Theology," 169–86.

4. The phrase comes from Tacitus *Annals* 1.1; text and trans. from Clifford H. Moore and John Jackson, *Tacitus: The Histories, The Annals* 2.244–45. It is also used by Schulz-Flügel and Mattei, *Tertullien Le voile des vierges*, 97.

5. Barnes, *Tertullian*, 25, 58.

By birth and education, he belonged to the literary circles of Carthage.[6] He was probably not of high social standing by birth but acquired wealth and social status through his literary achievements.[7] He was not born to a Christian family but became Christian as a young man.[8] He married a Christian woman and belonged to the laity of the church.[9] The oldest evidence for African Christians is the *Acts of the Scillitan Martyrs*.[10] It attests to the martyrdom of some Christians from a village at the hands of Vigellius Saturninus, proconsul in 180–181 during the reign of Commodus. In terms of social status, the martyrs were peasants. According to Timothy Barnes, this document expresses "the dominant motif of African Christianity: uncompromising rejection of an alien world." The later persecutions of Decius and Diocletian and the schism of Catholics and Donatists were further defining moments of the African church.[11]

The issues of chastity, continence, and even life-long celibacy were current in African Christian communities in Tertullian's time as they were elsewhere.[12] Paul already affirms the continence of the unmarried state as superior to marriage in 1 Cor 7:7–9. He also attests the practice of continence by married members of the community in Corinth, a practice he seeks to restrain and regulate (1 Cor 7:1–5). The author of Luke advocates continence by changing Mark's statement, "When they rise from the dead, they neither marry nor are given in marriage," to "The children of this age marry and are given in marriage, but those who are considered worthy to experience that age [the age to come] and the resurrection from the dead neither marry nor are given in marriage."[13] In the third and fourth centuries, continence and virginity were highly valued among Christians throughout the Mediterranean world.[14]

6. Ibid., 195–96.

7. Ibid., 69, 138, 242–43.

8. Ibid., 26, 245–47, 252.

9. On his marriage: ibid., 25, 58–59, 136–38; on his status as a layman: ibid., 11, 117.

10. Text and translation in Musurillo, *Acts of the Christian Martyrs*, 86–89.

11. Barnes, *Tertullian*, 60–63; quotation from 62.

12. Schulz-Flügel and Mattei, *Tertullien Le voile des vierges*, 69, 73–76.

13. Cf. Mark 12:24–25 with Luke 20:34–35. See also Acts 21:9 concerning the virgin daughters of Philip, who prophesy in Caesarea.

14. Schulz-Flügel and Mattei, *Tertullien Le voile des vierges*, 95–96; Cloke, *"This Female Man of God."* See the review by Harrison, *Theological Studies*, 694–700.

Tertullian's language about women varies depending on the audience and rhetorical purpose of each work. It should not be read and discussed in isolation from his language about men. Furthermore, he expresses a variety of views related respectively to the original created state of Adam and Eve, their state after their disobedience in the garden of Eden, the descent of the angels and their marriages with human women and the results of this event, the state of men and women in Christ, and their future state in the eschatological future.[15]

Daniel Hoffmann makes a significant contribution to the interpretation of Tertullian when he points out that he says many of the same things about disobedient Adam that he says about disobedient Eve.[16] His attempt, however, to show "that Tertullian's views toward women, when considered within his own cultural and theological context, were not unusually negative, but were relatively positive" suffers from the use of global, overly general terms like "negative" and "positive" and from lack of attention to the rhetorical purposes of the various works.[17] Similarly, his claim that "there are several statements that support the idea that he considered women ontologically equal with men" is unhelpful because it does not place Tertullian's remarks sufficiently clearly in the appropriate contexts of his discourse, that is, men and women as created, fallen, redeemed, and transformed in the eschatological future.[18]

These problems are evident in the interpretation of *Against Marcion* 2.11.[19] When Tertullian states in this passage, "Woman is at once condemned to bring forth in sorrow, and to serve her husband," he is summarizing the Marcionite view that after the fall of man God became a judge both severe and cruel. His remarks to the effect that "Bearing children should have been 'without pain' and Eve 'had been destined to be a help and not a slave to her male partner,'" are part of his summary of the Marcionite argument and do not necessarily support the view "that the curse is something that should and could be

---

15. The story about the descent of the angels and their marriages is based on Gen 6:1-4 and is elaborated in the Book of the Watchers (*1 Enoch* 1-36).

16. Hoffmann, *The Status of Women and Gnosticism in Irenaeus and Tertullian*, 153-59.

17. Quotation from ibid., 148.

18. Quotation from ibid., 152. Both of these remarks are cited without comment in Madigan and Osiek, *Ordained Women in the Early Church*, 199-200 n. 24.

19. Hoffmann, *Status*, 159-60.

overcome in Christ."²⁰ It would surely be overcome in the eschatological future but probably not during Christian life in this age. Most clearly pain in childbirth continues among women in Christ.

On the Veiling of Virgins

The work *On the Veiling of Virgins* belongs to the late period of Tertullian's literary activity when he was deeply influenced by Montanist ideas and practices.²¹ This, the main section of the essay, will consider the rhetorical aims of the author and, as far as possible, infer from his arguments the ideas and practices that he was opposing.²² It will also attempt to discern the underlying symbolic universe or system that Tertullian presupposes in this work as he constructs a social space for women to inhabit.²³

In chapter one, Tertullian advocates the position that virgins ought to be veiled from "the time that they have passed the turning-point of their age," that is, from puberty (1.1).²⁴ To make his case, he argues that this practice is supported by truth (*veritas*), whereas the opposite practice, virgins of all ages participating in the liturgy with bare heads, is supported only by custom (*consuetudo*) (ibid.).²⁵ It would seem that those who advocated the position that virgins should participate unveiled in the liturgy argued on the basis of custom. Ironically, Paul had argued *against* the same practice on the basis of the lack of such a custom (συνήθεια) in 1 Cor 11:16.

20. Ibid., 160.

21. Barnes dates the work to 208–9 (*Tertullian*, 55). On Tertullian's relation to Montanism, see ibid., 42–44, 82–84; cf. Hoffmann, *Status*, 146–48. Schulz-Flügel and Mattei date the work after 213 (*Tertullien Le voile des vierges*, 41–46). Christoph Stücklin dates it to 206; *De virginibus velandis*, 103.

22. For an approach based on the New Rhetoric and aiming at reconstructing the ideas and practices of the Corinthian female prophets, see Wire, *Corinthian Women Prophets*.

23. My thinking about how discourse constructs a social world and symbolic space within it has been stimulated by Newsom, *Self as Symbolic Space*.

24. Trans. from Thelwall, "On the Veiling of Virgins," 4.27, col. 1. For a Latin text and a German trans., see Stücklin, *De virginibus velandis*, 12–13. For a Latin text and a French trans., see Schulz-Flügel and Mattei, *Tertullien Le voile des vierges*, 128–29.

25. On the issue being bare heads in the liturgy, see Barnes, *Tertullian*, 140; Stücklin, *De virginibus velandis*, 102; Schulz-Flügel and Mattei, *Tertullien Le voile des vierges*, 36, 38.

Tertullian argues that truth is beyond temporal change, the influence of persons, and the special laws of regions. In contrast it is in these things, because of ignorance or simplicity, that custom finds its beginning (1.1). He then argues from scripture (John 14:6) that Christ is Truth, not Custom. Since Christ is eternal, so also is truth (1.2). Truth may sometimes appear to be novel, but it is truth that convicts heresies, not novelty (1.3).

He then introduces a new argument in relation to the rule of faith (*regula fidei*) (1.3) or law of faith (*lex fidei*) (1.4), which he elaborates with a form of the creed (1.3). He argues that the rule or law of faith is constant whereas matters of discipline and morals (*disciplina et conversatio*) admit "novelty" insofar as they may be corrected by the grace of God that continues to be active until the end (1.4).[26]

Tertullian supports the idea that the grace of God continues to be active with two arguments. The first takes as a premise that the devil (*diabolus*) is continually at work and multiplies his evil inventions daily.[27] This premise reveals that the account in Genesis 3 of the disobedience of Adam and Eve, incited by the serpent, has been elaborated and included in a master narrative encompassing all of creation and history, in which the devil incites all human beings to do evil, as he incited Adam and Eve through the serpent.[28] The second argument is that the Lord has sent the Paraclete (*Paraclitum*), the Holy Spirit, the representative of the Lord, so that church discipline may be directed, ordered, and brought to perfection. This gradual process is necessary because the limitations of human beings prevent them from grasping everything at once. This argument assumes the ongoing fulfillment of Christ's promise that the Father would send the Paraclete, the Holy Spirit, in Christ's name and that the Paraclete would teach the followers of Jesus all things.[29] Tertullian follows the Montanists in the conviction that the Paraclete has indeed been sent and that he continues the process of revelation. He then sums up this second argument, "What, then, is the Paraclete's

---

26. Stücklin, *De virginibus velandis*, 1.4 (pp. 14–15); Schulz-Flügel and Mattei, *De uirginibus* 1.5 (pp. 130–31).

27. *On the Veiling of Virgins* 1.4 (pp. 14–15) (in Stücklin's edition); 1.6 (pp. 130–31) (in that of Schulz-Flügel and Mattei).

28. On the traditional practice of constructing a master narrative on the basis of the Bible as a whole, in which all Christian readers participate and find their identity, see Frei, *Eclipse of Biblical Narrative*, 1–3.

29. John 14:26; see also 14:16–17; 16:12–13.

administrative office but this: the direction of discipline, the revelation of the Scriptures, the re-formation of the intellect, the advancement toward better things?"[30] This summary shows that for Tertullian the veiling of virgins after puberty is the teaching of scripture according to the hemeneutical principle that the Paraclete reveals the appropriate practices of church discipline through the interpretation of scripture by those with a properly re-formed intellect. This point is made explicitly at the end of chapter 1: "Those who have received [the Paraclete] set truth before custom. They who have heard Him prophesying even to the present time, not only his ancient prophecies, cover virgins."[31] It is noteworthy that this introductory chapter (especially at its beginning and end) speaks about virgins in the third person. Tertullian is not attempting to persuade the virgins themselves directly but apparently addressing the (male) leaders of the communities in Carthage. Since the first version of this work was written in Greek, some have argued that it was intended also for leaders of communities in the east.[32] Barnes, however, has argued persuasively that the Greek versions of this and other works were written "for the Greek-speaking Christians of the African metropolis."[33]

In chapter two, Tertullian, for the sake of argument, considers the practice of women veiling their heads as a custom rather than a matter of truth. He does this to compare one custom (bareheaded virgins in the liturgy in Carthage) with another (the veiling of women in Greece and adjoining regions) (2.1).[34] Tertullian says that the virgins are veiled in communities founded by apostles or the pupils and associates of the apostles. He refers, subtly and pejoratively, to other founders who reject the custom. He then argues that "we" should choose the custom of veil-

30. Trans. (slightly modified) from Thelwall, *ANF*, 4.27, col. 2. Cf. Stücklin, *De virginibus velandis*, 1.4 (pp. 14–15); Schulz-Flügel and Mattei, 1.8 (*Tertullien Le voile des vierges*, 130–31).

31. Trans. (modified) from Thelwall, *ANF*, 4.28, col. 1. Cf. Stücklin, *De virginibus velandis*, 1.6 (pp. 16–17); Schulz-Flügel and Mattei, 1.11 (*Tertullien Le voile des vierges*, 132–33).

32. Schulz-Flügel and Mattei argue that the conclusion of the work implies that Tertullian composed it for circulation beyond the Christian context in Carthage (*Tertullien Le voile des vierges*, 36).

33. Barnes, *Tertullian*, 68–69, 253.

34. The adjoining regions may be Asia Minor; so Stücklin, *De virginibus velandis*, 17, n. 12.

ing because the communities of apostolic foundation and the ones in Africa belong to the one church (2.2). In this argument he comes close to Paul's argument based on custom in 1 Cor 11:16.

Reverting to an argument closer to those of chapter one, he then asks, in the case of doubt and uncertainty, which custom ought to be followed. The custom should be chosen that is "more compatible with the discipline of God" (2.3).[35] He concludes that the custom of veiling must be chosen because it conceals the virgins who are thus known only to God.[36] Such is fitting because one ought to seek glory from God and not human glory. This is an argument from scripture (John 5:44, 12:43).

The concluding argument of this chapter is a subtle critique of those virgins who attend the liturgy bareheaded and those leaders who approved such a custom. The virgins who seek such a privilege are shameless and thus belie their virginity. The men who approve it manifest lust since they crave to look upon these women.[37]

In chapter three, Tertullian develops further his arguments regarding truth and the work of the devil. He says that until recently in Carthage each virgin could choose whether to be covered or to be exposed (*prostitui*), just as marriage is neither required nor forbidden (3.1). Hinting at the work of God through the Paraclete, Tertullian suggests that an increase in human understanding brought about recognition that one custom was better than the other. Straightaway, however, the adversary did his work so that the virgins who sought human glory (*virgines hominum*) attempted to persuade men to make their rivals, the virgins who sought glory from God (*virgines Dei*), subordinate to them (3.2).

If we attempt to reconstruct the self-understanding of the women Tertullian maligns as virgins who sought human glory, we must have some working hypothesis about the symbolic significance of wearing a veil. Schulz-Flügel and Mattei have argued that the practice was once common in Rome and signified a married woman's acceptance of her husband's authority as the *paterfamilias*. The practice was adopted in

---

35. Trans. from Thelwall, *ANF*, 4.28, col. 1. Cf. Stücklin, *De virginibus velandis*, 2.3 (pp. 18–19); Schulz-Flügel and Mattei, 2.4 (*Tertullien Le voile des vierges*, 134–35).

36. Cf. Matt 6:1–6.

37. Stücklin, 2.3 (*De virginibus velandis*, 18–19); Schulz-Flügel and Mattei, 2.4–5 (*Tertullien Le voile des vierges*, 134–35).

Carthage with the same significance. Under the empire the practice fell into disuse in Roman circles but endured in Carthage.[38] For a time, apparently, some virgins wore the veil in Carthage both in public and in church, while others did not. At some point those virgins who did not wear the veil in church proposed that all the virgins should participate in the liturgy with unveiled heads as an indication of their status as virgins not subject to a man's authority. According to Schulz-Flügel and Mattei, they were demanding that all the virgins follow their practice in order to let the rest of the community know in this way that the ascetics are "exclusively servants of Christ," enjoying Christian freedom more than any other.[39]

Tertullian, however, characterizes this social pressure as equivalent to the forced, public unveiling of those virgins who veiled themselves. This shameful act is equivalent to rape. In fact, it is worse than physical rape because the very spirit of the virgin is violated. She is no longer a virgin in her own eyes (3.4–5).[40] He concludes chapter three with an apostrophe to Truth, upon whom he calls to demonstrate that Truth itself is the coverer of virgins by interpreting Truth's own scriptures (3.5).[41] This figure of speech introduces the arguments from scripture in chapters four through eleven and characterizes them as in accordance with the divine will.

In 4.1 Tertullian says that those who argue that all virgins should participate in the liturgy unveiled support their argument with reference to Paul's instructions about the veil (1 Cor 11:2–16). They claim that he refers only to (married) women. If he intended to instruct virgins to be veiled, he would have said so explicitly, just as he explicitly mentions virgins in his instructions about marriage (1 Corinthians 7). Tertullian argues to the contrary that when Paul does not distinguish "(married) woman" and "virgin," the term "woman" (*mulier*) refers to community of condition. Thus in the passage on veiling all adult females are meant (4.2–4).[42]

---

38. Schulz-Flügel and Mattei, *Tertullien Le voile des vierges*, 90.

39. Ibid., 38.

40. Stücklin, 3.4–5 (*De virginibus velandis*, 20–23); Schulz-Flügel and Mattei, 3.6–8 (*Tertullien Le voile des vierges*, 136–39).

41. Stücklin, 3.5 (*De virginibus velandis*, 22–23); Schulz-Flügel and Mattei, 3.9 (*Tertullien Le voile des vierges*, 138–39).

42. Stücklin, 4.2–4 (*De virginibus velandis*, 24–27); Schulz-Flügel and Mattei, 4.2–8 (*Tertullien Le voile des vierges*, 140–43).

In chapter five Tertullian supports the conclusion of chapter four by arguing that Eve is called "woman" (*mulier*) while she is still a virgin. Several important implications follow from this argument. First, he emphasizes that both Adam and Eve were virgins before they disobeyed. Thus virginity represents the original state of humanity intended by God. Second, the woman is subordinate to the man already according to the order and nature of her creation. She is the second kind of human being or the kind of human being that follows the first kind that is man (5.2).[43] She "was made by God for man's assistance" (ibid.).[44] She was made from the substance of man (5.5).[45]

In chapter six Tertullian argues that Paul speaks of Mary, the mother of Jesus, as a woman (Gal 4:4) (6.1). Since she was a virgin, this makes clear that "virgin" belongs to the class "woman" (6.4).[46] In chapter seven, he examines Paul's reasons for instructing women (*feminae*) to wear a veil to see whether they apply to virgins as well. First he argues, "If 'the man is head of the *woman* (*mulier*)' [1 Cor 11:3], of course (he is) of the *virgin* too, from whom comes the *woman* who has married; unless the *virgin* is a third generic class, some monstrosity with a head of its own" (7.2). Second, "If 'it is shameful for a *woman* to be shaven or shorn' [1 Cor 11:6], of course it is so for a *virgin*" (7.3).[47]

After the second argument, Tertullian states in an aside, "Therefore, let the world (*saeculum*), the rival of God, beware if it deceitfully says that it is fitting for a virgin to have her hair cut short in the way that is permitted for a boy" (7.3).[48] This remark, like those about the devil in 1.4 and 3.2, is evidence that Tertullian presupposed a master narrative characterized by a struggle between God and opposing forces for hu-

---

43. Thelwall translates "this kind of second human being" (*ANF*, 4.30, col. 1); Stücklin "dieses zweite menschliche Geschlecht" (*De virginibus velandis*, 29); Schulz-Flügel and Mattei "le genre feminine, humanité venue après" (*Tertullien Le voile des vierges*, 145).

44. Thelwall, *ANF*, 4.30, col. 1.

45. Ibid., 4.30, col. 2; cf. Stücklin 5.5 (*De virginibus velandis*, 30–31); Schulz-Flügel and Mattei, 5.6 (*Tertullien Le voile des vierges*, 146–47).

46. So Thelwall (*ANF* 4.31, col. 2); Stücklin 6.4 (*De virginibus velandis*, 36–37). Note that Schulz-Flügel and Mattei take the last sentence as part of 7.1 (*Tertullien Le voile des vierges*, 150–53).

47. Trans. from Thelwall (*ANF*, 4.31, col. 2). Both quotations are part of 7.2 in the edition of Schulz-Flügel and Mattei (*Tertullien Le voile des vierges*, 152–53).

48. Trans. by author; this sentence belongs to 7.2 in the edition of Schulz-Flügel and Mattei (*Tertullien Le voile des vierges*, 152–53).

man loyalty and obedience. Since it is unlikely that it was typical for (adult) virgins among non-Christians in Carthage to wear their hair cut short like a boy, the "world" in this remark may represent a practice by Christians in that city who also advocate the position that (adult) virgins ought to attend the liturgy bareheaded. The short hair may signify that, by overcoming their female sexuality, these women have become like males in a spiritual sense. Another possibility is that the image is a rhetorical construct that sets up Tertullian's own argument. In contrast, he thus argues that it is as fitting for those (adult virgins) to be veiled as it is unfitting for them to have shorn hair (7.3).[49]

He then puts forth a third argument, "If 'woman is a man's glory' [1 Cor 11:7], how much more is a virgin (a man's glory), who is also a glory to herself; if 'woman (is) from man' and 'on account of man' [1 Cor 11:8–9], that rib of Adam was first a virgin; if 'woman ought to have power upon her head' [1 Cor 11:10], it is even more proper for a virgin, to whom that which is decisive here pertains" (7.4–6).[50] His line of argument becomes clear when he goes on to say that (woman ought to have power upon her head) "on account of angels" (1 Cor 11:10). He then interprets the story about the angels who came down from heaven and married human women.[51] He infers, reasonably, that it was not married women but virgins who excited the eager desire (*concupiscentia*) of the angels. He even remarks that their virginal innocence (*flos*) excuses human desire (*libido*) in the present time (7.6).[52] His conclusion is "So perilous a face, then, ought to be shaded, which has cast stumbling stones even so far as heaven: that, when standing in the presence of God, at whose bar it stands accused of the driving of the angels from their (native) confines, it may blush before the other angels as well; and may repress that former liberty of its head—(a liberty) now to be exhibited not even before human eyes" (7.7).[53] It is clear from this line of argumentation that in Tertullian's master narrative women,

---

49. This statement belongs to 7.2 in the edition of Schulz-Flügel and Mattei (ibid.).

50. Trans. by author; these remarks belong to 7.3 in the edition of Schulz-Flügel and Mattei (ibid.).

51. This story is based on Gen 6:1–4 and the Book of the Watchers (*1 Enoch* 1–36), as noted above.

52. These remarks belong to 7.4 in the edition of Schulz-Flügel and Mattei (*Tertullien Le voile des vierges*, 152–53).

53. Trans. from Thelwall, *ANF*, 4.32, col. 1.

especially virgins, were the cause of the angels' sinning. So women and virgins who do not take care to avoid placing a snare before the feet of angels and men by displaying their beauty in an unveiled state are as guilty of sin as are the lustful angels and men.

In chapter eight Tertullian elaborates these arguments *e contrario* and concludes with the observation, "In fact, at this day the Corinthians do veil their *virgins*. What the apostles taught, their disciples approve" (8.5).[54] In chapter nine he argues that the practice of veiling is consistent with the other precepts of church discipline for women and that they apply to virgins as well. First he takes up the rule, "It is not permitted to a *woman* to speak (*loqui*) in the church [1 Cor 14:34]; but neither (is it permitted her) to teach [1 Tim 2:12], nor to baptize, nor to offer, nor to claim to herself a lot in any manly function, not to say (in any) sacerdotal office" (9.2).[55] Tertullian explains these rules as deriving from the necessity of humility for women. The reason for this necessity will be discussed in the Conclusion below. He suggests that the virgin is allowed to dispense with the veil so that the sanctity of her flesh may be honored. Since, however, she is a woman, and women must cultivate humility, "nothing in the way of public honour is permitted to a *virgin*" (9.4).[56]

In chapter ten Tertullian argues that it is also uncivil (or barbarous) for women, who are supposed to be subordinate to men in all things, to bear (or wear) an honorable sign of their purity that can be seen, which gives them admiration, respect, and reverence among the brethren, whereas there are so many men who are virgins, so many who have made themselves eunuchs voluntarily, who keep their distinction hidden in that they bear nothing on themselves that allows them to stand out. Since male virgins deserve more honor than female virgins yet receive none, female virgins should cease to claim it for themselves. In chapter eleven he argues that it is only after puberty that females must be veiled. In chapter twelve he vividly describes how girls who have reached puberty change the way they wear their hair and stick a

54. Trans. from ibid., 4.33, col. 1. This observation belongs to 8.8 in the edition of Schulz-Flügel and Mattei (*Tertullien Le voile des vierges*, 158–59).

55. Trans. from Thelwall, *ANF*, 4.33, col. 1. For the evidence that women did exercise sacerdotal or priestly office (as "presbyters"), see Madigan and Osiek, *Ordained Women*.

56. Trans. from Thelwall, *ANF*, 4.33, col. 2. This statement belongs to 9.6 in the edition by Schulz-Flügel and Mattei (*Tertullien Le voile des vierges*, 162–63).

more conspicuous pin in their hair. They show that they have become women in various aspects of their behavior. It is only by keeping their heads bare that they still want to count as virgins (or unmarried girls). In chapter thirteen he argues that they should veil their heads also in church, as they do in the presence of unbelievers. If they fear outsiders, they should also be afraid of the brethren. Or else they should have the courage to appear also in the village as virgins since they dare to do so in the church. I would praise their strength, he says, if they would also offer for sale (*nundinor*) at least something of their virginity in the presence of unbelievers. Then the inner and the outer would be the same. The arguments of chapters eleven through thirteen are based on the premise that men and women in Christ share the weaknesses of the flesh experienced by unbelievers. It is only in the eschatological future that such weaknesses will be overcome definitively.

Next Tertullian claims, in chapter fourteen, that the practice of virgins coming unveiled to church is dangerous in a number of ways. First, it aims at encouraging other young women to choose virginity. This aim discloses a bad motivation, namely, the quest for glory. Second, if emulation is the motivation, rather than piety, they become weak and are easily seduced. When they become pregnant, they hypocritically continue bareheaded, styling themselves virgins to avoid being discovered as long as they can. Third, the desire not to remain hidden is already unchaste since they feel something in that desire that does not suit a virgin, namely the urge to awaken pleasure, especially in men. Even when she awakens so much good will, she endangers herself unavoidably by her own appearance in public, when she is met by many dubious glances and is titillated by the fingers pointing at her, when she is all too glad to be seen and grows hot when she is hugged and kissed continuously: in this way her forehead is hardened, her sense of shame is blunted and disappears, and so she learns to want to please in another way. These arguments, especially the third, presuppose that the appropriate attitude for women is shame or modesty, an attitude related to that of humility, advocated in chapter nine.

Fear is another related attitude, advocated in chapter fifteen. The virgin should fear the envy of the adversary on the one hand and the judgment of God upon haughtiness on the other. She should find joy in being known (as a virgin) to herself and to God alone and block the pathway against temptations. "For who would dare to fasten his eyes on a reserved face, a face without feeling, a face that is, so to speak, sad? Every bad thought would shatter right away on the hardness of such a face. Those who hide their virginity also deny their womanly nature" (15.3).[57] Denying their womanly nature here is obviously a good thing to do.

Chapter sixteen begins with a summation indicating that scripture, nature, and discipline all support the veiling of virgins, and all of these come from God. Tertullian continues, "Nothing is more dear to God than modesty, nothing more welcome than humility, and nothing more hateful than a passion for glory and the desire to please other human beings" (16.1).[58]

In the rest of chapter 16, Tertullian at last addresses the virgins themselves, calling them "mother," "sister," and "daughter," in accordance with their respective ages. He urges them to veil themselves, "if a mother, for your sons' sakes; if a sister, for your brethren's sakes; if a daughter for your fathers' sakes. All ages are periled in your person" (16.2).[59] This exhortation presupposes the cultural system of honor and shame and fits with Paul's claim, "Woman is man's glory" (1 Cor 11:7). The behavior of women increases or threatens the honor of the men to whom they are related, either by birth and marriage or by association in the Christian community. He then advocates that they adopt modesty, bashfulness, and strict control over their own looking and the looking of others at them; in short, they are to wear the full garb of (married) women in order to preserve their standing as virgins. In 2.3 and 13.2 he had alluded to Matt 6:1–4, arguing that the exposure of the virgins' glory in church (signified by their bare heads) was incompatible with the teaching of Jesus to do good in secret for God alone and not to trumpet forth that which ought to be done for

---

57. Trans. by author; cf. Stücklin 15.3 (*De virginibus velandis*, 64–65). These remarks belong to 15.4 in the edition by Schulz-Flügel and Mattei (*Tertullien Le voile des vierges*, 178–79). They suggest that the reference to the sad face of the virgin in this section is based on the practice among Greeks and Romans of covering the head as a sign of mourning (p. 89). For Tertullian mourning is appropriate for women because of the guilt that they inherit from Eve and from the women who seduced the angels; see the conclusion below.

58. Trans. by author; cf. Stücklin 15.1 (*De virginibus velandis*, 66–67). This sentence belongs to 15.3 in the edition of Schulz-Flügel and Mattei (*Tertullien Le voile des vierges*, 178–79).

59. Trans. from Thelwall, *ANF*, 4.37, col. 1.

God and not for human glory. Similarly, in 16.2 he urges the virgins directly to belie their virginity by wearing the veil, as married women do, "in order to exhibit the truth to God alone."[60] He concludes this chapter with the argument that they are in fact married women: they are brides of Christ. Since Christ (in 1 Corinthians 11) bids women to be veiled, the virgins should do the will of their husband, especially as his own wives. This last argument clearly grants that Christian women, at least the virgins, do have a direct relation to Christ and through him to God.[61] By means of this direct address and the metaphor of marriage to Christ, Tertullian proposes a way in which the virgins may exercise agency even though they give up the special privilege and honor of participating in the liturgy with bare heads.

In the final chapter of the work, Tertullian instructs married women to wear a proper veil that covers all of the hair and the neck. It is the whole head (presumably not including the face) that must be subjected, and on account of it a woman needs a "power" (*potestas*) over her head (1 Cor 11:10). The veil is its yoke (17.1).[62] The claim that women must take a yoke upon themselves seems at first glance to be incompatible with Paul's teaching in Gal 5:1, "For freedom Christ has liberated us; stand firm therefore and do not take upon yourselves again the yoke of slavery."[63] The image of the yoke here and in Matthew, however, refers to observance of the law.[64] In its use in chapter seventeen of *On the Veiling of Virgins*, however, the image is used in a more social sense, analogous to 1 Tim 6:1, "Let as many as are slaves under the yoke consider their masters worthy of every honor in order that the name of God and the teaching not be reviled."[65] Slaves who are in Christ are still living in this age. For this reason they are under the power of their masters. Likewise married women are under the power of their husbands.

---

60. Trans. from ibid. This exhortation is found in 16.5 in the edition of Schulz-Flügel and Mattei (*Tertullien Le voile des vierges*, 180–81).

61. Contra Stücklin, *De virginibus velandis*, 190; and Schulz-Flügel and Mattei, *Tertullien Le voile des vierges*, 92–93.

62. This instruction occurs in 17.1–3 in the edition of Schulz-Flügel and Mattei (*Tertullien Le voile des vierges*, 180–83).

63. Trans. by author.

64. In Matt 11:29–30, the yoke refers to the law as interpreted by Jesus.

65. Trans. by author.

Conclusion

The language about subjection and the yoke in chapter seventeen is related to the humility of women advocated in 9.2. As noted above, in Tertullian's master narrative, women are subordinate to men because of the order of creation.[66] Although he does not discuss this topic in *On the Veiling of Virgins*, it is likely that the account of the disobedience of Adam and Eve in Genesis 3 plays a role here as well. In another work that concerns the behavior of women, he says that women should: "go about in humble garb and [instead of a gladsome or ostentatious style of dress] rather to affect meanness of appearance, walking about as Eve mourning and repentant, in order that by every garb of penitence she might the more fully expiate that which she derives from Eve,—the ignominy, I mean, of the first sin, and the odium (attaching to her as the cause) of human perdition."[67]

A third reason for women to be humble and modest is another event in Tertullian's master narrative, the marriages of the fallen angels with human women. As discussed above, Tertullian views this event almost as the seduction of the angels by human women.[68]

Paul's position in 1 Cor 11:2–16 is nuanced. Although in the beginning woman was created from man and for man (vv. 8–9), now man comes through woman (v. 12). In Christ woman is not independent of man, and man is not independent of woman (v. 11), and all things come from God (v. 12). Tertullian's master narrative and symbolic system, however, also contain the teaching of 1 Cor 14:34–35, according to which women are to be silent in the assemblies of the saints and to be subordinate, and 1 Tim 2:11–12, which mandates even greater restrictions on women. Tertullian does not temper these restrictions in light of the mutuality affirmed in 1 Corinthians 11. Rather he elaborates them to include prohibitions of women's baptizing, offering the eucharist, and claiming for themselves a lot in any "manly" function, especially not any sacerdotal office.[69]

---

66. See the discussion of chapter 5 above. See also 10.1.

67. *On the Apparel of Women* (*De cultu feminarum*) 1.1; trans. by S. Thelwall, *ANF* 4.14, col. 1. See also Stücklin, *De virginibus velandis*, 188.

68. See the discussion of chapter 7 above. See also Schulz-Flügel and Mattei, *Tertullien Le voile des vierges*, 95.

69. See the discussion of chapter 9 above. See also Schulz-Flügel and Mattei, *Tertullien Le voile des vierges*, 98–99.

According to Schulz-Flügel and Mattei, Tertullian, as a man of his century and province, was conservative. He stands in the line of critical writers with regard to Roman society and its morals. He deplored the abandonment of the ancient ideas concerning the position of women (*Apol.* 6.4–6; *De pallio* 4.9). His version of Christianity reinforced these conservative tendencies. His conservatism is evident, not only in his anthropological conceptions, but also in his assertions about the position of women in the church—he forbade them every priestly activity, and more broadly, every governing activity (cf. *De baptismo* 17.2; *Virg.* 9.1). On the second point in particular, there was nothing in the Montanism that he knew that was capable of changing him: to grant that a woman could receive the gift of prophecy did not amount, for him, the recognition of the right to administer baptism and the eucharist—a right moreover, as far as we know, the two prophetesses who were assistants of Montanus, Prisca and Maximilla, never exercised.[70]

In the private domain in contrast, in the practical relations that he had with his "sisters," Tertullian considered women to be responsible human beings, capable of having a direct relation to God. He deemed them worthy to benefit from the charisms and able to attain virtue. It is striking that he is apparently the first Christian writer to address himself specifically to women in certain short moral works: *To His Wife, On the Apparel of Women*, and *On the Veiling of Virgins*. The so-called misogyny of Tertullian is explicable by means of his rigorism, which applies to both men and women, for our author does not teach a double morality (cf. *De monogamia* 10.7).[71]

As we have seen, Tertullian constructed a master narrative and a symbolic universe on the basis of scripture and tradition. This symbolic system influenced his reception of Paul's instruction about women. At the same time, the social values and perspectives that he brought with him when he adopted Christian faith and the influence of the Montanists no doubt affected that construction and reception. The gradual evolution of a recognized order of those practicing continence within the church was considered by the Montanist party to be incompatible with their ecclesiological conceptions. Tertullian agreed with them that the church is a spiritual reality in which ranks and functions do not lead to any privileges. The ethical requirements of the Christian existence

70. Ibid.
71. Ibid.

apply to all the members without exception. Furthermore, virginity is a grace and not, like other forms of continence, an achievement. Virgins should not aspire to any honor or particular rank. Rather they should live with their families, following a custom that remained lively at the time.[72] Tertullian's personal experience no doubt also played a role. He was happily married for some part of his adult life but apparently his wife died before him. His commitment to monogamy in the sense of one marriage in one's lifetime led him to live as a continent widower for the rest of his life. The struggle to maintain this commitment may have played a role in his instructions regarding female modesty.[73]

72. Schulz-Flügel and Mattei, *Tertullien Le voile des vierges*, 39–40.
73. Barnes, *Tertullian*, 25, 136–39.

Bibliography

Barnes, Timothy David. *Tertullian: A Historical and Literary Study*. Oxford: Clarendon, 1971. Rev. ed. 1985.

Cloke, Gillian. *"This Female Man of God": Women and Spiritual Power in the Patristic Age, AD 350–450*. London: Routledge, 1995.

Frei, Hans. *The Eclipse of Biblical Narrative*. New Haven: Yale University Press, 1974.

Harrison, Verna E. F. Review of Gillian Cloke, *"This Female Man of God." Theological Studies* 48 (1997) 694–700.

Hoffmann, Daniel L. *The Status of Women and Gnosticism in Irenaeus and Tertullian*. Studies in Women and Religion, 36. Lewiston, NY: Mellen, 1995.

Madigan, Kevin, and Carolyn Osiek. *Ordained Women in the Early Church: A Documentary History*. Baltimore: Johns Hopkins University Press, 2005.

Miles, Margaret R. "Patriarchy as Political Theology: The Establishment of North African Christianity." In *Civil Religion and Political Theology*, edited by Leroy S. Rouner, 169–86. Notre Dame: University of Notre Dame Press, 1986.

Moore, Clifford H., and John Jackson. *Tacitus: The Histories, The Annals*. 3 vols. New York: Putnam, 1925–1937.

Musurillo, Herbert. *The Acts of the Christian Martyrs*. Oxford: Clarendon, 1972.

Newsom, Carol A. *The Self as Symbolic Space: Constructing Identity and Community at Qumran*. Studies on the Texts of the Desert of Judah 52. Leiden: Brill, 2004.

Osiek, Carolyn, R.S.C.J. *Beyond Anger: On Being a Feminist in the Church*. New York: Paulist, 1986.

Schulz-Flügel, Eva, and Paul Mattei. *Tertullien Le voile des vierges (De uirginibus uelandis)*. Sources Chrétiennes 424. Paris: Cerf, 1997.

Stücklin, Christoph. *Tertullian, De virginibus velandis: Übersetzung, Einleitung, Kommentar: Ein Beitrag zur altkirchlichen Frauenfrage*. Europäische Hochschulschriften 23/26. Frankfurt: Lang, 1974.

Thelwall, S. "On the Veiling of Virgins." In *ANF* 4.27, col. 1.

Wire, Antoinette Clark. *The Corinthian Women Prophets: A Reconstruction through Paul's Rhetoric*. 1990. Reprinted, Eugene, OR: Wipf & Stock, 2003.

14

Women's Ordination in Hippolytus' Commentary *On the Song of Songs* and the Question of Provenance

Yancy W. Smith

PROFESSOR CAROLYN OSIEK PROVIDED GUIDANCE TO MANY STUDENTS in pointing out areas of research needing more attention. I am grateful that she guided me toward Hippolytus, and especially his commentary *On the Song of Songs*. Initial discussions became a term paper on this difficult text and eventually morphed into a dissertation—including a translation of the relevant texts.[1] Hippolytus' *On the Song of Songs* has sparked understandable interest and varied interpretations because of his supposed advocacy of early Christian female ordination and apostleship. The views of the exegete on the participation of women in salvation history raises important issues. But does Hippolytus also advocate an idiosyncratic view of the role of women in the leadership of Hippoltyus' church that should be read against disputes about the role of women during the early period of the Montanist renewal?[2] Or are the figures of Martha and Mary in Hippolytus a symbol of the apostolic ministry of the church as a whole?[3] What are the antecedents of the Martha and Mary tradition in Hippolytus? Does the tradition depend upon historical remembrances of Martha and Mary as a figure of apostolic authority in the Johannine community?[4]

---

1. See Smith, "Hippolytus' Commentary on the Song of Songs."
2. Cerrato, *Hippolytus*, 209.
3. Weyermann, "Typologies," 622–23, citing Peppa, *Die Töchter der Kirche Christi*, 69–76.
4. Ernst, "Martha from the Margins," 409.

Christ and His Two Wives

Hippolytus continued in *On the Song of Songs* the spiritual narrative of a love triangle between Christ, the synagogue, and the church of the Gentiles begun in his commentary *On Proverbs*.[5] His image of the beloved of the Song is complex indeed. Sometimes the beloved is Israel, sometimes the church of the Gentiles, sometimes the believing synagogue, sometimes the unbelieving synagogue. When the words of the beloved permit an interpretation of jealousy, the beloved is Israel jilted by Christ for the Gentiles: "'Tell me, you whom my soul has loved,' [means], 'tell me, Christ; respond, O Word, to me I beg you.' 'Where do you pasture, where do you rest at midday? You abandoned me and left me alone, you went away to the Gentiles. I remained behind as an orphan'" (*In Cant.* 6.1).

The symbolism in *On the Song of Songs* of two mates of Christ recalls the fourth- and fifth century Roman iconography of twin female figures representing the church of the Gentiles and the church of the Circumcision. Hippolytus' bride of Christ—in reality two brides—anticipates later distinctly Roman iconography. The famous fifth century mosaic in the church of Santa Sabina has the two women, the first of which holds a Bible written in Greek characters, the other holds one with Hebrew letters, on either side of the dedicatory inscription of the

---

5. Συναγωγή in *On Proverbs* also represents the Jewish people as a rival mate of Jesus opposite the church of the Gentiles, represented as a slave girl. According to the LXX, a slave who replaces her mistress is one of four things that shake the world. Commenting on Prov. 30:21, καὶ παιδίσκη ἐὰν ἐκβάλη τὴν ἑαυτῆς κυρίαν, καὶ γυνὴ μισητὴ ἐὰν τύχη ἀνδρὸς ἀγαθοῦ "a female domestic if she throws out her mistress, and a hateful woman if she finds a good husband," Hippolytus says, "The Lord-murdering [Jewish] synagogue that crucified the flesh of Christ outside the gate" is the παιδίσκη that cast out her mistress, the σάρξ of Christ" (*Frag. In Prov.* 54.31 Achelis; cp. *Frag. In Prov.* 61.1 Richard), while "the hateful (or lusty) woman that finds a good man" is the church of the Gentiles who belongs to Christ. Again, the same theme appears: "the church of the gentiles, who thought she was a slave girl and a stranger to the promises, 'cast out' the matron and lady of the house and herself became the lady of the house and bride of Christ" (*Frag. In Prov.* 26vat1.23 Richard; cp. 62.1–2 Richard). Τουτέστιν ἡ ἐπίγειος Ἰερουσαλήμ· παιδίσκη πάντων ἐθνῶν γεγενημένη ἐξέ-βαλετὴν ἑαυτῆς κυρίαν, τὴν ἁγίαν σάρκα κυρίου, κυριοκτόνος γενομένη. "Which means, the earthly Jerusalem. Once domestic slave, all gentiles, came, she cast out here own matron, since she had become a lord killer (husband killer) with respect to the flesh of the Lord." So she herself becomes the μισήτη "hated" woman, while the previously hated woman becomes the bride, the church of the Gentiles (cf. *Dem. adv. Jud.* 19:31).

church.⁶ The inscriptions indicate how these figures are to be understood. The "two figures are distinguished plainly . . . by their dress: the woman representing the church of the Gentiles is dressed as a Roman matron . . . The books they hold are distinguished by the lettering as Hebrew and Greek, the Old Testament and the New."⁷ A fourth-century (restored) mosaic in the church of Santa Pudenziana has two women placing garlands (*coronae*) upon the heads of Peter and Paul, representing the mission to the Jews and to the Gentiles (cf. *In Cant.* 8.8).⁸ The ornately carved door of Santa Sabina has a similar motif that mirrors the versatility of the woman/women—church/synagogue symbolism in Hippolytus. The door represents the *una ecclesia sancta* with one woman holding garlands in both hands and crowns both Peter and Paul at the same time.

Positive Mention of Women in the Commentary

Apart from the distinctive Roman motif of Christ's two mates, key passages in *On the Song of Songs* mention women in a positive way. Of course, the mention of women may be quite distinct from an acknowledgment of their significant contributions to the life of the church.⁹ The ambivalence of Hippolytus' "attitude" toward women and the liturgical practices he portrays them as performing—namely, anointing Christ (*In Cant.* 2.29) and using their bodies in an effort to acquire the anointing (*In Cant.* 2.18) or become one with him (*In Cant.* 25.4)—make

---

6. Text and translation available online from Unknown, "Dedication Mosaic (Detail)," (2008). Online: http://www.sacred-destinations.com/italy/rome-santa-sabina-photos/slides/xti_9514pa80.htm.

7. See Lowrie, *Art in the Early Church*, 68, 146.

8. See image in Spier, *Picturing the Bible*, figure 81, 113. See Kessler, "The Meeting of Peter and Paul in Rome," who traces origin of images of Peter and Paul together to the fourth or fifth century. Hippolytus is witness at least to an earlier textual tradition. The reference in *In Cant.* 8.8 seems to have two suggestions: a fraternal mission, held up as an example for Jews who would believe, and *concordia*, a central theme of *In Cant.* 8. Hippolytus describes Peter as "like a shepherd" and Paul as swift "like a steed." The reference in *In Cant.* 8.8 conveys the notion of *concordia apostolorum*, but uses a motif frequently employed in late antique art to express the idea of a fraternal mission, suggesting Castor and Pollux, an image frequently found in domestic decorations. The interpretation as Peter and Paul, however, is clearly a western phenomenon, ibid., 266, "either Roman or Italian."

9. Baumbach, personal correspondence, 2-26-2010.

it difficult to assess his view of their role in the ministry of the early church. If anything, Hippolytus views the role of women as liminal, risky, and dangerous but ultimately necessary to the salvation of both male and female in harmony with his notion of *apokatastasis* derived from Irenaeus.

The theology of the *myrrhophores*, Martha and Mary, in *In Cant.* 24–25, however, is clearly idiosyncratic—a repeated theme the author injects into his interpretation of at least one other surviving text, his commentary *In Exodum*.[10] The odd (but textually erroneous) reference to the "mystery of Martha" (*In Cant.* 25.3),[11] as well as the reference to Martha in Hippolytus' *In Exodum*, are eucharistic texts. Whatever other associations the passage may generate, Hippolytus applies the figure of the *myrrhophores* to the previously mentioned triangular conjugal relationship between "synagogue," church (*In Cant.* 25.10), and Christ.

Women populate the pages of the commentary in striking ways. Hippolytus praises Martha of Bethany—a role-model for believers—as the woman who anointed Christ, while he scorns Judas for hating the anointing (*In Cant.* 2.29).[12] He praises the Shunammite for preparing a couch for the prophet because from that couch she received her son back from the dead (*In Cant.* 27.2). Hippolytus even praises "blessed Tamar," who made herself appear as a harlot in order to take hold of the anointing (*In Cant.* 2.18). Hippolytus ignores the canonical role played by Mary Magdalene as witness to the resurrection. Instead, Martha and Mary seek for and find Christ. He identified them as the women whom Jesus met and who took hold of his feet (Mat 28:9), commissioned as

---

10. Brock, "Some New Syriac Texts," 177–200. While Brock doubts the attribution to Hippolytus the exegete, Cerrato, *Hippolytus*, 180 is correct to assert that the mention shared with the *In Cant.* that Mary and Martha were primary witnesses of the resurrection is a strong indicator of authenticity.

11. Cerrato's reading of *In Cant.* 25.3 must be amended to read "mystery of righteousness" rather than "counsel of Martha." Cp. Garitte, *Traités d'Hippolyte* (CSCO 264), 46 who reads *justum mysterium*, corrects the "mystery/counsel of Martha" to the "mystery of righteousness" by emending the Georgian *martayssa* (of Martha) to *martalsa* (of righteousness). The parallel Armenian and Paleo-Slavic texts both read "righteous mystery" ('das gerechte Geheimnis'), Bonwetsch, "Kommentar," 64. The phrase "great mystery" and "righteous mystery" appear elsewhere (*In Cant.* 2.29; 2.32; 8.1; 17.2; 26.3). See also Ernst, "Martha From the Margins," 160.

12. Similarly, Cyril of Jerusalem contrasted the women favored to be witnesses of the resurrection with the chief priests who remained ignorant (*Cat.* 14.14).

"apostles to the apostles" (*In Cant.* 24.2; 25.1, 3; cf. Matt 28:10).[13] For Hippolytus, the apostolic ministry of Martha and Mary recapitulates the disaster caused by Eve in the Garden, thus restoring women to legitimate service to Adam, who represents males. Eve, representative of women, now makes a new offering of herself in obedience to her husband, Adam.

Is Montanism the Milieu of *On the Song of Songs?*

In Cerrato's watershed work on Hippolytus, he argued that his teaching on women not only points to female church leadership, but is an indicator of provenance. Simply stated, the argument runs as follows. In *On the Antichrist* and the commentaries, Hippolytus exhibits a view of the role of women which is more positive than other second-century patristic literature, such as Tertullian and Clement of Alexandria.[14] His positive mentions of women without prescriptions about women's social and domestic roles express an open attitude toward women as church leaders. For example, Eve is called an apostle. The New Prophecy, centered in Phrygia near Asia Minor, indicates an eastern provenance. Other "eastern" traditions in the commentary support this notion. Cerrato concluded that Asian Christianity, influenced by Montanism, is the context for the commentary *On the Song of Songs*.

Cerrato's literary analysis of the episode of the *myrrhophores* is sound.[15] Apart from his acceptance of the erroneous "mystery of Martha," unless further evidence should surface to establish the original Greek text, his reading of the text (*In Cant.* 2.29; 24.2; 25.1) seems quite correct.[16] Scholars unfamiliar with the textual tradition of *On the Song of Songs* earlier rejected the reading "Martha" in these texts, led

---

13. Hippolytus' reading of the resurrection does not follow any one gospel account, but depends upon a harmonistic reading. Only on such a reading does Matthew 28:9–10 raise the question of the separate identity of these women. Hippolytus' readings of the gospel may indicate he used Justin's written harmonization of the Matthew, Mark, and Luke that formed the basis of Tatian's *Diatessaron*. See Koester, *Introduction to the New Testament*, 2:344. Hippolytus may have known Tatian's work. An early third century fragment of the *Diatessaron* was found near the Christian building in Dura Europos, see Kraeling, *A Greek Fragment of Tatian's Diatessaron*, 1–5.

14. Cerrato, *Hippolytus*, 210.

15. Ibid., 184. The following outline is adapted from Cerrato.

16. Ibid., 179–83.

astray by a commitment to the canonical figure of Mary Magdalene as "the apostle to the apostles."[17] The pair appears more than once in the commentary and in three textually independent versions (Georgian, Armenian, Paleo-Slavic). They are also witnesses of the resurrection in a Syriac fragment of Hippolytus' *In Exodum*.[18]

Hippolytus quotes nearly the entire text of Song 3:1–4 in *In Cant.* 24–25.[19] His exposition may be analyzed in three parts:[20]

- Martha and Mary represent the synagogue-church in search of the body of Christ and meet with angels at the tomb.
- The women encounter the risen Christ at the tomb.
- The women try to delay the ascension by clinging to his feet.
- The women beg for Christ to allow spiritual union with him and to be taken to heaven with him.
- Martha warrants their request by asking Christ to present Eve as a new sacrifice.
- Eve is now purified of deception (represented by the fig-leaf), and she is clothed with an incorruptible garment through the Holy Spirit.
- Christ, the New Adam, was also dressed in his resurrection with peace and incorruptibility.
- He was not naked.
- The synagogue makes its confession through the women.

---

17. Chappuzeau, "Die Auslegung," 56 n. 80 suggested that here Hippolytus' text is corrupt because neither Mat 28:1 nor any other canonical gospel names Martha among the women at the tomb, rather "Mary Magdalene, and the other Mary." So Nurnberg, "*Apostolae Apostolorum*," 228, and Haskins, *Mary Magdalen*, 63 argue that Hippolytus has either fused or mixed the identities of the women. The fact that Mary Magdalene has become such an important figure in current feminist research should inspire caution in reading her into a text where she is not once named. See Ernst, "Martha from the Margins," 153.

18. Brock, "Some New Syriac Texts,"199: "the angels to both Mary and Martha gave the news that the Bread had been sent from the resurrection."

19. One important omission, noted by Cerrato, is the phrase "on my bed" from Song 3:1, ἐπὶ κοίτην μου ἐν νυξὶν ἠγάπησεν . . .

20. I expand here on Cerrato's analysis to better represent the flow of thought, clarifying several contextual details along the way for a more accurate understanding of the text, Cerrato, *Hippolytus*, 185.

- The women cry out for spiritual union with Christ as his body, "Mix this my body with your body, drink it as wine;" "Accept Eve."
- Rather than take them to heaven, Christ gives the women a mission as "apostles to the apostles."
- The apostles initially reject the news by the women because Eve was "in the habit of" deception.
- Christ appears in order to establish the testimony of the women/Eve to the resurrection.
- The disciples/Adam receive spiritual nourishment from the tree of life via the women/Eve, thus reversing the disaster of Eden.
- Once again Eve becomes a helper to her husband. Once again Adam leads Eve.
- This is why the women announced the Gospel to the disciples.
- Conclusion: it is clear from these things that Christ brings peace to the synagogue and the church is glorified.
- *On the Song of Songs* 25.4b: Martha invites Christ to mix her heart with the Spirit and to mix Christ's body with hers so that she may ascend to heaven with him.

On the basis of this eucharistic symbol of the wine mixed by Christ and the diffusion of his life to women, Martha begs to be taken away from temptation with Christ to heaven. In the Syriac fragment of *In Exodum*[21] commenting on the "quails and manna" of Exodus 16, Hippolytus says that the angel gave the news to both Mary and Martha that the Bread, that is Jesus, had been sent from the resurrection (*In Ex* 3.19). That section of the commentary ends with an encouragement about receiving the bread at the Eucharist: "Recognize this bread when you take it, O faithful, as the heavenly [bread]." Cerrato is correct to suggest that, "The commentary is homiletical in character and may well have been composed for use in the course of the liturgy of the Eucharist."[22] Indeed, this describes what appears to be a liturgical act conducted by females:

---

21. Brock, "Some New Syriac Texts," 199.
22. Cerrato, *Hippolytus*, 181, n. 21.

25.4 For this reason she says: "When I withdrew a little . . . I found him, the one whom my soul loves" (Song 3:4). Receive, O my heart! Be mixed with the Spirit, strengthen it, perfect it, so that it also may be able to join with the heavenly body. Mix this my body with [the] heavenly body. Drink it as wine, taken it, make it go up to heaven then a newly mixed cup," that [the woman] may follow the one she desires and not go astray, no longer with a bruised heel nor having touched the wood[23] of knowledge (cf. Gen 3:15). But from now on [she is] victor[24] over the tree through death . . .

25.5 Receive Eve, that no longer gives birth with sighs, for pain has been driven out, as well as sighing and distress (Is 35:10). "From now on receive Eve who now walks in proper order, receive her and know this offering which has been provided to the Father. Make Eve a new offering, no longer is she naked, no longer clothed with the fig leaf. No, but clothed through the Holy Spirit, she has put on a good garment, of which there is no corruption."[25] From now on receive Eve who now walks in proper order, receive her and know this offering which has been provided to the Father." Make Eve a new offering, no longer is she naked, no longer clothed with the fig leaf. No, but clothed through the Holy Spirit, she has put on a good garment, of which there is no corruption."[26]

25.8 From now on she will no longer either crave or proffer to men food that corrupts; she has received incorruptibility; from now on she is in unity and [is] a helper, for Adam leads Eve.[27] O good helper, with the gospel offering (or sacrificing) [it] to her husband![28] This is why the women evangelized the Disciples . . .

---

23. Or "tree," not collective.

24. Lit. "having conquered" or "one who has conquered."

25. Ambrose *De Isaac et Anima Or.* 5.43b (PL 14.542–3).

26. Ibid.

27. Bonwetch, *Hippolytus Kommentar*, 69 translates: "Adam ist Führer für Eva"; Garitte, *Traités d'Hippolyte* (CSCO 264), 48, translates "*Adam Evam ducit*," as in NTI John Ap Rev 7:17 "he leads them to springs of living water." The verb in this case is a common verb *dzghola*. I am grateful to Dr. Jeffrey Childers for this reference. Less likely, but possible, is that *udzghos* is derived from a rarer verb, *dzghoma*, and functions like verbs of loving, perceiving, feeling, having. In this case the translation would be: "Eve satisfies Adam."

28. Lit. "with the gospel to husband an offering (or with offerings)."

25.10 Now, beloved, it is clear from these things that he pacifies (*or* brings peace to) the synagogue and the church is glorified.[29]

Christian funerary art depicts women lifting a cup in the Roman catacombs in remarkable similarity to this passage.[30] Especially important are the representations in the catacomb known as *SS. Marcelino e Pietro*. Eight banquet scenes appear in the frescoes with painted inscriptions from the late third or early fourth century for the burial chambers of wealthy Roman Christians.[31] Janet Tulloch discusses the importance of these frescoes, implements of celebrations such as tables, plates, cups, amphorae and bowls, as well as the symbolism of the use of wine in the celebration of the dead as an act that affirms and strengthens the deceased family member's new status as a divine being.[32] Christians were instructed that wine was appropriately consumed in celebrations of the dead, "otherwise it would be a reproach of what God made for cheerfulness." Christians, however, were not to drink to excess, since that lead to "sorrow," "unease," and "babbling" (*Const. ap.* 8.44).[33]

The private, family nature of rites for the dead did not require the presence of a priest. According to Tulloch, "Since there were no institutionalized rites for death that would require the presence of a priest, the path was clear for women to act as leaders in funerary ceremonies and the commemoration rites after burial."[34]

Tulloch's analysis includes a selection of banquets scenes whose gestures and inscriptions suggest the representation of women offering words of benediction over the meal and toasts over the wine. On that basis, she is able to reconstruct a toast dialogue between the guest and the host in the case of two of the paintings.

---

29. Cf. Cyril of Alexandria, *Fragmenta in Canticum canticorum* (PG 69: 1285.33–46).
30. Tulloch, "Family Funerary Banquets," 165, 166.
31. Ibid., 164.
32. Ibid., 172.
33. The language of this passage is also used in *On the Song of Songs* 3.3.
34. Tulloch, "Family Funerary Banquets," 172.

Guest 1: *Misce nobis*	(Mix wine for us ...)
Host 1 *Agape*	(Love and Affection!)
Guest 2: *[P]org[e] c[a]lda*	(Offer warm water ...)
Host 2: *Irene*	(Peace!)
Guest 1: *[Po]orge calda*	(Offer warm water ...)
Host 1: *Agape*	(Love and affection!)
Guest 2: *Misce*	(Mix [wine] ...)
Host 2 *Irene*	(Peace!)

On the Song of Songs 25 has a similar dialogical scene of the two *myrrhophores* expressing desire to be taken up to heaven rather than be left to their fate on the earth. The passage does not replicate a dialogue, but appears to be based upon a toast-dialogue like that reconstructed by Tulloch.

Thus, it is true that Hippolytus establishes a theological basis for praising the *myrrhophores* as examples of the apostolicity of women in recapitulating[35] the disastrous effects of Eve's deception of Adam.[36] However, Garitte's Latin translation of the Georgian text of *In Cant.* 25.5[37] misled Cerrato and others to assume Hippolytus intended to provide theological warrant not only for female redemption but for the practice of ordaining women to ministry.[38] Taking Tulloch's research on women's funerary rites into account, Hippolytus may well be affirming an important female funerary role, while attempting to redeem that role from the influence of heretics. However, the reach of Cerrato's belief in Hippolytus' vision of women as church leaders exceeds justification. He avers that "[w]hile the commentaries are not exempt from the culture in which they were composed, signs of an attempt to transcend elements

---

35. "Recapitulate" used in the sense of "give a new head."

36. Ibid., 184.

37. *Excipe abhinc Evam in-ordinationem ambulantem*, Garitte, CSCO 264.

38. According to Cerrato, *Hippolytus*, 193, n. 21, depends on the expression "counsel of Martha" to elevate Martha as the central figure of female redemption ([*In*] *Cant.* 25.3). The redemption of woman transpires in the post-resurrection events as divine and pre-planned "counsel" (cf. "the economy of Martha"), actualized through the obedience of Martha and Mary and their vocation as "apostles to the apostles" ([*In*] *Cant.* 25.3).

of patriarchy appear."³⁹ It is going too far to suppose that the mention in *Comm. Dan.* 1.26 of both men and "women and virgins" is anything other than descriptive.⁴⁰

Hippolytus' positive view of male and female equality in relation to the *Logos* (*Antichr.* 3) is a common place with a specific application to catechesis. Part of the attractiveness of Christian teaching was this ethical appeal to people of all social stations. All have equal access to the *Logos*. Accordingly, a bit of skepticism is appropriate. Only if no other explanation will suffice must one accept the idea that Hippolytus' view of the status of women in the mission of the church truly sets the commentaries apart from their environment. *On the Song of Songs*, in its Georgian version, affirms the apostolicity of the *myrrhophores* (*In Cant.* 24–25), but what is the rhetorical function of this claim?⁴¹ One must regard as dubious Cerrato's claim that the commentary elevates the status of women in a way that accords well with the milieu of Montanism and therefore Asia Minor.

The suggestion that Hippolytus builds upon Phrygian Montanism rests on the basis of the fourth century report of Epiphanius that the Montanists esteemed Eve and ordained women (*Pan.* 49.2).⁴² Epiphanius described that Montanists χάριν διδόντες τῇ Εὐᾳ, ὅτι πρώτη βέβρωκεν ἀπὸ τοῦ ξύλου τῆς φρονήσεως "grace to Eve because she first ate of the tree of knowledge" (*Pan.* 49.2).⁴³ A little further on Epiphanius adds,

κἄν τε γὰρ γυναῖκες παρ' αὐτοῖς εἰς ἐπισκοπὴν καὶ πρεσβυτέριον καθίστανται διὰ τὴν Εὔαν, ἀκούσωσι τοῦ κυρίου λέγεντος «πρός τὸν ἄνδρα σου ἡ ἀποστροφή σου καὶ αὐτός σου κυριεύσει» "even if women among them are appointed to the office of bishop and presbyter because of Eve, they hear the Lord saying, 'Your resort shall be to your husband, and he shall rule over you.'" The resemblance to *In Cant.* 25.5–6 is stunning. However, Epiphanius is not a reliable guide for early Montanism. So, Cerrato is correct to question whether the influence is from Montanism to Hippolytus or from Hippolytus to Montanism.

---

39. Ibid.

40. Ibid. Cerrato does not, however, note that here they are seen as the particular prey of heretics.

41. Ibid.

42. Ibid., 208.

43. Heine, *Montanist Oracles and Testimonia*, 135.

His earlier suggestion, "that the Montanists of the fourth century used this Hippolytan text, or other earlier sources like it, to develop their Eve ordination argument," is surely more correct.[44] Therefore, "the commentary predates the development of the [Montanist] argument for the ordination of women."[45] Since the argument for the ordination of women appears to have been a rather late development, then the evidence of Epiphanius is useless as an indicator of the Asian provenance of *On the Song of Songs*. It is possible, however, that Epiphanius gives an indication of the Asian reception of Hippolytus' commentary in Montanist circles in the fourth century at roughly the same time that Ambrose in the West and Cyril of Jerusalem in the East were also making use of the *On the Song of Songs* in their catechetical writings.

In many respects, Cerrato's argument appears impressive. However, its application to the provenance of *On the Song of Songs* is weakened because Cerrato fails to integrate the episode of the *myrrhophores* into the rhetorical and theological framework of the commentary as a whole and to the situation in which the commentary was likely used, which, Cerrato rightly surmises, is the setting involving the Eucharist in the context of Passover initiatory rites.[46] The formal and material weaknesses of the argument should give pause. A closer look at the commentary will not support this reading. Rather, the views expressed in the commentary are consistent with a church setting in which competition for the patronage of élite women shaped a positive characterization of women within a traditionally androcentric church. So, the positive characterization of women in *On the Song of Songs* may be entirely consistent with a third century Roman setting. Furthermore, it is not likely Hippolytus himself was influenced by the New Prophecy; nothing in his exegetical writings supports such a claim.

An Issue of Translation: Ordination or Sub-ordination of Eve?

Most unfortunate for Cerrato's analysis is that Hippolytus' supposed support for female ordination is based upon a faulty translation of the

---

44. Cp. Cerrato, "Hippolytus' on the Song of Songs and the New Prophecy," 271 with item, *Hippolytus between East and West*, 208.

45. Ernst, "Martha from the Margins," 167.

46. Cerrato, *Hippolytus*, 141–45.

Georgian text. When properly understood, Hippolytus' support for women's ordination evaporates entirely.[47] The Latin translation upon which Cerrato based his interpretation has misrepresented the meaning of the Georgian text that reads:

> From now on receive Eve who now walks in proper order, 48 receive her and know this offering which has been provided to the Father. Make Eve a new offering, no longer is she naked, no longer clothed with the fig leaf. (*In Cant.* 25.5)

This translation may be compared with the reading of the Paleo-Slavic tradition:

> Receive Eve once more, the *one living firmly* ("strongly") and henceforth not naked and clothed with fig leaves.[49]

Cerrato interpreted Garitte's "*Excipe abhinc Evam in-ordinationem*[50] *ambulantem*" to mean "Receive Eve who from now on walks in

---

47. Cerrato, "Hippolytus' on the Song of Songs and the New Prophecy," 268–73. Some streams of the New Prophecy as early as the second and early third century may have supported the ordination of women as presbyters, though evidence of the practice only turns up much later. See Klawiter, "Role of Martyrdom and Persecution," 251–61.

48. See trans. n. 3 *In Cant.* 25.5.

49. Bonwetch, *Hippolytus Kommentar*, 69, my translation of the German translation. The Armenian adaptation does not represent this text and rewrites it or summarizes rather completely.

50. Cerrato's argument seems to presuppose a particular view of ordination. However, the language of ordination in ancient Christianity is difficult to pin down. Ordination has to do with ascribed honor. The difficulty of discerning when official, sacramental ordination arises out of the diversity of Christian thought and practice is illustrated by the scholarly understanding of χειροτονεία. On this issue, see Madigan and Osiek, *Ordained Women in the Early Church*, 5, 10, who note that Turner, "Cheirotoneia, cheirothesia, cheirōn," 496–504, argues that χειροτονεία was a general word for appointment, while χειρωθεσία was more specific, while Vagaggini, "L'ordinazione," 146–89, argues the opposite case. See also Tertullian, *Treatises*, 122. Tertullian used appointment language and speaks of "ordination" of widows "*cum uiduam adlegi in ordinem nisi uniuiram non concedit*" (*Ad. ux.* 1.7) but the honor of their selection or recognition was not through a rite conferring grace and office. Conversely, *Trad. ap.* 11.1–5 has "widow" being "appointed [but] not ordained (χειροτονεία) but she shall be chosen by name ... Let the widow be instituted by word only ... But she shall not be ordained, because she does not offer the oblation nor has she a liturgical ministry (λειτουργία). But ordination is for the clergy on account of their liturgical ministry. But the widow is appointed for prayer, and this is a function of all Christians." Similarly, a confessor is said to not have need of "having hands laid" upon him in order to be either deacon or presbyter. The case of Callistus himself, in *Haer.* 9.7, conforms to this tradition. When released from Sardinia, he ceases to be a slave and passes directly into freed status and

ordination."⁵¹ To support this translation, Cerrato cites the text that follows several lines below, "O new consolations! Eve has been called an apostle!" Against this translation is the consideration that the word translated *in-ordinationem* (*c'esierebit*) has the usual semantic range: "orderliness, propriety, decorum, lawfulness." A comparison with the Paleo-Slavic tradition further weakens the translation "*ordinationem*" as "ordination," especially since the material that follows immediately in both Georgian and Paleo-Slavic versions is the discussion of the clothing of the naked Eve with a beautiful garment of incorruption by the Holy Spirit. Looking more closely at the lexical issue, the Georgian text of 1 Tim 2.9 (*NTI Paul AB*)⁵² translates ἐν καταστολῇ as *c'esierebisa* = "appropriate" referring to the modesty of the woman's dress.⁵³ So, a text that also speaks of man-woman relations in terms of Adam-Eve typology used the same Georgian word, but with no hint of "ordination." If anything, both texts speak of subordination. The Georgian text of Hippolytus speaks of Eve's full restoration to her status as a lawful, non-deceptive helper of her husband, Adam. Martha and Mary are called "apostles to the apostles," but this title is not connected with the "*in-ordinatione*" of this passage in the way Cerrato imagined. The combination of *in-ordinatione . . . munus* in Garitte's translation unfortunately suggested Hippolytus was speaking of female ordination.

The notion of ordination implied in the argument appears to be anachronistic and ordination—to what office? Female apostleship? Hippolytus' text concerns witness to the resurrection—evangelism—and not prophecy. The authors concerns lie elsewhere: in recapitulating and correcting the misdeeds of the fall, providing female converts to Christianity with laudable moral examples and mission within the context of their families, and, especially pacifying the synagogue and glorifying the church. Influence from the New Prophecy is not a factor.⁵⁴

---

becomes a salaried deacon for Zephyrinus, taking care of one of his residences and then later, under Victor, director of the cemetery.

51. Cerrato's translation is perhaps a misunderstanding of Garitte's Latin translation may also mean "in regulation." Note that McConvery, "Hippolytus' Commentary," 219, corrects to "walks in order."

52. *Novum Testamentum iberice Epistolae Beati Pauli Apostoli* (Redaction AB). TITUS version by Jost Gippert, Frankfurt a/M, 14.10.1998 / 26.12.1999 / 1.6.2000 / 15.12.2002 / 16.10.2005 / 15.9.2007.

53. Thanks to Dr. Jeff Childers for alerting me to this reference.

54. McConvery, "Hippolytus' Commentary," 222, makes an appropriate comment

The Mystagogical Context of the Commentary and Female Redemption

Whatever provenance "eastern" traditions in *On the Song of Songs* may indicate, a simpler and more elegant explanation for Hippolytus' positive statements about women is available. Both *On the Song of Songs* and *On the Antichrist* are integral parts of Hippolytus' program of instruction for new Christians. Positive statements about women, together with the doctrine of the Antichrist, are a hallmark of his catechetical instruction and, indeed, later catechesis like that of Cyril of Jerusalem.[55] Candidates for baptism represented in their nakedness (*In Cant.* 7.3; 25.5) their equality before God in the radical death-and-birth baptismal rite.[56] John Chrysostom's famous words on "the abundance" of God's goodness in his first instruction for people awaiting baptism recall what seems to have been a *topos* in Christian catechetical instruction going all the way back to Hippolytus:

> Come to me all, not only rulers but also their subjects, not only the rich but also the poor, not only the free but also slaves, not only men but women, not only the young but also the old, not only those of sound body but also the maimed and those with mutilated limbs, all of you, He says, come! For such are the Master's gifts; He knows no distinction of slave and free, nor of rich and poor but all such inequality is cast aside. Come, He says, all you who labor and are burdened.[57]

Chrysostom used rhetorically balanced couplets to typify the acceptable group/identity, followed by the group/identity of some who may be disparaged and suffer rejection. Within cultural settings of the era, one group/identity is ordinarily deemed superior to another.[58]

---

at this juncture. To say that the Montanists "developed a high view of the ecclesiastical status of women, as presbyters, bishops and ministers of other ranks, runs the risk of making them just a little too modern!" Cerrato, *Hippolytus between East and West*, 212, suggested that the women of the movement were "bookish, composing and publishing literature" and that "they appear to have been concerned with the interpretation of Scripture, perhaps including exegetical commentary," but little evidence suggests this.

55. Cerrato, "Hippolytus and Cyril," 154–59.

56. See Guy, "Naked Baptism," 133–43.

57. Chrysostom, *Baptismal Instructions* 1:27 (Harkin, 1963, 33). Cf. *In Cant.* 2.9; 4.1; 6.2; 19.1; 23.1; 27.1ff.

58. Baumbach, personal communication, 2/26/2010.

The gospel ostensibly changes all of that. A comparison of this text to the famous text on equality in *On the Antichrist* reveals a similar, if not completely balanced, pairing:

> [The Word] does not esteem the rich man more highly than the poor, nor does He despise the poor man for his poverty. He does not disdain the barbarian, nor does He set the eunuch aside as no man. He does not hate the female on account of the woman's act of disobedience in the beginning, nor does He reject the male on account of the man's transgression. But He seeks all, and desires to save all, wishing to make all the children of God, and calling all the saints unto one perfect man. For there is also one Son of God (θεοῦ παῖς), by whom we too, receiving the regeneration through the Holy Spirit, desire to come all unto one perfect and heavenly man. (*Antichr.* 1.3=TLG 3.20)

The conclusion is difficult to avoid that such comparisons in the context of the open invitation to baptismal initiation were a commonplace in Christian catechetical and mystagogical instruction even a century before the Edict of Milan.

In his *Catechetical Lectures* Cyril seems to have been partly dependent upon Hippolytus. Like Hippolytus, he introduced the doctrine of the Antichrist to his hearers (*Cat.* 15.11 et passim) and took a similar approach in his treatment of women.[59] So, Cyril explicitly also mentions both men and women in his audience (*Cat.* 4.33). Like Hippolytus, Cyril teaches that both life and death come from a woman (*Cat.* 12.15, 2, Eve and Mary). Women had received the crown of martyrdom (*Cat.* 12.34). Jesus was pierced in the side specifically for the redemption of women (*Cat.* 13.22).

Cyril believed that the woman, as represented by Eve, was weaker than man and thus was susceptible to the temptation of the serpent (*Cat.* 12.5). Hippolytus appears to hold the same opinion, since Martha begs to be taken to heaven so that she will no longer be susceptible to straying, as Eve was susceptible to the serpent (*In Cant.* 25.3). Hippolytus likely believed, as did Tertullian and Cyril, that the souls of males and females are equal for salvation, but different with respect to "person," πρόσωπον or "status" (*Cat.* 4.20, 21; Tert. *De bapt.* 18). During exor-

---

59. Whether or not Ambrose may have known Cyril's *Catechetical Lectures*. See Yarnold, "The Ceremonies of Initiation," 453–63; Yarnold, "Did St. Ambrose Know the *Mystagogic Catecheses*," 184–89. It is certain Ambrose knew Hippolytus' *On the Song of Songs*.

cisms or times of waiting during the period of catechetical instruction, men and women are to occupy themselves, the men reading something, women praying or singing silently, though the women were to pray silently in order to avoid speaking in the church (1 Cor 14:34; *Procat.* 14; cp. Ambrose *De sacr.* 17). Cyril, like Hippolytus, places a high value upon confession of sin.

> Rahab is an example of sinners to whom salvation is available through repentance. Perhaps even among the women someone will say: "I have committed fornication and adultery. I have defiled my body with every excess. Can there be salvation for me?" Fix your eyes, woman, upon Rahab, and look for salvation for yourself too. For if she who openly and publicly practiced fornication was saved through repentance, will not she whose fornication preceded the gift of grace be saved by repentance and fasting (*Procat.* 2.9)?

The prophetic word concerning Jesus' death and Passover bring consolation to both apostles and women (*Cat.* 13.25). Men and women are part of the story of the resurrection so that both men and women may see themselves in the story (*Cat.* 13.39). Hippolytus is surely the source of Cyril's allusion to Song 3:2 as "the women who sought him and found him not and afterwards found him and rejoiced" (*Cat.* 14.2). Unlike Hippolytus, Cyril follows the gospel accounts that report Mary Magdalene was the primary witness of the resurrection (*Cat.* 14.12) but, like Hippolytus, he sees the events of the resurrection predicted in the Song 3:1–5. Rather than ascribe a women the status of "apostles to the apostles," Cyril suggests that God favored the women at the sepulcher above the male chief priests who lacked understanding (*Cat.* 14.14). He affirms that women were equal to the apostles as witnesses of the resurrection (*Cat.* 14.22), but women were especially susceptible to heretical influence (*Cat.* 16.8 cf. *In Cant.* 25.8–9).

During the time of Hippolytus, the appeal of Christianity to women, especially elite women, was on the increase. Furthermore, if a date early in the third century for *On the Song of Songs* is correct, it was written during the years of the Severan dynasty in which women *de facto* ruled the Empire. Thus, strong social reasons led Hippolytus to exhibit a positive attitude toward women, particularly if he were writing this commentary in Rome. A healthy dose of skepticism should be directed against too easily arguing from Hippolytus' glorification of

Martha and Mary and a historical argument supposing he supported women's ordination.

Methodologically, it is perilous to derive the historical reality from theological categories. Theology is often difficult to correlate with social reality. The rhetorical function of Hippolytus' *exempla* in *On the Song of Songs* should put the reader on alert to his persuasive purposes. One who uses Hippolytus' *exempla* for historical reconstruction must proceed with caution and attend to the rhetorical situation of the commentary. The meaning of the exegete's comments must constantly be sought in their concrete application to his audience: the church-school gathered to welcome new converts and initiate them into the mysteries of their new faith.

On the Song of Songs and Female Patronage

What is language concerning the apostleship of Martha and Mary about if not about the kind of female ordination to church leadership later practiced among the Montanists? Cerrato entertains the idea that the early traditions of Martha are more ancient, perhaps even first-century, memories of local female patronage.[60] However, female patronage in the late second and early third century church is more relevant. Martha and Mary may symbolize female patrons (or matrons) of the church so that behind the prominence of women in *On the Song of Songs* in general, and in chapters 24–25 in particular, is a tension in the community between Hippolytus and female patrons of the community.[61] Peter Brown and Charles Bobertz point to tensions between official, male clergy and patrons of the community in late antique Christianity, particularly in Rome. These "patrons" of the community were, according to Brown, often female. Women as heads of household in such a position of influence represented a danger and possible threat to the male leaders in the Christian community.[62] Bobertz traced tension

---

60. Or, "matronal loyalty," see ibid., 200.

61. See Brown, *The Body and Society*, 140–59.

62. For example Irenaeus reports (*Adv. haer.* 1.25.6) that Marcellina, a female teacher with some relation to Carpocrates, went to Rome during the time of the presbyter-bishop Anicetus (155–160 AD). She and her followers apparently used images, including images of Christ, and gave them honor. Images were completely unremarkable in Greco-Roman culture. As the so-called "statue of Hippolytus" suggests, the use of images by Christians may not have been as rare as is often thought in the early church.

between clergy and patrons as part of the motivation in the *Apostolic Tradition* for regulating meal celebrations of patrons and matrons involved in distributing needed relief among the poor through the practice of celebratory meals.[63] Osiek points out that many of the cemeteries that eventually became the property of the Roman church may have begun as private cemeteries in which some Christians were allowed to bury their dead.[64] Many of the early cemeteries in Rome bear the names of women and indicate significant Christian dependence upon female patronage in the early third century.[65] During the late second and early third centuries, as much as male church-school leaders might have wished to snub the protectresses of the community, patronesses were necessary for the survival of the house churches.[66] Some Christian women became powerful through their connection to powerful men, like Commodus' concubine Marcia, who was a Christian sympathizer if not a Christian. Others, through inheriting an estate from a wealthy husband or father, were vitally important for churches dependent upon family networks.[67] The encouragement that such women (as well as men) received to remain celibate after the death of a spouse not only ensured the house churches of a pool of vital wealth for the support of its poor, it also blurred the spiritual status between the official male leaders and matrons and patrons of the community. That the official church-school leaders were willing to accept gifts from more well-to-do members is one central economic factor that accounts for the slow rise of the developing mainstream church at the expense of churches with more radical attitudes toward wealth and marriage. Such groups had "no possibility of accumulating resources for the church and of producing generations of children reared in Christian families."[68] A distinctive of Christian history is how clergy strove to define their own position in relation to the benefactors of the Christian community. Early Christians ascribed to their leaders recognizable and perpetual tokens of superiority to the laity. Among others were evidence of a charismatic calling, the

63. Bobertz, "The Role of Patron in the *Cena Dominica*," 170–84.
64. Osiek, "Roman and Christian Burial," 257–60.
65. Ibid.
66. Brown, *Body and Society*, 146.
67. Jewish synagogues also depended upon and honored their patronesses. See Brooten, *Women Leaders*.
68. Brown, *Body and Society*, 144.

practice of perpetual continence, ordination and proper ceremonies of succession. "This in turn, gave them an exclusive role in the celebration of the Eucharist that was the central rite of the Christian community. By these precautions, the clergy ensured that leadership of the church would not gravitate unthinkingly into the hands of its wealthiest and most powerful lay benefactors."[69]

A dismissive attitude exhibited toward women benefactors (1 Tim 2:12–15) was at times and places no longer possible in 200 CE, when the inheritance of wealthy women could serve to support the clergy, the poor, and the widows of the church. Therefore, it is not debates over the participation of women in church leadership in Asia Minor in the second and third century, specifically in the context of the New Prophecy"[70] that are the background of Hippolytus' teaching about women. Rather fusses about celibacy, patronage and worries about the susceptibility of women to heretical teaching hover in the background of the teaching about women in *On the Song of Songs*. Perhaps the delicate situation of some believing women in Hippolytus' period explains why the commentary does not *condemn* the sexual activity of Tamar. Rather, Hippolytus extols the continence of Joseph (2.18, 19). It is therefore appropriate to assume that Martha and Mary—whose husbands receive no mention and who beg to be united to Christ (25.3)—represent women patronesses of the community. Such women who were also independently wealthy could edge closer to the status of clergy, if they remained celibate, than many men who were sexually active with female partners.[71] By the mid-third century, the Roman Church supported 1,500 widows and destitute persons (Eusebius, *Hist. eccl.* 6.43.11). Not all widows, however, were of low status, and such women were often mobile, active, and sometimes the only lay persons who were able to accumulate all the respected attributes of holy, clerical status.[72] They were often the most active members of the church, and, according to the references in *On the Song of Songs* 24–25 and *Comm. Dan.* 1.26, they were sometimes

---

69. Ibid.

70. Ernst, "Martha from the Margins," 166, follows Cerrato, stating: "[The statements about the ordaining of Eve and Martha and Mary as apostles to the apostles] need to be heard in the context of the debates over the participation of women in church leadership in Asia Minor in the second and third century, specifically in the context of the New Prophecy."

71. Ibid., 146.

72. Ibid.

the most willing to learn from and give support to a teacher. In the list of works found on the side of the throne of the so-called "statue of Hippolytus" is one work dedicated to a woman.

In *On the Song of Songs* 24–25, Eve is given the soteriological-typological distinction of "apostle" because of the "apostolic service" of Mary and Martha to the apostles. Eve, in this way, is an apostle to her husband Adam. Is it possible to transfer this symbolic category directly to life in Hippolytus' church-school? Or is it possible, from language and within the mental horizon of Hippolytus, to infer an official ecclesiastical status conferred on particular women in Hippolytus' church-school?

The text actually mentions nothing more than esteemed service to the apostles.[73] Is ordination to church office—perhaps like that possibly practiced later among Montanists—shining like a star, glimmering in the horizon of the commentary?[74] For his part, Cerrato speculates freely about the literary relationship between Hippolytus' Martha tradition and other possible sources. Thus, for Cerrato, Hippolytus the exegete's preference of Martha as a resurrection witness has to come from the knowledge of a tradition found in *The Epistle of the Apostles*.[75] This document, he avers, could only have been composed in the East,[76] and it is Hippolytus' source of the Martha story. At the same time Cerrato affirms that the promotion of Martha in *On the Song of Songs* must be a polemical rejection of the gnostic Christian preference of Mary Magdalene as a resurrection witness.[77] In addition, Cerrato sees connections in the

---

73. Ibid., 200.

74. Cerrato, *Hippolytus*, 208. Scholten, "John A. Cerrato, *Hippolytus between East and West*," 89, who rightly observes that unfortunately no early sources support the official activity of women in early Montanism. Nor do any early anti-Monanist authors indicate female ordination among them. Only the probably fictitious testimony of Epiphanius in the fourth century supports this claim. Cerrato dutifully reports the fact that the epigraphic evidence of early Montanism is barely preserved (ibid., 206); however, he again raises the dubious inscriptions as if they were accurate historical documents (ibid., 207). Moreover, his emphasis is on female office bearers and not female prophets, which does not fit the profile of Montanism.

75. Ibid, 198. See Scholten, 89.

76. Ibid., 257.

77. Cerrato, *Hippolytus*, 196–98; Scholten, 89. Ernst, *Martha from the Margins*, 293–303, has shown that the celebration of the resurrection of Lazarus the week before Easter in the liturgical traditions of Jerusalem and early reports of pilgrimage offer a better explanation for the spread of the tradition of Martha and Mary as witnesses of the resurrection.

commentary with specific "gnostic" *texts* (2 *ApcJac* [NHC V, 3 and V, 4] and 1 *ApcJac*) from Syrian Jewish Christianity, close neighbor to Asia Minor in the East!

Methodologically it is important to remember, "theology is always earthed in a context,"[78] and that a context affects local theology in complex ways. It will not do to reconstruct the context of *On the Song of Songs* from a single, brief passage in his commentary (*In Cant.* 24–24). Nor is the context of the commentary a few theological ideas, gnostic texts and Montanist practices. Rather, scholars must always come back to earth to social realities in houses-churches, baptismal initiation during the Passover season, audience and teacher relations, and to the purpose of the commentary in context, that is to its rhetorical situation. Like the modern crime scene investigator, scholars need to look for signs of transfer between text and context that help build up a pattern of evidence for provenance.

Hippolytus directed his commentary to the newly baptized in a situation in which women, both elite and non-elite, in larger numbers than men, were coming to the Christian faith.[79] Some of them may have been widows seeking the comfort of community and the promise of significance and belonging in the church. The point of the interpretation of Song of Songs 3:1–7 for Hippolytus is to commend Eve, symbolizing women who are blessed to participate in the community, because she has been transformed through a reversal brought about by Martha and Mary. Now Eve is restored as a helper to her husband, Adam. Now she can truly satisfy him with life-giving food (the gospel) and she can be clothed with a "garment of virtue," that replaces temporary fig leaves. If there is an ordination to female apostleship for women in *In Cant.* 25 is not the high honor of hierarchy. It is the "ordination" given to women who are active in the church, sometimes patronesses with or without influential husbands, some of whom are not believers. These women, then, are commended in the crucial role played by Martha and Mary. They honor the dead through appropriate liturgy, they "offer" the gospel to their husbands, on behalf of the church, or they even consult with the clergy, who represent the "apostles." Hippolytus may have in mind the apostolic succession in the male leaders of his church. So for Hippolytus

---

78. Young, *Theology of the Pastoral Letters*, 1.
79. Ibid.

in *On the Song of Songs*, the men, like the apostles do well to remain wary and look to confirmation from Christ alone.

> 25.9 And because of this they regarded them as deceived, because they doubted. But the reason was that it was the custom of Eve to report deception and not truth. What is this new announcement of the resurrection, O women? This is why they reckoned and (i.e., even) them as deceived. But in order that they might not appear as deceivers, but as speaking the truth, Christ was displayed to them at that time and said to them: "Peace be with you," (Jn 20:15) by this he taught that, "It was my desire, I who appeared to these women, to send them also as apostles to you."

In this way the evil effects of the fall are reversed by the recapitulation wrought through the woman: Eve. In other words, the evil initiated by Eve is reversed through Eve's representatives, Martha and Mary. In terms of social realities in the church, however, little needed changing. Hippolytus' point does not, after all, go far beyond the exhortations of 1 Peter 3:1–6. And yet, Hippolytus' emphasis provides a much more positive interpretation of what is essentially the teaching represented in 1 Tim 2:11–15 and the other household codes (Col 3; Eph 5; 1 Pet 3; 1 Cor 14:34–35).

In order to understand Hippolytus' statements on women, an ideological critique informed by a poststructuralist perspective is useful.[80] Using theory, or "any standpoint from which we might challenge a text's self understanding,"[81] helps fill in gaps left by the social-historic approach in this book and to contextualize the surprising but ultimately conventional statements of Hippolytus (*In Cant.* 25–27).

Conclusion

The synagogue and church move in and out of the spiritual narrative of the commentary in complex ways as the two mates of Christ. Like the local tradition of Peter and Paul, this third century teaching motif appears to have contributed to later Roman representations of the one church as two matrons: the church of the Circumcision and the church of the Gentiles. The mission of Martha and Mary as "apostles to the

---

80. Clark, *History, Theory, Text*, 176–81.
81. Strohm, *Theory and the Premodern Text*, xiv.

apostles" is the climax of the commentary and represents a healing of the fractious relationship of church and synagogue, Adam and Eve and the overcoming of Satan by recapitulating the disaster brought by the deceitfulness of woman in Eden.

Previous assessments of the commentary that see it as celebrating female ordination to church office based on Montanist models is misguided. A healthy skepticism informed by feminist approaches to the history of ancient Christianity provides needed perspective. The rhetorical equation of women and Eve makes use of a *topos* of Christian preaching, the universalizing and naturalizing concept of "woman." Like Hippolytus, other patristic authors saw woman's subjection to man as "natural," and the amalgamation of all women with Eve is a prime example of this *topos*.[82] In the same way as 1 Tim 2:11–15 shifts blame to Eve for the limitations placed upon women's activities and authority, Hippolytus "appeal[s] to the identification of women with Eve as a justification for their submission to men,"[83] and ultimately Hippolytus' text has nothing to do with office-holding in "the church" as conceived by him. Still, overlapping domestic roles and church roles provided rich areas of potential conflict. At issue would have been "what is church"? The commentarie's exaltation of women served, by way of compensation, as a justification for woman's "*exclusion* from priesthood and public teaching office."[84] There is no "ordination" of women *In Cant.* 25, rather, congratulation are given to the "ladies." So the question arises whether Hippolytus truly contrasts with the tone of other church fathers, Tertullian in particular:

> You are the Devil's gateway; you are the unsealer of that tree; you are the first foresaker of that divine law; you are the one who persuaded him whom the Devil was not brave enough to approach; you so lightly crushed the image of God, the man Adam; because of your punishment, that is, death, even the Son of God had to die. And you think to adorn yourself beyond your "tunics of skins" (Gen 3.21) (Tertullian, *Cult. fem.* 1.1, 2; CCL 1.343)?

---

82. Clark, ed. *Ascetic Piety*, 31–2.

83. "The Church's ever-increasing need for funds opened an avenue for women to gain importance in Christian circles despite their decisive exclusion from positions of ecclesiastical leadership," Clark, "Patrons, Not Priests," 253–74; Clark, "Ideology, History, and the Construction of 'Woman,'" 177.

84. Ibid.

Tertullian's famous "gateway" passage (quoted in Simone de Beauvior's *The Second Sex*[85]) may not be as far from Hippolytus the exegete's treatment of women as one might like to think.[86] What Hippolytus gives with one hand during catechetical instruction to beginners, he could easily take back with the other hand during a controversy with women he considered unruly or too demanding. Finally, the way Hippolytus used the characterization of women as a mode of thought fits well within a Roman milieu at the beginning of the third century.

---

85. De Beauvoir, *The Second Sex*, 167.
86. On Tertullian's gateway passage, see Church, "Sex and Salvation," 83–101.

Bibliography

Ambrose. *Expositio psalmi CXVIII: Pars V*. 2nd ed. Ambrosius Opera: Ambrosius 5. Edited by M. Petschenig and Michaela Zelzer. Corpus scriptorum ecclesiasticorum latinorum 62. Vienna: Verlag der österreichischen Akademie der Wissenschaften, 1999.

Baumbach, Gerard F. University of Notre Dame, personal correspondence, 2/26/2010.

Beauvoir, Simone de. *The Second Sex*. Translated and edited by and H. M. Parshley. New York: Knopf, 1953.

Bobertz, Charles A. "The Role of Patron in the *Cena Dominica* of Hippolytus' Apostolic Tradition." *Journal of Theological Studies* 44 (1993) 170–84.

Bonwetsch, G. Nathanael. "Studien zu den Kommentaren Hippolyts zum Buche Daniel und Hohen Liede." *Texte und Untersuchungen zur Geschichte der altchristlichen Literatur* 16.2. Leipzig: Hinrichs, 1897.

———. "Hippolyts Kommentar zum Hohenlied auf Grund von N. Marrs Ausgabe des Grusisinischen Textes." *Texte und Untersuchungen*, NF 8.2c (1902) 1–108.

Brock, Sebastian. "Some New Syriac Texts Attributed to Hippolytus." *Museon* 94.1–2 (1981) 177–200.

Brooten, Bernadette J. *Women Leaders in the Ancient Synagogue: Inscriptional Evidence and Background Issues*. Brown Judaic Studies 36. Chico, CA: Scholars, 1982.

Brown, Peter. *The Body and Society: Men, Women, and Sexual Renunciation in Early Christianity*. Lectures on the History of Religions 13. New York: Columbia University Press, 1988.

Cerrato, John A. "Hippolytus' On the Song of Songs and the New Prophecy." *Studia Patristica* 31 (1997) 268–73.

———. *Hippolytus between East and West: The Commentaries and the Provenance of the Corpus*. Oxford Theological Monographs. Oxford: Blackwell, 2002.

———. "Hippolytus and Cyril of Jerusalem on the Antichrist: When Did an Antichrist Theology First Emerge in Early Christian Baptismal Catechesis?" In *Apocalyptic Thought in Early Christianity*, edited by Robert Daly, 154–59. Holy Cross Studies in Patristic Theology and History. Grand Rapids: Baker Academic, 2009.

Clark, Elizabeth A. "Patrons, Not Priests: Gender and Power in Late Ancient Christianity." *Gender & History* 2 (1990) 253–74.

———. *History, Theory, Text: Historians and the Linguistic Turn*. Cambridge: Harvard University Press, 2004.

Chappuzeau, Gertrud. "Die Auslegung des Hohenliedes durch Hippolyt von Rom." *Jahrbuch für Antike und Christentum* 19 (1976) 45–81.

Chrysostom, John. *Catecheses baptismales = Taufkatechesen*. Fontes Christiani 6. Edited by Reiner Kaczynski. Freiburg: Herder, 1992.

Church, F. Forrester. "Sex and Salvation in Tertullian." *Harvard Theological Review* 68 (1975) 83–101.

Cyril of Alexandria, *Fragmenta in Canticum canticorum*. PG 69: 1285.33–46.

Ernst, Allie M. "Martha from the Margins: An Examination of Early Christian Traditions about Martha." PhD dissertation, University of Queensland, 2006.

———. *Martha from the Margins: the Authority of Martha in Early Christian Tradition*. Supplements to Vigiliae Christianae. Leiden: Brill, 2009.

Garitte, Gérard, editor. *Traités d'Hippolyte sur David et Goliath, sur le Cantique des cantiques et sur l'Antéchrist.* Corpus Scriptorum Christianorum Orientalis; Sriptiores Iberici 15 263. Louvain: Sécretariat du CorpusSCO, 1965.

Guy, Laurie. "Naked Baptism in the Early Church: The Rhetoric and the Reality." *Journal of Religious History* 27.2 (2003) 133–43.

Haskins, Susan. *Mary Magdalen: Myth and Metaphor.* New York: Harcourt, Brace, 1994.

Heine, Ronald E. *The Montanist Oracles and Testimonia.* Patristic Monograph Series 14. Macon, GA: Mercer University Press, 1989.

Kessler, Herbert L. "The Meeting of Peter and Paul in Rome: An Emblematic Narrative of Spiritual Brotherhood." *Dumbarton Oaks Papers* 41 (1987) 265–75.

Klawiter, Frederick C. "The Role of Martyrdom and Persecution in Developing the Priestly Authority of Women in Early Christianity: A Case Study of Montanism." *Church History* 49 (1980) 251–61.

Koester, Helmut. *Introduction to the New Testament.* 2 vols. Rev. ed. Berlin: de Gruyter, 2000.

Kraeling, Carl H. *A Greek Fragment of Tatian's Diatessaron from Dura [Texts and Documents III].* SD 3. Edited by Kirsopp Lake and Silva Lake. London: Christophers, 1935.

Lowrie, Walter. *Art in the Early Church.* Pantheon, 1947.

Madigan, Kevin, and Carolyn Osiek. *Ordained Women in the Early Church: A Documentary History.* Baltimore: Johns Hopkins University Press, 2005.

McConvery, Brendan. "Hippolytus' Commentary on the Song of Songs and John 20: Intertextual Reading in Early Christianity." *Irish Theological Quarterly* 71 (2006) 211–22.

Novum Testamentum iberice Epistolae Beati Pauli Apostoli [The Old Georgian Version of St. Paul's Epistles] (Redaction AB). ed. K. Dzoçenidze and K. Danelia, Pavles epistoleta kartuli versiebi / Gruzinskie versii poslanij Pavla, Tbilisi 1974 (dzveli kartuli enis katedris šromebi, 16) ed. by Jost Gippert and Vaxtang Imnaišvili, Frankfurt a/M and Tbilisi, 1988–1998; v.l. ed. by Sopiko Sardzeladze and Daredzan Tvaltvadze, Tbilisi, 2005; TITUS version by Jost Gippert, Frankfurt, 14.10.1998 / 26.12.1999 / 1.6.2000 / 15.12.2002 / 16.10.2005 / 15.9.2007.

Nurnberg, Rosemarie. "Apostolae Apostolorum: Die Frauen am Grab als erste Zeuinnen der Auferstehung in der Väterexegese." In *Stimuli*, edited by G. Schöllgen, C. Scholten and E. Dassmann, 228–42. Jahrbuch für Antike und Christentum 23. Münster: Aschendorff, 1996.

Osiek, Carolyn. "Roman and Christian Burial Practices and the Patronage of Women." In *Commemorating the Dead: Texts and Artifacts in Context: Studies of Roman, Jewish and Christian Burials*, edited by Laurie Brink and Deborah Green, 243–70. Berlin: de Gruyter, 2008.

———. "Patronage of Women in Early Christianity." In *Feminist Companion to Patristic Literature*, edited by Amy-Jill Levine and Maria Mayo Robbins, 173–92. FCNT. London: T. & T. Clark, 2008.

Marcel Richard, "Les fragments du commentaire de S. Hippolyte sur les Proverbes de Salomon: Museon" 78 (1965) 257–90; 79 (1966) 61-94.

Peppa, Constantina. *Die Töchter der Kirche Christi und die frohe Botschaft des Sohnes Gottes: Eine Studie über die aktive Präsenz der Frauen und ihre besonderen*

Dienste in Frühchristentum und Gemeinden der ungeteilten Alten Kirchen. Athens: Epektas, 1998.

Schöllgen, Georg, Clemens Scholten, and Ernst Dassmann, editors. *Stimuli: Exegese und ihre Hermeneutik in Antike und Christentum. Festschrift für Ernst Dassmann.* Jahrbuch für Antike und Christentum 23. Münster: Aschendorff, 1996.

Scholten, Clemens. "Hippolytus Between East and West: the Commentaries and the Provenance of the Corpus." *Vigiliae christianae* 59 (2005) 85–92.

Smith, Yancy. "Hippolytus' Commentary *On the Song of Songs* in Social and Critical Context." PhD dissertation, Brite Divinity School at Texas Christian University, 2009.

Spier, Jeffrey. *Picturing the Bible: The Earliest Christian Art.* New Haven: Yale University Press, 2007.

Strohm, Paul. *Theory and the Premodern Text.* Medieval Cultures 26. Minneapolis: University of Minnesota Press, 2000.

Tulloch, Janet H. "Women Leaders in Family Funerary Banquets." In *A Woman's Place: House Churches in Earliest Christianity*, by Carolyn Osiek and Margaret Y. Macdonald, 164–93. Minneapolis: Fortress, 2006.

Turner, Charles H. "*Cheirotoneia, Cheirothesia, Cheirōn* and the Accompanying Verbs." *Journal of Theological Studies* 24 (1922–23) 496–504.

Tertullian, *Treatises on Marriage and Remarriage: To His wife, An Exhortation to Chastity, Monogamy.* Translated by W. P. Le Saint. Westminster, MD: Newman, 1951.

Vagaggini, Cipriano. "L'ordinazione delle diaconesse nella tradizione greca e bizantina." *Orientalia christiana periodica* 40 (1974) 146–89.

Weyermann, Maja. "The Typologies of Adam-Christ and Eve-Mary, and their Relationship to One Another." *Anglican Theological Review* 84 (2002) 609–26.

Yarnold, Edward J. "The Ceremonies of Initiation in the *De Sacramentis* and *De Mysteriis* of St. Ambrose." In *Studia Patristica* 10, edited by F. L. Cross, 453–63. Berlin: Akademie, 1970.

———. "Did St. Ambrose Know the *Mystagogic Catecheses* of St. Cyril of Jerusalem?" *Studia Patristica* 12, edited by E. Livingstone, 184–89. Berlin: Akademie, 1975.

Young, Frances M. *The Theology of the Pastoral Letters.* New Testament Theology. Cambridge: Cambridge University Press, 1994.

Index of Ancient Sources

FIRST TESTAMENT

Genesis

1:1	93
1:27	110, 112, 112n36
2:7	202
2:24	110–12, 112n36
3	307
3:15	318
3:21	334
6:1–4	295n15, 302n51
20:11	135
24:10–61	196
29:1–20	196
38:11	124

Exodus

2:16–22	196
7:4	131
12:12	131
15:20	259
16	317
17:6	197n19
22:22	127

Leviticus

18:25	109
18:28	109
19:14	135
19:32	135

Numbers

12:1–15	259
20:11	197n19
31:2–3	131

Deuteronomy

4:10	135
10:18	127
24:19–21	127
27:19	127
32:18	198
32:35	132

Judges

4:4	259
11:12	236n15
15:7	131
16:28	131

1 Samuel

27:3	124
30:5	124

2 Samuel

2:2	124
3:3	124
14:5	124

1 Kings

3:13	236n15
17	124, 141–42
17:9	141
17:12	141
17:18	141, 236n15

2 Kings
2:23–24	159
22:14	259

2 Chronicles
19:7	135
34:22	259
35:21	236n15

Nehemiah
6:12–15	259
6:14	259

Job
31:16–19	127
38:28–29	199

Psalms
2:7	198
22:9–10	199
94:6	127
111:10	135
146:9	127

Proverbs
1:7	135
20:30	137
25:15	132

Song of Songs
3:1–7	332
3:1–5	327
3:1–4	316
3:4	318

Isaiah
1:17	127
26:17–18	198
26:19	198
35:10	318
42:14	198
49:15	199
66:7–8	198
66:9	199
66:12–13	199

Jeremiah
7:6	127
22:3	127
23:28	142

Ezekiel
13:17–23	260
13:7–9	260
13:18	262
22:7	127
36:25–27	195, 195n13
37:5	202
44:22	127
47:1	197n19

Daniel
1:20	82n8
2:37–45	82n8
6:4	82n8

Hosea
14:8	236n15

Joel
3:1	255, 260

Zechariah
7:9–10	127

Malachi
3:5	127

SEPTUAGINT

Deuteronomy
1:17	135

Ruth
4:16	193

Job
32:21	135

SECOND TESTAMENT

Matthew
1:2–20	192
1:18–25	109
1:18–19	109
4:17	93
5:16	95
5:25	131
5:31–32	109
5:32	109n25
5:34	92
5:40	138
5:44–45	93
5:44	94
5:45	81, 91, 93–94, 97
5:48	94
6:1–6	299n36
6:1–4	305
6:1	94
6:4	94
6:6	94, 95
6:8	91
6:9–13	93, 97
6:9–10	82
6:9b–10	93
6:9	95–96
6:10	93–95, 97
6:11	93
6:12	93
6:13	93
6:14–15	92–3
6:15	94
6:18	94
6:26	91, 93, 97
6:32	92
7	130
7:21	94–95
7:36–50	130
7:37	130
9:9–13	152n3
10:2	108n20
10:3–5	108n20
10:7–8	94
10:15	94
10:16–31	94
10:20	95
10:29	92–93
10:31	92, 94
10:32–33	94, 97
10:32	94
11:25	93, 95–96
11:25–26	95
11:25–27	94–95, 98–99
11:27	93
11:29–30	306n64
12:50	94–95
13:11	113
13:43	82, 94
15:13	94–95, 97
15:17	197n18
15:21–28	140, 144
16:17	94
16:22–23	258
18:2	110
18:10	95
18:14	94
18:18–20	99
18:29	92
18:35	93–94
19–20	93, 98n49, 103
19	103, 105–8, 118–19
19:3–15	103–4, 116–21
19:3–12	97n46
19:3–9	105–6, 118
19:3–5	121
19:3	108, 110

Matthew (cont.)

19:4–6	110–11, 117
19:4	110
19:5	110
19:6	111, 114, 118
19:7	108
19:7–9	108, 110
19:7–8	107
19:8–9	108–9
19:9	109, 109n25
19:10–12	105, 117–18
19:11–15	116
19:11	112–13
19:12	112–15, 117–18
19:12	107
19:13–15	106, 110, 118
19:14	107, 115, 277
19:16–30	104
19:16–22	105
19:16	107
19:23	107
19:24	107
19:27	105, 106, 144
19:28	107
19:29	106
20:23	94
21:15	217
22:1–3	117
22:7	117
22:23–28	143
23:9	93, 95–6
24:36	94–95
25:29	94
25:34	82, 93–94, 97–98
25:42	94
26:6–13	152n2
26:29	95
26:39	94–95
26:42	94–95
26:53	93, 95, 98
27:45	199
28:9	314
28:10	315
28:18–20	95

Mark

2:13–17	152n3
7:19	197n18
7:24–30	140
8:29	236
8:32–33	258
9:37	277
10	108, 108n20
10:13–16	116
10:28	144
11:18	227
11:24	236
12:19–33	143
12:24–25	294n13
12:40	143
14:3–9	152n2
14:61–64	228
15:34	199

Luke

1:3	155
1:5–6	257n18
1:27	256
1:41	197n18
1:44	197n18
2:7	201
2:21	197n18
2:22–38	265
2:25	257n18, 260
2:36	140, 260
2:36–38	124, 140
2:36–37	140
2:37–38	140
2:37	260
2:38	140, 260
3:5	201
4:10	201
4:25–27	124
4:25–26	140–41
4:26	124
4:34	228
4:39	139
5:11	144
5:28	144

Luke (cont.)

5:29	152n3
5:29–39	152
5:30	152n3
6:19	263
6:21	142
6:29	138
6:37	138
7:11–17	140
7:11–15	257n18
7:12	142
7:13	142
7:15	142–3
7:36–50	151n1, 152, 152n2, 153, 162
7:36–42	139
7:37–50	257n18
7:38	201
7:39	162
7:41–42	162
7:43	162
7:44–46	162
7:47	162
8:1–3	139, 139n54
8:19	139
8:21	139
8:26–39	257n18
8:41–56	257n18
8:44	263
9:49	267
10:5–7	172
10:30	142
10:33	142
10:38–42	139
10:38	257n18
11	137n46
11:7	136
11:15	266
11:19	138
11:27–28	140
11:27	197n18
11:37–54	151n1, 152, 152n2, 153, 158, 162
11:39–44	158, 163
11:42	158
11:43	158
11:44	158
11:45	158
11:46–52	163
11:46	158
11:47	158
11:48	158
11:49	158n39
11:53–54	158, 160
12:13	128
12:14	138
12:16–21	144
12:16–20	138
12:42–46	138
12:58	131, 138, 148
14:1–24	151, 151n1, 152, 152n2, 153, 162–64, 169
14:1	164
14:2–6	164
14:2	165
14:3	163
14:4	165
14:5	163, 165
14:6	163, 165
14:7–11	165, 166n72
14:8–11	167
14:8–10	165
14:11	166–67
14:12–15	167
14:15	168
14:16–24	168
14:17	168
14:18–19	168
14:20	168
14:21	168n81
14:24	169
14:44–46	162
15:11–32	138
15:16	197n18
15:18	136
15:21	136
15:20	142
15:24	142

Luke (cont.)

15:30	143
16:1–8a	137–38
16:19–31	144
16:23	193
17:11–16	124
17:22	139
18:1–8	125, 131, 140, 144
18:1	124, 138
18:2–5	125, 127
18:2	134
18:3–5	126
18:4	134, 136
18:5	124, 136
18:6	131, 142
18:7	124, 138
18:8	132, 138–39
18:15–17	116
18:18–25	143
19:2	257n18
19:22	138
19:30	201
20:9–16	138
20:27–33	124
20:28–33	140, 143
20:33	143
20:34–35	294n13
20:35	143
20:46–47	143
20:47	124, 128, 140
21:1–4	140, 143–44
21:2–3	124
21:3–4	144
22:14–38	152n2
22:56	258
22:66	228
23:2	228
23:5	228
23:28	140
23:29	197n18
23:50–51	257n18
24:30–32	152n2
24:36–49	152n2

John

1–4	235
1–2	259
1:3	192–93
1:12–13	192–93
1:12	201
1:13	193, 193n6, 205
1:14	205, 210
1:18	193, 193n9
1:24	216n2
1:26–34	194
2:1–11	194, 201, 234
2:3	194
2:4	194, 237
2:4a	235
2:11	194
2:13–25	217
2:13–22	228
2:13	221
2:18–25	217
2:18	221
2:19–20	221
2:21–22	221
2:23	221
2:36–28	261
3:1–21	201
3:1–2	221
3:3	192n5, 195
3:3–8	195
3:4	192, 195
3:5–8	192n5
3:5	195, 205
3:7	195
3:16–17	220
3:16	219n10
3:22	225
3:29	196
4	140, 221
4:1–3	223
4:1	221–22
4:2	221
4:4–42	196
4:9	196
4:10	196

Index of Ancient Sources   345

John (cont.)

4:12	196
4:14	196
4:15	196
4:20	217
4:39	196
5:15	196
5:16–18	221
5:16	223
5:18	221, 223, 225
6:1	225
6:14–15	222
6:14	222
6:30	222
6:42	246
6:51	219n10, 231
7:1–9	240
7:1	222, 225
7:5	241
7:15	222
7:19–31	222
7:19	222
7:20	222, 225
7:25–31	223
7:25–26	222
7:30	194, 222
7:31	222
7:32–52	222
7:32	216n2, 223, 225
7:32	216n2, 222
7:37–52	223
7:37–39	197
7:37–38	197, 197n19
7:40–52	228
7:43–44	222
7:45–52	216n2, 222
7:45	216n2, 222
7:53	222
8:20	194
8:37	225
8:41	192n5
8:48	225
9:2	192n5
9:13	216n2
9:15	216n2
9:16	216n2, 222–23, 228
9:19	192n5
9:20	192n5
9:22	223
9:32	192n5
9:34	192n5
9:40	216n2
10:11	219n10
10:15–16	219n10
10:15	219n10, 231
10:18	226
10:24–25	228n17
10:31–39	223
10:31	223
10:33–39	223
10:33	221, 223
10:36	228n17
10:38–42	225
10:39–42	223
10:39	223, 225
10:40	225
10:41–42	223
11	215
11:42–43	228
11:45–53	215, 217, 220–24, 226–28, 230–31
11:45–46	216
11:47–48	223
11:47	216, 216n2, 217, 219
11:48	217
11:50–52	217
11:49	218
11:49–50	218
11:50	231
11:51	219
11:51–52	220
11:52	219
11:53	216, 219
11:54	219, 225
11:57	194, 216n2, 219, 225
12:1	219
12:9–11	223
12:19	216n2, 228

John (cont.)

12:23	194
12:36	223
12:37	223
12:42–43	223
12:42	216n2
13	215
13:1	194, 220, 226
13:32	193n9
14:6	297
14:16–17	297n29
14:26	297n29
15:12–13	220, 226
16:12–13	297n29
16:20–22	194, 198, 200
16:21–22	198
16:21	192
17:20–22	219n10
18:3	216, 216n2, 224n14
18:12–24	224
18:12	224n14
18:13	218
18:14	218, 218n8
18:19	228
18:24	218
18:25–28	224
18:28–31	229
18:28	218
18:33	224
18:35	217–18
18:36	224
18:37	192n5, 224
18:39	224
19	246
19:1–3	224
19:12	224
19:14–16	224
19:15	224
19:16	224
19:19–22	224
19:25–27	234–37
19:25	201
19:26	194
19:27	194
19:30	195, 195n12, 226
19:34–35	201n29
19:34	191–92, 193n7, 195, 197, 201, 248n57
19:35	194
19:39	201
19:40	201
20:1–2	200
20:2	200n25
20:11–18	200
20:15	333
20:19–23	202
20:20	200
20:22	202
21	248n58

Acts

1:14	210n57
2	258–59
2:9	255
2:16–21	255, 268
2:17–20	260
3:2–8	257n18
3:18	261
3:21	261
3:24–25	261
5:1–6	257n18
5:34	257n18
5:44	299
6:1–6	140n56
7:42	261
7:52	261
8:9–13	267
8:9	257n18
8:18–19	267
8:27	257n18
8:40	253n3
9	258n22
9:1–9	287n55
9:10–17	257n18
9:12	287n55
9:30	253n3
9:33	257n18
9:36	257n18

Index of Ancient Sources 347

Acts (cont.)
9:39–41	140n56, 185
10	253
10:1—11:18	172
10:1–2	257n18
10:1	253n3
10:24	253n3
10:42	138
10:43	261
11:11	253n3
11:27	261
11:28	261
12:4–10	255n10
12:13	182, 258
12:12–17	180
12:12	4
12:15	259
12:19	253n3
12:43	299
13:1	261
13:6	257n18, 261
13:15	261
13:27	261
13:40	261
14:8–18	267
14:8–10	257n18
14:11–13	255n10
15	253n4
15:15	261
15:27	261
15:32	261
16	180–81
16:1–2	257n18
16:11–15	172
16:14–15	257n18
16:14	255n10
16:15	4, 177
16:40	4
16:16–18	259
16:23–29	255n10
16:25–34	172
17:6	138
18:1–11	172
18:2	255n10
18:2–3	184
18:2–4	257n18
18:9–11	287n55
18:15	138
18:18—9:1	184
18:18	184
18:21	257n18
18:22	253n3
19:2	268
19:12	264
19:13–16	267
19:24	255n10, 257n18
19:27	255n10
19:38	255n10
20:7–12	183
20:9–12	257n18
21:4	265
21:7–18	256
21:8–9	182
21:8	253n3, 254n6
21:9	256, 258, 261, 294n13
21:10	261
21:11	256
21:13	269
21:16	253n3
22:3–16	287n55
22:6–16	258n22
22:17–21	287n55
23:11	287n55
23:16–19	183
23:23	253n3
23:33	253n3
24:10	138
24:14	261
25:1	253n3
25:4	253n3
25:6	253n3
25:13	253n3
26:9–18	287n55
26:12–18	258n22
26:22, 27	261
27:13–44	253n3
28:4–6	255n10
28:23	261

Romans

12:19	131
16:1	4
16:3–5	184
16:3	184

1 Corinthians

1:11	183n38
1:16	172
4:14	135
6:13	197n18
6:16	111
6:19	184
7	108, 300
7:1–5	294
7:7–9	294
7:12–16	173
8:1–3	xxxv
9:27	137
10:27–33	xxxv
11	306–7
11:2–16	300, 307
11:3	301
11:5	260
11:7	302, 305
11:8–9	302, 307
11:10	302, 306
11:12	307
11:16	296, 299
14:19	286
14:30	xxxiv
14:34–35	307, 333
14:34	260, 303, 327
16:15	172

2 Corinthians

2:6	276
2:7	276
10–13	275–78, 285, 287
10:1	276
10:2	277
10:4	277
10:7	277
10:9–11	276
10:11	276–77
11:1—12:28	285n51
11:1—12:18	285
11:1—12:10	285n51
11:1	276
11:5	277, 287
11:17	276
11:12–13	276
11:12	276
11:13	276–77
11:21b–23	285n51
11:24–27	285n51
11:28–29	285n51
12	278
12:1–10	272, 274, 279–81, 285, 287
12:1–6	274, 284
12:1b–4	285n51
12:2–10	275
12:2–4	272, 274–75, 277, 281, 285–86, 288
12:2–3	275–77
12:3	276–77
12:4	283
12:5	276–77, 286
12:7–10	272, 274–75, 284–87, 287n55
12:7–9	285n51
12:9a	286, 288
12:10	278
12:11	287

Galatians

1:6–9	278
1:12ff.	287n55
2:11	253n4
3:1ff.	278
3:28	xxxvi
4:4	192, 301
4:19	209
5:1	306
5:16–26	278
5:17	278
6:1	277–78

Ephesians

5	333
5:21—6:9	176
5:21–33	176
5:32	111

Philippians

1:1	4, 44
1:1–2	4
2:3–4	44
3:28	xxxiii
4:2	4, 44
4:4–7	xxxiii
4:15	45
4:18	45
4:21–31	xxxiii
5:1–13	xxxiii

Colossians

3	333
3:18—4:1	5, 44
4:15–16	5
4:15	4, 44, 173

1 Thessalonians

1:3	139
2:7	209
2:13	139
5:17	139

2 Thessalonians

3:14	135

1 Timothy

2:9	324
2:11–15	333–34
2:11f.	260, 307
2:12–15	330
2:12	303
3:11	4, 256
4:11–15	44
5	130
6:1	306
6:1–2	173

2 Timothy

1:3	139

Titus

2:8	135

Philemon

20	45

Hebrews

10:30	132

1 Peter

3	333
3:1–6	333
3:1	173

1 John

5:6–8	201n29

Revelation

2:14	xxxv
2:20	xxxv, 261
7:17	318n27
10:9	197n18
12:1–6	xxxvii
16:13	261
19:20	261
20:10	261

~

APOCRYPHA

Judith

9:2	131
16:22	141

Wisdom of Solomon

6:7	135
15:11	202

1 Maccabees

1:6	82n8
1:16	82n8
1:41	82n8
8:18	82n8
11:1	82n8

Sirach

1:1–10	xxxvii
4:11–18	xxxvii
4:22	135
6:18–31	xxxvii
24:1–12	xxxvii
24:13–14	xxxvii
24:19–21	xxxvii
32:12	135
35:15b–25	131
35:17–18	131
35:17	127
35:18	127

PSEUDE-PIGRAPHIA

1 Enoch

1–36	295n15
7:1	266
42:1–3	xxxvii

Testament of Job

6–7	263
21–26	263
46–52	263
46–53	264
47:11	263
48:1	263
48:2	263
48:3	263
48:4	263
49:2	263
50:1	263
51	263
51:1	263
51:3	263
52:1	263

EARLY JUDAIC DOCUMENTS

m. Baba Bathra

8:1	129

m. Ketubot

4:2	129

b. Sanhedrin

4b	134n35

m. Sanhedrin

1:1	134n35

y. Sanhedrin

7:9, 25d	266

DEAD SEA SCROLLS

1QH

3:7–18	200

EARLY CHRISTIAN DOCUMENTS

Aelred of Rievaulx

De institutione

31	203n38

Index of Ancient Sources   351

Aelred of Rievaulx (cont.)
Opera omnia
1:671   203n38

Ambrose
De Isaac et Anima Or.
5:43b   218n25
De sacramentis
17   327
On Virgins
1:5   202

Apostolic Constitution
8:44   319

Clement of Alexandria
The Instructor
1:6   202

Cyril of Jerusalem
Catechetical Lectures
4:20–21   326
4:33   326
12:15   326
12:34   326
13:22   326
13:35   327
13:39   327
14:2   327
14:12   327
14:14   327
14:22   327
15:11   326
16:8   327
25:3   326

Fragmenta in Canticum canticorum
1285:33–46   319n29

Procatechesis
2:9   327
14   327

Didache
11:8   261

Epiphanius
Panarion
49:2   321

Eusebius
Ecclesiastical History
3:30.1   256
3:39.9   269
6:43.11   330

Gospel of Thomas
21   116n49
22   104, 110, 114–21
22:1–7   116
22:1–3   116
37   116n49
114   113

Hippolytus
Expository Treatise against the Jews
19:31   312n5

Fragments on Proverbs
26vat1:23   312n5
54:31   312n5

On the Antichrist
1:3   326
3   321

On Daniel
1:26   321, 330–31

Hippolytus (cont.)

On Exodus
3:19	317

On the Song of Songs
2:9	325n57
2:18–19	330
2:18	313–14
2:29	313–14, 314n11, 315
2:32	314n11
3:3	319n33
4:1	325n57
6:1	312
6:2	325n57
7:3	325
8:1	314n11
8:8	313, 313n8
14:14	314n12
17:2	314n11
19:1	325n57
23:1	325n57
24–25	314, 316, 321, 328, 330, 332
24:2	315
25	320, 332, 334
25:1	315
25:3	315
25:3	314, 315, 320n38, 330
25:4	313, 318
25:4b	317
25:5–6	321
25:5	318, 320, 323, 325
25:8–9	327
25:8	318
25:9	333
25:10	314, 319
25–27	333
26:3	314n11
27:1f.	325n57
27:2	314

Refutatio omnium haeresium
9:7	323n50

Traditio apostolic
11:1–5	323n50

Irenaeus

Adversus haereses
1:25.6	328n62

Jerome

Epistles
108:8	269

John Chrysostom

Baptismal Instructions
1:27	325n57

Origen

Contra Celsus
1:28	266
1:71	266
2:32	266
2:48	266
2:55	181

Shepherd of Hermas

Mandata
11:2	262
11:3	262
11:5	262, 262n29
11:8–12	261
11:8	262
11:12	262
11:17	262

Visions
2.4.3	44

Tatian

Fragments of the Diatessaron
1–5	315n13

Tertullian

Ad uxorum
1:7	323n50

Against Marcion
2:11	295

Apologeticus pro Christianis
6:4–6	308

De cultu feminarum
1:1	334
1:2	334

De baptismo
17:2	308
18	326

De monogamia
10:7	308

De pallio
4:9	308

On the Veiling of Virgins
1:1	296–97
1:2	297
1:3	297
1:4	297
2:1	298
2:2	299
2:3	299, 304
3:1	299
3:2	299
3:4–5	300
3:5	300
4:1	300
4:2–4	300
5	307n66
5:2	301
5:5	301
6:1	301
6:4	301
7	307n68
7:2	301, 302n49
7:3	301–2, 302n50
7:4	302n52
7:6	302
7:7	302
8:5	303
9	307n69
9:1	308
9:2	303, 307
9:4	303
10:1	307n66
13:2	305
15:3	305
16:1	305
16:2	305–6
17:1–3	306n62
17:1	306

GRECO–ROMAN SOURCES

Aeschylus

Choephori
	20n35

Appian

Cival Wars
2:16.106	83n16
2:20.114	83n16

Aristeas

Letters
2:10–11	154n18
2:32	154n17
187–294	155n21

Aristophanes

Acharnesnses
366	165n70

Ecclesiazusae
136	165n70

Equites
87	165n70
157	165n70
344	165n70

Nubes
825	165n70

Thesmophoriazusae
206	165n70

Aristotle

Poetics
5:1449a	159n47

Politics
1:1.5–12	81
1:5.1–7	81

Rhetoric
2:2.12	159n48

Athenaeus

Deipnophistae
3:9	154
3:74f–75a	155n21
3:96–97	157n28
3:97a	157n29
3:97c	157n30
3:99e	157n31
3:100b	157n32
4:156a	157n33
4:157a–158d	157n34
4:158d	157n35
4:159a–b	157n36
4:159c	158n37
4:159e	158n38
4:4:165–67	155n21
4:128, 143–56	154n12
5:193c–d	154n12

Augustus

Res Gestae
1	85–87
1, 7	86
2	87
3	85–86, 88
4	88
4–6	88
5	86, 87–88
6	87
8	87
10	88
11	88
12	86, 88
13	86–8
14	88
15	86–87
16	86, 88
17	86
18–21	86
18	86
22–23	86
24	86
25–30	87
25	86, 88
26	86
27	86
28	88
29	86, 87
31	87
32	87
30	86
31–33	86
31–32	88
34	87–88
35	84–85, 88

Index of Ancient Sources

Cicero
De Domo Sua
94	84n20

De oratore
2:58.236	160n51
2:60.244–45	160n52

In Defense of Rabirius
27	83n15

In Pisonem
6	83n15

On Divination
1:3	83n14

Pro Sestio
121	83n15

Dio Cassius
44:4.4	83n16
43:17.2	84
43:17.5–6	84
43:17.6	84
53:18.3	91

Dio Chrysostom
De compotatione
27:1–4	159n42
27:3	159n41
30:33–36	159n42

Diogenes Laertius
Lives
1:69–70	159n43
1:93	159n44
6:39	281n33

Ennius
Annals
113:5	83n14

Euripides
Opera Omnia
584–91	284n48

Selected Papyri (fragment)
126–29	284n48

Greek Anthology
102–3	282n41

Homer
Iliad
6:154–206	282n38

Horace
Carmen saeculare
22–24	91n35
29–32	91n35

Odes
1.2.2	82n11
1.12.13–17	82n11
4.21–28	282n40

Josephus
Against Apion
1.150	82n8
2.199	176

Antiquities of the Jews
10.83	136n41
12.160–85	159
12.168–83	160n57, 161n58
15.8.5	253n2
18.3.1	229n18

18.4.1–2	229n18	Pausanius	
18.120	82n8	*Description of Greece*	
20.34–48	175	2.3.5	284n47
20.173–78	253n2		

Jewish War

		Philostratus	
1.4.2	253n2	*Apollonius*	
1.40	82n8	7.3	93n44
2.9.2	229n18		
2.9.4	229n18	Pindar	
5.409	82n8	*Isthmian Odes*	
7.44	82n8	7.43–48	282n37

Livy

		Olympian Odes	
1.16.3	83n14	1.55–63	282n46
5.49.7	83n15	13.83–94	282n40

Lucian

Icaromenippus

		Plato	
1.1	280n29–30, 281n32	*Leges*	
1.22	283n43	11.935	159n45
1.22–23	283n42		
2.267–323	280n28	*Philebus*	
		45d–e	159n46

Ovid

Fasti

		Symposium	
2.127–34	89n26	172b	154n13
		174a	154n13

Metamorphosis

		179a–b	155n21
8.1–151	20n35	197e	155n22
		197b–e	155n21

Tristia

		197e–198a	155n23
2.37	82n11	209a–b	155n21
2.39–42	89n26		
2.157–58	89n26	Pliny the Elder	
2.181	89n26	*Natural History*	
		35.40.147–48	8n18

Remedies of Love

		Pliny the Younger	
53–54	5	*Epistles*	
		4.19	176n16
		7.24	xxxiii

Panegyrics

2.3	84n20, 90n34
57.5	90n34
67.1	90n34
67.3	90n34
88.8	82n11

Plutarch

Advice to the Bride and Groom

17	243n46
20	243n47
36	243n48

Cicero

22.5	83n15
23.6	83n15

Marius

27.9	83n15

Quaestionum convivialum libri IX

2.1.4.631	160n50

Septem sapientium convivium

146	154n15
147–48	161n61
147f.	155n26
147f–148a	161n60
148a	161n63, 163n68, 164n69
148–149	166n73
149a	166n74
148e–149a	167n78
148e	166n72
149b	166n75–77, 167n78

Quintillian

Institutio oratoria

6.3.6	160n54
6.3.7	160n56
6.3.34	160n55

Seneca

The Controversiae

7.7.12	247n54

De Beneficiis

3.31.4–5	91
4.26.1	91

Epistles

6.5–6	8n18
52.8	8n18

Statius

Silvae

3.4.20	93n44
4.2.14–15	93n44

Suetonius

Deified Augustus

58	85

Deified Julius

76.1	83n16
85	83n18

Tacitus

Annals

1.1	293n4
2.244–45	293n4
14.17	37
15.44	266

Xenophon

Cyropaedia
2.2.12–14   160n49

Oeconomicus
3.15   243n44
7.14–15   243n44

Symposium
1.1   156n24
3.4—4.4   155n21
4.28   156n25

Index of Modern Authors

Abrahamsen, V. A., 175
Achelis, Hans, 312
Ackerman, David A., xviii, xxviii
Aletti, Jean-Noël, 174
Alföldy, Andreas, 82
Alter, Robert, 265
Anderson, Herbert, xxiii, xxvi
Anderson, Janice C., 104, 119
Ando, Clifford, 84, 89
Aquino, María Pilar, 205
Ascough, Richard S., 177, 179
Aspegren, Kerstin, xix
Atkins, Margaret, xxvii
Aune, David E., 266, 272, 280, 288

Babbitt, F. C., 154
Bagnall, Roger, xxvii
Bailey, Randall C., 70
Baird, William, 272
Bakke, O. M., xxvii
Balch, David L., xv, xvii, xx, xxiii, xxvi, xxxii, 8, 26, 44, 103, 183
Bammel, Ernst, 216
Barnabei, Lorenzo, 35–36
Barnes, Timothy D., 293–94, 296, 298, 309
Barrett, C. K., 217, 231, 240, 254, 257–58, 268
Barrier, Jeremy W., xxxvii, xxxviii
Barringer, Judith M., 29–32
Barth, Markus, xxv
Bartsch, Carla, 62
Bauckham, Richard, 140–41, 149, 269

Baumbach, 313, 325
Beauvoir, Simons de, 335
Bednarz, Terri, ix, xxxvii, xxxviii, 153, 156, 159, 161
Belle, G. van, 227
Bergant, D., xv
Bergmann, Betina, 9
Bernabé, Carmen, xxviii
Berrino, N. F., xxvii
Berry, Paul, xxii
Bertram, Robert W., xv
Best, E., 175
Betz, Hans Dieter, xxiv, 92, 274–75, 279
Beutler, Johannes, 219
Bevans, Stephen B., 71
Bingemer, Maria C., 204–6
Blanke, Helmlut, xxv
Blankenhorn, David, xxvi
Blasi, Anthony J., xix, xxv, xxxiii
Blass, Friedrich, 277
Blomberg, Craig L., 234
Bobertz, Charles A., 329
Boismard, M.-É., 265
Bonwetsch, G. N., 314, 318, 323
Boomershine, Thomas, 53, 54
Borman, Lukas, xxii
Bosworth, Brian, 86
Botha, Eugene, 53, 62
Botha, Pieter J. J., 55
Bovon, François, 136
Bowe, Barbara, ix, xix, xx, xxxvii, xxxix, 253

Index of Modern Authors

Bragantini, Irene, 5–7, 10, 13, 20–21, 23, 26, 41,
Branigan, Renée, xxviii
Brenner, Athalya, xxv
Brilliant, Richard, 32
Brink, Laurie, xxiv, xxviii, 253
Brock, Ann Graham, xxvi
Brock, Sebastian, 314, 316–17
Brooten, Bernadette, 179
Brotherton, Anne, xxi
Brown, Raymond E., xvi, xvi, xix, 194, 197, 201, 216–18, 224, 228, 235, 256
Brown, Peter, 328–29
Browning, Don, xxvi, 3
Brox, Norbert, xx
Bruce, F. F., xvi
Brueggemann, Walter, xiii
Bultmann, Rudolf, 234–35
Burnett, Andrew, 90
Burrus, Virginia, 177–79, 182
Buttrick, David, 139
Bynam, Caroline W., 203, 207
Byrne, Lavinia, xxii

Caquot, A., xvii
Callahan, Sidney, 204
Campbell, Ken M., xxvi
Carr, Anne, xviii
Carson, D. A., 52, 234
Carter, Warren, 83, 92–94, 97–99, 104, 116, 119, 139, 229
Castrén, Paavo, 36
Cerrato, John A., 311, 314–17, 320–25, 330–31
Chappuzeau, G., 316
Charlesworth, James H., 101, 170, 211
Charlesworth, Martin, 84
Childers, Jeffrey, 318, 324
Chilton, Bruce, 82
Church, E. Forreters, 336
Ciardello, Rosaria, 33
Clark, Elizabeth A., 333–34

Clarke, Andrew D., 171
Cloke, Gillian, 294
Cohen, Shaye J. D., xxii
Collins, Adela Yarbro, xvi, xvi, xxiv
Collins, John J., xxvii, 279
Coloe, Coloe, 237
Connell, Martin F., xxiii
Conway, Colleen M., 105, 112, 117
Cooley, Alison E., 35, 37–40, 44
Cooley, M. G. L., 35, 37–40, 44
Cosgrove, Charles H., 52, 68
Cotter, Wendy, 125, 130, 132, 135–36
Cotton, Hannah M., 130
Countryman, L. William, xv, xvii
Cribiore, Rafaela, xxvii
Crook, Zeba A., xxvii, xxviii
Crosby, Michael H., 104
Crossan, John Dominic, xxiii, 133
Culpepper, R. Alan, 236–37
Curkpatrick, S., 125, 132, 144
Cwiekowski, F. J., xviii

Daly, Robert J., xvi
D'ambra, Eve, xxviii
D'Angelo, Mary Rose, xxv, 83, 254
Dassmann, Ernst, 272
Davies, Stefan L., xv
Davies, W. D., 96
Davis, Casey Wayne, 57
Davis, Stephen J., xxvi
DeBoer, Esther A., 139
Demaris, Richard E., xxix
Derrett, J. D. M., 135
deSilva, David A., xxv
de Vries, Lourens, 62
Dewey, Dennis, 56
Dickerson, Patrick L., 257
Dixon, Suzanne, 178
Dobbins, John J., 39
Dodd, C. H., 220
Donfried, Karl P., xxiii
Dudley, Carl S., xviii
Duhaime, Jean, xxxiii

Duke, Paul D., 218
Duling, Dennis C., 244

Eck, Werner, 84, 87
Edelman, Lee, 120
Edwards, Mark, 67
Edwards, W. D., 201
Eisen, Ute E., xxv
Elliott, John H., xxi, 58, 62
Elliott, Scott, 53
Ernst, Allie M., 311, 314, 316, 322, 330–31
Esquivel, Julia, 205
Esler, Philip E., 240, 278
Evans, Craig A., xvii

Fehribach, Adeline, 204
Ferlita, E., xiii
Fine, Elizabeth C., 68
Finlan, Stephen, 204
Fiocchi-Nicolai, V., xxviii
Fitzgerald, John T., xxiii
Fitzgerald, Timothy, xxiii
Fitzmyer, Joseph A., xxii, 256
Foley, John Miles, 67, 69
Ford, Josephine M., 194, 200–203, 207
Ford, Richard Q., 128, 138
Foster, Robert, 91
Foucault, Michel, 107
Franklin, J. L., Jr., 37–40
Frashetti, Augusto, xxv
Freed, Edwin D., 126, 132, 136
Frei, Hans, 297
Frend, W. H. C., xxiii
Freyne, Seán, xviii
Fry, Euan M.
Furey, Pat, xviii
Furnish, Victor Paul, 272, 277

Gabel, W. J., 201
Gafney, Wilda, 260
Garnsey, Peter, 99
Garrett, Susan R., 264

Garritte, Gérard, 314, 318, 320
Gaventa, Beverly R., 177, 268
Gebara, Ivone, 211
Gehring, Roger W., 172
Gell, William, 20, 26
Georgi, Dieter, 278
Giblin, C. H., 239, 245
Gilhus, Ingvild S., 153, 156
Gill, Carolos, xxviii
Gillett, Shirley, 206
Giordano, Carlo, 44
Gippert, Jost, 324
Gittins, Anthony, 71
Glancy, Jennifer A., 185
Gonzalez, Justo L., xix
Gooder, Paula, 272, 279
Goodman, Martin, 129
Gradel, Ittai, 84
Grammick, Jeannine, xviii
Grant, Mary A., 159–60
Grasso, Fiorenza, 20–21, 26, 41
Gray, Mary, 204
Green, Deborah, xxviii
Green, Joel B., 128, 132–33, 137
Greenfield, Jonas C., 129
Grimal, Pierre, 281–83
Grosh, Gerald R., xviii
Gryson, Roger, xxii
Guy, Laurie, 325
Guzzo, Pier Giovanni, 13, 29

Haenchen, Ernst, 247
Hafemann, Scott, xvii
Hagdorn, Anselm C., xxviii
Halliday, M. A. K., 239
Hammerton-Kelly, R. G., xxi
Hanson, John S., 279–80
Harnack, Adolf, 254
Harries, Jill, 135
Harrington, Daniel, xiv
Harrison, Verna E. F., 294
Harvey, David, 106, 108
Harvey, John D., 57
Hayter, Mary E., xvii

Hedrick, Charles W., 132–33, 135–37
Heim, Mark S., 204
Heine, Ronald E., 321
Helholm, David, xv
Hellerman, Joseph, xxv
Hengel, Martin, 246
Henne, Phillipe, xxi
Henten, J. W. van, xxv
Herrmann, Léon, 275
Herzog, William R., 137, 147
Heyward, Carter, 204
Hicks, John M., 125
Hilgert, Earle, xviii
Hills, Julian V., xxiii
Hock, Ronald F., xiv
Hoffmann, Daniel L., 295
Holhorst, A., xiii
Holmberg, Bengt, xx
Holmes, Michael W., 262
Hopkins, Julie, 269
Hoppe, L., xxii
Horrell, David G., 183, 185
Horsley, Richard, xix, xxii, xxiii, xxvii
Horst, van der, 164
Hosmer, F. E., 201
Howard, George, xiv
Hughes, Kathleen, xvii, xx, xxxvii
Hultgren, Arland J., 128, 132, 135–37
Humphrey, E. M., xxii
Hymes, Dell H., 68

Ilan, Tal, 207, 255, 266
Instone-Brewer, D., xxvi
Iovina, Paolo, xvii

Jackson, John, 293
Jeffers, James S., xx
Jenkins, Claude, 269
Jeremias, Joachim, 135
Jewett, Robert, xxvi
Johnson, Elizabeth A., 204–5, 207–8

Johnson, Luke T., xxiv, 128, 130, 135, 153, 155
Jones, Larry Paul, 194
Jónsson, Jakob, 166, 168
Joubert, Annekie, 68

Kahn, Isidoro, 44
Karam, Sharon, xx, xxxvii, xl
Katzoff, Ranon, 129
Kee, Howard Clark, xix
Keener, Craig S., 231, 234, 247
Kelber, Werner H., 54
Kennedy, George A., 285
Kessler, Herbert L., 313
King, Karen L., 256
Kitzberger, Ingrid R., 201, 205
Klauck, Hans-Josef, 266–67
Klawiter, Krederick, 323
Kloenkow, Anitra B., 268
Kloppenborg, John S., xxiii
Knies, Jerome, xiv
Kodell, Jerome, xviii
Koenig, John, xiv
Koestenberger, A. J., 218
Koester, Craig R., 194, 235–36
Kozakiewicz, Maria, 13
Kraeling, Carl H., 315
Kraemer, Ross S., xviii, xxv, 243
Kraiker, Wilhelm, 41–43
Kuefler, Matthew, 113
Kuhn, Thomas S., 53
Kurtz, William S., xx
Kyung, Chung Hyun, 204

Lamb, W. R. M., 154
Lamoreaux, Jason T., xxxii–xxxix
LaMouille, A., 265
Lampe, Peter, 44
Lee, Dorothy, 194
Leeuwen, M. S. van, xxvi
Leon, Harry J., xxii
Leutzsch, Martin, xx
Levine, Amy-Jill, xxviii
Levinson, Stephen H., 52
Lieu, Judith, 175

Lincoln, Andrew T., 174, 219, 231, 272, 278–79, 286
Lindars, Barnabas, 235
Lindboe, Inger M., xx
Lippolis, I. B., xxvi
Lista, Marinella, 33
Loisy, Alfred, 265
Longenecker, Bruce, 168
Loubser, J. A., 53
Lowrie, Walter, 313
Luz, Ulrich, 108–10, 112, 116

MacDonald, M. Y., xxiii, xxvii, xxviii, 4, 41, 44, 107, 173, 175, 177–78, 180–81, 185, 207
Mack, Burton L., xxi
MacLean, Berenson, 235
MacRae, George E., xvii
Madigan, Kevin, xxvii, xxxiv, 4, 41, 295, 303, 323
Maier, Harry O., xx
Malherbe, Abraham, 8
Malina, Bruce J., xxi, xxii, 106, 135, 238–39, 244
Maloney, Francis J., xxv, 241
Manson, T. W., 132, 136
March, Jennifer R., 281
Martin, Dale B., xix, 109, 113–14, 118
Mastroroberto, M., 13
Matson, David L., 173
Mattei, Paul, 293, 300–303, 307–9
Matthews, Mary W., 130, 133,
Matthews, Shelley, 175, 178–79, 181, 185
Mattingly, Harold, 89–90
Maxey, James A., 53, 61, 65–66, 68, 70–71
Mayer, Günter, 207–8
McConvery, Brendan, 324
McFague, Sallie, 205, 208–9
McGinn, Sheila E., xxvi
McHugh, John, 236
McLean, B. H., xxi

Meeks, Wayne A., xiv, xv, 110–11, 116
Meeus, X. de, 153
Meier, John P., 240
Merritt, Jason L., xxxviii, 233
Metzger, Bruce, xxv
Meyer, R. P., xiv
Meyering, Catherine, 253
Michael, Chester P., xvii
Miles, Margaret R., 293
Miller, Richard W., xxvi
Mitchell, Margaret, xxvii
Mollenkott, Virginia Ramey, 199
Moloney, Francis J., 235, 237
Moore, Clifford H., 293
Moore, Stephen D., 104, 197
Morray-Jones, C. R., 272–73
Mowery, Robert, 81, 92
Moxnes, Halvor, xxiv, xxvi, 110–14, 120, 171
Murphy, Cullen, xxv
Murphy-O'Connor, Jerome, xv, 183
Muscettola, Adamo, 35–36
Musurillo, Herbert, 294

Najbjerg, Tina, 29
Nathan, Geoffrey S., 176
Neufeld, Dietmar, xxix
Newlands, Carole E., 90
Newman, Jan, xxv
Newsom, Carol A., xx, 296
Neyrey, Jerome H., xxviii, 104, 135, 240–42
Niekerk, A. van, 62
Nikiprowetzky, V., xvii
Nissinen, Martti, xxviii
Norquist, Marilyn, xiv
Norrisey, Marie C., xvii
Noss, Philip, 50, 53, 60–62
Noy, David, 184
Nurnberg, R., 316

Oakes, Peter, xxvi
O'Connell, T. E., xvi

O'Day, Gail R., 178
Omerzu, Heike, 263, 265
Ong, Walter, 56, 64
Oporto, Santiago G., xxiv
Osbourne, Robin, xxvii
Osiek, Carolyn, v, ix, xiii, xviii, xxxii, xl, 3, 50, 8 1, 103, 106, 121, 130, 148, 151, 171, 173, 177–78, 180, 183, 185, 191, 207, 215, 234, 253, 272, 293, 295, 303, 311, 323, 329, and passim
Otranto, Georgio, xxxv

Patterson, Stephen J., 126
Pauw, C. J., 62
Pearson, Birger A., xx
Penna, Romano, xvi
Pennington, J., 81, 92
Peppa, Constantina, 311
Perkins, Pheme, 132
Pervo, Richard I., 148
Petersen, David L., xxvii
Petersen, Norman R., xvii
Peterson, John, xxvi
Peterson, Rena, xxvii
Phemister, M., 57
Pilch, John J., xxi
Piper, Ronald A., 224, 240
Pippin, Tina, xxi
Plaza, Maria, 161
Plummer, Alfred, 254
Pomerey, Sarah B., 173
Portefaix, Lillian, xix
Porter, Stanley E., 52–53
Powell, Mark Allen, 233
Provost, James H., xiv

Ragghianti, C. L., 41
Rankin, David, xxviii
Rawson, Beryl, 183–84
Reed, Jeffrey T., 52
Reid, Barbara E., 125, 128, 130, 132–33, 145–46, 185, 191, 254, 260

Reimer, Ivoni R., 175, 179, 184, 257
Rhoads, David, 51, 69
Richard, 312
Richardson, Herbert, xxiii
Richardson, L., Jr., 5–8, 10, 13, 20–21, 23, 26, 37–40
Ridderbos, Herman, 245
Ringe, Sharon H., xx, 137
Ringrose, Kathryn, 114
Robbins, Maria Mayo, xxviii
Robbins, Vernon K., 256
Rodriguez, Jeannette, 211
Roetzel, Calvin J., xviii
Rohrbaugh, Richard L., 238–39, 244
Romizzi, Lucia, 5–8, 10, 13, 20–21, 23, 26, 29, 36–37
Rossi, Mary Ann, xxxv
Rossing, Barbara, xxiv
Rudolph, Kurt, 91
Rushton, Kathleen, 207
Russell, Letty M., xvi
Ryder, Andrew, xxiv

Saldarini, Anthony J., 118
Saller, Richard, 177
Sampaolo, Valeria, 6–7, 41
Sanders, E. P., xvi
Sandt, Huub van de, 219
Satlow, Michael L., 111–12
Schaberg, Jane, xvii, xxvi, 254
Scheele, Barbara, 130, 145, 150
Schneiders, Sandra M., xvii, 195–96
Schoedel, William R., xvii, xvii
Scholem, Gershom G., 273
Scholten, Clemens, 331
Schottroff, Luise, xxii, xxiv, 128, 147, 175
Schreiter, Robert J., 71
Schrenk, G., 82
Schroer, Silvia, xxiv
Schulz-Flügel, Eva, 293–94, 296–303, 305–10
Schüssler-Fiorenza, Elisabeth, xv, xxi, xxi, xxiv, 204

Scott, Bernard Brandon, 62, 64, 131–32, 136
Seim, Turid Karlsen, 174, 254
Sellew, Philip, 137, 162
Senior, Donald, xv, xv, xviii, xxvii, 220, 226–27
Seyffert, Oskar, 284
Sherk, Gottlob, 89–90
Shiell, William D., 56, 62
Shiner, Whitney T., 58, 62, 64
Shutt, R. J. H., 154
Simon, John, 57
Sirano, Francesco, 41
Small, Alistair, 35–36
Small, Jocelyn P., 55
Smith, D. Moody, 219
Smith, Dennis, 153
Smith, Jonathan Z., 120
Smith, Morton, 275
Smith, Yancy W., xxxvii, 311
Snodgrass, Klyne R., 132, 144
Snyder, Graydon F., xxiii, xxiv
Soja, Edward W., 107, 110, 121
Spencer, F. Scott, 258–59
Spier, Jeffrey, 313
Spittler, R. P., 263
Stambaugh, John E., xvii
Steele, E. Springs, 151, 153, 162–63, 166
Stein, R. H., xiii
Stegemann, Erhard W., xxiv
Stegemann, Wolfgang, xxiv
Steinspring, W. F., xvii
Stevenson, Tom, 82
Stibbe, Mark W. G., 237
Stratton, Kimberly B., 267
Straus, Jean A., xxvii
Strohm, Paul, 333
Stücklin, Christoph, 296–300, 305–7
Stuhlmueller, Carroll, xiii, xv, xvii, xviii
Sullivan, Kathryn L., xxvii, xxvii
Swetnam, James, 195

Swidler, Arlene, xiii,
Swidler, Leonard, xiii

Talbert, Charles H., xviii, 236
Tedlock, Dennis, 68
Tetlow, Elisabeth, xiv
Thatcher, Tom, 220, 229
Theissen, Gerd, 43
Thelwall, S., 296, 298–99, 301–3, 305, 307
Thomas, Kenneth J., 61–62, 64, 67
Thomas, Margaret O., 61–62, 64, 67
Thomson, Mark W., 204
Thrall, Margaret E., 275, 286
Thurston, Anne, xxv
Tmyoczka, Maria, 58
Torelli, Mario, 35–36
Trainor, Michael F., xxv
Torjesen, Karen Jo, xxii, 177–79, 182, 269
Trelstad, Marit, 204
Tuck, Wm. Powell, xviii
Tulloch, Janet H., xxvii, xxviii, 319
Turcotte, P.-A., xxxiii
Turner, Charles H., 323
Turner, William B., 120
Tyson, Joseph B., 139

Ubieta, Carmen B. U., xxviii
Urto, Risto, xxviii

Vagaggini, Cipriano, 323
Valantasis, Richard, 117–18
VanderKam, James, 218
Varone, Antonio, 44
Varrialle, Ivan, 33

Wacher, Marie-Theres, xxiv
Walsh, Michael, xvii
Ward, Miriam, xvi
Weaver, Dorothy J., 129
Webb, Matilda, xxvi
Webster, Gary, 168
Weinstock, Stefan, 83

Weiss, Konrad, 137
Welborn, Laurence, 272, 283, 285
Welch, Katherine E., 35
Wendland, Ernst R., 61, 63–65, 67, 69–70
Westfall, Cynthia, 52
Weyermann, 311
White, L. Michael, xxii, xxv, xxv, 176
Whittaker, Charles, 98
Wilken, Robert Louis, xiv
Wilson, Robert R., 266
Wilson, Stephen G., xxiii
Wimbush, Vincent L., xvii

Winter, Bruce W., 176
Wire, Antoinette Clark, xx, 260, 296
Witherington, Ben, xix, 196, 256, 258
Wolff, Christian, 286

Yarbrough, O. Larry, xxii
Yarnold, Edward J., 326sx
Young, Brad H., 129, 132, 136
Young, Frances M., xxvii, 332

Zahn, Wilhelm, 21–22
Zimmer, Mary, 125
Zumstein, Jean, 227, 237

www.ingramcontent.com/pod-product-compliance
Lightning Source LLC
Chambersburg PA
CBHW071230290426
44108CB00013B/1354